MOHAMED RAMJOHN AND

UNLOCKING
EVIDENCE

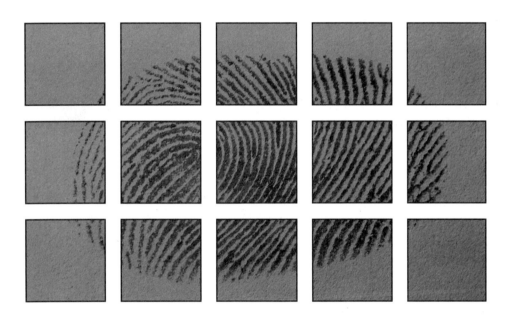

SERIES EDITORS:
JACQUELINE MARTIN & CHRIS TURNER

HODDER
EDUCATION
AN HACHETTE UK COMPANY

Orders: please contact Bookpoint Ltd, 130 Milton Park, Abingdon, Oxon OX14 4SB. Telephone: (44) 01235 827720. Fax: (44) 01235 400454. Lines are open from 9.00–5.00, Monday to Saturday, with a 24-hour message answering service. You can also order through our website www.hoddereducation.co.uk

If you have any comments to make about this, or any of our other titles, please send them to educationenquiries@hodder.co.uk

British Library Cataloguing in Publication Data
A catalogue record for this title is available from the British Library

ISBN: 978 0 340 972 922

First Edition Published 2009
Impression number   10 9 8 7 6 5 4 3 2 1
Year   2012 2011 2010 2009

Hachette UK's policy is to use papers that are natural, renewable and recyclable products and made from wood grown in sustainable forests. The logging and manufacturing processes are expected to conform to the environmental regulations of the country of origin.

Photo credit: Dennie Cody/Taxi/Getty Images
Index compiled by Dr. Laurence Errington, 15 Kirkhall Terrace, Edinburgh EH16 5DQ
Typeset by Phoenix Photosetting, Chatham, Kent.
Printed in Malta for Hodder Education, An Hachette UK Company, 338 Euston Road, London NW1 3BH

CONTENTS ∎

ACKNOWLEDGEMENTS ■

The authors would like to express their sincere gratitude to the staff at Hodder Arnold for their enormous patience and assistance in the completion of this edition. We are especially grateful to Colin Goodlad, Matthew Sullivan and Liz Wilson without whose assistance and encouragement the publication of this book would not have been possible. We would also like to thank all those who reviewed the book at proofs stage. Many of the suggestions made for the book's improvement have been taken on board. We are also grateful to our colleagues at Thames Valley University, who, although not making a direct contribution to the production of this book, gave us enormous and invaluable support during the production stage of this book.

This book is dedicated to my daughter, Nadia. **M.R.**

PREFACE ■

The *Unlocking the Law* series is an entirely new style of undergraduate law textbook. Many student texts are very prose dense and have little in the way of interactive materials to help a student feel his or her way through the course of study on a given module.

The purpose of this series, then, is to try to make learning each subject area more accessible by focusing on actual learning needs, and by providing a range of different supporting materials and features.

All topic areas are broken up into 'bite-size' sections, with a logical progression and extensive use of headings and numerous sub-headings. Each book in the series will also contain a variety of charts, diagrams and key facts summaries to reinforce the information in the body of the text. Diagrams and flow charts are particularly useful because they can provide a quick and easy understanding of the key points, especially when revising for examinations. Key facts charts not only provide a quick visual guide through the subject but are useful for revision purposes also.

The books have a number of common features in the style of text layout. Important cases are separated out for easy access and have full citation in the text as well as in the table of cases, for ease of reference. The emphasis of the series is on depth of understanding much more than breadth. For this reason, each text also includes key extracts from judgments, where appropriate. Extracts from academic comment from journal articles and leading texts are also included to give some insight into the academic debate on complex or controversial areas. In both cases these are indented to make them clear from the body of the text.

Finally, the books also include much formative 'self-testing', with a variety of activities ranging through subject-specific comprehension, application of the law, and a range of other activities to help the student gain a good idea of his or her progress in the course.

Symbols used in this series:

 This is a small extract from a judgment in a case. It may follow a case example or the case may be identified immediately above.

 This is a section from an Act.

 This is an Article of the EC Treaty or of the European Convention on Human Rights.

 This is a clause from a draft Bill or Code.

 Q This is a quote from a government paper, Royal commission report or similar.

Where a paragraph is indented, this is an extract from an academic source such as an article or a leading textbook.

Note also that for all incidental references to 'he', 'him', 'his', we invoke the Interpretation Act 1978 and its provisions that 'he' includes 'she' etc.

The law of evidence has developed over the centuries as essentially a case law subject interspersed by statutory intervention. The modern trend, however, has been to introduce widescale statutory reforms to the subject. Examples include the Youth Justice and Criminal Evidence Act 1999 and the Criminal Justice Act 2003. These developments are best charted and analysed by considering the precise words used in the statutes and the exposition of judges. The principal objectives of writing this book are to present the relevant principles of law, on civil and criminal evidence, in an intelligible and simplified form and to provide easy access to a collection of statutory provisions and extracts from judgments in an effort to facilitate understanding of the law and stimulate critical thought.

The law is stated as I believe it to be on 14th May 2009.

Mohamed Ramjohn
Jay Landa

TABLE OF CASES

TABLE OF STATUTES AND OTHER INSTRUMENTS

Statutes

Statutory Instruments

European Legislation

International Legislation

LIST OF FIGURES ■

AN INTRODUCTION TO THE LAW OF EVIDENCE

AIMS AND OBJECTIVES

In this chapter you will learn:

- What the law of evidence is

- About the historical development of the law of evidence and its exclusionary approach

- What different categories of evidence exist

- About the rules on admissibility of evidence

- About the role of the judge and jury in assessing evidence

- What the general rules are on exclusion of evidence.

1.1 Introduction

In summary the study of the law of evidence involves a rigorous examination of the lexicon of rules and exceptions, both in the civil and criminal law of evidence, set against the judicial discretion to exclude. These rules and exceptions co-exist, like pieces in a jigsaw puzzle, complementing each other and thereby creating an image of 'what happened' in a greater context. It would be salient to say that all lawyers, regardless of whether they are solicitors or barristers, need a sound appreciation of the substantive law of evidence. Remember this formula: the principles of the substantive law of evidence govern: how *facts* are proven in court, the rules on how evidence *should be put to* and *presented in* court along with rules on which evidence *should be excluded from* the court altogether. It is therefore important to appreciate that the parties to any action, whether it be a civil action or a criminal one, are not given blanket permission to put all the information that may assist their case before the court. Here is an important point: they are only permitted to put before the court evidence that is (a) relevant to a fact in issue and (b) admissible; even then the trial judge may decide to exclude it. It sounds like a tall order, does it not? We will cover all of this throughout the book.

Before we proceed with our discussion, here is a summary of all the various topics that we will discuss throughout the book:

- burdens and standards of proof

- competence and compellability of witnesses

- trial process (examination-in-chief, cross-examination and re-examination of witnesses

- privilege and public interest immunity

- silence

- hearsay

- confessions and illegally obtained evidence

- identification evidence

- corroboration and care warnings

- character evidence

- doctrine of similar fact

- opinion evidence

- documentary and real evidence.

It should be noted that the similar fact doctrine has been superseded by the relatively new rules in the Criminal Justice Act 2003; this is discussed later.

1.2 The English Law of Evidence: an exclusionary approach

In order to begin to understand the rules of evidence it is important to appreciate what evidence is and how it works; that is the aim of this chapter, thus the definitions used here appear throughout the book. Consider this scenario: Frank and Hilary have been married for over 20 years during which Frank has been repeatedly physically, mentally and verbally abusive towards her. One day Frank returns from work drunk; he starts to argue with Hilary, shouting at her. He begins to walk towards her, shaking his fists violently, and Hilary, fearing for her safety, picks up a frying pan and hits Frank over the head with it. Frank slumps to the floor in a pool of blood – unbeknown to Hilary, he has a thin skull which is easily fractured; he subsequently dies in hospital. Hilary is arrested and charged with murdering Frank. What happens next? How does Hilary prove that she was defending herself? Was her responsibility diminished? The job of counsel instructed to act for Hilary will be to advise her:

- on the case against her

- on any defences that she may raise

- on the likely prospect of successfully defending herself against this allegation.

Counsel for Hilary will want to challenge or test the evidence, ie the facts, which are stacked against her, thereby ensuring that any subsequent conviction is not unsafe. In summary, evidence can be described as facts used to prove or disprove something.

Many jurisdictions throughout the world admit all relevant evidence; in distinction the English Law of Evidence did not. The English system traditionally adopted a far more cautious and somewhat restrictive approach, thereby excluding evidence that may at first glance seem to be relevant. The foundations of this approach lie in trial by jury and the view that jurymen (and women) were generally unable to (a) correctly analyse evidence, (b) give certain types of evidence the correct weight, or (c) be prejudiced by it if it were not excluded. Studies of the criminal law prove exactly how harsh a penalty was imposed on a defendant found guilty of the commission of a criminal offence, it was therefore thought necessary to protect an accused from the inequity that would result from the jury's mishandling of the evidence. Trial judges were vigilant in excluding evidence that they suspected of having been concocted, fabricated or distorted.

In addition to this, a series of public policy reasons evolved to exclude certain types of evidence from being required to be disclosed, ie legal professional privilege which protects communications between a lawyer and their client, and evidence that could potentially damage national security; for example, certain types of military document.

What then is the role of the lawyer? It is their task to prepare and present the case on the basis of this test: is the evidence relevant? If yes, is it admissible, because only evidence that is relevant and admissible can be put to the court; notice, the test requires an assessment of relevancy first. Consider this: Counsel is presented with 50 pieces of evidence. Unbeknown to them, all 50 are technically admissible, but only 10 are relevant to prove their client's case. When determining what evidence could be used, should counsel assess the admissibility or the relevance of the evidence first? Assessing admissibility first means assessment of all 50 pieces of evidence; more logically, assessing relevancy first, limits the exercise to only relevant evidence. However, as will become obvious throughout the book, even relevant evidence may not be admissible. Remember this formula: evidence that is relevant, but not admissible, cannot be put to the court, regardless of how important it is to the success of the case.

KEY FACTS

The English Law of Evidence: an exclusionary approach

Evidence can be described as facts that are used to prove or disprove something.

1.3 Types of judicial evidence

Let us discuss the types of evidence that can be put before the court; a sound appreciation of all of the following types of evidence is required for assessment success:

- direct and percipient evidence

- circumstantial

- hearsay

- original

- primary

- secondary

- presumptive

- conclusive

- oral testimony

- documentary

- real.

1.3.1 Direct or percipient evidence

Let us begin with direct or percipient evidence. Direct evidence, referred to by HHJ Peter Murphy as percipient evidence, is that evidence which, if accepted by the court, does not require any further inferences to be drawn from it. Direct evidence will be a direct perception of a fact in issue by sight, sound, smell or taste. Let us have a look at an example: Raj's evidence of Martha singing a song is direct evidence of Martha's state. Here is another example: Michael gives evidence that he saw Jean shoot Ronald with a sawn-off shotgun.

1.3.2 Circumstantial evidence

In contrast to direct or percipient evidence, circumstantial evidence is evidence which, if accepted by the court, does require further inferences to be drawn from it. Here is an example; Raj's evidence that Martha was singing a song may be circumstantial evidence that she was intoxicated. Generally, the inference that is required to be drawn will be obvious; sometimes it is not so clear. What happens then? In that instance such circumstantial evidence can be supported by other circumstantial evidence. When considering whether the evidence proves something circumstantially, the jury will ask the following questions: are the relevant facts, or some of them, proven by the evidence? If yes, should the fact in issue be inferred by the existence of those relevant facts?

In *R v Exall* (1866) 4 F & F 922 Pollock CB formulated his now famous analogy between circumstantial evidence and the strands of a rope, stating:

> **J** '. . . one *single* strand of the cord may be insufficient to sustain the weight *of something*, but three *strands* stranded together may be of sufficient strength to do so'.

Let us take our example from above. Raj's evidence could further be strengthened if he had additionally witnessed and stated that Martha was clutching a half-drunk bottle of Bombay Gin. How does that affect the evidence? Raj's account of Martha singing would be considered to be direct evidence of her actions and his evidence of her clutching a half-drunk bottle of Bombay Gin both direct evidence of her action and circumstantial evidence to support the inference that she was drunk.

1.3.3 Hearsay

Hearsay evidence is witness evidence of the fact that something is true, unlike percipient evidence, not because they have perceived it through their senses, but by reason of them learning something by another. How? This can be either verbal or through another method of communication or through an actual document that they have seen. In summary, hearsay is a statement made by someone, on a prior occasion out of court which in the present proceedings is tendered as proof of the truth of the contents therein. The courts were extremely suspicious of such evidence and robustly excluded it, although exceptions to allow admittance were soon formulated by both the common law and statute. The law now takes an inclusionary approach to hearsay in that it is admissible in criminal cases where either one of the preserved common law exceptions or the Criminal Justice Act 2003 allow it. Hearsay evidence has been statutorily admissible in civil cases for far longer.

1.3.4 Original evidence

To recap, hearsay evidence is *a statement made by someone, on a prior occasion out of court which in the present proceedings is tendered as proof of the truth of the contents therein.* What if the statement is tendered for a reason other than to prove the truth of its contents? Correct; that statement will become original evidence. At this stage it becomes evident that a pattern emerges; the classification of a single piece of evidence depends on, amongst other reasons, why it is tendered and therefore it may be classified as a variety of types of evidence, ie hearsay as original evidence.

Here is a good example of how the rules work; in the case of *Woodhouse v Hall* (1980) 72 Cr App R 39 the prosecution sought to adduce the evidence of a police officer that whilst at the massage parlour, a masseuse employed by the accused had offered him sexual services in exchange for money. The accused argued that the evidence was inadmissible hearsay because it was in fact a statement that was allegedly made by the masseuse, on a prior occasion out of court which in the present proceedings was being tendered as proof of the truth of the fact that the massage parlour was in fact a brothel. The court decided against the accused and held that the evidence was not hearsay evidence because it was not being tendered to prove the truth of what the masseuse had said, ie that she would provide sexual services at a price, but to show that an offer for the provision of sexual services at a price had been made.

1.3.5 Primary and secondary evidence

Let us move on to primary and secondary evidence. Primary evidence is considered to be the *best* type of evidence; for example, an original deed, contract, tenancy or lease agreement would be classed as primary evidence. In contrast, secondary evidence is considered to be its inferior counterpart; examples of secondary evidence would include a photocopy of the original deed, contract, tenancy or lease agreement that we have just mentioned or a statement as to the contents of the original document by someone who had seen it. There was a time when the law insisted that a claimant provided primary evidence as proof. This is not the case now as many statutes make provision for the use of secondary evidence. It should be noted that the distinction between the two is important when it comes to evidential issues in relation to privileged documents; we will discuss this later in Chapter 4.

1.3.6 Conclusive evidence

Here is an interesting point: conclusive evidence is evidence that, by law, cannot be contradicted by the parties to the action. A good example of a rule that is conclusive evidence is *doli incapax,* which states that a child under the age of 10 is unable to form the requisite mental intention required to commit a criminal offence. Likewise, in s 13 of the Civil Evidence Act 1968, it is enacted that in defamation actions, proof that a person has been convicted of a criminal offence shall be 'conclusive evidence' that that person committed the offence.

1.3.7 Presumptive evidence

In contrast to conclusive evidence, the law provides rules known as presumptive evidence; these apply unless successfully challenged. Where the law provides such a rule and it is challenged, then it is for the court to decide whether or not the rule applies. An example of this is; Gina walked out on her husband John seven years ago. Neither John nor anyone Gina knew, including her family, has heard from her since. John, Gina's mother, Susan, and her friends have made numerous enquiries as to her whereabouts but to no avail. In this instance, because Gina has been missing for over seven years, she can be presumed dead. This rule is a presumptive rule of evidence because it can be challenged by adducing evidence that Gina is still alive.

1.3.8 Oral evidence

On occasion, oral evidence is also referred to as oral testimony. This is the evidence which a witness, whether for the prosecution or defence, gives from the witness box. The point is that this form of evidence comes directly from the witness, at court, in their own words. Note that oral evidence includes evidence given in chief, cross-examination and re-examination.

Although evidence that is tendered in the form of a document is normally classed as documentary evidence, in some instances the evidence will be treated as though it were oral evidence. The court may accept an affidavit, a written statement as oral evidence or allow the witness to give oral evidence outside of the courtroom by video link.

1.3.9 Real evidence

Real evidence is tangible evidence from which the court, that is, the judge and jury, can observe, inspect, perceive and draw inferences. Examples of real evidence include the murder weapon, ie a spanner, rope, knife or candlestick. Real evidence also includes photographs of the scene of the crime and the actual appearance of a witness. To distinguish whether a piece of evidence is real evidence, it must be something that is capable of making an impression on the court.

KEY FACTS

The English Law of Evidence: an exclusionary approach
Evidence can be described as facts that are used to prove or disprove something.

Types of judicial evidence

Direct or percipient evidence – evidence which, if accepted by the court, does not require any further inferences to be drawn from it, ie a direct perception of a fact in issue by sight, sound, smell or taste.

Circumstantial evidence – evidence which, if accepted by the court, does require further inferences to be drawn from it. The inference drawn will be obvious.

Hearsay – a statement made by someone, on a prior occasion out of court, which in the present proceedings is tendered as proof of the truth of the contents therein.

Original evidence – a statement made by someone, on a prior occasion out of court, which in the present proceedings is not tendered as proof of the truth of the contents therein but as proof of something else.

Primary and secondary evidence – primary evidence is considered to be the *best* type of evidence; for example, an original deed, contract, tenancy or lease agreement. Secondary evidence is considered to be its inferior counterpart, ie a photocopy of the original deed, contract and tenancy or lease agreement.

Conclusive evidence – evidence that, by law, cannot be contradicted by the parties to the action.

Presumptive evidence – rules of law that apply unless successfully challenged.

Oral evidence – evidence that a witness, whether for the prosecution or defence, gives from the witness box.

Real evidence – tangible evidence from which the court, that is, the judge and jury, can observe, perceive and draw inferences, ie the murder weapon.

1.4 Facts

Now that we have a grasp of the types of evidence that exist, it is important to appreciate why evidence is adduced. It was mentioned earlier that in every case there are a number of facts that will be in issue, which means that a party to the action will somehow need to either prove or disprove a fact in issue. This is done by adducing relevant and admissible evidence. Let us take a closer look at facts in issue in relation to criminal and civil cases.

1.4.1 Facts in issue: criminal cases

These tend to be the facts that the prosecution must prove to establish a defendant's guilt, ie the elements of an offence as well as facts constituting defences raised by the defendant. Additionally, the prosecution will have to adduce evidence in order to disprove any defence that the defendant has raised, for example provocation or diminished responsibility under the Homicide Act 1957. If the defendant makes a 'not guilty' plea, then the entire prosecution case will be in issue, which means that the prosecution will have to prove the commission of the entire offence, ie proving, where required, that the defendant committed the *actus reus* with the requisite *mens rea*. What happens if the prosecution fails to do so? Then the defence will succeed and the defendant will be acquitted.

1.4.2 Facts in issue: civil cases

Turning now to civil cases, a document known as the Particulars of Claim, also referred to as a Statement of Case, will contain a statement of the material facts on which party bases its claim. It is possible to ascertain which facts are in issue from this document. In summary, in civil cases, the facts that are in issue are *those facts that the claimant must establish in order to succeed* in their claim *and to disprove any defence* raised by the defendant, ie contributory negligence or *volenti non fit injuria*.

1.4.3 Facts in issue: formal admissions

A formal admission is an agreement between the parties indicating that the subject-matter of the admission does not require proof.

An interesting question arises at this point: what happens if a fact in issue, for example the existence of a duty of care, is formally admitted? Simple: the fact is no longer a fact in issue. In that instance the party who has the burden of proving the fact in issue will not have to adduce evidence to prove it and the court will not hear such evidence. The logic behind this is simple – there is no requirement to prove something that can be taken to have been already proven. To do so would be a waste of time and resources. A good example in criminal cases is a plea of guilty by a defendant that means no facts remain in issue. Less dramatic are partial admissions, ie 'I was at the scene of the crime but I did not do it'. The prosecution and defence can, in writing and at any stage before the trial, make such an admission. In civil cases formal admissions are normally made in the Particulars of Claim. The main reason behind making such admissions is the clarification of the actual issues, to speed up the time taken for an action to be completed and the saving of resources. This is particularly evident in civil claims; take a look at the overriding objective of the Civil Procedure Rules 1998, available at http://www.justice.gov.uk/civil/procrules_fin/contents/parts/part01.htm.

The effect of making a formal admission is that it is conclusive of the facts admitted. In short, evidence of such facts admitted is not admissible in those proceedings.

In criminal proceedings, formal admissions may be made by virtue of s 10 of the Criminal Justice Act 1967. This section enacts a self-contained code for the creation of formal admissions.

Section 10 of the Criminal Justice Act 1967 provides as follows:

'(1) . . . Any fact of which oral evidence may be given in criminal proceedings may be admitted . . . by or on behalf of the prosecution or defendant . . . and shall, as against that party, be conclusive evidence in those proceedings of the fact admitted.

(2) The admission may be made before or at the proceedings and shall be in writing save when made in court.

(3) An admission may be withdrawn with the leave of the court.'

1.4.4 Facts in issue: collateral facts

These are facts that affect the admissibility of evidence; for example, where a confession was obtained by oppressive means, the existence of the oppression is a collateral fact because it will affect whether or not the court allows the evidence to be adduced. Other collateral facts are those that affect the credibility of a witness or the weight given to a piece of evidence. Collateral facts will normally be put before the court before the evidence is presented, ie the defence will, in a *voir dire* or a trial with a trial, apply to have a confession obtained by oppression excluded.

1.4.5 Facts in issue: relevant facts

The next question is: how are facts in issue proven or disproven? Facts in issue are proven or disproven by what are known as relevant facts. In the case of the *DPP v Kilbourne* [1973] AC 729 the court stated:

'. . . relevant, ie logically probative or disprobative, evidence is evidence which makes the matter which requires proof more or less probable'.

The basic rule is that only relevant evidence can be admitted (*R v Turner* [1975] QB 834). Furthermore, such relevant evidence may be presented in the form of direct witness evidence or

circumstantial evidence. What happens if the evidence is irrelevant or insufficiently relevant to a fact in issue? Then the court will reject it (*R v Randall* [2004] 1 WLR 56). Remember, even if the evidence would have been sufficiently relevant, but the fact that was in issue has been admitted, and therefore is no longer in issue, the court will not hear this evidence.

The determination of relevance is dependent on whether the evidence tends to either prove or disprove a fact in issue. Counsel will normally ask this question: does this piece of evidence tend to prove or disprove a fact in issue? Alternatively, does this evidence have a probative effect? If the evidence does not tend to prove or disprove a fact in issue, or does not have a probative effect, then it is irrelevant and inadmissible. Contrast these two cases:

1. *Joy v Phillips, Mills & Co* [1916] 1 KB 849; evidence of a child being found with a halter and of its previous torment of a horse was admitted, it was relevant to this fact in issue; how the child was killed.

2. *Hart v Lancashire and Yorkshire Railway* (1869) 21 LT 261, the claimant alleged negligence when injured by a runaway train. His argument centred around the fact that the train company had recently changed the points on the track to avoid the type of event that had occurred. The court decided that this change in practice occurred after the accident and was irrelevant to proving or disproving negligence, all it showed was the company improving its safety standards.

In *Joy v Phillips, Mills & Co* [1916] 1 KB 849 Lord Cozens-Hardy stated that not to admit this evidence would be akin to 'shutting your eyes altogether to facts necessary for drawing the proper inferences'. In *Hart v Lancashire and Yorkshire Railway* (1869) 21 LT 261, the court stated that the evidence was irrelevant 'to hold that, because the world gets wiser as it gets older, therefore it was foolish before'.

CASE EXAMPLE

R v Sandhu [1997] Crim L 288

The Court of Appeal held that evidence that illustrated the defendant's state of mind at the time of committing a strict liability offence was irrelevant to prove the issue of the defendant's guilt. Why? Think back to your studies of criminal law, strict liability is imposed regardless of mental intention. Therefore, evidence proving or disproving a guilty intent is irrelevant as the mental intent of the defendant is not a fact in issue.

CASE EXAMPLE

R v Kearley [1992] 2 All ER 345 (HL)

The defendant was charged with being in possession of drugs with an intent to supply. In the defendant's absence and whilst searching his flat, police officers answered 15 telephone calls, 10 of which asked for the defendant and for drugs. In addition, nine individuals came to the flat asking for the defendant, seven of whom requested drugs. At the trial, the officers were given permission to give evidence of the calls and what was said. Mr Kearley was convicted and appealed to the House of Lords. The Law Lords decided that the evidence was inadmissible because it was (a) irrelevant and (b) inadmissible hearsay.

Let us look at the reasoning of the Lords: Lord Bridge stated that

> J '. . . the fact that the words were spoken may be relevant for various purposes, but most commonly they will be so when they reveal the state of mind of either the speaker or the person to whom the words were spoken when that state of mind is itself *a fact in* issue or relevant to *another* matter in issue. The state of mind of the person making the request for drugs is of no relevance at all to the question whether the defendant is a supplier.'

Lord Ackner stated that

> J '. . . each of those requests was, of course, evidence of the state of mind of the person making the request; *they* wished to be supplied with drugs and thought that *Mr. Kearley* would so supply *them*. It was not evidence of the fact that the appellant had supplied or could or would supply the person making the request. But the state of mind of the person making the request was not an issue at the trial; accordingly evidence of his request was irrelevant and therefore inadmissible.'

Lord Browne-Wilkinson, dissenting, stated

> J '. . . the evidence was, in my judgment, relevant because it showed that there were people resorting to the premises for the purpose of obtaining drugs from the appellant. Although evidence of the existence of such would-be buyers is not, in

CONTINUED ▸

itself, conclusive, the existence of a substantial body of potential customers provides some evidence which a jury could take into account in deciding whether the accused had *the requisite* intent to supply. The existence of a contemporaneous potential market to buy drugs from him, by itself, shows that there was an opportunity for the accused to supply drugs.'

Lord Oliver defined relevant facts as

'. . . any . . . facts . . . so related . . . proves or renders probable the past, present or future . . .'

The relevance of evidence is not always clear-cut; the relevancy of a piece of evidence may change as the trial progresses, for example where other evidence emerges. When preparing for trial the prosecution will normally try to anticipate any defences that may be put forward and therefore produce evidence, the production of which may not, at first sight, be clear. Normally, the judge will ask counsel to clarify the matter of relevance. Where the judge agrees, the evidence will be treated *de bene esse* or as being conditionally relevant. What happens if the evidence then turns out to be irrelevant? Then the judge will direct the jury to ignore it. This sounds simple; however, it is not. If the evidence turns out to be prejudicial, then the jury will have to be discharged and a new trial ordered.

KEY FACTS

Facts in issue: criminal cases – these are facts that the prosecution must prove to establish a defendant's guilt or disprove a defence.

Facts in issue: civil cases – these are facts that the claimant must establish in order to succeed in their claim and to disprove any defence raised.

Facts in issue: formal admissions – any facts in issue that are admitted do not have to be proven.

Facts in issue: collateral facts – these are facts that affect the admissibility of evidence, the credibility of a witness or the weight given to a piece of evidence.

Facts in issue: relevant facts – facts in issue are proven or disproven by what are known as relevant facts, that is, 'relevant, ie logically probative or disprobative, evidence is evidence which makes the matter which requires proof more or less probable'.

1.5 Admissibility, weight and discretion

Now that we have covered facts in issue, there are a number of additional topics that must be understood – admissibility and weight of evidence and the judge's discretion to exclude evidence.

1.5.1 Admissibility

Although relevance is a prerequisite to evidence being admissible, it is not the sole requirement that needs to be satisfied before evidence can be put before the court. If the evidence is relevant, ie it proves or disproves a fact in issue, the admission of the evidence will then depend on whether or not it falls foul of any of the exclusionary rules of the English law of evidence. These rules were, and are, originally designed to ensure (a) that the evidence is authentic, and (b) its fairness.

It should be noted that evidence can be admissible for some purposes and inadmissible for others; for example, if Jamie and Theo rob a bank and Jamie later confesses to the commission of the crime, his confession will be both relevant and admissible as evidence against him in court; however, it cannot be used as evidence against Theo. In these instances, it is likely that the defendants will be tried separately because of the risk that the co-defendant will be prejudiced. The rules regarding the use of juries in complex cases are changing; please refer to the website accompanying this book for updates.

1.5.2 Weight

Once it has been determined what facts in issue the evidence may prove or disprove (which means that it is relevant and that it is admissible), it is then down to the court or tribunal of fact (jury) to decide what weight to attach to it. What is meant by weight? Weight simply refers to whether the conclusion is proven or disproven by the evidence. The weight that the jury give a particular piece of evidence will be subjective, drawing on both logic and common sense when they determine what they do, or do not, believe. There are two possible outcomes: first, the evidence may be given no weight and therefore disregarded, or second, it may be given weight, thereby influencing the jury's decision concerning the extent to which they perceive its reliability, strength and truthfulness. Counsel simply cannot afford to concentrate on relevance and admissibility; they will inevitably have to consider the weight that is likely to be attached to the evidence. Considerations of the weight of evidence will have the following effects:

• the decision to prosecute or not

• the advice given to the accused as to the prospect of successfully defending the allegation

• whether or not there is a prosecution case for the accused to answer

• in civil cases, the weight of evidence will affect negotiation, ie as a bargaining chip.

Finally, on many occasions specific guidance on the weight that should be attached to certain types of evidence will be given in case law, ie identification evidence (*R v Turnbull* [1977] QB 224) or statute law as in the Civil Evidence Act 1995.

13

1.5.3 Discretion

Originally, the English law of evidence did not allow a judge the discretion to *include* inadmissible evidence, albeit some statutes allow this now; however, it did allow the judge to *exclude* admissible evidence. There are two provisions that must be taken into account when considering judicial discretion:

•   The court may, at common law, exclude prosecution evidence where its prejudicial effect outweighs its probative value; see *R v Sang* [1980] AC 402 and s 82(3) Police and Criminal Evidence Act 1984 (PACE).

•   Section 78 of the Police and Criminal Evidence Act (PACE) 1984 allows the court to exclude prosecution evidence if 'after having regard to, all the circumstances, including the circumstances in which the evidence was obtained, the admission of the evidence would have an adverse effect on the fairness of proceedings'.

There had been some curtailing of judicial discretion with the Criminal Justice Act 2003; this will be discussed later in the book with reference to hearsay.

KEY FACTS

Admissibility, weight and discretion

Admissibility – if the evidence is relevant, ie it proves or disproves a fact in issue, the admission of the evidence will then depend on whether or not it falls foul of any of the exclusionary rules of the English Law of Evidence.

Weight simply refers to whether the conclusion is proven or disproven by the evidence. The weight that the jury gives a particular piece of evidence will be subjective, drawing on both logic and common sense when they determine what they do or do not believe.

Discretion – the court may, at common law, exclude prosecution evidence where its prejudicial effect outweighs its probative value and s 78 of PACE 1984 allows the court to exclude prosecution evidence if 'after having regard to, all the circumstances, including the circumstances in which the evidence was obtained, the admission of the evidence would have an adverse effect on the fairness of proceedings.'

1.6 Judge and jury

It is important to appreciate the roles of the judge and jury in the trial process. In fact, the English mode of trial has its origins in trial by jury. Interestingly, the division of functions between judge and jury, and much of the procedure that exists today was formulated by reason of this. The distinction is important because questions of law or fact may arise. The trial judge or magistrates will determine all questions of law. However, lay magistrates are not legally qualified, and therefore they will only determine questions of law on the advice of their clerk, who is normally a legally qualified solicitor or barrister of at least 10 years' standing; see Practice Direction (Justices Clerk to Court) [1981] 1 WLR 1163. All questions of fact in the Crown Court will be determined by the jury, or by a single judge if sitting alone. In the Magistrates' Court, questions of fact will be determined by the magistrates. Finally, it is the responsibility of the trial judge to sum up the case to the jury and to ensure, like a manager, that the trial runs as smoothly as possible. Let us take a closer look at questions of law or questions of fact.

1.6.1 Questions of law

Generally, questions of law will relate to the definition of an offence, elements of an offence, rules of evidence, ie admissibility and existence of sufficient evidence allowing the jury to consider an issue.

What if no evidence that the defendant has committed the offence exists or the evidence is so tenuous that no properly directed jury could ever convict on its basis? Then counsel will make a mid-time submission that the defendant has *no case to answer* because the prosecution has failed to prove each element of the offence; see *R v Galbraith* [1981] 1 WLR 1039. The judge will then withdraw the case from the jury. In the Magistrates' Court the position is the same but governed by a 1962 Practice Direction issued by Lord Parker CJ in [1962] 1 WLR 227.

As mentioned earlier, questions of admissibility are questions of law which the judge would decide in the absence of the jury. What happens if counsel A objects to some of the evidence being tendered by counsel B? Is that evidence still admissible? In that instance, counsel A would inform counsel B, who would then not refer to the disputed evidence until the trial judge rules it admissible. How does the judge rule the evidence admissible? The trial judge will hear the legal arguments of both sides on the rules governing the admissibility of the evidence in question and then make a decision.

Issues of admissibility of disputed evidence will normally be settled at the outset of a case if, logically, the progression of the case would be affected. Alternatively, it can be dealt with whilst the case is proceeding in a *voir dire* (trial within a trial), this procedure is held in the absence of the jury. Witnesses are called to give evidence and the admissibility of the evidence may be dependent on a factual situation, for example on the existence of oppression in obtaining a confession. May counsel opposing the admissibility of evidence do so in a procedure other than a

voir dire? Yes, if counsel is of the opinion that a *voir dire* would, in effect, allow the witnesses to rehearse their evidence, ie a trial run, in response to the defence argument, then counsel can attack the admissibility of the evidence after it has been put to the jury; see *Ajodha v The State* [1982] AC 204. The only time that this is not possible and a *voir dire* must be held is where the admissibility of evidence that is disputed is that of a confession; s 76(2) of the PACE 1984 requires a *voir dire* to be held.

In summary, the trial judge would hold a *voir dire*, make a decision on admissibility of the evidence and then make no mention of it or the existence of the evidence in the presence of the jury. What happens if counsel does not object to the admissibility of disputed evidence at the outset of a trial or whilst the trial is proceeding? Then counsel can seek to appeal. However, the Court of Appeal has made it very clear that it is reticent to hear appeals based on the admissibility of evidence that remained unchallenged the first time around; see *The Tasmania* (1890) 15 App Cas 223. What if the trial judge makes an error whilst summing up, ie accidentally mentions the evidence, then counsel will normally remain silent and appeal on the basis of a misdirection; see *R v Cocks* (1976) 63 Cr App R 79.

The position on admissibility is slightly more complicated when it comes to cases where no jury is involved because the person determining admissibility of the evidence (the judge) and the decision as to the outcome (normally the jury) are the same. The problem concerns the risk that where the evidence is inadmissible, even though the trier of fact tries to put the evidence out of its mind, the decision will have been prejudiced. It may be that the evidence can be discussed generally, rather than specifically, but this does not solve the problems regarding admissibility after the evidence has already been heard. In non-jury trials a *voir dire* is basically redundant in preventing prejudice; see *F (an infant) v Chief Constable of Kent* [1982] Crim LR 682. Once again if the evidence in dispute is a confession, then a *voir dire* must be used. Finally, it should be noted that the use of a *voir dire* may be useful in a later appeal.

1.6.2 Questions of fact

Here are a couple of examples of questions of fact, questions relating to the weight of evidence, whether the evidence should be believed, ie is it credible, and a defendant's fitness to plead. For a discussion on the latter, reference should be made to the Insanity and Fitness to Plead Act 1991. As our earlier discussion revealed, in the Crown Court the jury will decide questions of fact. However, as an exception to the general rule, the judge will decide the following questions of fact:

* the definition of unusual terms used in a contract
* issues relating to foreign law.

Let us take a brief look at each of these, starting with defining terms. Where the question relates to the ordinary meaning or usage of words, then that question of fact will be decided by the jury (*Brutus v Cozens* [1973] AC 854). Such questions are subject to appellate control if the decision of the tribunal of fact is unreasonable and ought to be set aside. However, if the question relates to the use of the word in an unusual context, then the question will be determined by the judge. What about terms in statutes? This is in effect a question of law and therefore a question for the trial judge. A good example is defamation where the trial judge decides whether the words used are capable of bearing a defamatory meaning and the jury decides whether the words are in fact defamatory; see *Neill v Fine Arts and General Insurance Co* [1987] AC 68.

Furthermore, where the question relates to foreign law, the judge decides this issue as a question of fact. The law of other countries, including Scotland (for these purposes) and Commonwealth countries, is treated as foreign law. It is up to the trial judge to decide what foreign law is in issue based on expert evidence; the discussion of this is beyond the scope of this textbook; however, reference may be made to s 15 of the Administration of Justice Act 1920. Finally, you should note that, albeit the rule was substantially eroded, the trial judge was required to determine issues on the best evidence that was available. This was achieved by excluding evidence where better evidence was available; see *Omychund v Barker* (1745) 1 AtK 21 and *Garton v Hunter* [1969] 2 QB 37. The rule was not absolute and it seems that the final instance in which the rule applied, in relation to documents, has been finally laid to rest by the Court of Appeal's decision in *Springsteen v Masquerade Music Ltd* [2001] EMLR 654, where the court stated that '. . . the best evidence rule was recognized as no more than a rule of practice to the effect that the court would attach no weight to secondary evidence of the contents of a document unless the party seeking to adduce *it first accounted for not producing* the document itself . . . I would not recognize the continuing existence of the remaining instance of this old rule'.

1.7 Instances in which proof is unnecessary

There are a number of instances in which no evidence is required to prove something. To clarify, in general the court requires evidence in order to be satisfied that a fact in issue is proved or disproved. However, there are instances in which no proof will be required. We have already discussed one of them: formal admissions; the second instance is judicial notice. Judicial notice allows the courts to use their objective, general knowledge of the world – sounds like a contradiction – there are frequent articles in the tabloid press about judges asking questions regarding facts that are generally considered common knowledge. For example, a personal instance I can recollect involves a Family Court Judge enquiring what a treadmill was in the following terms '. . . is it like one of those things that hamsters run around on?' More famously, in an example cited by Roderick Munday in his book on Evidence, a judge questioned what a 'Tellytubbie' was. Not surprisingly this only seeks to propound the argument that judges do not live in the real world.

Rest assured that this is not a common state of affairs as the doctrine of judicial notice proves; it allows the judge to dispense with the need for evidence regarding notorious facts. In *Lumley v Gye* (1853) 2 E & B 216 Coleridge J stated:

'. . . Judges are not necessarily *ignorant in court* to what everybody else . . . out of court, are familiar with . . . we find in the year books *judicial reasoning* about the ability of knights . . . and gentlemen to maintain themselves without wages . . .'

The point is that some facts are so well known that requiring a party to prove the same would only result in a waste of court time; furthermore, it would not enhance the image of the courts in the eyes of the public. Let us take a look at some examples of facts that are judicially noted, that:

*   rain falls, *Fay v Prentice* (1845) 14 LJCP 298

*   the postal system is not infallible, *Sloan Electronics Ltd v Customs and Excise Commissioners* [1999] unreported

*   countries such as Thailand, Jamaica and Holland are areas with drug trafficking, dealing and supply problems, *R v Crown Court at Isleworth, ex p Marland* (1997) 162 JP 251.

From these examples it becomes obvious what types of fact are judicially noticed. The test is when the facts are so notorious that it would be an affront to the common sense of judges and the dignity of the court to require proof. There are two occasions when notice may be taken – automatically or after inquiry when the judge refreshes his memory. The difficulty with this principle concerns the limits of the doctrine. Some matters of 'common knowledge' vary with sections of the population, with particular age groups and the educational upbringing of the individual; but the test requires the judge to exercise an objective assessment of the popularity of the relevant facts. In *Hoare v Silverlock* (1848) 12 QB 624, the claimant had applied to a benevolent society for assistance and named the defendant as a referee. In supplying a reference, the defendant had said that 'her friends would realize the truth of the fable about the frozen snake'. The claimant sued the defendant for libel. The judge took judicial notice of the fable and that the words used by the defendant were defamatory. '. . . I may take judicial notice that the words "frozen snake" have an application very generally known indeed, which application is likely to bring into contempt a person against whom it is directed' (Erle J).

The justification for taking judicial notice after inquiry is that although the fact is notorious, the details cannot readily be recalled. The judge needs to refresh his memory by consulting works of reference or considering the views of experts. In *McQuaker v Goddard* [1940] 1 KB 687, the claimant was bitten by a camel whilst visiting the defendant's zoo. The question in issue was whether camels are *'ferae naturae'* (naturally fierce) or *'mansuetae naturae'* (naturally tame) for the purpose of the law relating to liability to animals. The judge ruled that he would take judicial notice of the issue and listened to five expert witnesses who gave evidence on the subject. The judge decided that camels came within the latter classification. Clauson LJ:

> **J** '. . . the judge takes judicial notice of the ordinary course of nature in regard to the position of camels among other animals. The reason why the evidence was given was, for the assistance of the judge in forming his view as to what the ordinary course of nature in this regard in fact is – a matter of which he is supposed to have complete knowledge.'

Likewise, in *DPP v Hynde* [1998] 1 All ER 649, the Divisional Court decided that a 'butterfly' knife in the possession of a person at Heathrow Airport was an offensive weapon under the Aviation Security Act 1982 partly because of consistency with the general offence under the Criminal Justice Act 1988.

On political and international matters, ie affairs of the state, the court may take judicial notice so that both the courts and the Government may act in unison. For this purpose, the court will inquire from the Minister of Foreign Affairs about the relevant issues, and a certificate, issued by that Department, will be conclusive of the information. In *Duff Development Company v Government of Kelantan* [1924] AC 797, the claimant company had obtained a judgment order against the defendant, the Government of Kelantan. The defendant applied for an order to set aside the judgment on the ground of sovereign immunity, ie that it was a sovereign independent state and not subject to British jurisdiction. The Secretary of State for the Colonies wrote to the judge, on request, to the effect that Kelantan was an independent state and the Sultan was its ruler. Viscount Finlay:

> **J** 'It is settled law that it is for the court to take judicial cognizance of the status of any foreign government. If there can be any doubt on the matter the practice is for the court to receive information from the appropriate department of his Majesty's Government and the information so received is conclusive . . . Such information is not in the nature of evidence: it is a statement by the Sovereign of this country through one of his Ministers upon a matter which is peculiarly within his knowledge.'

An interesting question concerns the extent to which the personal knowledge of the adjudicator (professional judge or lay magistrate) may influence his or her judgement. To a large extent, the general knowledge of judges, juries and magistrates (ie, professional lawyers or lay persons) plays a significant role in assessing the quality and weight of evidence adduced before a tribunal, for example the length of the skid marks, the type and age of the motor vehicle, the age of the driver may all combine in assisting the tribunal in determining by inference whether the vehicle

was travelling at speed, immediately before the collision. There simply is no way in which the tribunal may be prevented from drawing on their general knowledge in assessing the probabilities that exist.

How far may an adjudicator use his specialist, non-legal knowledge in the judicial process, for example, whether a judge or magistrate, who is also a medical doctor, may use his medical knowledge in adjudicating on the issue? The answer is that the tribunal (judge or lay magistrate) is never entitled to substitute its specialized experience for evidence. If the judge or lay magistrate has any relevant specialized knowledge, he is required to be sworn in and give evidence in the normal way. In *R v Fricker* (1999) *The Times*, 13th July, this principle was applied to a member of the jury who had specialized knowledge of the significance of the serial numbers on tyres. On a charge of handling stolen goods, namely a motor car tyre, the juror used his knowledge to influence his fellow jurors in the jury room and cast doubt on the defendant's case. On conviction, the appeal was allowed for the juror was unlawfully using his knowledge as a substitute for evidence.

In addition, a judge (but not a lay adjudicator) is not even entitled to rely on his specialized knowledge in a field other than law (eg medicine) in assessing the weight to be attached to evidence. In other words, a judge, who may be a medical doctor, is debarred from using his medical knowledge in assessing the medical evidence admitted in court. His legal training equips him to disregard his specialized non-legal knowledge and to rely on the evidence that has been admitted.

Lay justices (and juries), although prevented from relying on their specialist knowledge as a substitute for evidence, are nevertheless entitled to rely on their professional knowledge in assessing the weight and quality of the evidence adduced. In this respect a lay magistrate (or a juror) is not entitled to force his views on other members of the bench.

These principles were decided by the Divisional Court in *Wetherall v Harrison* [1976] QB 773. In this case, the defendant was charged with failing to provide a specimen without reasonable excuse, contrary to s 9(3) of the Road Traffic Act 1972 (since repealed and replaced). The defendant claimed that he could not give a blood sample because he had had a fit. The prosecution claimed that he was simulating it. Sitting on the bench was a doctor who gave his opinion (without forcing his views) to the other magistrates. The defendant was acquitted and the prosecution appealed. The court held that there was no error in law and the appeal was dismissed. Widgery CJ:

> **J** 'I do not think that the position of a justice of the peace is the same in this regard as the position of a trained judge. If you have a judge sitting alone, it is perfectly feasible and sensible that he should be instructed and trained to exclude certain

CONTINUED ▸

factors from his consideration. Justices are not so trained . . . I start with the proposition that it is not improper for a justice who has special knowledge . . . to draw on that special knowledge in interpretation of the evidence which he has heard. I stress that last sentence because it would be quite wrong if he went on to give evidence to himself, still more is he not there to give evidence to other justices; but that he can employ his basic knowledge in considering, weighing up and assessing the evidence given before the court is I think beyond doubt.'

The concept of notoriety, which is the hallmark for judicial notice, may change with time. For example, the fact that cats are domestic animals may change in years to come, therefore there is an element of speculation and cautiousness involved before a court will judicially notice a fact. Therefore, a court may depart from the need for evidence to prove facts that are general knowledge. It must not, however, do so from subjective, personal knowledge, ie something which the trial judge has personal knowledge. What is the difference between the two? It is very difficult to distinguish the two when on many occasions *local knowledge* will have been judicially noted.

CASE EXAMPLE

Ingram v Percival [1969] 1 QB 584

At first instance the justices used what seemed to be their personal knowledge of tidal waters in a locality judicially to notice that netting of migrating salmon and trout was unlawful.

CASE EXAMPLE

Carter v Eastbourne Borough Council (2000) 164 JP 273

This is another interesting case where the justices judicially noted the age of some trees that an accused had uprooted, based on their personal knowledge of woodland.

In *Mullen v Hackney Borough Council* [1997] 1 WLR 1103, a county judge took into consideration his personal knowledge of past breaches of repairing undertakings by the defendant council when fixing the penalty for a breach of an undertaking in question. The Court of Appeal ruled that the judge was entitled to take judicial notice based on his special local knowledge of how the council behaved.

Remember that the basic rule is: a fact must be notorious and the decision judicially to notice it will be made on a case-by-case basis. Finally, there are a number of statutes that specifically provide for the taking of judicial notice on a number of facts.

Section 3 of the Interpretation Act 1978 requires the court to take judicial notice that an HM Government Stationery Office copy of a public Act of Parliament is accurate and complies with the official pronouncement of Parliament. In addition, all statutes are *prima facie* presumed to be public until the contrary is proved, see s 3 of the Interpretation Act 1978. Likewise, s 4(2) of the European Communities Act 1972 provides for judicial notice to be taken of treaties and community decisions.

KEY FACTS

Judge and jury

The trial judge or magistrates will determine all questions of law. However, lay magistrates are not legally qualified and therefore they will only determine questions of law on the advice of their clerk. All questions of fact in the Crown Court will be determined by the jury or by a single judge if sitting alone. In the Magistrates' Court, questions of fact will be determined by the magistrates. The trial judge is responsible for summing up the case to the jury and to ensure, like a manager, that the trial runs as smoothly as possible.

Questions of law – will relate to the definition of an offence, elements of an offence, rules of evidence, ie admissibility and existence of sufficient evidence to allow the jury to consider an issue.

Questions of fact – include questions relating to the weight of evidence, whether the evidence should be believed, ie is it credible and a defendant's fitness to plead.

Instances in which proof is unnecessary

In general the court requires evidence in order to prove a fact in issue. However, there are instances in which no proof will be required: formal admissions and judicial notice. Judicial notice allows the courts to use their general knowledge of the world, allowing the judge to dispense with the need for evidence to prove notorious facts.

1.8 The binding nature of judicial findings

An interesting question arises: what happens to judicial findings on issues that have been previously litigated, ie where a judge has already decided on an issue? Were this to arise the English law of evidence, in promoting consistency and preventing the continuous resurgence of the same issues, often requires such findings to be taken as binding a subsequent court of the same or lower jurisdiction, although further discussion on this point is beyond the scope of this book; however, reference may be made to the topic of *Estoppel*.

KEY FACTS

The binding nature of judicial findings

Judicial findings are binding as this promotes amongst other things consistency, and to prevent the continuous resurgence of issues the English law of evidence sometimes accepts judicial findings, ie in previous litigation, as binding a subsequent court of the same or lower jurisdiction.

1.9 Procedural rules: criminal and civil

The introduction of the Civil Procedure Rules (CPR) in 1998, and more recently, in 2005, the Criminal Procedure Rules (CrPR) have had the effect of restricting the amount of evidence that is admitted for trial. The rules promote the fact that the trial judge has responsibility of *effectively managing a case* and thereby ensuring efficient use of court resources. The full range of CPR can be accessed at http://www.justice.gov.uk/civil/procrules_fin/menus/rules.htm and the CrPR at http://www.justice.gov.uk/criminal/procrules_fin/rulesmenu.htm. In summary both sets of rules promote what is known as 'active case management' which includes dealing with a case efficiently and expeditiously, minimizing delay, ensuring that any evidence is presented in a logical way, ie short and clear, encouraging open communication and dealing with a number of issues at the same hearing, thereby avoiding pointless additional hearings. The full impact of the CrPR is not clear; however, what is clear is that the presiding judge has considerable discretion to achieve the aims of the over-riding object of the rules; see *K and Others* [2006] EWCA Crim 835.

ACTIVITY

Self-test questions

1. Was the traditional approach of the English law on evidence inclusionary or exclusionary?

2. What is meant by the terms 'direct' and 'percipient' evidence?

3. List two examples of circumstantial evidence.

4. What is hearsay?

5. How do presumptive and conclusive evidence differ?

6. Is all relevant evidence admissible?

7. What do the terms real and oral evidence mean?

8. Outline the difference between primary and secondary evidence.

9. Define the roles of the judge and jury.

10. What are facts in issue?

11. What is meant by the terms 'relevant' or 'collateral' facts?

12. Who decides question of law and questions of fact?

13. Give two examples of a question of law and a question of fact?

14. What is 'weight' in reference to evidence?

15. Who decides issues on foreign law, the judge or the jury?

16. What is judicial notice?

17. How do judicial notice and personal knowledge differ?

18. Explain what is meant by the term 'best evidence'.

19. Explain how the English law of evidence treats judicial findings.

20. How do the CPR and CrPR affect evidence in trials?

Further reading

Cornish W. and Sealy P., *Juries and the Rules of Evidence* [1973] Crim LR 208.

Gallanis, *The rise of Modern Evidence Law*, 84 Iowa L Rev 499 (1999).

Munday, R. (2008). *The Law of Evidence*. Oxford: Oxford University Press.

Ormerod D. and Birch D., *The Evolution of the Discretionary Exclusion of Evidence* [2004] Crim LR 767.

Internet links

CPR: http://www.justice.gov.uk/civil/procrules_fin/menus/rules.htm

CrPR: http://www.justice.gov.uk/criminal/procrules_fin/rulesmenu.htm

chapter 2 THE LAW OF EVIDENCE. THE BURDENS AND STANDARDS OF PROOF

AIMS AND OBJECTIVES

By the end of this chapter you should be able to:

- Comprehend and distinguish the various types of burdens of proof in civil and criminal cases

- Understand the principles concerning the different standards of proof

- Identify the incidence of the legal burdens of proof and the exceptions to the general rule

- Understand the function of the burdens of proof in litigation.

2.1 Introduction

In any legal dispute it is important to determine which party has the obligation to prove a point in contention, ie the incidence of the legal burden of proof. It is also necessary to decide how much evidence is needed to prove the particular point in contention or the degree of cogency required of the evidence to satisfy the court on the point in issue, ie the standard of proof. The term 'burden of proof' is connected with the general proposition that in legal proceedings the axiom is: 'He who asserts must prove', ie a party who makes a positive allegation is required to prove his case. In addition, in criminal cases an automatic presumption of innocence is required to be drawn. Accordingly, on a charge of murder the accused is presumed to be innocent until the contrary is proved. It is therefore incumbent on the prosecution to prove that the defendant caused the death of the victim with the appropriate *mens rea*. Thus, the prosecution (or the Crown) will bear the legal burden of proof to establish all the elements of the offence. Similarly, in civil cases the party making the assertion is put to proof, for example in an action for negligence the claimant is required to prove that the defendant caused the relevant injuries in breach of a duty of care.

2.1.1 Several burdens

In many prosecutions or causes of actions there may be a multiplicity of issues that the parties may wish to raise in the court. On a charge of murder the defendant may wish to raise the

defences of provocation and diminished responsibility. On whom would the burden of proof lie and what is the nature of the burden? On the issue of provocation the defendant does not bear a legal burden but merely a duty to adduce sufficient evidence to raise the issue. The prosecution bears a legal burden to rebut such defence beyond a reasonable doubt. In other words, the defendant does not bear a legal burden to prove the defence of provocation but only an evidential burden to raise the defence. The defendant is only required to adduce sufficient evidence to raise the issue of provocation to the satisfaction of the judge. On the issue of diminished responsibility, by statute (see s 2 of the Homicide Act 1957) the accused bears a legal burden to prove the elements of the defence on a balance of probabilities. Thus, the phrase 'burden of proof' is ambiguous. It is generally accepted that there are two burdens of proof – 'legal' and 'evidential'.

2.1.2 Legal burden

The phrase 'legal burden' was coined by Lord Denning and may be vindicated by the fact that its incidence is determined by substantive law. This appears to be the most popular expression and will be used in this book. Other expressions used from time to time include 'the burden of proof on the pleadings' (Phipson), 'the risk of non-persuasion' (Wigmore), 'persuasive burden' (Glanville Williams), 'probative burden'.

The legal burden of proof is the obligation to prove a point in contention, or fact in issue, in order to convince the tribunal of fact of the truth of the assertion. If a party fails to discharge a legal burden of proof to the satisfaction of the tribunal of fact he will, as a matter of course, lose the case. Thus, if the prosecution fails to prove the guilt of the accused beyond a reasonable doubt the accused is entitled to an acquittal. Equally, in a negligence action if the claimant fails to prove the elements of negligence, judgment will be given for the defendant.

The legal burden is fixed at the beginning of the trial and remains unchanged throughout the trial and never shifts to another party. Thus, in a criminal case, the various elements that constitute the offence are required to be proved by the prosecution. Failure on the part of the prosecution to prove one or more elements of the offence will result in an acquittal of the accused. The general rule regarding a fixed burden on the prosecution remains the same even though exceptionally, a legal burden on a different issue may also be imposed on the accused, for example on a charge of murder the accused may raise the defence of diminished responsibility. In this case the prosecution will have a legal burden to prove the respective elements of murder, but the accused will have the legal burden of proving the elements of the defence. These are separate issues and consistent with the principle that the parties bear separate burdens.

2.1.3 Evidential burden

In addition, a party may bear an evidential burden. This is the obligation to put sufficient evidence of a point in contention before the court, to justify to the court or tribunal considering the matter, ie a duty to raise a *prima facie* case or adduce sufficient evidence to the satisfaction of the tribunal of law that an issue ought to be considered ultimately by the tribunal of fact. The discharge of the evidential burden is for the judge to decide in a case tried by judge and jury.

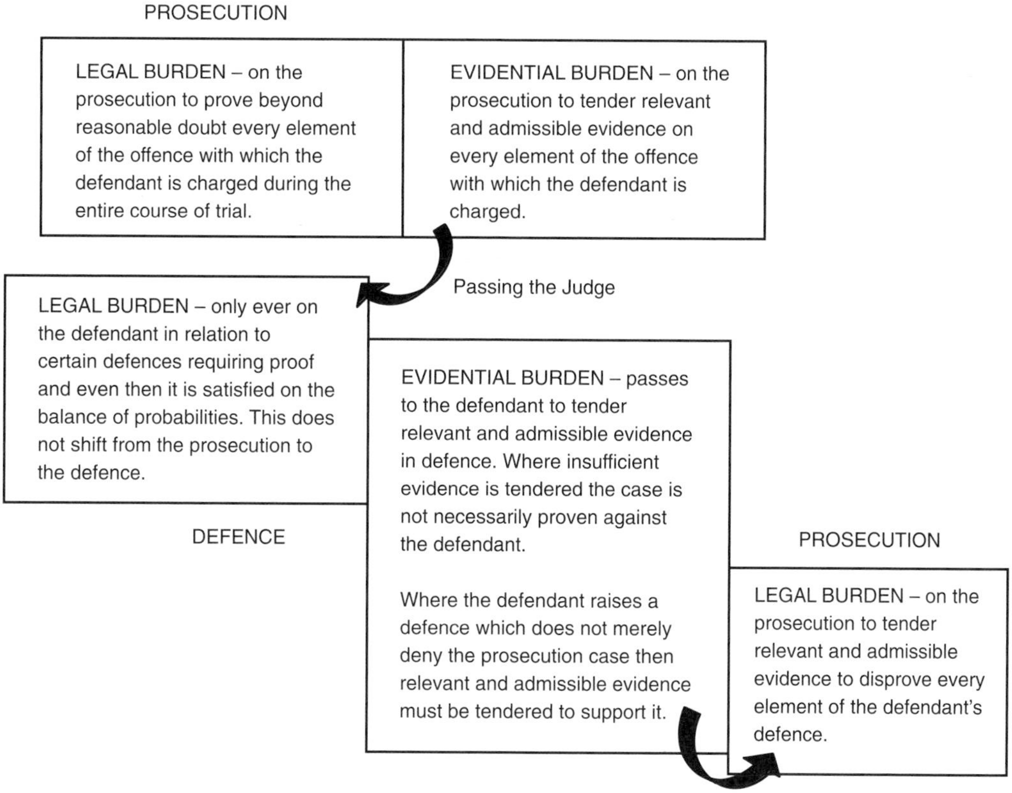

PROSECUTION

| LEGAL BURDEN – on the prosecution to prove beyond reasonable doubt every element of the offence with which the defendant is charged during the entire course of trial. | EVIDENTIAL BURDEN – on the prosecution to tender relevant and admissible evidence on every element of the offence with which the defendant is charged. |

Passing the Judge

| LEGAL BURDEN – only ever on the defendant in relation to certain defences requiring proof and even then it is satisfied on the balance of probabilities. This does not shift from the prosecution to the defence. |

DEFENCE

EVIDENTIAL BURDEN – passes to the defendant to tender relevant and admissible evidence in defence. Where insufficient evidence is tendered the case is not necessarily proven against the defendant.

Where the defendant raises a defence which does not merely deny the prosecution case then relevant and admissible evidence must be tendered to support it.

PROSECUTION

LEGAL BURDEN – on the prosecution to tender relevant and admissible evidence to disprove every element of the defendant's defence.

Figure 2.1 Distinction between legal and evidential burdens of proof

2.1.4 Evidential burden of proof?

There is some judicial disquiet concerning the expression 'evidential burden'. Some judges do not regard this concept as a burden of proof as such. The reason is that a party with an evidential burden is not under an obligation to convince the tribunal of fact of anything. Such a party may rely on the evidence to suggest that certain facts exist, for example in a criminal case the defendant may rely on discredited evidence adduced by the Crown to argue that a reasonable doubt exists. Lord Devlin in *Jayasena v R* [1970] AC 618:

> '. . . it is misleading to call it a burden of proof, whether described as legal or evidential or by any other adjective, when it can be discharged by production of evidence that falls short of proof.'

The issue here is whether a party with the evidential burden has a duty to raise the issue as part of its case, or more broadly, whether the issue exists on the facts of the case, whether or not raised by a specific party.

In *R v Gill* (1963) 47 Cr App R 166, Edmund Davies J expressed himself as if the issue is required to be raised by the relevant party:

> J
>
> 'The accused either by cross examination of the prosecution witnesses or by evidence called on his behalf or by a combination of the two, must place before the court such material as makes [the defence] a live issue fit and proper to be left to the jury. But once he has succeeded in doing this [and thereby discharged his evidential burden] it is then for the Crown to destroy that defence in such a manner as to leave in the jury's minds no reasonable doubt that the accused cannot be absolved on the grounds of the alleged [facts constituting the defence].'

Whereas Lord Tucker in *Bullard v R* [1957] AC 635 adopted the broader view to the effect that the relevant issue is not treated as the responsibility of a party:

> J
>
> 'It has long been settled law that if on the evidence, whether of the prosecution or of the defence, there is any evidence of provocation fit to be left to a jury, and whether or not this issue has been specifically raised at the trial by counsel for the defence and whether or not the accused has said in terms that he was provoked, it is the duty of the judge, after a proper direction, to leave it open to the jury to return a verdict of manslaughter, if they are not satisfied beyond a reasonable doubt that the killing was unprovoked.'

It is submitted that the correct approach was that stated by Lord Tucker. It matters not how the issue was raised or indeed who raised the issue, provided that it was raised in the trial, the evidential burden may be discharged.

Lord Bingham in *AG's Reference (No 4 of 2002)* [2004] 3 WLR 976 refers to the phrase as a 'burden of raising' an issue in the trial as opposed to a 'burden of proof' *simpliciter*:

> J
>
> 'An evidential burden is not a burden of proof. It is a burden of raising, on the evidence in the case, an issue as to the matter in question fit for consideration by the tribunal of fact. If an issue is properly raised, it is for the prosecutor to prove, beyond reasonable doubt, that that ground of exoneration does not avail the defendant.'

On the other hand there is judicial support for the expression evidential burden: Clarke LJ in
DPP v Sheldrake [2004] QB 487 declared:

> **J** 'It is … sensible to continue to use it [evidential burden] provided that it is
> recognized that all that is required to discharge the burden is to identify evidence
> raising the issue.'

2.1.5 Party with legal and evidential burdens

In addition, the party with a legal burden of proof also bears an evidential burden on that issue,
subject to a few exceptions such as presumptions, formal admissions and judicial notice. This
means that the party with the legal burden has a duty to adduce sufficient evidence to raise the
issue. This is inevitable in the sense that the greater burden includes the lesser burden. At the
same time, different tribunals decide on the different burdens. The tribunal of fact decides
whether the legal burden has been discharged, whereas the tribunal of law decides whether the
legal burden is discharged. Moreover, the discharge of the evidential burden is determined before
the discharge of the legal burden. The effect is that failure to discharge the evidential burden on
an issue will mean that the judge will rule that there is insufficient evidence of the existence of
the issue and must reject the allegation or withdraw it from the jury. On the other hand, the
successful discharge of the evidential burden does not automatically mean that that party will
discharge the legal burden. Discharging the evidential burden means only that the opponent runs

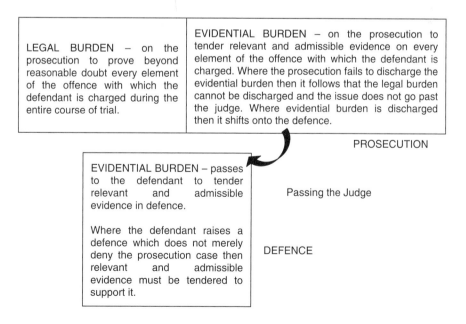

Figure 2.2 Party with both legal and evidential burdens of proof

a risk of an adverse finding by the tribunal of fact on that issue. At the end of the day the court (tribunal of fact) is required to decide whether the party has proved his case.

2.1.6 Separate evidential burden

A party may bear an evidential burden without a corresponding legal burden, for example on a charge of murder the defendant may raise the defences of provocation or duress or self-defence. With respect to such defences the accused bears only an evidential burden without a corresponding legal burden. The obligation on the accused is to adduce sufficient evidence to convince the judge that the defence(s) ought to be considered by the jury. The defendant may convince the judge (discharge his evidential burden) but may or may not convince the jury of the existence of such defence(s).

Incidence of the legal burden of proof – civil cases

Factors to be considered:
- rules of substantive law
- statements of the case (pleadings)
- rules of convenience

Examples
- *Sutton v Sadler*
- *Constantine Steamship v Imperial Smelting Co*
- Validity and reliance on an exclusion clause in a contract – *The Glendarroch*, allegation of a fundamental breach *Levison v Patent Carpet Cleaning, Munro v War Risks Association, Hurst v Evans*

Figure 2.3 Party with evidential burden of proof

2.1.7 Importance of distinguishing legal and evidential burdens

As a final introductory remark, it is essential that the legal and evidential burdens are distinguished for the following four reasons:

(a) to ascertain which party has the right to begin, ie to open his case and call the evidence. This is the party with the legal burden of proof. This burden is cast on the party at the beginning of the trial and stays with him until the end of the trial

(b) when a party (perhaps the defendant) makes a 'no case' submission at the close of a claimant's or prosecution's case the judge will rule on whether the evidential burden (cast on the party with the legal burden) has been discharged. A successful 'no case' submission would result in a failure on the part of the opponent to discharge the evidential burden

(c) when the tribunal of fact is in doubt after all the evidence has been adduced. The issue here is whether the legal burden has been discharged. This in turn will depend on the type or degree of doubt that has been entertained by the tribunal of fact

(d) when the appellate court is required to decide on the correctness of a summing up or judgment dealing with the burden of proof. The question here is whether or not the trial judge's ruling on the incidence of the burden of proof is accurate.

2.2 Incidence of the legal burden of proof

The incidence of the legal burden of proof involves the principles applied by the courts (and statute) to allocate the legal burden of proof on a party. The fundamental principle is based on the motto 'he who asserts must prove'. In criminal cases the basic principle is derived from the automatic presumption of innocence. It follows that in criminal cases the prosecution is required to prove all the elements of the offence.

2.2.1 Civil cases

In civil cases the party who substantially asserts the affirmative will bear the legal burden of proof. In any particular case this would depend on the circumstances in which the claim arises. This rule is adopted principally because it is fair that those who invoke the aid of the law ought to be put to proof and partly because a negative is more difficult to establish than an affirmative. The principle may be summarized in the latin maxim, *ei qui affirmat, non ei qui negat, incumbit probatio* (the burden of proof lies upon he who affirms and not upon he who denies).

In deciding which party makes an affirmative allegation, consideration is required to be given to the substance of the issue and not merely to the form in which the issue is presented. It is probably true to say that a positive assertion, in theory, can always be converted into a negative statement by appropriate linguistic manipulation, for example a claim for damages for breach of a repairing covenant may be expressed either that the defendant did not repair the house or that he allowed the house to become dilapidated. The mode of expressing the claim does not disguise the issue that, in substance, the legal burden is borne by the claimant for it is he who makes the assertion. A test laid down in *Abrath v NE Rly* (1883) 11 QBD 440, is, 'If the assertion of a negative is an essential part of the plaintiff's case, the proof of the assertion still rests upon the plaintiff' (Bowen LJ). In this case the claim was for malicious prosecution. The court decided that the legal burden of absence of reasonable and probable cause rested on the claimant, *per* Bowen LJ:

J 'Whenever litigation exists, somebody must go on with it; the plaintiff is the first to begin; if he does nothing, he fails; if he makes a prima facie case, and nothing is done to answer it, the defendant fails. The test, therefore, as to the burden of proof or onus of proof, whichever term is used, is simply this: to ask oneself which party will be successful if no evidence is given, or if no more evidence is given than has been given at a particular point of the case, for it is obvious that as the controversy involved in the litigation travels on, the parties from moment to moment may reach points at which the onus shifts, and at which the tribunal will have to say that if the case stops there, it must be decided in a particular manner.'

In determining whether an affirmative allegation has been made and the nature of that allegation, and therefore the incidence of the legal burden of proof, the courts apply a number of principles. The principal issue involves rules of substantive law. If this principle is not decisive the courts will have regard to the statements of the case and as a last resort, a balance of convenience. In practice, the determination of this question is based on precedent.

CASE EXTRACT

Sutton v Sadler (1857) 3 CBNS 87

The heir at law claimed to be entitled to the deceased's estate as opposed to the devisee under the testator's will. The basis of the claim by the heir was that the will was invalid on the ground that the testator was insane. The trial judge decided that the legal burden of proof rested on the claimant, heir at law. On appeal, this was considered to be a misdirection. The devisee, defendant, bore the legal burden of proof, for it was he who was making the allegation that the will was valid. The devisee may discharge his evidential burden by relying on a presumption, namely, that the will appeared to be rational on the face of it.

Cresswell J:

J 'If, indeed, a will, not irrational on the face of it, is produced before a jury and the execution of it proved, and no other evidence offered, the jury would be properly told that they ought to find for the will, and if the party opposing the will gives some evidence of incompetency, the jury may, nevertheless, if it does not disturb their belief in the competency of the testator, find in favour of the will and in each case the presumption in favour of competency would prevail. But that is not a mere presumption of law, and, when the whole matter is before the jury on evidence given on both sides, they ought not to affirm that a document is the will of a competent testator, unless they believe that it really is so.'

CASE EXTRACT

Joseph Constantine Steamship v Imperial Smelting Corporation [1942] AC 154 (HL)

In this case the charterers of a ship claimed damages from the owners for breach of contract in failing to load the ship by a specific date. The owners defended on the ground that the contract was frustrated by the destruction of the ship owing to an explosion. In contract law, frustration is a defence to a claim for breach of contract, but only if the frustrating event occurred without the fault of the defendant. The question was, which party bore the legal burden of proof on the issue of fault. The court decided that the legal burden of proof rested on the claimants to prove that the defendants were at fault.

Viscount Maugham:

> 'I think the burden of proof in any particular case depends on the circumstances under which the claim arises. In general, the rule which applies is *ei qui affirmat non ei qui negat incumbit probatio*. It is an ancient rule founded on considerations of good sense and it should not be departed from without strong reasons. The position as to proof on non-responsibility for the event in such a case as the present is not very different from the position of a plaintiff in an action for negligence where contributory negligence on his part is alleged. In such a case the plaintiff must prove that there was some negligent act or omission on the part of the defendant which caused or materially contributed to the injury, but it is for the defendant to prove affirmatively, if he so contends, that there was contributory negligence on the part of the person injured . . .
>
> If, however, I am right in the opinion above expressed that the onus of establishing absence of default did not rest on the appellants [original defendants], the mere possibility of default on their part is not sufficient to disentitle them to rely on the principle of frustration.'

It should be noted that, in this case, the court also considered that it would have been difficult for the defendants to prove the negative, ie that they were not at fault. Accordingly, the balance of convenience played a material part in deciding the incidence of the legal burden of proof.

In respect of claims for breaches of contracts containing exclusion clauses the claimant is required to establish the existence of the contract, breach and resulting loss. The defendant will claim that

33

the exclusion clause had been validly incorporated into the contract and protects him from the claim for breach of contract. In short, the party seeking to rely on a clause in a contract limiting his liability will bear the legal burden of proof. However, an allegation of a fundamental breach of the contract may have the effect of destroying the defence based on the exclusion clause. The issue that was raised in *Levison v Patent Carpet Cleaning* was, which party had the legal burden of proof with respect to the exclusion clause? On the one hand, it was argued that fundamental breach was part of the claim in respect of breach of contract. On the other hand, it was argued that fundamental breach affects the enforcement of the exclusion clause and therefore required the defendant to bear the legal burden of proving that the loss did not constitute a fundamental breach, ie a negative. The Court of Appeal decided that it was the defendant who bore the legal burden of proof.

CASE EXTRACT

Levison v Patent Carpet Cleaning [1977] 3 All ER 98

The claimant deposited his expensive Chinese carpet to the defendants for cleaning. The contract, signed by the claimant, contained a clause exempting the defendants from liability for negligence. The defendants failed to return the carpet to the claimant on the ground that it was lost. In an action for breach of contract the defendants claimed that the exclusion clause protected them from liability. The claimant alleged that the non-delivery of the goods amounted to a fundamental breach of the contract by the defendants and deprived them of the benefit of the exclusion clause. The issue was, which party had the burden of proof regarding fundamental breach? The County Court Judge decided against the claimant who appealed to the Court of Appeal.

It was held that the defendant bore the legal burden of proof to show that the loss suffered by the claimant did not amount to a fundamental breach.

Lord Denning MR:

'This brings me to the crux of the case . . . On whom is the burden to prove that there was fundamental breach?

Upon principle, I should have thought that the burden was on the cleaners to prove that they were not guilty of a fundamental breach. After all, Mrs Levinson does not know what happened to it. The cleaners are the ones who know, or should know, what happened to the carpet, and the burden should be on them to say what it was . . .

CONTINUED ▶

J '. . . I am clearly of the opinion that, in a contract of bailment, when a bailee seeks to escape liability on the ground that he was not negligent or that he was excused by an exception or limitation clause, then he must show what happened to the goods. He must prove all the circumstances known to him in which the loss or damage occurred. If it appears that the goods were lost or damaged without any negligence on his part, then, of course, he is not liable. If it appears that they were lost or damaged by a slight breach − not going to the root of the contract − he may be protected by the exemption or limitation clause. But if he leaves the cause of loss or damage undiscovered and unexplained − then I think he is liable, because it is then quite likely that the goods were stolen by one of his servants; or delivered by his servant to the wrong address; or damaged by reckless or wilful conduct; all of which the offending servant will conceal and not make known to his employer. Such conduct would be a fundamental breach against which the exemption or limitation clause will not protect him.'

It may be noted that in this case the court had regard to the balance of convenience principle. If the legal burden of proving fundamental breach was imposed on the claimant, she would have found it difficult to discharge; whereas, the defendants ought to have known what happened to the carpet.

The claimant bears the legal burden of proving that the loss complained of falls within a proviso to a valid exclusion clause; see *The Glendarroch* [1894] P 226. The claimants brought an action for the non-delivery of goods shipped under a bill of lading. The goods had been damaged by sea water. The bill of lading exempted the defendants from liability for loss or damage occasioned by perils of the sea, provided that the defendants were not negligent. The Court of Appeal held that the claimants bore the legal burden of proving that the damage was caused by the defendants' negligence, *per* Lord Esher MR:

J 'When you come to the exceptions, among others there is the exception of perils of the sea. There are no words which say 'Perils of the sea not caused by the negligence of the captain or the crew'. You have got to read those words in by a necessary inference. How can you read them in? You have got the plain words, in their ordinary sense, that the ship-owner is relieved if the loss is a loss by perils of the sea in the ordinary sense of the word. But then you have to read in the other.

CONTINUED ▸

> You can only read it in, in my opinion, as an exception upon the exceptions. You must read in 'Except the loss is by perils of the sea, unless or except that loss is the result of the negligence of the captain or sailors of the owner.' That being so, I think that, according to the ordinary course of practice, each party would have to prove the part of the matter which lies upon him. The plaintiff would have to prove the contract and the non-delivery. If he leaves that in doubt, of course he fails. The defendant's answer is, 'Yes, but my case was brought within the exception, within its ordinary meaning.' That lies upon him. Then the plaintiff has a right to say there are exceptional circumstances – viz, that the damage was brought about by the negligence of the defendant's servants, and it seems to me that it is for the plaintiff to make out that second exception.'

A different result was reached with reference to the law of marine insurance law. In *Munro, Brice and Co v War Risks Association* [1918] 2 KB 78, a claimant whose ship had been lost claimed under an insurance policy insuring it against loss by perils of the sea, subject to a proviso excepting loss by capture, seizure and consequences of hostility. The court held that the defendant bore the legal burden of proving that the loss fell within the proviso. The court took the view that once the claimant (assured) proved that its ship had been lost at sea he had made out a *prima facie* case under the policy against the defendants. The latter was required to prove that the loss was excepted under the hostilities clause.

However, a decision that is difficult to justify is *Hurst v Evans* [1917] 1 KB 352. The claimant, a jeweller, had an insurance policy in respect of loss or damage to his stock except where caused by any servant in his exclusive employ. He suffered loss and sued on the policy. The defendants claimed that the loss was caused by the theft of M, a servant in the claimant's exclusive employ. Evidence was admitted that M had been seen two days before the theft in a public house with three highly skilled safebreakers known to the police. The court held that the onus of proof was on the claimant to prove his loss was not due to one of the exceptions and he had not discharged his burden.

This case was disapproved in *Munro*, although not overruled. It is difficult to reconcile with *Munro*, save for the fact that the policy in *Hurst* was a special risks insurance policy. On a balance of convenience the decision could be justified because only the claimant could explain, or ought to be able to explain, how the loss occurred; but placing the legal burden on the claimant required him to prove a negative.

Parties may make provision in a contract for the legal burden on certain issues to lie on one or other of them. At common law such clauses are valid but will have to be clearly expressed. A contractual term which alters the normal rules on the burden of proof counts as an exemption clause for the purposes of the Unfair Contact Terms Act 1977, see s 13(1)(c).

2.2.2 Criminal cases – general rule – the 'golden thread' theory

In criminal cases the fundamental rule is that the prosecution is required to prove all the elements of the offence to the satisfaction of the jury or tribunal of fact. Another way of expressing the principle is that there is an automatic presumption of innocence in favour of the accused. This principle has been affirmed in Art 6(2) of the European Convention on Human Rights, but is an integral part of the common law. The general rule may be illustrated by *Woolmington v DPP* [1935] AC 462.

ASE EXTRACT

Woolmington v DPP [1935] AC 462

On a charge of murder by shooting, the accused raised the defence of accident. The judge directed the jury that once the Crown had proved the killing at the hands of the accused, it must be presumed to be murder and that it was for the accused to prove circumstances which would excuse the homicide as an accident. The accused was convicted of murder and appealed. It was held that this was a misdirection and the conviction was quashed.

Lord Sankey LC:

J

'While the prosecution must prove the guilt of the prisoner, there is no such burden laid on the prisoner to prove his innocence and it is sufficient for him to raise a doubt as to his guilt: he is not bound to satisfy the jury of his innocence . . . Throughout the web of the English criminal law one golden thread is always to be seen that it is the duty of the prosecution to prove the prisoner's guilt subject to . . . the defence of insanity and [statutory exceptions]. If, at the end of and on the whole of the case, there is a reasonable doubt, created by the evidence given by either the prosecution or the prisoner, as to whether the prisoner killed the deceased with a malicious intention, the prosecution has not made the case and the prisoner is entitled to an acquittal. No matter what the charge or where the trial, the principle that the prosecution must prove the guilt of the prisoner is part of the common law of England and no attempt to whittle it down can be entertained. When dealing with a murder case the Crown must prove (a) death as the result of a voluntary act of the accused; and (b) malice of the accused. When evidence of death and malice has been given (this is a question for the jury) the accused is entitled to show, by evidence or by

CONTINUED ▶

J examination of the circumstances adduced by the Crown, that the act on his part which caused death was either unintentional or provoked. If the jury are either satisfied that this explanation or, upon a review of all the evidence, are left in reasonable doubt whether, even if his explanation be not accepted, the act was unintentional or provoked, the prisoner is entitled to [the benefit of the doubt].'

The *Woolmington* principle puts to rest any doubt as to the appropriate starting point in criminal prosecutions. This is the 'golden thread' theory that the prosecution bears the legal burden of proof. For the avoidance of doubt it must follow that if the prosecution fails to discharge its evidential burden, ie fails to make out a *prima facie* case, the accused is entitled to an acquittal, for it would be clear that the prosecution will not be able to discharge its legal burden. The decision in *Woolmington* also classifies the exceptional circumstances when a reverse burden of proof will be cast on the accused. This will be considered later.

The effect of placing the legal burden on the prosecution results in the jury or fact-finding tribunal deciding whether the onus had been discharged. This is done at the end of the trial when all the evidence had been adduced. The governing principle also has the added advantage of assessing the risks of misdirection on the part of the judge. This involves a question of law for the courts to decide. The general principle is justified on the grounds that a high value is placed on the human rights of individuals, and the resources available to the Crown in the detection and presentation of the case against the accused far outweigh the facilities available to the individual.

2.2.3 Exceptions in criminal cases

Common law exception – insanity

The only common law defence in which the accused bears the legal burden of proof is insanity. The reason for this exception lies in the presentation of the rules in *McNaghten's* case (1843) 10 Cl and F 200. It was assumed by the judges that the accused ought to bear the legal burden of proving insanity. Today, it is extremely doubtful whether there are any sound policy reasons for placing the legal burden on the accused, as opposed to an evidential burden.

The McNaghten Rules are: 'The jurors ought to be told in all cases that every man is presumed to be sane and to possess a sufficient degree of reason to be responsible for his crimes, until the contrary be proved to their satisfaction; and that to establish a defence on the grounds of insanity, it must be clearly proved that, at the time of the committing of the act, the party accused was labouring under such a defect of reason from disease of the mind, as not to know the nature and quality of the act he was doing; or, if he did know it, he did not know he was doing what was wrong.'

Difficulty may sometimes arise where there is evidence of both insane automatism and non-insane automatism of the accused at the time of the alleged commission of the offence. It is imperative that the judge in his summing up to the jury distinguish between these two defences, for the incidence of the legal burden of proof differ. In respect of insane automatism raised by the accused, the defence will bear the legal burden of proof on a balance of probabilities. With regard to non-insane automatism the accused bears an evidential burden of raising the issue, but once there is sufficient evidence of the defence the legal burden to rebut the defence lies with the prosecution.

In *R v Burns* [1973] 58 Cr App R 364, Stephenson LJ said 'It is not for the defence to prove automatism, it is for the prosecution to negative it once the defence lays a foundation for it. Nowhere does the judge draw that distinction . . .'

In any event, *prima facie* evidence of the probable existence of the defence(s) must be established by the accused before the judge becomes duty bound to direct the jury of the incidence of the burden of proof regarding that issue. If there is insufficient evidence to support the defence of sane automatism, the judge is entitled to withdraw the issue from the jury. In short, if the defence fails to discharge its evidential burden, the issue may be withdrawn from the trial.

In *Bratty v AG for N.I* [1963] AC 386, Viscount Kilmuir said: '. . . Not only must automatism be expressly put forward as a defence, but also a proper foundation must be laid for it . . . In my view . . . it is necessary that a proper foundation be laid before a judge can leave automatism to the jury. That foundation is not forthcoming merely from unaccepted evidence of a defect of reason from a disease of the mind. There would need to be other evidence on which a jury could find non-insane automatism.' In this case the charge was murder and the accused raised defences of insane and non-insane automatism. There was insufficient evidence of non-insane automatism and the judge rejected the defence. The jury rejected the defence of insane automatism and found him guilty of murder. His appeal was dismissed.

Express statutory reversal of the burden

Lord Sankey in *Woolmington v DPP* referred to statutory exceptions to the general rule. These include both express and implied statutory exceptions or reverse burdens created by statute. There are a number of occasions when Parliament has expressly imposed a legal burden on the accused to prove a defence and sometimes the issue may concern an element of the offence.

Much depends on the wording of the statute. The statutory provision may expressly state that it is for the accused to prove the relevant defence such as s 2(2) of the Homicide Act 1957 in respect of diminished responsibility, which states 'on a charge of murder, it shall be for the defence to prove that the person charged is by virtue of this section not liable to be convicted of murder.'

Alternatively, the statutory provision may declare that an offence shall be 'deemed to be committed unless the contrary be proved'. The effect is the same as if the statute had declared

that it shall be for the accused to prove to the contrary. On a charge under the Prevention of Corruption Act 1906, s 2 of the Prevention of Corruption Act 1916 enacts,

S 'Where in any proceedings against a person for an offence under the [1906] Act, it is proved that any money, gift or other consideration has been paid, given to or received by a person in the employment of HM Government or any Government Department
. . . the money, gift or consideration shall be deemed to have been paid or given . . .
corruptly . . . unless the contrary is proved.'

It may be noted that this provision concerns an element of the offence, namely, corruption or corrupt payments. A multitude of other statutory enactments have achieved the same. Many of these provisions will need to be reviewed in view of the approaches adopted by the House of Lords in *R v Lambert* [2001] 2 Cr App R 511, see later under the 'Impact of the Human Rights Act 1998'.

In those cases where the accused bears a legal burden of proof (either at common law or by statute), the standard of proof does not exceed a balance of probabilities; see *R v Carr-Briant.*

CASE EXTRACT

R v Carr-Briant [1943] KB 607

The accused, a director in a firm, was charged under the Prevention of Corruption Act 1906 in that it was alleged that he gave or loaned £60 to an engineer employed in a Govt. department. The defence was that the payment had not been made corruptly. The judge directed the jury that the standard of proof imposed on the accused was beyond a reasonable doubt. He was convicted and appealed.

The Court of Appeal allowed the appeal and decided that the judge had misdirected the jury as to the standard of proof which ought to have been on a balance of probabilities.

Humphreys J:

J 'In our judgment where, either by statute or at common law, some matter is presumed against the accused person "unless the contrary is proved", the jury should be directed that it is for them to decide whether the contrary is proved; that the burden of proof required is less than that required at the hands of the prosecution in proving the case beyond a reasonable doubt, and that the burden may be discharged by evidence satisfying the jury of the probability of that which the accused is called upon to establish.'

Implied statutory reversal of the legal burden

There are a number of cases where an enactment may be construed as impliedly imposing a legal burden on the accused. In other words the provisions may be treated as equivalent to occasions when Parliament expressly intended to impose a legal burden on the accused.

Section 101 of the Magistrates Courts Act 1980 lays down the general principle in respect of summary offences. Similar provisions had existed long before the *Woolmington* case. Section 101 of the Magistrates Courts Act 1980 states:

S 'Where a defendant to an information or complaint relies for his defence on any exception, exemption, proviso, excuse or qualification, whether or not it accompanies the description of the offence or matter of complaint in the enactment creating the offence or on which the complaint is founded, the burden of proving the exception, exemption, proviso, excuse or qualification, shall be on him; and this notwithstanding that the information or complaint contains an allegation negativing the exception, exemption, proviso, excuse or qualification.'

The effect of the section is that where the conduct of the accused creates an offence but in circumstances where the statute creates a defence in respect of an exception, exemption, proviso, excuse or qualification, the burden of proving that the conduct comes within the exception, exemption, etc. will be placed on the accused. The section makes clear that it does not matter whether the provision relied on forms part of the clause creating the offence or whether it appears elsewhere in the statute. The principle originates partly from the notion that it is easy or easier for the accused to prove that he falls within the exception, exemption, etc. because of access to the relevant information and partly from the original provision enacted in s 39(2) of the Summary Jurisdiction Act 1879.

Section 101 is concerned with cases where the defendant is charged with doing an act which is not outright unlawful but becomes unlawful in certain circumstances, such as driving a motor vehicle on a public road without a valid licence; see *John v Humphreys* [1955] 1 WLR 325. In such a case, driving a motor vehicle on a public road is not an unlawful act *per se*, but becomes unlawful when the driver does not have a valid licence. The non-possession of a valid licence is not part of the offence requiring the prosecution to prove the negative but requires the accused, if he wishes, to prove the existence of a valid licence. The predominant application of such provisions is in respect of regulatory offences for which a licence or permission is required. The prosecution retains the legal burden of proving that the accused committed the prohibited act. If the prosecution fails to discharge the evidential burden that is attached to the legal burden, the accused is not put to proof and is entitled to be acquitted. In *Gatland v Metropolitan Police Commissioner* [1968] 2 QB 279, the accused had been charged that without lawful authority or excuse he had deposited a thing, namely, a builders' skip, on a highway in consequence whereof a user of the highway had been endangered. It was held that, although it was for the accused to establish any lawful authority or excuse, and although he failed to do so, it was for the

prosecution to prove, first that the article in question had been deposited upon the highway, and second, that in consequence thereof a user of the highway was injured or endangered. As there had been no evidence that any user of the highway had been injured or endangered in consequence of the deposit, the prosecution had failed to discharge its legal burden and the conviction was quashed.

In *Nagy v Weston* [1965] 1 All ER 78, the charge was under s 121(1) of the Highways Act 1959 (now s 137(1) of the Highways Act 1980) which provides that it is an offence 'to wilfully obstruct the highway without lawful authority or excuse'. The court decided that this provision placed a legal burden of proof on the prosecution to prove a negative; namely, that the defendant did not have lawful authority or excuse. Section 101 (or its predecessor) was not applicable. The effect is that there has been little consistency in the approach to s 101 provisions.

In *Hirst v Chief Constable of West Yorkshire* [1987] Crim LR 330, the court endorsed the construction of the provision adopted in *Nagy*. In *Hirst*, the charge was under s 137(1) of the Highways Act 1980. The case concerned an alleged obstruction of the highway by protesting animal rights supporters. The court decided that the Crown bore a legal burden of proof to show lack of lawful excuse for the obstruction. It could be argued that these cases can be reconciled on the ground that in *Gatland*, to deposit an object, especially a large object, on the highway was *prima facie* capable of endangering life until the accused proves to the contrary; whereas, in *Nagy* and *Hirst*, being on the highway *per se* is not unlawful until the Crown proves to the contrary. Such cases have prompted JC Smith, '*The Presumption of Innocence*' (1987) 38 Northern Ireland Legal Quarterly, to state that, 'to deduce from this that Parliament intended to exclude the effect of s 101 from the obstruction offence, though not from another offence under the same statute, in respect of which Parliament has used exactly the same language, would seem to be to indulge in fiction of an arbitrary and undesirable kind.'

It is a question of construction of the statutory provision to determine whether the prohibited conduct, the subject-matter of the complaint, is to be treated as part of the offence imposing a legal burden on the prosecution, ie a negative pre-condition, or, whether the act is to be treated as a defence. In commenting on the predecessor to s 101 of the 1980 Act, in *Shehan v Cork JJ* [1908] 2 IR 1, Gibson J said:

> **J** 'Does the section [creating the charge] make the act described an offence subject to particular exceptions, qualifications, etc, which, where applicable, make the *prima facie* offence an innocent act, or does the statute make an act *prima facie* innocent an offence when done under certain conditions? In the former case the exception need not be negatived; in the latter words of exception may constitute the offence.'

Much turns on the wording of the statute in question. Words such as 'unless', 'except', 'other than' or 'provided always' indicate that the offence is within s 101, but the section as a whole is required to be construed. In *Nimmo v Alexander Cowan & Sons Ltd* [1968] AC 107, the House of Lords took the opportunity to offer general guidance on the construction of provisions. It was an offence not to comply with s 209 of the Factories Act 1961. This section provided that a workplace should be a safe place for employees . . . 'so far as is reasonably practicable'. In *Nimmo*, the Court had to consider whether this provision created an 'excuse, exemption . . . etc'. causing the burden of proof to be placed on the defendant, or whether the prosecution continued to bear the burden. The House of Lords held that the burden was on the defendant. In determining this, it was necessary . . . 'to direct attention to the substance and effect . . . of the enactment'. By a 3:2 majority, the House of Lords held that once the prosecution had established that the workplace was unsafe, it was for the defendant to excuse himself by proving that it was not 'reasonably practicable' to make it safe. The Court was entitled to look beyond the linguistics of the section, 'at the mischief at which the Act was aimed and practical considerations affecting the burden of proof, and, in particular, the ease or difficulty that the respective parties would encounter in discharging the burden', and that 'exceptions are to be set up by those who rely on them'. In other words the question in *Nimmo* was, on construction of the provision, whether it was unlawful to provide an unsafe work place or whether it was only unlawful to fail to take all reasonably practicable steps to make it safe? Normal rules of statutory construction were required to be applied to determine what was prohibited.

In respect of trials on indictment s 101 of the 1980 Act has no direct application but the defendant may impliedly bear the legal burden of proof. Rule 6C of the Indictment Rules 1971, lays down that where the alleged offence is one which the relevant statute provides a defence by way of exception, exemption, proviso, excuse or qualification, it is not necessary for any of these to be specified in the indictment. In *R v Edwards* [1975] QB 27, the Court of Appeal decided that there was a common law rule which was the same as s 101 of the 1980 Act, although it did not express the rule as clearly as the section. In addition, the court reviewed the leading authorities reversing the legal burden and decided it was a question of construction of the provision, *per* Lawton LJ:

> **J** '. . . the common law, as a result of experience and the need to ensure that justice is done both to the community and to defendants, has evolved an exception to the fundamental principle of our criminal law that the prosecution must prove every element of the offence charged. This exception . . . is limited to offences arising under enactments which prohibit the doing of an act save in specified circumstances or by persons of specified classes or with specified qualifications or with the licence or permission of specified authorities. Whenever the prosecution seeks to rely on this exception, the court must construe the enactment under which the charge is laid. If the true construction is that the enactment prohibits the doing of acts, subject to proviso's, exceptions and the like, then the prosecution can rely upon the exception . . . it is for the defendant to prove that he was entitled to do the prohibited act. What rests on him is the legal, or as it is sometimes called, the persuasive burden.'

In this case the defendant was charged with selling intoxicating liquor without holding a justices' licence, contrary to s 160(1) of the Licensing Act 1964. The prosecution proved a sale by the defendant of intoxicating liquor but omitted to adduce evidence that the defendant did not hold a licence, even though the register of licences was available to the police at any reasonable time. The accused was convicted and appealed. The Court of Appeal dismissed his appeal on the ground that, on construction of the Act, the legal burden was cast on the defendant to prove that he had a valid licence.

In respect of the construction of the statutory provision the court is not restricted to the four corners of the statute but may take into consideration extraneous factors. Such guidance had been given by Lord Griffiths in *R v Hunt* [1987] 1 All ER 1, where he said:

> **J** '. . . their Lordships were in agreement that if the linguistic constructions of the statute did not clearly indicate upon whom the burden should lie, the court should look to other considerations to determine the intention of Parliament such as the mischief at which the Act was aimed and practical considerations affecting the burden of proof and, in particular, the ease or difficulty that the respective parties would encounter in discharging the burden. I regard this last consideration as one of greatest importance for surely Parliament can never lightly be taken to have intended to impose an onerous duty on a defendant to prove his innocence in a criminal case, and a court should be slow to draw any such inference from the language of a statute.'

In this case the accused was charged with the unlawful possession of morphine, contrary to s 5 of the Misuse of Drugs Act 1971. Under the Misuse of Drugs Regulations 1973, it is provided that s 5 shall not apply in relation to any preparation of morphine containing not more than 0.2% of morphine (a *de minimis* principle). The prosecution had adduced no evidence as to the proportion of morphine in the powder found in the possession of the accused. At the trial the defence made a 'no case' submission which was rejected by the judge and the accused changed his plea to guilty and appealed. The Court of Appeal dismissed his appeal, but the House of Lords allowed the accused's appeal and quashed his conviction on the following grounds:

- On construction of the statute, the case did not fall within the formula stated by Lawton LJ in *Edwards*.

- If, on construction of a statute, there is no indication that the burden of proof rested on the defendant, the court is entitled to have regard to policy and practical considerations – such as the mischief behind the passing of the statute, the gravity of the offence, the ease or difficulty in discharging the burden of proof.

- In this case, if the accused had a burden of proof it would have been extremely difficult for him to discharge. The substance was seized by the police and the accused has no statutory entitlement to a proportion of it for analysis; whereas, it would be less inconvenient for the prosecution to discharge a burden of proving that the substance exceeded the prescribed limit of morphine.

Impact of the Human Rights Act 1998

Today, all occasions involving reverse burdens of proof on the accused, whether at common law or expressly or impliedly imposed by statute, are required to be construed in compliance with the Human Rights Act 1998 (HRA) which incorporates the European Convention for the Protection of Human Rights and Fundamental Freedoms (ECHR). Article 6(1) of the ECHR states that 'In the determination . . . of any criminal charge against him, everyone is entitled to a fair and public hearing within a reasonable time by an independent and impartial tribunal established by law . . .' and Article 6(2) declares, 'Everyone charged with a criminal offence shall be presumed innocent until proved guilty according to law.' Section 3(1) of the Human Rights Act 1998 enacts as follows, 'So far as it is possible to do so, primary legislation and subordinate legislation must be read and given effect in a way which is compatible with the Convention rights.' Section 4(2) of the HRA declares, 'If the court is satisfied that the provision is incompatible with a Convention right, it may make a declaration of that incompatibility.' Section 4 (6) enacts, 'A declaration [of incompatibility] under this section . . . (a) does not affect the validity, continuing operation or enforcement of the provision in respect of which it is given; and (b) is not binding on the parties to the proceedings in which it was made.' The appellate courts have, on several occasions, been faced with arguments that by placing a legal burden of proof on a defendant in a criminal case contravenes Article 6(2) of the Convention. The essence of the argument is that if the defendant faces the possibility of a conviction on the basis that the specified offence presumes (or deems) certain facts to exist unless the defendant can prove to the contrary, this derogates from the presumption of innocence and is contrary to Article 6(2). The same argument can be advanced if a statute requires that a defendant be convicted unless he can prove certain facts as part of his defence. On these occasions the solutions that may be adopted by the courts are first, to decide whether the provision imposing a legal burden on the accused (reverse legal burden) may be 'read down' within s 3(1) of the HRA to impose an evidential burden only on the accused. Second, if this is not possible, then the court may issue a declaration of incompatibility within s 4(2) of the HRA. The effect of such declaration is stated in s 4(6) of the HRA 1998.

The issue that was raised in *R v Lambert* [2002] 2 AC 545, was whether s 5(3) of the Misuse of Drugs Act 1971 compromised the presumption of innocence and whether s 3 HRA 1998 was applicable. In *Lambert*, the accused was charged and convicted of possessing cocaine with intent to supply contrary to s 5(3) of the 1971 Act. Section 28 of the Act afforded a defence if the defendant could prove that 'he neither believed nor suspected that the substance was a controlled drug'. The defendant possessed a bag but alleged that he was not aware of all of its contents. He was convicted and appealed. The House of Lords decided that the events occurred before the coming into force of the 1998 Act but in an *obiter* pronouncement declared that s 28 of the Act

enacted that *prima facie* knowledge of the contents of the bag was not an ingredient of the offence which the prosecution was required to prove. In order to demonstrate lack of knowledge, according to the section, the defendant was required to prove this element, and in so enacting, the section had the tendency to undermine the presumption of innocence. However, in accordance with s 3(1) of the HRA 1998, it was possible to 'read down' s 28 of the Misuse of Drugs Act 1971 so as to impose only an evidential burden on the defendant. In other words, the 'reading down' of the section was because the court decided that the imposition of a legal burden on the defendant was a disproportionate means of achieving the justified aim of easing the difficult task of the prosecution in proving the defendant's knowledge in this type of case, namely, where the drugs are in a container. The court adopted the approach of the European Court of Human Rights (ECrtHR) in arriving at its decision in *Salabiaku v France* (1988) 13 EHRR 379. The approach was:

- Member states were free to enact criminal rules and to define constituent elements of criminal conduct.

- Reverse burdens (or presumptions) operate in every jurisdiction. The European Convention does not prohibit such presumptions in principle, but requires the reverse burdens to be kept within certain limits.

- The limits concerning such reverse burden provisions require the State to take into account the right of the defendant to a fair trial and to strike a balance between the interests of the State and the rights of the defendant.

The tests laid down by Lord Steyn in *R v Lambert* concerning reverse legal burdens and the duty to ensure a fair trial were (a) justification of the legislative provision, ie the mischief at which the provision was aimed, and (b) proportionality, ie the provision must not be greater than is necessary to deal with the mischief.

The test of justification or the pursuit of a legitimate aim involves Parliament enacting a provision (creating a crime) in order to rid society of a particular type of conduct, ie the relevant mischief. This mischief is required to be clearly identified. In *Lambert*, the mischief involved sophisticated drug dealers and couriers concealing drugs in containers, thereby enabling the suspect to claim that he was unaware of the contents, if apprehended. The test of proportionality requires the State to demonstrate that the imposition of the legal burden on the defendant meets the legitimate aims of the provision and does not exceed that goal and compromise the presumption of innocence. The imposition of a legal burden of proof on the accused to prove the relevant issue on a balance of probabilities is a drastic measure. This may result in the conviction of the defendant if he is incapable of proving a relevant fact, even though there might be a reasonable doubt as to his guilt. In a way, it could be argued that *prima facie* reverse burdens compromise the presumption of innocence, subject to the justification and proportionality requirements.

The impact of *Lambert* on the law regarding reverse burdens of proof may be summarized as follows:

1. Such provisions, without more, do not necessarily violate the presumption of innocence. In other words, some reverse burden provisions may be justified as legitimate.

2. States are required to keep such provisions 'within reasonable limits'.

3. The test of whether such provisions are within reasonable limits will depend on whether a proper balance has been struck between the interests of the public with regard to the issues at stake and the rights of the defendant.

4. A specific provision would be required to satisfy the test of proportionality. This involves asking whether there was a pressing need for the burden to be imposed on the defendant.

5. In appropriate cases a statutory provision that the defendant 'prove' an issue may, in appropriate cases, be construed as imposing an evidential, as opposed to a legal, burden on the defendant. Thus, 'reading down' the provision.

6. These considerations apply equally to legal burdens impliedly imposed by Parliament on the defendant. Thus the guidelines laid down in *R v Hunt* need to be read subject to Art 6(2) of the Convention.

Lord Steyn's opinion was elaborated on by Lord Nicholls in *R v Johnstone* [2003] 1 WLR 1736. In this case, the House of Lords upheld a provision under the Trademarks Act 1994 imposing a legal burden on the defendant to prove that 'he honestly and reasonably believed that there was no infringement of the registered trademark'. He was found guilty. The leading opinion was delivered by Lord Nicholls who referred to a number of factors that are required to be taken into account in deciding whether a reverse burden of proof had been legitimately imposed on the defendant. These are:

- the serious nature of the offence and the punishment that may be meted out on a guilty defendant. The more serious the offence and punishment, the more compelling must be the reasons for imposing a legal burden on the defendant

- the extent and nature of the factual matters required to be proved by the defendant and their importance relative to matters required to be proved by the prosecution

- whether the burden relates to facts which are readily provable by the defendant, such as matters within his knowledge.

Lord Nicholls added that in evaluating these factors the court's role is one of review. Parliament, not the court, is charged with the primary responsibility for deciding, as a matter of policy, what should be the constituent elements of an offence. The court will reach a different conclusion from the legislature only when the legislature attached insufficient importance to the presumption of innocence. Of course, at the risk of stating the obvious, Lord Nicholls was dealing with a different statutory provision from Lord Steyn.

In *AG Reference (No 1 of 2004)* [2004] EWCA 1025 (there were five consolidated appeals concerning reverse burdens), Lord Woolf CJ observed that there was a significant difference in opinion between Lords Steyn in *Lambert* and Lord Nicholls in *Johnstone* and suggested that Lord

Nicholls's view ought to be followed. The Court of Appeal also laid down a number of guidelines for the benefit of the lower courts (see para 52 of Lord Woolf's judgment).

In *AG Reference (No 4 of 2002)*; *Sheldrake v DPP* [2004] All ER (D) 169, (two consolidated appeals), Lord Bingham referred to Lord Woolf's guidelines (in *AG Ref (No 1 of 2004)*) and decided that the differences in emphasis by Lords Steyn and Nicholls were explicable by reference to the different subject-matter in the two cases under consideration and rejected Lord Woolf's guidelines in so far as they are inconsistent with the guidelines laid down in the current case. Lord Bingham then reviewed the leading cases and proceeded to lay down a definitive set of guidelines (see para 21 of Lord Bingham's judgment):

1. The over-riding concern is that the trial of the defendant should be fair.

2. The Convention does not outlaw presumptions or reverse burdens, but requires these to be kept within reasonable limits.

3. It is the prerogative of each State to define the constituent elements of a criminal offence excluding the requirement of *mens rea*.

4. The substance and effect of any presumption adverse to the defendant must be examined and be reasonable. The test for compatibility with Convention rights is 'reasonableness' and 'proportionality'.

5. Factors that are to be taken into account to evaluate reasonableness include maintenance of the rights of the defence; flexibility in the application of the presumption; retention by the court of a power to assess the evidence; the extent and nature of the factual matters required to be proved by the accused, and their importance relative to the matters required to be proved by the prosecution; the extent to which a burden on the accused relates to facts which, if they exist, are readily proved by him as to matters within his own knowledge or to which he has ready access.

6. Security concerns do not absolve member states from their duty to observe basic standards of fairness.

7. The justifiability of any infringement of the presumption of innocence may only be resolved by an examination of all the facts and circumstances of the particular provision, as is applicable in the particular case.

8. A sound starting point is to remember that if an accused is required to prove a fact on a balance of probability to avoid conviction, this may permit the accused to be convicted in spite of the fact-finding tribunal having a reasonable doubt as to the guilt of the accused. This consequence of a reverse burden of proof should colour the court's approach when evaluating the reasons as to why the public interest will be served to an extent that justifies placing the legal burden on the accused. The more serious the offence and punishment that might flow from a conviction, the more compelling must be the reasons.

9. The interpretative obligation of the court under s 3 of the Human Rights Act 1998 is a very strong and far-reaching task and may require the court to depart from the legislative

intention of Parliament. The court will reach a different conclusion from the legislature only when it is apparent that the legislature has attached insufficient importance to the fundamental right of an individual to be presumed innocent until proved guilty.

10. A Convention-compliant interpretation under s 3 HRA 1998 is a primary remedial measure and a declaration of incompatibility under s 4 of the 1998 Act is an exceptional course for the court to take. During the passage of the Bill (Human Rights) through Parliament, the promoters of the Bill told both Houses of Parliament that it was envisaged that the need for a declaration of incompatibility would rarely arise.

11. There is a limit beyond which a Convention-compliant interpretation is not possible, for it would change the substance of the provision completely. In these circumstances a declaration of incompatibility would be appropriate. This would be a measure of last resort.

Lord Bingham then declared that the task of the court is never to decide whether a reverse burden of proof ought to be imposed on the defendant, but always to assess whether a burden enacted by Parliament unjustifiably infringes the presumption of innocence. This involves balancing the interests of the defendant to a fair trial with the needs of the public to be adequately protected.

Application of the principles to the facts of the cases

In *AG Reference (No 4 of 2002)*, the defendant was indicted on two counts under s 11(1) of the Terrorism Act 2000, namely, being a member of a proscribed organization, ie Hamas and professing to be a member of that organization. Section 11(2) used the expression, 'defence to prove' and this has the effect of imposing a legal burden on the defendant. At the conclusion of the case of the prosecution the judge ruled that there was no case to answer and a verdict of not guilty was entered in respect of each count. The Attorney General took a reference and the issue was whether the defence within s 11(2) imposed a legal rather than an evidential burden on the defendant, and if a legal burden was imposed, whether it was compatible with the Convention. The House of Lords decided that s 11(2) of the Act *prima facie* imposed a legal burden of proof on the defendant. Adopting the 'justifiability' and 'proportionality' considerations the statutory provision went beyond what was necessary for the protection of society and impinged on the presumption of innocence. The court decided that it may well be all but impossible for the defendant to prove that he had not taken part in the activities of such an organization. Organizations that promote terror throughout the world, by definition, do not keep minutes of meetings, records or documents other members would be unlikely to come forward and testify on his behalf, it is possible that the defendant may have been a member before the organization became proscribed (this eventuality was not provided for in the statutory provision). Applying s 3 HRA 1998, the interpretative function of the court was to adopt a construction which was compatible with Art 6(2) of the Convention. Accordingly, s 11(2) would be 'read down' and construed as imposing only an evidential burden on the defendant.

In *DPP v Sheldrake*, the defendant was convicted of being in charge of a motor vehicle in a public place after consuming so much alcohol that the proportion of it in his breath, blood or

urine exceeded the prescribed limit contrary to s 5(1)(b) of the Road Traffic Act 1988. Section 5(2) enacted a defence for the accused to *prove* that at the time of the alleged commission of the offence there was no likelihood of his driving the vehicle while the proportion of alcohol exceeded the prescribed limit. The justices ruled that s 5(2) imposed a legal burden on the defendant and this did not interfere with the presumption of innocence. The defendant was convicted and appealed to the High Court by way of case stated. The High Court by a majority (2 to 1) allowed the appeal and decided that the provision will be 'read down' to impose only an evidential burden on the defendant. On appeal, the House of Lords unanimously allowed the appeal and decided that s 5(2) created a legal burden of proof and was not incompatible with Art 6(2) of the Convention. The section pursued a legitimate aim and was proportionate.

2.3 Evidential burden

The evidential burden is the obligation to adduce sufficient evidence to raise an issue to the satisfaction of the tribunal of law. In a case tried by judge and jury, the discharge of the evidential burden is for the judge to decide. In contrast, the discharge of the legal burden is for the jury to decide. Thus, a party with a legal burden of proof is required to surmount two hurdles. First, he must adduce sufficient evidence to prevent the judge from withdrawing the issue from the jury, ie to discharge the evidential burden. Second, the party is required to convince the tribunal of fact of the truth of the assertion, ie discharge his legal burden. If the evidential burden has not been discharged, based on a ruling by the judge, it follows that the legal burden attached to that issue will equally not be discharged. In addition, a party may bear an evidential burden without a corresponding legal burden, such as a defence of self-defence, provocation or duress in a criminal case. In such a case, if the defendant fails to discharge his evidential burden, the issue will not be considered by the tribunal of fact; but if the evidential burden imposed on the accused has been discharged, a duty is imposed on the judge to leave the defence to the jury. Normally this will be done through the defendant actively asserting a defence, but the same result will be achieved if evidence emerges at the trial suggesting the presence of a defence even though not put forward by the defendant. In *R v Calvert* [2000] All ER (D) 2071, the Court of Appeal quashed the defendant's conviction for rape on the ground that, despite counsel for the defendant not positively raising the defence of consent, the existence of some evidence of consent required the judge to direct the jury on the evidence.

2.3.1 Shifting of the evidential burden

The burden of adducing sufficient evidence to justify a favourable finding may be distributed between different parties during the course of a trial. The concept of the 'shifting' of the evidential burden refers to the risk of an adverse finding run by an opponent when a party discharges his evidential burden, for example where the prosecution has discharged its evidential burden by a rejection of a no-case submission by the defendant, the defendant runs the risk that the jury may find him guilty of the offence if he does not adduce any evidence. However, such a proposition may only be supported if it is assumed that:

(a) there is only one issue to be tried. In a criminal case there is a general issue of whether the defendant is guilty but there are multiple specific issues that involve the evidential burden that answer the general question; and

(b) that the evidence adduced by the prosecution in discharge of the evidential burden is sufficient to convict the defendant.

There is no such indication before the jury's verdict. On the contrary, there are multiple issues in a trial and the evidential burden on these issues does not shift as a matter of substantive law.

2.4 Standards of proof

The term 'standard' or 'quantum' of proof refers to the extent to which the judge and the jury, as separate bodies, are required to be satisfied that the proponent has made out his case. This applies to both the legal and evidential burdens of proof. The expression 'standard of proof' is referable to the quality of evidence adduced in support of the relevant allegation.

It follows that the party bearing the legal burden is required to adduce more persuasive evidence on a point than his opponent. If the evidence adduced on both sides is equally persuasive or credible, the proponent must lose the case. Similarly, if the opponent has raised a serious doubt about the accuracy of the facts as alleged by the proponent, the latter has not proved his case.

The question in issue is by how much must the evidence of the proponent exceed the evidence supporting the opponent's case in order to justify a favourable result for the proponent? In other words, what is the proportionate amount and quality of evidence required to be adduced by the proponent? This varies with criminal and civil cases.

2.4.1 Criminal cases

The standard of proof imposed on the prosecution in order to discharge the legal burden of proof is 'beyond reasonable doubt'. This is the highest standard recognized in law and has been adopted for policy reasons, namely that it is better to allow guilty persons to be set free rather than allow an innocent person to be wrongfully convicted. The phrase 'beyond reasonable doubt' does not mean 'beyond a shadow of a doubt'. This is much too high a standard. Likewise, the phrase does not mean a 'preponderance of probability' or a 'balance of probabilities'. This is the civil standard of proof and is treated as too low to be used to rebut the presumption of innocence. Denning J in *Miller v Minister of Pensions* [1947] 2 All ER 372, explained thus:

> **J** 'It [the criminal standard] need not reach certainty, but must carry a high degree of probability. It does not mean beyond a shadow of a doubt. The law would fail to protect the community if it admitted fanciful possibilities to deflect the course of justice. If the evidence is so strong against a man as to leave only a remote possibility in his favour which can be dismissed with the sentence, "Of course it is possible, but not in the least probable", the case is proved beyond reasonable doubt, but nothing short of that will suffice.'

Several misdirections have been detected in the past because judges have adopted a variety of different phrases in place of the time-honoured expression 'beyond reasonable doubt', for example 'satisfied' in *R v Hepworth* (1955) 2 QB 600; the jury was told that they need to be 'satisfied, anything less will not do' in *R v Gourley* (1981) Cr LR 334; 'pretty certain' in *R v Law* (1961) Cr LR 52; 'reasonably sure' in *R v Head* (1961) 45 Cr App R 225; 'you must be satisfied so that you are reasonably sure' in *R v Sweeney* (1983) *The Times* 22nd October; 'reasonably satisfied' in *R v Kritz* [1950] 1 KB 82.

The phrase 'satisfied so that you can feel sure' of the accused's guilt is an acceptable alternative to the time-honoured formula. In *R v Summers* (1952) 36 Cr App R 14, Lord Goddard said,

> **J** '. . . If a jury is told that it is their duty to regard the evidence and see that it satisfies them so that they can feel sure when they return a verdict of guilty, that is much better than using the expression, "reasonable doubt" and I hope in future that that will be done. I never use the expression when summing up. I always tell the jury that, before they convict they must feel sure and must be satisfied that the prosecution have established the guilt of the prisoner.'

The courts have offered advice on many occasions to the effect that the criminal standard of proof is not a matter of some precise formula or particular form of words used by the judge, provided that the correct standard of proof had been conveyed to the jury. In *Ferguson v R* [1979] 1 WLR 94, Lord Scarman observed: '. . . though the law requires no particular formula, judges are wise, as a general rule, to adopt one'.

Moreover, it appears that not only the formula of words used by the judge will be examined by the appellate court, but the effect of the summing up as a whole to the jury, *per* Lord Goddard in *R v Kritz* [1950] 1 KB 82:

J

'. . . It is not the particular formula that matters: it is the effect of the summing up. If the jury are made to understand that they have to be satisfied and must not return a verdict against a defendant unless they feel sure, and that the onus is all the time on the prosecution and not the defence, then whether the judge uses one form of language or another is neither here nor there. In the present case, the judge told the jury that they must be reasonably satisfied and did not use the words, "satisfied beyond a reasonable doubt", he was not sufficiently stating the onus of proof.'

Occasionally, judges attempt to explain the type of doubt involved in the time-honoured formula, 'beyond reasonable doubt'. It is necessary to depict the type of doubt accurately. In *R v Stafford* [1968] 3 All ER 752, Edmund Davies LJ said,

J

'We do not agree with the trial judge when directing the jury upon the standard of proof he told them to remember that a reasonable doubt is "one for which you could give reasons if you were asked", and we dislike such a description or definition.'

In *R v Gray* (1974) 58 Cr App R 177, the trial judge inaccurately summed up to the jury thus: 'The standard of proof is sometimes said to be, beyond a reasonable doubt, and that means simply a doubt based upon good reason and not a fanciful doubt. It is the sort of doubt which might affect you in the conduct of your everyday affairs.' The Court of Appeal held that this was a misdirection: 'If the learned judge had referred, for example, to the sort of doubt which may affect the mind of a person in the conduct of *important* affairs, then there could be no proper criticism . . . But in this case, the direction is open to legitimate criticism. The reference to 'conduct of your everyday affairs' might suggest to a jury too low a standard of proof, because a doubt which would influence a decision on an important matter might sensibly be disregarded in a decision on some everyday affair' (Megaw LJ).

2.4.2 Discharge of the legal burden by the accused

In criminal cases the prosecution bears the legal burden of proof. In exceptional cases explored earlier, the accused may bear a legal burden of proof on a separate issue from the prosecution, for example the defence of insanity on occasions when Parliament expressly or impliedly impose a legal burden on the accused. In these cases, the discharge of the legal burden requires the accused to prove the issue to the satisfaction of the jury or the tribunal of fact on a balance of probabilities.

CASE EXTRACT

R v Carr-Briant [1943] KB 607

The accused, a director in a firm, was charged under the Prevention of Corruption Act 1906 in that it was alleged that he gave or loaned £60 to an engineer employed in a government department. The defence was that the payment had not been made corruptly. The judge directed the jury that the standard of proof imposed on the accused was beyond a reasonable doubt. He was convicted and appealed.

The Court of Appeal allowed the appeal and decided that the judge had misdirected the jury as to the standard of proof which ought to have been on a balance of probabilities.

Humphreys J:

> 'In our judgment where, either by statute or at common law, some matter is presumed against the accused person "unless the contrary is proved", the jury should be directed that it is for them to decide whether the contrary is proved; that the burden of proof required is less than that required at the hands of the prosecution in proving the case beyond a reasonable doubt, and that the burden may be discharged by evidence satisfying the jury of the probability of that which the accused is called upon to establish.'

2.4.3 Discharge of the legal burden in civil cases

In civil proceedings the traditional standard of proof imposed on the party with the legal burden is a balance of probabilities or a preponderance of probability, ie the proponent is required to prove that his case is more probable than his opponent. It follows that if the probabilities are equally balanced the party with the legal burden will not succeed. The explanation of the phrase, balance of probabilities was made out in *Miller v Minister of Pensions* [1947] 2 All ER 372, by Denning J thus:

> '. . . If at the end of the case the evidence turns the scale definitely one way or the other, the tribunal must decide accordingly, but if the evidence is so evenly balanced that the tribunal is unable to come to a determinate conclusion one way or the other, then the man must be given the benefit of the doubt . . . The case must be proved on a reasonable degree of probability, but not so high as is required in a criminal case. If the evidence is such that the tribunal can say: "We think it more probable than not," the burden is discharged, but, if the probabilities are equal, it is not.'

Crime alleged in civil proceedings

There are many instances in civil proceedings where a crime is alleged to have been committed by a party, for example the allegation by the insurer that the insured created the loss by arson in respect of a claim under a fire insurance policy. The issue that will be considered here is the standard of proof that is imposed on the party making an allegation that the other party committed a crime. The solution today is that, after a great deal of conflicting decisions, the standard of proof remains the traditional civil standard of a balance of probabilities.

CASE EXTRACT

Hornal v Neuberger Products Ltd [1957] 1 QB 247

In this case, the claimant in an action for breach of contract alleged that one of the directors of the defendant company made a fraudulent representation to the claimant. The alleged fraudulent representation was that a lathe sold by the defendant had been reconditioned. The County Court Judge had stated that he was satisfied that the allegations were proved on a balance of probabilities but would not have been satisfied if the criminal standard had applied. The Court of Appeal decided that the judge had applied the correct standard. The justification for the rule was stated by Denning LJ, as follows:

Denning LJ:

> '. . . I think it would bring the law into contempt if a judge were to say that on the issue of warranty he finds the statement was made and that on the issue of fraud he finds it was not made . . . the judge had reviewed all the cases and held rightly that the standard of proof depends on the nature of the issue. The more serious the allegation the higher the degree of probability that is required: but it need not, in a civil case reach the very high standard required by the criminal law.'

The reference by Lord Denning to 'the higher degree of probability that is required' where the allegation is more serious has the appearance of creating degrees of probabilities within the traditional standard with regard to more serious allegations, a sort of sliding scale. This is a contradiction in terms. Indeed in the same case, Morris LJ explained that the issue does not involve a sliding scale of probabilities but rather, the weight or credibility of the evidence needed to tip the balance of probabilities.

Morris LJ:

> **J** 'Though no court and no jury would give less careful consideration to issues lacking in gravity than to those marked by it, the very elements of gravity become a part of the whole range of circumstances which have to be weighed in the scale when deciding as to the balance of probabilities.'

Perhaps the most serious criminal allegation in civil proceedings is murder and again the standard of proof is a balance of probabilities, see *Re Dellow's Will Trust* [1964] 1 All ER 771. In this case, the issue was whether a wife (beneficiary under a will) had murdered her husband, a testator. The court decided that the standard of proof was a balance of probabilities, *per* Ungoed Thomas J:

> **J** 'It seems to me that in civil cases it is not so much that a different standard of proof is required in different circumstances varying according to the gravity of the issue, but the gravity of the issue becomes part of the circumstances which the court has to take into consideration in deciding whether or not the burden of proof has been discharged. The more serious the allegation the more cogent is the evidence required to overcome the unlikelihood of what is alleged and thus to prove it. This is perhaps a somewhat academic distinction.'

CASE EXTRACT

Re H (Minors) [1996] AC 563

An application for a care order was made by a local authority in respect of a girl who alleged that her stepfather had sexually abused her over a considerable period of time. The stepfather was charged with indecent assault on the girl and was acquitted at his trial. The issue before the court was, despite his acquittal, whether a care order ought to be made. In particular, the standard of proof to be imposed on the local authority. The House of Lords decided that the standard of proof is the traditional standard of a balance of probabilities, but subject to the proviso that the more serious the allegation, the clearer should be the evidence, *per* Lord Nicholls.

Lord Nicholls:

> **J** 'When assessing the probabilities the court will have in mind a factor that the more serious the allegation the less likely it is that the event occurred and hence the stronger should be the evidence before the court concludes that the allegation is established on a balance of probability. Fraud is usually less likely than negligence. Deliberate physical injury is usually less likely than accidental physical injury . . . Built into the preponderance of probability standard is a generous degree of flexibility in respect of the seriousness of the allegation.'

Third standard of proof?

There appears to be a number of anomalous civil proceedings where a different standard of proof is required to be achieved. These are:

- Claims for rectification of documents. In such cases 'strong, irrefragable evidence' is required to be adduced; see *Roberts v Leicestershire County Council* [1961] Ch 555.

- Proof of change of domicile. A person who is required to prove that his domicile has changed is obliged to adduce 'clear and unequivocal evidence'; see *Re Fuld's Estate (No 3)* [1968] p 675.

- A party who intends to rebut the presumption in favour of the formal validity of a marriage is required to adduce 'strong, distinct and satisfactory' evidence; see *Piers v Piers* (1849) 2 HL Cas 331.

- Contempt of court in civil proceedings must be proved beyond reasonable doubt; see *Re Bramblevale Ltd* [1970] Ch 128.

- Proceedings before the solicitors' disciplinary tribunal for professional misconduct are required to be proved to the criminal standard; see *Re A Solicitor* [1993] QB 69.

2.4.4 Discharge of the evidential burden

The discharge of the evidential burden is a question of law for the judge to decide. The question is whether the proponent has adduced sufficient evidence of the issue to justify the judge putting the issue before the jury or the tribunal of fact. No precise formula has been laid down concerning the standard of proof or the quantum of evidence needed to discharge this burden.

Alternatively, where the evidential burden cast on a party has not been discharged, the issue will not be put to the jury or considered by the tribunal of fact, for lack of sufficient evidence. The judge exercises a filtering power to distinguish occasions when there is some evidence to support an allegation and occasions when the allegation is unsupported by evidence. This judicial function concerns the evidential burden.

To ascertain the standard of proof required, it is necessary to distinguish five types of cases:

(a) the position where the accused bears the evidential burden without the legal burden of proof

(b) occasions where the accused bears both the evidential and legal burdens of proof

(c) the situation where the prosecution bears the evidential and legal burdens of proof

(d) in civil cases when a party bears the evidential and legal burdens of proof

(e) in civil cases when a party bears only the evidential burden of proof.

Accused bears solely the evidential burden

These are occasions where the accused bears only the evidential burden without the corresponding legal burden on the same issue, such as provocation, duress, self-defence, etc. In these circumstances, it is only necessary for him to adduce sufficient evidence of the issue which, in the view of the judge, may create the possibility of a reasonable doubt as to his guilt.

Per Lord Morris in *Bratty v AG for Northern Ireland* [1963] AC 386 (on the issue of non-insane automatism): 'There was no sufficient evidence, fit to be left to the jury, on which a jury might conclude that the appellant had acted unconsciously and involuntarily or which might leave a jury in reasonable doubt whether this might be so' (Lord Morris).

Accused bears both the evidential and legal burden

In the exceptional circumstances when an accused bears a legal burden (either in respect of the defence of insanity or a statutory reversal of the legal burden, see earlier) the discharge of the evidential burden is dependent on the accused satisfying the judge that there is sufficient evidence of the issue on which a jury might be convinced on a balance of probabilities. In other words, the judge decides whether there is sufficient evidence of the defence to be put to the jury.

Whether the jury is satisfied on a balance of probabilities is a separate question from the discharge of the evidential burden and the former burden involves the discharge of the legal burden of proof. Whether the legal burden imposed on the accused has been discharged may sometimes be detected in the verdict, for example on the issue of diminished responsibility the judge may decide that the accused's evidential burden had been discharged and puts the issue before the jury, but the jury may ultimately reject the defence.

Where the prosecution bears both evidential and legal burdens

This involves the traditional case where the prosecution bears both the evidential and legal burdens. The discharge of the evidential burden is dependent on the judge deciding that there is a possibility of sufficient evidence adduced by the Crown which may convince the jury beyond reasonable doubt.

Per Lord Devlin in *Jayasena v R* [1970] AC 618,

'The Crown is required to discharge the burden by adducing such evidence as, if believed, and if left uncontradicted and unexplained, could be accepted by the jury as proof.'

In this respect the judge acts as a barometer to determine whether the jury *may* convict on the evidence. A procedure to determine whether the prosecution has discharged its evidential burden involves the accused making a 'no case' submission at the close of the prosecution's case. A rejection by the judge of such a submission results in the discharge of the evidential burden by the prosecution.

The modern equivalent to the test for deciding whether the prosecution has discharged its evidential burden was stated by Lord Lane CJ in *R v Galbraith* [1981] 1 WLR 1039, thus:

'(1) If there is no evidence that the crime alleged has been committed by the defendant there is no difficulty – the judge will stop the case. (2) The difficulty arises where there is some evidence but it is of a tenuous character, for example, because of inherent weakness or vagueness or because it is inconsistent with other evidence. (a) Where the judge comes to the conclusion that the prosecution evidence, taken at its highest, is such that a jury properly directed could not properly convict upon it, it is his duty, upon a submission being made, to stop the case. (b) Where, however, the prosecution evidence is such that its strength or weakness depends on the view to be taken of a witness's reliability, other matters which are generally speaking within the province of the jury and where on one possible view of the facts there is evidence upon which a jury could properly come to the conclusion that the defendant is guilty, then the judge should allow the matter to be tried by the jury.'

In *R v Pryer* [2004] EWCA Crim 1163, the Court of Appeal decided that the *Galbraith* test involved the judge making an assessment of the whole of the prosecution case and not parts of it, such as the credibility of an individual witness. The test did not mean that the judge is entitled to 'pick out all the plums and leave the duff behind'. The credibility of individual witnesses does play a part in determining this question, but essentially the question concerns the case of the prosecution as a whole. In *Brooks v DPP* [1994] 1 AC 568, the Privy Council said that (in the context of committal proceedings) questions of credibility, except in the clearest of cases, do not normally result in a finding that there is no *prima facie* case.

Such submissions of 'no case' to answer are generally made at the close of the prosecution's case, although some attempts have been made by the defence to renew such application during the defence case. The position today, as clarified in *R v Brown (Davina)* [2002] 1 Cr App R 5, is that the judge has the power to decide that there is insufficient evidence to convict the defendant and consequently withdraw the issue from the jury. This is the position even after the close of the prosecution case, but it was said by the Court of Appeal that such a power should be exercised sparingly.

Civil proceedings where a party bears the legal burden

In civil proceedings, when a party bears a legal burden and a corresponding evidential burden, the discharge of the evidential burden is based on the adduction of sufficient evidence to satisfy a reasonable trier of fact on a balance of probabilities. In other words, the judge (tribunal of law) is required to decide whether there is sufficient evidence to justify the tribunal of fact to make a finding in favour of the proponent. In the event of a 'no case' submission by the opponent the judge will postpone his ruling until all the evidence has been adduced.

Civil proceedings where the party does not bear the legal burden

In civil proceedings where the party bears only the evidential burden, the obligation here is to adduce sufficient evidence to leave the tribunal of fact in a state of equilibrium. This inevitably means that the party with the legal burden would be incapable of discharging it.

59

2.5 Tactical burden

Some commentators describe what has been referred to as the evidential burden as a 'tactical' burden. The notion concerns those occasions where a party does not bear a legal burden on an issue, but only an evidential or tactical burden. In these cases, strictly speaking there is no 'burden' cast on the party in the sense that he is not obliged to raise or prove an issue in order to succeed. Such a party may simply rely on the party with the legal burden not discharging the burden on a balance of probabilities; but in doing so, he runs a risk that the party with the legal burden may discharge it to the satisfaction of the tribunal of fact. Neither party has any decisive way of knowing before the end of the trial whether the legal burden of proof will be discharged. A party may merely speculate as to this possibility. Thus, the party without the legal burden, ie the party with a tactical burden, may reduce the risk of an adverse finding by adducing evidence of the issue. For example, on a charge of murder the defendant may sit back and rely on the prosecution failing to discharge its legal burden of proof, but he has no way of knowing if this possibility may materialize until the jury returns its verdict. To reduce the risk of an adverse finding he may adduce evidence that the deceased died accidentally. He is not obliged to do so, for this is not a fresh issue in the trial. The accused would be best advised to raise any defences available to him.

ACTIVITY

Self-test questions

1. What do you understand by the expressions 'legal burden of proof', 'evidential burden of proof', 'tactical burden of proof', the 'incidence of the legal burden of proof', 'reverse legal burdens of proof' and 'standards of proof'?

2. In civil cases, what factors are relevant in determining which party bears a legal burden of proof?

3. To what extent is there clarity in the phrases 'beyond a reasonable doubt', 'balance of probabilities' and making out a *prima facie* case?

4. In criminal cases, what standard of proof is required to be discharged by the prosecution when the defendant makes a 'no case' submission?

5. In criminal cases, when would a defendant bear a legal burden of proof?

6. 'The real concern is not whether the accused must disprove an element or prove an excuse, but that an accused may be convicted while a reasonable doubt exists. When that possibility exists, there is a breach of the presumption of innocence' (*per* Dickson CJ, Canadian Supreme Court in *R v Whyte* (1988) 58 DLR 481).

   Discuss this statement in the light of the current judicial approaches towards reverse legal burdens of proof.

Further reading

Ashworth, A. and Blake, M. 'The presumption of innocence in English criminal law' [1998] Crim LR 306

Bennion, F. 'Statutory Exceptions: A Third Knot in the Golden Thread' [1988] Crim LR 31

Birch, D. 'Hunting the snark: the elusive statutory exception' [1988] Crim LR 221

Dennis, I. 'Reverse onuses and the presumption of innocence: in search of principle' [2005] Crim LR 901

Dingwall, G. 'Statutory exceptions, burdens of proof and the Human Rights Act 1998' (2002) 65 MLR 450

Hamer, D. 'The presumption of innocence and reverse burdens: a balancing act' (2007) 66 CLJ 142

Healey, P. 'Proof and Policy: No Golden Threads' [1987] Crim LR 355

Lewis, P. 'The Human Rights Act 1998: shifting the burden' [2000] Crim LR 667

Mirfield, P. 'The legacy of Hunt' [1988] Crim LR 19

Padfield, N. 'The burden of proof unresolved' (2005) 64 CLJ 17

Roberts, P. 'Taking the burden of proof seriously' [1995] Crim LR 783

Roberts, P. 'The presumption of innocence brought home/*Kebilene* deconstructed' (2002) 118 LQR 41

Smith, J.C. 'The presumption of innocence' (1987) 38 NILQ 223

Tavros and Tierney, 'Presumption of innocence and the Human Rights Act' (2004) 67 MLR 402

Williams, G. 'The evidential burden: some common misapprehensions' (1977) 127 NLJ 156

Williams, G. 'Evidential burdens on the defence' (1977) 127 NLJ 182

Zuckerman, A. 'The Third Exception to the Woolmington Rule' (1976) 92 LQR 402

chapter 3 TESTIMONY OF WITNESSES ■

AIMS AND OBJECTIVES

By the end of this chapter you should be able to:

- Appreciate the preparatory rules leading up to *viva voce* evidence in court

- Understand the occasions when a witness may give sworn and unsworn evidence in court

- Comprehend the test of competence and compellability of witnesses in both civil and criminal cases

- Recognize the occasions when special measures directions may be available to assist the witness in the presentation of his testimony.

3.1 Introduction

In this chapter we will be dealing with the most popular mode of proof of relevant facts, namely, live evidence (*viva voce*) or testimony presented in court in both civil and criminal cases. The witnesses may be encouraged or forced to attend the proceedings. Once the witness has attended the proceedings, the primary question is whether he is competent to testify. Additional issues concern the presentation of his testimony on oath or subject to a solemn affirmation. Exceptionally, a witness may give unsworn evidence. Finally, the individual may require some assistance in order to testify. The judge has jurisdiction to make special measures directions that may assist the witness.

3.2 Attendance of witnesses at court

In both civil and criminal cases the parties will make arrangements with their witnesses to attend the court. Prior to the date of the trial, the witness would have made a witness statement in writing and it would be on the basis of such assertions that the party wishes the witness to testify. There is no general principle that the witness is not allowed to see his statement within a short while before testifying. The process of testifying is not designed to be a test of memory, but an effort to present the truth in court, subject to rules of admissible evidence.

If a party is aware that a potential witness who is compellable, but unwilling to attend the court in order to avoid testifying, that party may apply for a witness summons or order requiring the witness to attend on the relevant dates; see s 97 of the Magistrates Court Act 1980 and s 2 of the Criminal Procedure (Attendance of Witnesses) Act 1965, as amended. The following two conditions are required to be satisfied before a court issues a summons:

- that the person is likely to be able to give material evidence

- that his presence in court is necessary in the interests of justice.

If the person named in the witness order fails to attend the proceedings without lawful excuse, a warrant will be issued for his arrest in order to secure his attendance. Where the witness, without lawful excuse, refuses to answer questions put to him, he may be guilty of contempt of court. The court has a range of powers for dealing with contempt, including imprisonment, see *R v Haselden* [2000] All ER (D) 56.

3.3 Order of presentation of evidence

The general rule is that it is the duty of the legal representative to decide what evidence is called and in what order to call the witnesses. In criminal proceedings, it is the practice to call the defendant before any other defence witnesses.

In civil proceedings, the practice is that the witnesses are entitled to remain in court before he or she testifies in the proceedings. This rule is subject to any orders made by the judge in his discretion to exclude a witness before he gives his testimony.

In criminal proceedings, the general practice is that all witnesses are excluded from the court until after they have given testimony. The purpose of the rule is that all witnesses should be examined out of the hearing of other witnesses who have yet to give their evidence. If a witness remains in court before he testifies or after an order had been made to exclude the witness, and a party wishes to call the witness to testify, it appears that the judge has no discretion to exclude the testimony of that witness, see *R v Kingston* [1980] RT 51, *per* Edmund Davies LJ:

> **J** 'No rule of law requires that in a trial the witnesses to be called by one side must all remain out of court until their turn to give testimony arises. This is purely within the discretion of the court. Indeed, if the court rules that witnesses should be out of court and a witness nevertheless remains in court . . . the judge has no right to refuse to hear his evidence.'

Of course the weight of the testimony of the witness may be severely affected and it is a matter for the court to decide how credible such evidence will be.

In addition, no party has any 'property' in the evidence of a witness. Accordingly, if a party makes a contract with a witness, to the effect that the witness agrees to give his services exclusively to that party, that agreement is treated as contrary to public policy and is unenforceable. Thus, such a witness is compellable to testify for the other party, see *Harmony Shipping Co v Saudi Europe Line Ltd* [1979] 1 WLR 1380; see later; but, in criminal proceedings, once a witness has given evidence for the prosecution he cannot be called to testify for the defence, see *R v Kelly* (1985) *The Times*, 27th July.

3.4 Evidence: sworn/unsworn or solemn affirmation

The starting point is that the testimony of all witnesses in both civil and criminal cases is required to be presented in court after the witness has been sworn in or he has made a solemn affirmation. There is an exception with regard to the evidence of children. The justification for taking the oath dates back to the days when it was thought that there was a divine sanction for speaking the truth. This remains the rationale today and the motivation for speaking the truth is purely subjective. If the witness wilfully tells lies under oath or having made a solemn affirmation, he may face perjury charges.

3.4.1 Oath

Section 1 of the Oaths Act 1978 declares the manner in which the oath may be administered. The witness taking the oath is required to hold the New Testament or, in the case of a Jew, the Old Testament, in his uplifted hand, and shall say or repeat the words, 'I swear by Almighty God that the evidence which I shall give shall be the truth, the whole truth and nothing but the truth'. Unless the witness objects, the court officer is entitled to adopt the procedure as outlined above. The modern practice is that the appropriate officer inquires what oath the witness accepts as binding on him and he is then sworn in accordingly.

Section 1(3) of the Oaths Act 1978 enacts:

 'In the case of a person who is neither a Christian nor a Jew, the oath may be administered in any lawful manner.'

This procedure would involve the appropriate Holy Book being held by the witness, who then repeats a prepared oath similar to the one above, but adapted to the tenets of the relevant religion. Whether the oath was administered in a 'lawful manner' as laid down in s 1 of the Oaths Act 1978, does not depend on the intricacies of the religion in question, but rather on whether the oath appeared to the court to be binding on the conscience of the witness and, if so, whether the witness himself considered the oath to be binding on his conscience; see *R v Kemble* [1990] 3 All ER 116. In this case, the witness, a Muslim by religion, had taken the oath using the New Testament. On conviction, the defendant appealed contending that s 1 of the

Oaths Act 1978 had not been complied with and that the witness was not properly sworn in. The Court of Appeal dismissed the appeal and laid down the test as stated above. Lord Lane CJ:

> **J** 'We take the view that the question of whether the administration of the oath is lawful does not depend upon what may be the considerable intricacies of the particular religion which is adhered to by the witness. It concerns two matters and two matters only in our judgment. First of all, is the oath an oath which appears to the court to be binding on the conscience of the witness? And, if so, secondly, and most importantly, is it an oath which the witness himself considers to be binding upon his conscience?
>
> So far as the present case is concerned, quite plainly the first of those matters is satisfied. The court did obviously consider the oath to be one which was binding upon the witness. It was the second matter which was the subject so to speak of dispute before this court. Not only did we have the evidence of the professor, the expert in Muslim theology but we also had the evidence of the witness himself. He having on this occasion been sworn upon a copy of the Koran in Arabic gave evidence before us that he did consider himself to be bound as to his conscience by the way in which he took the oath at the trial. Indeed, he went further. He said, "Whether I had taken the oath upon the Koran or upon the Bible or upon the Torah, I would have considered that to be binding on my conscience" . . . that he did consider all of those to be holy books, and that he did consider that his conscience was bound by the form of oath he took and the way in which he took it. In other words we accept his evidence.'

There are special forms of oaths for jurors and interpreters.

3.4.2 Solemn affirmation

As an alternative to the taking of the oath in both civil and criminal cases, a witness may make a solemn affirmation. Section 5 of the Oaths Act 1978 lays down the principle that a solemn affirmation may be made if the witness objects to taking the oath or that it is not reasonably practicable without inconvenience or delay to administer the oath in accordance with the religious tenets of the appropriate faith. The solemn affirmation has the same force and effect as the oath. Thus, the witness may commit perjury if he wilfully lies from the witness box following his solemn affirmation.

Subject to the evidence of children, where the potential witness is incapable of taking the oath or making a solemn affirmation, his account will not be admitted in court because he is treated as incompetent to testify in proceedings; see below.

3.5 Competence and compellability of witnesses

A witness is competent to give evidence if his testimony is receivable in court, subject, of course, to the rules of admissibility. A witness is compellable where he can be obliged to testify, even against his will. The sanction is a contempt of court for failing to testify without lawful cause. Likewise, it is a contempt of court for a witness to refuse, without lawful authority, to answer questions put to him.

The modern test for the competence of witnesses varies with the nature of the proceedings (civil or criminal) and the status of the witness (child, adult, accused, accused's spouse, person of defective intellect).

3.5.1 Civil cases

In *Omychund v Barker* (1745) 1 Atk 21, and a series of statutes, individuals were made competent to testify in civil proceedings. In *Omychund v Barker,* the court decided that non-Christians were competent to testify. The Evidence Act 1843 abolished the rule of incompetence on the ground that a person had been convicted or had an interest in the outcome of the proceedings. These are matters that are capable of affecting the weight of the evidence. The Evidence Act 1851 rendered the parties to civil proceedings competent and compellable to testify. The Evidence (Amendment) Act 1853 had the same effect with regard to the spouses of parties. The effect today is that all adults who do not suffer from defective intellect are competent and compellable to testify in civil proceedings. There are special rules created by statute that enact that sovereigns and diplomats are not compellable to testify.

3.5.2 Sworn evidence

At common law the test for competence to testify involved the test for the giving of sworn testimony, subject to an exception created to accommodate the evidence of children. This test is known as the *Hayes* test, derived from the case *R v Hayes* [1977] 1 WLR 234. The rule was originally applicable to both criminal and civil proceedings and remains the test today for civil proceedings. The test for criminal proceedings is currently to be found in the Youth Justice and Criminal Evidence Act 1999; see below.

The *Hayes* test involves a cumulative two-tier requirement for the judge to decide whether:

• the intended witness appreciates the solemnity of the occasion
• he is of sufficient intelligence to understand that the taking of the oath involves an obligation to tell the truth, over and above the ordinary duty of doing so. Knowledge or belief in God is not essential.

In *R v Hayes* the charges involved indecency with four small boys. The youngest, a nine-year-old, who testified, was ignorant of the significance of God and the existence of Jesus, but appreciated the necessity of speaking the truth whilst testifying. The question in issue was whether the child was competent to give sworn testimony. The Court of Appeal decided that he was capable of giving sworn evidence. Bridge LJ:

> J 'It is unrealistic not to recognise that, in the present state of society, amongst the adult population the divine sanction of an oath is probably not generally recognised. The important consideration, we think, when a judge has to decide whether a child should properly be sworn in, is whether the child has a sufficient appreciation of the solemnity of the occasion, and the added responsibility to tell the truth, which is involved in taking an oath, over and above the duty to tell the truth which is an ordinary duty of normal social conduct.'

3.5.3 Unsworn evidence of children in civil cases

The current position of competence in civil cases is that the witness is required to give sworn evidence or make a solemn affirmation. An exception to this rule regarding sworn evidence was created by s 96 of the Children Act 1989 authorizing the admissibility of unsworn evidence of children provided that they are incapable of giving sworn evidence.

The test for giving unsworn evidence in civil proceedings is enacted in s 96(2) of the 1989 Act, which states as follows:

'The child's evidence may be heard by the court if, in its opinion –
(a) he understands that it is his duty to speak the truth; and
(b) he has sufficient understanding to justify his evidence being heard.'

A child for these purposes is a person under the age of 18; see s 105 of the 1989 Act.

The effect of this provision is that in civil proceedings a child may give unsworn testimony as a last resort, if he is incapable of giving sworn testimony.

3.5.4 Criminal cases

The test for competence of a witness in criminal proceedings is a cumulative, two-tiered test as laid down in s 53(3) of the Youth Justice and Criminal Evidence Act 1999, which states:

'A person is not competent to give evidence in criminal proceedings if it appears to the court that he is not a person who is able to –
(a) understand questions put to him as a witness, and
(b) give answers to them which can be understood.'

It should be noted that this general rule is applicable to all witnesses (including the defendant and his or her spouse) in criminal proceedings. When an issue concerning the competence of a

witness is raised by a party in the proceedings of the court, the judge will rule on the issue in the absence of the jury. The legal burden of proof that the witness is competent to testify lies on the party calling the witness and the standard of proof is on a balance of probabilities. Interestingly, expert evidence may be called in order to determine the competence of the witness, see s 54 of the Youth Justice and Criminal Evidence Act 1999.

In *R v Sed* [2004] EWCA Crim 1294, the Court of Appeal decided that the test of competence was satisfied even though the witness did not have a 100 per cent understanding of the questions put to her and could not give answers which were 100 per cent understandable. The real issue is whether the witness was capable of giving a coherent account of the events for the benefit of the jury. The credibility and reliability of the evidence were matters for the jury to decide. In this case, an allegation of rape was made by an 81-year-old woman suffering from Alzheimer's disease. The prosecution made an application to admit her evidence by means of a video-taped interview. The defence objected and called two psychiatrists who testified to the effect she was suffering from moderate to severe Alzheimer's disease and she was not competent to testify and her interview should not be admitted. The judge ruled that the taped interview was admissible. The Court of Appeal dismissed the appeal and decided that her evidence was sufficiently coherent to admit in the proceedings. Auld LJ:

> **J** 'It should be noted that s 53 does not, in terms, provide for 100 per cent mutual comprehension of material exchanges giving rise to potential evidence. And, in our view, depending on the length and the nature of the questioning and the complexity of the matter the subject of it, it may not always require 100 per cent, or near 100 per cent, mutual understanding between questioner and questioned as a pre-condition of competence. The judge should also make allowance for the fact that the witness's performance and command of the detail may vary according to the importance to him or her of the subject matter of the question, how recent it was (in this case the interview took place within two days after the alleged attempted rape) and any strong feelings that it may have engendered.'

In *DPP v R* [2007] EWHC 1842 (Admin), it was decided that a 13-year-old complainant of indecent assault, and who was severely mentally handicapped, was interviewed on video tape which constituted her evidence-in-chief. She was unable to recall anything of the incident in cross-examination. The Divisional Court decided that she was competent to testify, despite her lapse of memory. Hughes LJ:

J 'The girl may have had learning difficulties. Her evidence may have needed treating with some care in consequence, but the problem at trial was not capacity to understand or to give intelligible answers, it was loss of memory. Recollection is quite different from competence.

[This girl] could understand the questions and she could give intelligible answers. The problem was that her perfectly intelligible answer was, "I cannot remember." She was not incompetent. It may be that she could not, for lack of memory, give useful evidence by the time of trial, but that is a different question.'

3.5.5 Sworn/unsworn evidence

In criminal proceedings the general rule is that, subject to two exceptions, only the sworn evidence of witnesses are admitted in court. The decision whether a witness is entitled to give sworn evidence is made by the judge, see s 55(1) of the Youth Justice and Criminal Evidence Act 1999.

The test for determining whether a witness may be sworn is laid down in s 55(2)(b) of the 1999 Act. This involves the common law, cumulative, two-tiered test that was known as the *Hayes* test (see above), namely whether the witness 'has a sufficient appreciation of the solemnity of the occasion and of the particular responsibility to tell the truth which is involved in taking the oath'. There is a presumption to the effect that the witness has a sufficient appreciation of the solemnity of the occasion and the duty to speak the truth, if he is able to give intelligible testimony, see s 55(3) of the 1999 Act. The test of 'intelligible testimony' is laid down in s 55(8) and is the same test for competence, namely, whether the witness understands questions put to him and may give answers which can be understood. The legal burden of proof lies on the party calling the witness to testify and the standard of proof is a balance of probabilities; see s 55(4). The questioning of the witness is conducted in the absence of the jury, and expert evidence may be called by the party.

The two exceptions to the sworn evidence rule are stated in s 55(2) of the 1999 Act, thus;

1. the witness is under the age of 14

2. the witness is incapable of satisfying the test for sworn evidence.

In respect of these exceptions the witness is entitled to give unsworn evidence. In respect of the first exception, ie the witness is under the age of 14, the witness is not permitted to give sworn evidence. The second exception (incapacity to give sworn evidence) involves a last-resort method of receiving the evidence of the witness. However, the legislation does not lay down a test to determine whether the witness may give unsworn evidence. This is a matter within the trial judge's discretion. Presumably, this is dependent on whether the witness is capable of giving a coherent account of the facts.

3.5.6 The defendant

In criminal cases the original rule at common law was that the defendant was not competent to testify, not even on his own behalf. The reasons commonly accorded for this incapacity were an interest in the proceedings and the over-riding principle of not incriminating himself. However, the Criminal Evidence Act 1898 changed the law and made the defendant a competent witness for the first time, but only for or on behalf of the defence, ie for the defendant and any co-defendants. At the same time the defendant was not compellable to testify on his behalf and was accordingly entitled to refuse to testify. The common law rule of incompetence governed the defendant's capacity to be a witness for the prosecution.

The modern law concerning the competence of the defendant and other witnesses in criminal cases is laid down in s 53(1) of the Youth Justice and Criminal Evidence Act 1999. This Act repeals the Criminal Evidence Act 1898 and enacts the general rule in s 53(1) to the effect that all persons, irrespective of age, are competent to give evidence. This principle includes the defendant, ie the person charged.

In addition, the defendant (or person charged) is not treated as a competent witness for the prosecution, whether charged solely or jointly with others. This is an affirmation of the common law rule as stated above. Section 53(4) of the 1999 Act declares as follows:

'A person charged in criminal proceedings is not competent to give evidence in the proceedings for the prosecution (whether he is the only person, or is one of two or more persons, charged in the proceedings).'

Section 53(5) of the 1999 Act defines a person charged as not including 'a person who is not, or is no longer, liable to be convicted of any offence in the proceedings (whether as a result of pleading guilty or for any other reason)'.

The effect of this provision is that a 'person charged' is one who is currently on trial on indictment or summarily and pleads not guilty.

Moreover, the common law rule is applicable to the effect that the defendant is not compellable to testify in his defence. Thus, whether the defendant chooses to testify in his defence is a decision he will take after considering advice from his legal adviser. There is no compulsion on his part to testify, this is known as the defendant's right of silence (in court). The possible consequences of remaining silent will be considered later under the right of silence, but in a nutshell, if the defendant fails to testify in the circumstances enacted in s 35 of the Criminal Justice and Public Order Act 1994, the judge may direct the jury 'to draw such inferences as appear proper'.

Techniques available to the prosecution to call an accomplice

There are various devices available to the prosecution who wishes to call as a witness, a person who has been allegedly implicated in the crime. In these circumstances the individual will be treated as an ordinary witness and may be competent and compellable to testify for the prosecution. These devices are:

- where a *nolle prosequi* is entered against a defendant
- where a successful application is made for an order of separate trial
- where the defendant pleads guilty.

Nolle prosequi

This is a technique that is available to the prosecution where the defendant (D) is charged together with others (E and F) with the commission of one or more offences, and the prosecution wishes to call one defendant (D) to testify against other defendants (E and F). The prosecution may 'offer no evidence' against the defendant (D) and the judge or magistrates will formally acquit the defendant for the relevant offence. In these circumstances, D will be treated as an ordinary witness and will be both competent and compellable to testify for the prosecution.

Section 17 of the Criminal Justice Act 1967 provides as follows:

'Where a defendant arraigned on an indictment or inquisition pleads not guilty and the prosecutor proposes to offer no evidence against him, the court before which the defendant is arraigned may, if it thinks fit, order that a verdict of not guilty shall be recorded without any further steps being taken in the proceedings, and the verdict shall have the same effect as if the defendant had been tried and acquitted on the verdict of the jury or a court.'

Although the section declares that the court 'may' enter a finding of 'not guilty', the word 'may' suggests that the court can refuse the prosecution application. In practice, however, the court is unlikely to reject the prosecution's application and force the prosecution to prove its case. Indeed, in *R v Grafton* [1993] QB 101, the Court of Appeal said that the decision whether or not to continue the prosecution had to be that of the prosecution, and the trial judge had no power to refuse to permit the discontinuance of the prosecution.

Application for separate trials

The trial judge retains a discretion to order separate trials of defendants who are accused of committing an offence jointly. Factors which militate against a separate trial are the saving of time and the convenience to witnesses in having one trial; the desirability of the jury having a full picture of the occurrence of the event in a single trial and the risk of different verdicts being returned by different juries on similar facts in the event of separate trials; see *R v Moghal* (1977) 65 Cr App R 56. The decision is ultimately one for the discretion of the judge and the Court of Appeal is unlikely to interfere with the decision of the judge provided that there is no miscarriage of justice.

Guilty plea by one defendant

In a trial with more than one defendant if one defendant pleads guilty he is no longer treated as a 'person charged'. The effect is that such a person may be required to testify for the prosecution. In these circumstances, it is desirable that the guilty defendant be sentenced before testifying for the prosecution. The reason for the practice of sentencing the defendant before he testifies is to avoid the temptation of the defendant colouring his testimony in the hope of receiving a lighter sentence. At the same time, if the judge is unclear as to the significance of the defendant's role in the commission of the offence, he may postpone the time of sentencing until the conclusion of the trial of the co-defendant.

In *R v Payne* [1950] 1 All ER 102, Payne (P) and two co-defendants, A and B were indicted on a charge of burglary. On arraignment on the first day of the trial, P pleaded guilty and the others pleaded not guilty. P was sentenced to two years' imprisonment and then testified for the prosecution. The two other defendants were found guilty the following day and were sentenced to 12 and 15 months' respectively. P appealed against his sentence. The Court of Appeal allowed the appeal and reduced P's sentence to 15 months. Lord Goddard CJ:

> **J** 'It may be a very convenient course to sentence on the first day prisoners who plead guilty but that ought not to apply where two or more men are indicted together. If one pleads guilty and the other not guilty, the proper course is to postpone sentence on the man who pleaded guilty until the others have been tried and then to bring up all the prisoners to be dealt with together because by that time the court will be in possession of the facts relating to all of them and will be able to assess properly the degree of guilt of each. This man received a heavier sentence than the other two because he was tried in a different court on a different day. This is a most inconvenient practice and it ought to cease ... But what I have said does not apply in the exceptional case where a man who pleads guilty is going to be called as a witness. In those circumstances it is right that he be sentenced there and then so that there can be no suspicion that his evidence is coloured by the fact that he hopes to get a lighter sentence.'

3.5.7 The defendant's spouse/civil partner in criminal cases

At common law not only the defendant, but his or her spouse was incompetent to testify in both civil and criminal proceedings. In a series of statutory provisions the general rule has been abrogated in both civil and criminal cases. In criminal proceedings, the test concerning a witness's competence is enacted in s 53(3) of the Youth Justice and Criminal Evidence Act 1999. This involves a test that is applicable to *all witnesses* in criminal proceedings, ie whether the person understands questions put to him and may give answers which can be understood; see above. In addition, the extent to which the spouse (including a registered civil partner) is

compellable to testify in criminal proceedings is dealt with in s 80 of the Police and Criminal Evidence Act 1984. The principle enacted here is dependent on which of three parties involved in criminal proceedings calls the spouse of the defendant to testify. The three parties involved are:

- the defendant who is the spouse (or civil partner) of the witness
- the spouse (or civil partner) of a co-defendant, who is charged in the proceedings, being called by the defendant
- the prosecution who wishes to call the spouse (or civil partner) of any of the defendants.

It is important to note that the rules concerning the compellability of the defendant's spouse that are applicable to the latter two categories are identical. In other words, whether the defendant's spouse (or civil partner) is compellable to testify for the co-defendant or the prosecution is subject to the same principles as laid down in s 80 of the 1984 Act.

A spouse of the defendant has not been defined in the Act but is a person who, at the time of being called to testify, had contracted a valid marriage. The legislation has been amended to include the registered civil partner of the defendant. In both cases there is no requirement that the parties live with each other. However, persons living with each other without going through valid ceremonies of marriage or registered civil partnerships are not spouses, etc for these purposes, and will be treated as ordinary witnesses and compellable to testify for any party in the proceedings.

Spouse (civil partner) of the defendant

Section 80(2) of the 1984 Act lays down the rule that the defendant's spouse (or civil partner) is, subject to one exception, compellable to testify on his or her behalf in respect of *any criminal charges*. For example, H, who is married to W, is charged with common assault on X. W is compellable to testify on behalf of H. The same principle applies if the alleged assault is on W.

The only exception to this principle of compellability at the instance of a spouse (civil partner) is the occasion when the spouse (civil partner) is also a defendant in the same proceedings; see s 80(4) of the 1984 Act. This is an obvious exception which would have been implied in any event on the ground that an accused person is never compellable to testify in criminal proceedings; see above.

Spouse (civil partner) of co-defendant/or being called by the prosecution

Where the spouse (civil partner) of a co-defendant is called by a defendant to testify on his behalf, the general rule is that the spouse, etc of the co-defendant is not compellable to testify on his behalf. For example, where H and D are charged with theft from X, W, the wife of H, is not compellable to testify for the defendant, D. The same principle is applicable where the prosecution wishes to call the spouse (civil partner) of an accused. In the example above, W is not compellable to testify for the prosecution against H or D.

Exceptionally, where the charge in respect of the defendant is within a 'specified offence' identified in s 80(3) of the 1984 Act, the spouse (civil partner) of the defendant is compellable to testify for either the co-defendant or the prosecution in the criminal proceedings; see ss 80(2A)(a) and (b) of the 1984 Act.

Section 80(3) declares:

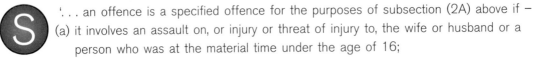

'. . . an offence is a specified offence for the purposes of subsection (2A) above if –
(a) it involves an assault on, or injury or threat of injury to, the wife or husband or a person who was at the material time under the age of 16;
(b) it is a sexual offence alleged to have been committed in respect of a person who was at the material time under that age; or
(c) it consists of attempting or conspiring to commit, or of aiding, abetting, counselling, procuring or inciting the commission of, an offence falling within paragraph (a) or (b) above.'

Thus, the compellability of a spouse (civil partner) of a defendant to testify on behalf of a co-defendant or the prosecution is dependent on the type of offence with which the defendant is charged. Section 80(3)(a) uses the expression 'involves', ie the offence 'involves' an assault, etc, which is much broader than 'against'. In other words, the spouse of the defendant or a person under the age of 16 may be a victim of the assault, directly or indirectly. It is arguable that charges of blackmail and kidnapping against a spouse may involve an assault on that spouse and be within the definition of a 'specified offence'.

A person may be understandably reluctant to testify against his or her spouse or civil partner; but there is strong public interest in favour of certain offences being prosecuted and it will be difficult to secure evidence of these offences otherwise than from the defendant and/or his or her spouse or civil partner, hence the need to introduce an element of compulsion within s 80.

The decisive moment to determine whether a person is a spouse or registered civil partner of a defendant is at the time that the witness is called to testify in the criminal proceedings. A person who has been but is no longer married to the defendant (or the discontinuance of a civil partnership) is not treated as a spouse for the purpose of these provisions; see s 80(5) of the 1984 Act. Thus, an ex-spouse or ex-civil partner will be treated as an ordinary witness and will be compellable to testify for any of the parties. On the other hand, once the individuals satisfy the legal tests for being spouses or civil partners, it is irrelevant that they are not living with each other at the time that the witness is called to testify.

In addition, a 'person charged in the proceedings' for the purposes of s 80 does not include a person who is not, or is no longer, liable to be convicted; see s 80(4A) of the 1984 Act. Thus, a defendant who has been acquitted or pleaded guilty is outside this definition and is treated as an ordinary witness.

Acaster warnings

Where a spouse (civil partner) of the defendant who is competent, but not compellable, to testify for the prosecution and is called by the prosecution to testify on its behalf, the judge may be required to exercise his discretion to warn the potential witness, in the absence of the jury, that he or she is not compellable to testify. This is known as an *Acaster* warning derived from the case *R v Acaster* (1912) 7 Cr App R 187.

Darling J:

'In any case where the spouse of the accused comes to give evidence against her husband, the judge ought to ask her "Do you know you may object to give evidence?" . . . That I imagine is what other judges will do for the present, though there is no decision which binds us to do it ...'

In *R v Pitt* [1983] QB 25, the Court of Appeal decided that although there was no rule of law to the effect that the judge should issue the warning, the matter would be treated as an exercise of the discretion of the judge. In this case, the defendant's wife, a competent but not compellable witness (as the law existed at that time), reluctantly testified for the prosecution against her husband. She gave answers that were inconsistent with her statement and was made a hostile witness and cross-examined by the prosecution. Her husband was convicted, but the Court of Appeal quashed the conviction on the ground that the wife did not appreciate that she was not a compellable witness and could not be taken to have waived her right not to testify without full knowledge of her rights, *per* Pain J:

'This case illustrates very powerfully why it is necessary for the trial judge to make certain that the wife understands her position before she takes the oath. Had that been done here, there would have been no difficulty . . . Up to a point where she goes into the witness box, W has a choice: she may refuse to give evidence or waive her right of refusal. The waiver is effective only if made with full knowledge of her right to refuse. If she waives her right of refusal, she becomes an ordinary witness . . . Once W has started upon her evidence, she must complete it. It is not open to her to retreat behind the barrier on non-compellability if she is asked questions that she does not want to answer. This makes it particularly important that W should understand when she takes the oath that she is waiving her right to refuse evidence . . . It seems to us, desirable that where W is called as a witness for the prosecution of H, the judge should explain to her in the absence of the jury, that, before she takes the oath she has the right to refuse to give evidence, but that if she chooses to give evidence she may be treated like any other witness . . .'

In the event of a failure to warn a competent, but not compellable witness, that she is not required to testify for the prosecution of the co-accused, the Court of Appeal will take into consideration all relevant factors, such as:

* whether the witness was reluctant or enthusiastic to testify against her husband
* whether she was called to testify for the co-defendant or the prosecution
* the significance of her testimony.

Where the spouse exercises his or her right not to testify, the prosecution is not entitled to comment on his or her silence; see s 80A of the 1984 Act. This statutory restriction does not extend to the co-defendant and the judge. As far as the co-defendant is concerned, there is no restriction as to the presentation of his case, including the co-defendant's right to comment on the defendant's right of silence.

The trial judge has a restricted freedom to comment on the defendant's spouse not testifying in the case. The power of the judge to comment is dependent on the exercise of discretion, and the overriding duty is to ensure a fair trial. Indeed, in exceptional circumstances, the judge may use the summing up to rectify a breach by the prosecution. In *R v Naudeer* [1984] 3 All ER 1036, under the predecessor to s 80A, the court decided that where the prosecution makes an unauthorized comment, the judge, subject to the circumstances of each case, is entitled to remedy the breach in his summing up.

3.6 Special measures directions

Sections 16–33 of the Youth Justice and Criminal Evidence Act 1999 lay down a number of provisions designed to assist young, disabled, vulnerable or intimidated witnesses to give evidence in criminal proceedings. Procedural rules that govern the process of applying for a special measures direction have been created by the Criminal Procedural Rules 2005.

There are four categories of witness who are eligible for assistance. These are:

* a witness who is under the age of 17 at the time of the hearing; see ss 16(1) and 21 of the 1999 Act. In the latter case, a special measures direction may be made in respect of a child witness who is in need of special protection, as defined. The special measures direction may take the form of presenting the witness's evidence by means of a video recording. Where this is not possible the evidence must be given by means of a live television link. In *R v Camberwell Green Youth Court* [2003] 2 Cr App R 257, the court decided that the presentation of evidence of a child witness in a room where the defendant was not present did not infringe the defendant's right to a fair trial
* a witness who suffers from a mental or physical disorder or otherwise has a significant impairment of intelligence, s 16(2) of the 1999 Act

- a witness whose evidence is likely to be affected on grounds of fear or distress about testifying, s 17(1) of the 1999 Act

- The complainant as a witness in respect of a sexual offence, s 17(4) of the 1999 Act.

The prosecution or defence may apply to the court for a special measures direction or the court may, of its own motion, make such a direction; see s 19 of the 1999 Act. The court is required to determine whether any, and, if so, which, of the special measures available would be likely to improve the quality of the evidence of the witness; see s 19 of the 1999 Act. In deciding this question the court is required to consider all the circumstances of the case, including any views expressed by the witness. Finally, the court is required to state in open court its reasons for giving, varying, refusing or discharging a special measures direction, s 20 of the 1999 Act.

The 1999 Act lays down a variety of special measures that may be ordered by the court. These are specified in ss 23–30 of the 1999 Act and are as follows:

Screening witnesses from the defendant. The court may direct that a witness, while giving testimony, may be prevented by means of a screen or other arrangement from seeing the defendant. However, the witness must be positioned in such a way that he is seen by the judge (or justices), the jury, legal representatives and any court interpreters; see s 23 of the 1999 Act.

Evidence by live link. A special measures direction may take the form of giving evidence by a live link. Such a link has been defined as a live television link or other arrangement whereby the witness, whilst absent from the courtroom, is able to see and hear a person there and to be seen and heard by the judge (or justices), the jury, legal representatives and any court interpreters; see s 24 of the 1999 Act. The effect is that the witness is treated as being constructively present in the court.

Evidence given in private (in camera). A special measures direction may order that certain individuals be excluded from the court while the witness testifies. The direction may not exclude the defendant, his legal representatives and interpreters acting for the witness. This direction may only be used where the proceedings relate to a sexual offence, or there are reasonable grounds to believe that the witness has or will be intimidated by any person other than the defendant, see s 25(4) of the 1999 Act.

Removal of wigs and gowns. A direction may be issued for the wearing of wigs and gowns to be dispensed with, while a witness gives his evidence, see s 26 of the 1999 Act.

Video recorded evidence. Section 27 of the 1999 Act provides for a video recording of an interview of the witness to be admitted as the evidence-in-chief of that witness. However, the court is not entitled to make such a direction if, having regard to all the circumstances of the case, the recording ought not to be admitted in the interests of justice. Where a recording is admitted, the witness must be called by the party tendering the recording in evidence, unless a direction has been made for the witness's cross-examination to be given otherwise than by testimony, or the parties have agreed to dispense with the witness's presence.

Video recorded cross-examination or re-examination. Where a video recording is admitted as the witness's examination-in-chief as stated above, a direction can provide for any cross-examination or re-examination of the witness to be recorded before trial by means of a video-recording. Such a recording must be made in the presence of the judge or justices and legal representatives, but in the absence of the defendant. The defendant, however, must be able to see and hear the examination of the witness, probably by use of a live link; see s 28 of the 1999 Act.

Examination through an intermediary. This special measures direction may provide for any examination of the witness to be conducted through an interpreter or other intermediary. The intermediary's function is to communicate questions put to the witness, answers given by the witness to any person asking such questions and provide an understanding of the questions and answers to the witness or person in question; see s 29 of the 1999 Act.

Aids to communication. This special measures direction provides for any device, mechanical or otherwise, which will enable questions or answers to be communicated to or by the witness, despite any disability or disorder or other impairment which the witness suffers from; see s 30 of the 1999 Act.

3.7 Court's inherent powers

Witnesses who fall outside the four statutory categories as specified in the Youth Justice and Criminal Evidence Act 1999 may still be assisted through the court's inherent powers. These have been preserved by s 19(6)(a) of the 1999 Act. Under this head, directions may be made to ensure that the witness remains anonymous and a direction may be made regarding voice modulation. This is an extremely complicated issue, and it is of paramount importance that the order, made by the judge, does not severely disadvantage the defendant to such an extent that it compromises a fair trial.

ASE EXTRACT

R v Davis [2008] 3 All ER 461 (HL)

The accused was charged with murder by shooting. The defendant denied the shooting. The witnesses for the prosecution, who claimed to have identified the defendant as the gunman, claimed to be in fear for their lives if it became known that they had given evidence against him. Their claims were investigated and accepted as genuine. To ensure the safety of these witnesses and to induce them to give evidence, the trial judge made a variety of special measures directions: (1) they were each to give evidence under a pseudonym; (2) their addresses and personal details were to be

CONTINUED ▶

withheld from the defendant and his legal advisers; (3) the defendant's counsel was prohibited from asking the witnesses questions which might enable any of them to be identified; (4) the witnesses were to give evidence behind screens; (5) the witnesses' natural voices were to be heard by the judge and jury but not by the defendant or his counsel. On conviction, the defendant appealed ultimately to the House of Lords.

The Court allowed the appeal and quashed the conviction on the following grounds:

The protective measures compromised the long-established principle of English common law that the defendant in a criminal trial should be confronted by his accusers in order that he might cross-examine them and challenge their evidence. The directions adopted in this case were not compatible with the defendant's human rights. The conduct of the defence was unlawfully hampered to such an extent to have rendered the trial unfair. It was not open to the courts to modify the common law rights of the defendant to the extent envisaged by this case. There was nothing in the Strasbourg jurisprudence that required states in their national law to balance anonymity against defendants' rights. In relation to the convention, the use of anonymous evidence had not satisfied the requirements of Art 6. Not only had the evidence been the sole or decisive basis on which the defendant could have been convicted, but effective cross-examination had been hampered.

Lord Bingham:

J

'To decide whether the protective measures operated unfairly in this case it is necessary to consider their impact on the conduct of the defence. For that purpose it cannot be assumed at the outset that the defendant is guilty and all that he says false. The appellant denied that he was the gunman. Why, then, did witnesses say that he was? His answer, on which his instructions to counsel were based, was that he believed the false evidence to have been procured by a former girlfriend with whom he had fallen out. Mr Swift duly sought to pursue this suggestion in cross-examination of the unidentified witnesses, but was gravely impeded in doing so by ignorance of and inability to explore who the witnesses were, where they lived and the nature of their contact with the appellant. When, eventually, subject to the protective measures, a female witness was called whom the appellant believed to be the girlfriend it was at least doubtful whether she was or not, but this was a question that could not be fully explored. If the jury concluded that she was probably not the former girlfriend, they would also conclude that the defence had been based on a false premise. But this was an unavoidable risk if the defence were obliged, to

CONTINUED ▸

J take blind shots at a hidden target. A trial so conducted cannot be regarded as meeting ordinary standards of fairness.

I feel bound to conclude that the protective measures imposed by the court in this case hampered the conduct of the defence in a manner and to an extent which was unlawful and rendered the trial unfair. I would accordingly allow this appeal.'

Lord Mance:

J 'I do not believe that the Strasbourg court would accept that the use of anonymous evidence in the present case satisfied the requirements of art 6. Not only was the evidence on any view the sole or decisive basis on which alone the defendant could have been convicted, but effective cross-examination in the present case depended upon investigating the potential motives for the three witnesses giving what the defence maintained was a lying and presumably conspiratorial account. Cross-examination was hampered by the witnesses' anonymity, by the mechanical distortion of their voices and by their giving evidence from behind screens, so that the appellant (and, since he was not prepared to put himself in a position where he had information that his client did not, his counsel) could not see the witnesses. Assuming that the sole or decisive nature of the evidence is not itself fatal, it is on any view an important factor which would require to be very clearly counter-balanced by other factors. Here there are none. The other factors are here very prejudicial in their impact on effective cross-examination.

So, if the matter rested with the Strasbourg jurisprudence, I would allow the appeal. However, on the basis that there is in the present Strasbourg jurisprudence nothing that requires states in their national law to balance anonymity against defendants' rights, the primary question is whether English domestic law permits anonymous evidence in any circumstances. The defence would be precluded from knowing or asking questions disclosing the officer's [witness's] true identity and background; and it would become difficult to draw the line between this and more radical inroads into the basic common law rule.

In this situation, I have been persuaded that any further relaxation of the basic common law rule, requiring witnesses on issues in dispute to be identified and

CONTINUED ▸

J cross-examined with knowledge of their identity and permitting the defence to know and put to witnesses otherwise admissible and relevant questions about their identity, is one for Parliament to endorse and delimit and not for the courts to create. Parliamentary legislation is the means by which common law principles regarding the admission of documentary evidence have been modified. It may well be appropriate that there should be a careful statutory modification of basic common law principles. It is clear from the Strasbourg jurisprudence discussed in this judgment that there is scope within the Convention on Human Rights for such modification. I would allow this appeal accordingly.'

Warning by the judge. Where a special measures direction has been issued, the judge is required to issue a warning to the jury to the effect that the direction does not prejudice the defendant; see s 32 of the 1999 Act.

3.8 Miscellaneous

Persons of defective intellect

The competence of a person with defective intellect is determined in the usual way, by reference to the test laid down in s 53 of the Youth Justice and Criminal Evidence Act 1999. In appropriate cases, in criminal law, expert evidence will be permitted to assist the court in determining the competence of the witness. The additional factor with mentally defective individuals depends on the exact nature of the mental defect, ie whether the witness may give a coherent account of matters not connected with their derangement.

CASE EXTRACT

R v Hill (1851) 2 Den 254

On a charge of manslaughter, W, a witness and patient in a lunatic asylum was called to testify for the prosecution. To counter the defence objection the prosecution called a medical officer at the asylum who testified to the effect that although the witness believed that a number of spirits spoke to him, he was quite capable of giving an account of any transaction that he experienced. The court held that the witness was competent to testify.

CONTINUED ▸

Lord Campbell:

'It is for the judge to see whether the party tendered understands the nature and sanction of an oath and then if the judge admits him as a witness, it is for the jury to say what degree of credit is to be given to his testimony . . . but the witness may be *non compos mentis* and yet understand the sanction of an oath and be capable of giving material testimony. He had a clear apprehension of the obligation of an oath and was capable of giving a trustworthy account of any transaction which took place before his eyes and he was perfectly rational upon all subjects except with respect to his particular delusion.'

Temporary mental incapacity, due to transitory illness or intoxication, may lead to an adjournment of the proceedings.

Sovereigns and diplomats

Sovereigns, heads of states as well as diplomats and consular officials are competent but not compellable to testify in civil and criminal proceedings.

3.9 Training or coaching of witnesses/ familiarization

In *R v Momodou and Limani* [2005] 2 Cr App R 6, the Court of Appeal decided that there was a dramatic distinction between witness training or coaching on the one hand, and on the other hand, witness familiarization. Witness training for criminal trials was prohibited but witness familiarization was permissible.

The rule avoided the possibility that one witness might tailor his evidence in the light of what anyone else said, and equally, avoided any unfounded perception that he might have done so. Those risks were inherent in witness training.

That principle did not preclude pre-trial arrangements to familiarize a witness with the layout of the court, the likely sequence of events when the witness was giving evidence and a balanced appraisal of the different responsibilities of the various participants. None of that, however, involved discussions about proposed or intended evidence.

In the context of an anticipated criminal trial, if arrangements were made for witness familiarization by outside agencies, not, for example, that routinely performed by or through the Witness Service, the following broad guidance should be followed.

In relation to prosecution witnesses, the Crown Prosecution Service should be informed in advance of any proposal for familiarization. The proposals for the intended familiarization programme should be reduced into writing, rather than left to informal conversations.

If, having examined them, the Crown Prosecution Service suggested that the programme might be in breach of the permitted limits, it should be amended.

If the defence engaged in the process, it would be extremely wise for counsel's advice to be sought in advance, and again with written information about the nature and extent of the familiarization.

In any event it was a matter of professional duty on counsel and solicitors to ensure that the trial judge was informed of any familiarization process organized by the defence using outside agencies, and it would follow that the Crown Prosecution Service would be made aware of what had happened.

The familiarization process should normally be supervised or conducted by a solicitor or barrister, or someone who was responsible to a solicitor or barrister with experience of the criminal justice process, and preferably by an organization accredited for the purpose by the Bar Council or Law Society.

None of those involved should have any personal knowledge of the matters in issue and records should be maintained. If discussion of the current criminal proceedings began, as it almost inevitably would, it had to be stopped and advice given about precisely why it was impermissible, with a warning against the danger of evidence contamination and the risk that the course of justice might be perverted. No documents used in the process should be destroyed. Judge LJ:

> **J**
> 'There is a dramatic distinction between witness training or coaching, and witness familiarisation. Training or coaching for witnesses in criminal proceedings (whether for the prosecution or defence) is not permitted. This is the logical consequence of the well-known principle that discussions between witnesses should not take place, and that the statements and proofs of one witness should not be disclosed to any other witness: see *R v Richardson* [1971] 2 QB 484, *R v Arif*, *The Times*, 22nd June 1993, *R v Skinner* (1993) 99 Cr App R 212 and *R v Shaw* [2002] EWCA 3004. The witness should give his or her own evidence, so far as practicable uninfluenced by what anyone else has said, whether in formal discussions or informal conversations. The rule reduces, indeed hopefully avoids, any possibility that one witness may tailor his evidence in the light of what anyone else said, and equally, avoids any unfounded perception that he may have done so . . .

CONTINUED ▸

> **J** This principle does not preclude pre-trial arrangements to familiarise witnesses with the layout of the court, the likely sequence of events when the witness is giving evidence, and a balanced appraisal of the different responsibilities of the various participants. Indeed such arrangements, usually in the form of a pre-trial visit to the court, are generally to be welcomed. Witnesses should not be disadvantaged by ignorance of the process, nor when they come to give evidence, taken by surprise at the way it works. None of this however involves discussions about proposed or intended evidence. Sensible preparation for the experience of giving evidence, which assists the witness to give of his or her best at the forthcoming trial is permissible.'

ACTIVITY

Self-test questions

1. In criminal cases when is a witness competent to testify?

2. What is the test for competence of witnesses to testify in civil proceedings?

3. In criminal cases, when is a witness compellable to testify for the prosecution?

4. In what circumstances may an accomplice to a criminal charge be both competent and compellable to testify for the prosecution?

5. When may a defendant's spouse (or civil partner) be compellable to testify for the co-defendant or prosecution in criminal proceedings?

6. What are special measures directions? When may a judge make such a direction?

7. May a judge protect the anonymity of a witness, and if so, what conditions must be satisfied?

Further reading

Birch, D. 'Children's Evidence' [1992] Crim LR 262

Birch, D. 'A Better Deal for Vulnerable Witnesses?' [2000] Crim LR 223

Cooper, D. 'Pigot Unfulfilled: Video Recorded Evidence under section 28 of the YJCEA 1999' [2005] Crim LR 456

Creighton, P. 'Spouse Competence and Compellability' [1990] Crim LR 34

Gillespie, A. 'Compellability of a child victim' J Crim L, Vol 64, no 1, 98

Hoyano, L. 'Variations on a Theme by Pigot: Special Measures Directions for Child Witnesses' [2000] Crim LR 250

Hoyano, L. 'Striking a Balance between the Rights of Defendants and Vulnerable Witnesses: Will Special Measures Directions contravene Guarantees of A Fair Trial?' [2001] Crim LR 948

Jones, D. 'The Evidence of a Three Year Old Child' [1987] Crim LR 677

Munday, R. 'Sham Marriages and Spousal Compellability' [2001] J Crim L, Vol 65, no 4, 336

chapter 4 DISCLOSURE OF EVIDENCE AND PROTECTION FROM DISCLOSURE; PRIVILEGE AND PUBLIC INTEREST IMMUNITY ■

AIMS AND OBJECTIVES

By the end of this chapter you should be able to:

■ Understand the requirements for disclosure of evidence

■ Recognize the rules regarding the privilege including the types, their basis, extent and when privilege is lost

■ Identify the rules designed to protect documents from disclosure on the grounds of public interest immunity

■ Evaluate which public policy issues underpin public interest immunity.

4.1 Introduction

In this chapter we will discuss three related topics; disclosure, privilege and public interest immunity. We will begin our discussion with a general look at the rules on disclosure. Moving on to discuss privilege – the privilege against self-incrimination, legal professional and journalistic privileges. In relation to these we will discuss when it applies, its limitations, loss, waiver and the statutory exceptions. We will then discuss public interest immunity, the instances in which it applies, how it can be challenged and any restrictions that might be available. We will also discuss the public policy reasons behind public interest immunity, its role in the detection of crime, its waiver and statutory exceptions.

4.2 Disclosure

In both criminal and civil cases the general rule is that all relevant evidence is admissible. In criminal cases both the prosecution and defence are required to make disclosure at the pre-trial stage. Prior to the amendments introduced by the Criminal Justice Act 2003, disclosure under the Criminal Procedure and Investigations Act 1996 (CPIA) had four main parts:

UNLOCKING
EVIDENCE

- statutory duty on the investigating officer to record and retain information
- a primary disclosure by the prosecution
- disclosure by the defence
- a secondary disclosure by the prosecution.

Section 23(1) of the CPIA provided for the Secretary of State to create a code of practice to accompany the Act which included the requirement that all investigating police officers record and retain any information and material gathered or generated during the investigation of a criminal offence, such as crime reports, notebooks, custody records, interview records, communications and records derived from tapes or messages. The material must be retained at least until a decision has been made as to whether or not to institute proceedings against a person. For further research, readers are referred to the Code of Practice 2005 that accompanies the CPIA 1996, copies of which are readily downloadable from the Internet.

The prosecution's initial duty to make a primary disclosure used to be far more limited than it is at present. Prior to the amendments introduced by the CJA 2003 under s 3(1)(a) of the CPIA 1996, the duty of the prosecutor was limited to disclosure of any material which in the prosecutor's opinion might have undermined the prosecution case against the accused. This triggered defence disclosure which required the accused to disclose in general terms the nature of their defence, outlining any alibi and issues that they wish to raise at the trial. If this requirement was complied with, the prosecution would, if necessary, make a secondary disclosure that involved any 'material which might reasonably be expected to assist the defence'. This process was modified by the Criminal Justice Act 2003, which amended the 1996 Act and introduced a single objective test for the disclosure of unused prosecution material. Section 3(1) of the Criminal Procedure and Investigations Act 1996 (CPIA) now reads:

'. . . s 3(1) The prosecutor must (a) disclose to the accused any prosecution material which has not previously been disclosed to the accused and which might reasonably be considered capable of undermining the case for the prosecution against the accused or of assisting the case for the accused, or (b) give to the accused a written statement that there is no material of a description mentioned in paragraph (a) . . . (2) For the purposes of this section prosecution material is material (a) which is in the prosecutor's possession, and came into his possession in connection with the case for the prosecution against the accused, or (b) which, in pursuance of a code operative under Part II, he has inspected in connection with the case for the prosecution against the accused . . . (6) Material must not be disclosed under this section to the extent that the court, on an application by the prosecutor, concludes it is not in the public interest to disclose it and orders accordingly.'

From a reading of this provision it is obvious that there are now three main parts to disclosure; a statutory duty on the investigating officer to record and retain information, prosecution disclosure and defence disclosure in the form of a detailed defence statement. What then must the defence statement include? Section 6A(1) (inserted into the CPIA 1996 by the CJA 2003 and the Criminal Justice and Immigration Act 2008 (CJIA)) states that:

> '... s 6A(1) ... a defence statement is a written statement (a) setting out the nature of the accused's defence, including any particular defences on which he intends to rely, (b) indicating the matters of fact on which he takes issue with the prosecution, (c) setting out, in the case of each such matter, why he takes issue with the prosecution (ca) setting out particulars of the matters of fact on which he intends to rely for the purposes of his defence, and (d) indicating any point of law (including any point as to the admissibility of evidence or an abuse of process) which he wishes to take, and any authority on which he intends to rely for that purpose.'

It should be noted that the prosecution's duty to disclose continues from initial disclosure through to the determination of the case.

In addition s 6A(2) provides the extent of disclosure where the defence statement discloses an alibi, stating:

> '... s 6A(2) A defence statement that discloses an alibi must give particulars of it, including (a) the name, address and date of birth of any witness the accused believes is able to give evidence in support of the alibi, or as many of those details as are known to the accused when the statement is given; (b) any information in the accused's possession which might be of material assistance in identifying or finding any such witness in whose case any of the details mentioned in paragraph (a) are not known to the accused when the statement is given.'

In civil cases the requirements for disclosure are determined by the track on which the case is listed. This diagram summarizes how cases are allocated to a track.

Claims track	Reason for allocation
Small	Cases valued at less than £5,000 in total value (or where the damages for pain, suffering and loss of amenity in personal injury claims are less than £1,000 and in housing disrepair where the claim is valued at less than £1,000). Costs follow the outcome, ie the winner can recover fixed costs.
Fast	Cases valued at between £5,000 and £15,000 in total value. A trial on this track will last no longer than one day. Costs follow the outcome, ie the winner can recover fixed costs.
Multi	All other cases and those worth less than £5,000 if complex and technical.

■ Figure 4.1 How cases are allocated to a case management track

Part 31 of the Civil Procedure Rules 1998 (CPR) lays down standard disclosure requirements in cases listed on the fast and multi-tracks, on the small claims track only that evidence that will be relied on at trial need be disclosed. CPR 31.6 states:

S CIVIL PROCEDURE RULE '. . . standard disclosure requires a party to disclose only (a) the documents on which he relies and (b) the documents which (i) adversely affect his own case, (ii) adversely affect another party's case, or (iii) support another party's case, and (c) the documents which he is required to disclose by a relevant practice direction.'

Let us take a look at this in a little more depth. Part 31.6 requires a party to make standard disclosure of the following documents:

- those upon which they propose to rely
- those which adversely affect their own or another party's case
- those that support another party's case
- any documents that are required to be disclosed by a Practice Direction.

Part 31 of the CPR is available to download freely at http://www.justice.gov.uk/civil/procrules_fin/contents/parts/part31.htm#IDA4XIR. In addition, readers should regularly check the website that accompanies this book for regular updates on relevant issues. Having discussed the general rules on disclosure, the next part of this chapter will examine two related grounds upon which evidence may be excluded; this time, not necessarily by the court, but by the party who wishes to suppress the evidence that is otherwise admissible; privilege and public interest immunity.

KEY FACTS

Disclosure

The *general* rule in both criminal and civil cases is that all relevant evidence is admissible.

In criminal cases, there are three parts to disclosure: a statutory duty on the investigating officer to record and retain information, prosecution disclosure and defence disclosure in the form of a detailed defence statement.

In civil cases, Part 31 of the CPR lays down the requirements for standard disclosure, that is, documents upon which the parties will rely, those which adversely affect their own or another party's case, those that support another party's case and those that are required to be disclosed by a Practice Direction – in these cases disclosure is dependent on track allocation.

4.3 Privilege

The rest of the discussion in this chapter will focus on the protection from disclosure of evidence on the grounds that it is subject to privilege, which will be discussed in this part, and public interest immunity which is discussed at section 4.6. Privilege, where claimed successfully, protects evidence from being disclosed. As the discussion later will reveal, unlike public interest immunity, privilege attaches to evidence by reason of a justification in reference to an individual. The rationale of privilege is to protect the interests of a party which the law recognizes as being in need of protection in the limited circumstances surrounding the claim to privilege. The privilege belongs to a party to the proceedings and must be claimed by that party or his agent. Otherwise, the admissible evidence will be disclosed.

The English common law of evidence had contained protection of evidence from disclosure on the grounds that it is privileged by limiting it to specified situations which were:

- the privilege against self-incrimination
- legal professional privilege
- without prejudice negotiations
- journalistic privilege
- matrimonial communications.

The latter of these (matrimonial communications) was abolished in relation to civil proceedings in 1968 by s 16(3) of the Civil Evidence Act 1968 and by s 80(9) of the Police and Criminal Evidence Act 1984, in criminal proceedings.

4.3.1 Privilege against self-incrimination

At common law, no witness was required to answer any question or produce any document in court proceedings, if the answer or document would have a tendency to expose him to a criminal charge. The privilege was applicable to both civil and criminal proceedings and is part of the general right of silence. In criminal cases the general rule is summarized in the Latin maxim, '*nemo tenetur prodere se ipsum*', meaning 'no one is obliged to give himself away'. The general rule was stated as per Lord Goddard LJ in *Blunt v Park Lane Hotel Ltd* [1942] 2 KB 253, as:

'. . . No one is bound to answer any question if the answer thereto would, in the opinion of the judge, have a tendency to expose the deponent to any criminal charge, penalty or forfeiture which the judge regards as reasonably likely to be preferred or sued for.'

This particular type of privilege attaches to the witness themselves and that means that a party may not be able to obtain evidence through cross-examination because the witness has successfully claimed privilege. However, the party opposing the privilege can prove the same matter in a different way if such party has the relevant evidence or is able to prove the fact by a different method, such as a witness. The traditional position in both criminal and civil cases was outlined in *Blunt v Park Lane Hotel Ltd* [1942] 2 KB 253; the answers given by a witness in court could be used as evidence against him to determine his guilt in the proceedings and in relation to any future offences committed by him.

The Criminal Evidence Act 1898 (CEA) makes it clear that a defendant cannot refuse to answer incriminating questions in relation to the offence charged or their guilt which are put to them in cross-examination, although this is now subject to s 101 of the Criminal Justice Act 2003, concerning the admissibility of a defendant's bad character. Section 1(2) of the CEA 1898 states:

> **S** '. . . a person charged in criminal proceedings who is called as a witness in the proceedings may be asked any question in cross-examination notwithstanding that it would tend to criminate him as to any offence with which he is charged in the proceedings.'

Can a witness refuse to answer a question that incriminates him in respect of another offence, ie an offence with which he is not charged? If the witness answers such a question, that answer would be classified as a confession. The discussion in Chapter 8 reveals how confessions are admissible against their maker. The general rule is that there is a privilege against self-incrimination unless the contrary is expressly stated such as occasions where statute may preclude such a privilege – this is discussed later in this chapter. Where a claim for a privilege against self-incrimination is successful, the witness may leave unanswered any question that incriminates him to a criminal charge, other than one for which he is currently charged. The extent of the privilege includes protection from:

- the risk of future criminal proceedings
- directly or indirectly incriminatory questions.

The privilege against self-incrimination protects the witness from the *risk* of future criminal proceedings or forfeiture in England, Wales and Scotland; this does not include civil proceedings. The penalties covered include those under UK criminal law and any European penalties or sanctions. Reference may be made to the European Communities Act 1972, information in relation to which can be freely downloaded from the Office of Public Sector Information website at http://www.opsi.gov.uk/Acts/acts1972/ukpga_19720068_en_1.

In *Rio Tinto Zinc Corporation and Others v Westinghouse Electric Corporation* [1978] AC 547, Westinghouse, an American company, was sued in Virginia, USA for a breach of a contract to build nuclear power stations. The company alleged that the contracts could not be performed for two reasons; first, owing to a shortage of uranium, and second, steep price rises and price-fixing by an international cartel of uranium producers, including two English companies, one of whom was the Rio Tinto Zinc Corporation. The judge in the Virginia Court, on an application by Westinghouse, issued letters rogatory (formal request) to the High Court in London requesting it to order that certain named individuals, connected as officers or directors with both English companies, appear at the US consular office before an officer so that they could be examined on oath. It also requested that the High Court order that the claimant produce certain documents or classes of document. Both orders were made. However, the individuals from the Rio Tinto Zinc Corporation contended that some of the documents were privileged as they could render the Corporation liable to being fined under the EEC Treaty, which had been enshrined into English Law.

The claim for privilege was upheld in the UK, the judge from the Virginian Court also upheld a claim to privilege by the individual witnesses under the Fifth Amendment to the United States Constitution, on the ground of self-incrimination. Then the Virginian judge was informed by the United States Department of Justice that it now required the evidence of the witnesses for a grand jury investigation into breaches of United States anti-trust law by the alleged cartel with the possibility of initiating criminal proceedings. The United States Department of Justice applied to the Virginian judge for an order compelling the witnesses to give evidence under the United States Constitution s 6002/2 which applies where the privilege against self-incrimination is claimed. However, any evidence cannot be used against the witness in a subsequent criminal case. The Virginian judge made the order – the individuals appealed. The Court of Appeal held:

J '. . . that the master's order rightly gave effect to the letters rogatory in respect of the production of documents, subject to amendments to confine their operation to areas allowed by English law and further (Viscount Dilhorne dissenting) that the order rightly gave effect to them as regarded the witnesses sought to be examined but (*per* Lord Wilberforce) subject to the disallowance of certain witnesses . . . that the companies were entitled to claim privilege against self-incrimination under section 14(1) of the Civil Evidence Act 1968 in respect of the documents required to be produced, since production would tend to expose them to fines under articles 85, 189 and 192 of the European Economic Community Treaty, which cover penalties imposed by administrative action and recoverable in England by "proceedings . . . for the recovery of a penalty" within section 14(1) . . . that, in accordance with the ruling of the judge of the Virginian court, upholding the right of the individual witnesses to claim privilege against self-incrimination under the Fifth Amendment to the US Constitution, they could not, in consequence of section 3(1)(b) of the Evidence (Proceedings in Other Jurisdictions) Act 1975, be

CONTINUED ▶

J compelled to give evidence . . . that the intervention of the Department of Justice, converting the letters rogatory into a request for evidence for the purposes of a grand jury investigation, changed their character, seeking to use the Act of 1975 for purposes for which it was not intended by extending the grand jury's investigations internationally in a manner which was impermissible as being an infringement of United Kingdom sovereignty, a context in which the courts were entitled to take into account the declared policy of Her Majesty's Government.'

Section 14(1) of the Civil Evidence Act 1968 makes it clear that the privilege does not extend to the exposure to the risk of proceedings in foreign civil or criminal court proceedings. For example, Jetoya Lackson is charged with the offence of aggravated burglary. She cannot claim a privilege against a direct or indirect question that may expose her to the risk of being charged with the criminal offence in relation to smuggling drugs in Peru.

The privilege against self-incrimination covers answers to questions that directly or indirectly incriminate the witness, either because the actual answer incriminates him, or it would lead to evidence being recovered that would incriminate him; see *Rank Film Distributors v Video Information Centre* [1982] AC 380. On a claim for breach of copyright, the court decided that the defendant was entitled to claim a privilege against self-incrimination with regard to questions concerning the supply and sale of the infringing copies. See also *Tate Access Floors Inc v Boswell* [1990] 3 All ER 303.

It is clear that the witness's assertion of privilege is not sufficient to attract the privilege. The judge is required to examine all the circumstances of the case in order to ascertain whether there is a 'real and appreciable danger' that a prosecution may follow if the witness answers the question.

In *R v Boyes* (1861) 30 LJQB 301, a witness declined to answer a question on the ground that the answer would incriminate him. He was then handed a pardon and so could not be prosecuted, but, in theory, was liable to be impeached. The Court of Appeal decided that the privilege was not available. Cockburn CJ:

J '. . . To successfully claim the privilege of silence, the court must see, from the circumstances of the case and the nature of the evidence which the witness is called upon to give, that there is a reasonable ground to apprehend danger to the witness from his being compelled to answer . . . the danger apprehended must be

CONTINUED ▸

J real and appreciable with reference to the ordinary operation of law in the ordinary course of things; not a danger of an imaginary and substantial character, having reference to some extraordinary and barely possible contingency, so improbable that no reasonable man would suffer it to influence his conduct. We think that a merely remote and naked possibility, out of the ordinary course of the law, and such that no reasonable man would be affected by, should not be suffered to obstruct the administration of justice.'

In *A&T Istel v Tully* [1993] AC 45, the House of Lords decided that where the CPS made an offer not to prosecute the defendant in respect of any frauds revealed, this amounted to sufficient protection and the defendant was not entitled to claim the privilege.

The application of the privilege against self-incrimination is not retrospective. Where a witness has already been charged or has already provided the information, they cannot then assert the privilege.

The judge may warn a witness that he is not obliged to answer incriminating questions, but there is no rule of law to that effect. It follows that if the witness answers questions or produces a document in ignorance of his right to refuse to answer or produce the document, the court may, nevertheless, rely on the evidence. An appeal cannot be maintained on this ground. However, where a witness is forced to answer questions in relation to which he was entitled to privilege, then the answer will be inadmissible as evidence against him in future proceedings, the reason being that his answers are treated as analogous to involuntary confessions; see *R v Garbett* (1847) 1 Den CC 236.

Statutory exceptions to the privilege against self-incrimination

There exist a number of statutory exceptions to the privilege against self-incrimination, in summary these are:

- s 31 Theft Act 1968
- s 72 Supreme Court Act 1972
- s 2 Criminal Justice Act 1987
- s 98 Children Act 1989.

This table summarizes the effect of the three most important:

Act	Effect
Section 31 Theft Act 1968	A witness must answer questions relating to the recovery or administration of property – the answers cannot be used as evidence in subsequent proceedings under the Act
Section 72, s 72(3) and Supreme Court Act 1972	The privilege is of no application to civil proceedings related to a dispute concerning intellectual property – the answers cannot be used as evidence in subsequent criminal proceedings unless they are for perjury or contempt of court
Section 2 of the Criminal Justice Act 1967	The DPP of the Serious Fraud Office has broad powers to investigate persons in respect of offences of serious fraud. Persons investigated may be required to answer questions or provide documentation.
Section 98 Children Act 1989	A witness must answer questions in proceedings relating the care, supervision or protection of a child – the answers cannot be used as evidence in subsequent criminal proceedings

Figure 4.2 The effect of the statutory exceptions to the privilege against self-incrimination

Privilege against self-incrimination and human rights

The European Court of Human Rights (EctHR) has been unequivocal in stating that the privilege against self-incrimination is a fundamental part of the right to a fair trial, enshrined in Art 6 of the European Convention on Human Rights and Fundamental Freedoms. The text of this Convention can be downloaded from http://www.echr.coe.int/echr/. See also *Saunders v UK* (1997) 18 EHRR CD 23. This led to the amendment of the Companies Act 1985 (now the Companies Act 2006) and hence judges must consider the right to a fair trial when seeking to exclude evidence.

KEY FACTS

Privilege

This protects evidence from being disclosed by reason of a justification in reference to an individual. Evidence will be immune from disclosure on the grounds that it is privileged. Privilege is limited to specified situations which include the privilege against self-incrimination, legal professional privilege, without prejudice negotiations and journalistic privilege.

Privilege against self-incrimination

The general rule is that there is a privilege against self-incrimination unless otherwise provided. On occasion, statute may preclude such a privilege. In *Blunt v*

CONTINUED ▸

KEY FACTS

Park Lane Hotel Ltd [1942] 2 KB 253 stated that the answers given by a witness in court could be used as evidence against them to determine their guilt in the proceedings and in relation to any future offences committed by them.

Section 1(2) of the CEA 1898 makes it clear that a defendant cannot refuse to answer incriminating questions in relation to the offence charged, or their guilt put to them in cross-examination – see s 101 of the CJA 2003. The extent of the privilege includes protection from the risk of future criminal proceedings and direct or indirect incriminatory questions.

Section 14(1) of the Civil Evidence Act 1968 states that this privilege does not extend to the exposure to the risk of proceedings in foreign civil or criminal court proceedings.

Statutory exceptions to the privilege against self-incrimination
Section 31 of the Theft Act 1968, s 72 of the Supreme Court Act 1972, s 2 of the Criminal Justice Act 1987 and s 98 of the Children Act 1989.

4.3.2 Legal professional privilege

In contrast to the privilege against self-incrimination which concentrates on the individual, legal professional privilege focuses on two issues:

- the communications between a lawyer and his client in the normal course of legal practice, ie giving or obtaining legal advice

- the communications between a lawyer (and/or his client) and a third party, in contemplation of litigation, for example an expert witness's report.

Thus, communications falling into either one of these will be privileged and immune from disclosure, if claimed by a party, regardless of the timing of the litigation. Taylor CJ explained the rationale behind this privilege in *R v Derby Magistrates Court, ex parte B* [1996] 3 WLR 681 as:

> '. . . a man must be able to consult his lawyer in confidence, since otherwise he might hold back half the truth . . . he must be sure that what he tells his lawyer in confidence will never be revealed without his consent . . . legal professional privilege is thus much more than an ordinary rule of evidence, limited in its application to the facts of a particular case . . . it is a fundamental condition on which the administration of justice as a whole rests.'

Where the communication between the lawyer and his client is in the usual course of legal practice, it will be privileged and immune from disclosure unless the client wishes it to be disclosed. The rule covers communications between a solicitor, barrister, legal executive and paralegal with their client, so long as they are acting in the course of a professional relationship. Remember this formula: no relationship of lawyer/client equals no legal professional privilege. Consider this scenario: Samir writes to his friend Jay, who happens to be a barrister, for *one off* advice on buying shares in the Royal Bank of Iceland and the related legal repercussions regarding company tax. Is this communication privileged? In *Minter v Priest* [1930] AC 558, the House of Lords made clear that any advice obtained must be legal advice and that it will be privileged even if subsequently Jay refuses to act as Samir's barrister or if Samir appoints Marc to act for him instead, *per* Lord Buckmaster:

'. . . the relationship of solicitor and client being once established, it is not a necessary conclusion that whatever conversation ensued was protected from disclosure. The conversation to secure this privilege must be such as, within a very wide and generous ambit of interpretation, fairly referable to the relationship, but outside that boundary the mere fact that a person speaking is a solicitor, and the person to whom he speaks is his client affords no protection.'

Per Viscount Dunedin:

'. . . now, if a man goes to a solicitor, as a solicitor, to consult and does consult him, though the end of the interview may lead to the conclusion that he does not engage him as his solicitor or expect that he should act as his solicitor, nevertheless the interview is held as a privileged occasion.'

A claim for legal professional privilege will only be successful if the following is satisfied:

- the communications between the lawyer and their client is confidential in nature
- if not made in the course of a lawyer and client relationship it must have been made with a view to establishing one.

Once a party has successfully claimed privilege they must continue to ensure that it remains intact. Generally, communications that are immune from disclosure by reason of privilege will remain so, unless:

- it is shown that the communication itself was obtained to further either a crime or a fraud
- it is waived.

Where it is shown that the communication itself was obtained to further either a crime or a fraud that means it was seeking advice or was actually a step in furtherance of the crime or fraud, privilege will be lost. In *R v Central Criminal Court ex parte Francis and Francis* [1989] AC 346 the court confirmed that it is of little relevance who intends the crime or fraud, thus the crime or fraud of the lawyer, client or even a third party can cause legal professional privilege to be lost. Similarly, where the police have obtained a search warrant under s 8 of the Police and Criminal Evidence Act 1984 allowing them to enter, search and seize property, then s 10 of the same Act prevents them from seizing anything that is protected by legal professional privilege, unless, of course, the 'thing' is in furtherance of a crime or fraud.

Where a defendant obtains privileged information through trickery or by means of fraud, then a claimant may apply for an injunction preventing them from using the information; see *Lord Ashburton v Pope* [1913] 2 Ch 469. What of a lawyer acting for joint parties? In that instance communications must be disclosed to all those involved, ie A and B, and only then can such communication attract immunity from disclosure by reason of legal professional privilege; see *Buttes Gas & Oil Co v Hammer (No. 3)* [1981] 1 QB 223.

Legal professional privilege is personal in nature and thus may be waived but only by the person entitled to it. The wilful, ignorant or inadvertent disclosure of evidence will result in the evidence being rendered admissible so long as it is relevant. Where a communication is waived by the lawyer's professional negligence, ie they forget to claim privilege, then privilege will be lost, unless obtained through a crime or fraud. Consider this scenario: Ben decides to waive privilege to document A; however, unbeknown to him document A contains references to documents B, C and D. Does waiver of privilege in relation to document A mean that privilege, if any, in relation to documents B, C and D is also waived? The answer is no. Further, it should be noted that legal professional privilege will not simply end on the termination of the lawyer and client relationship. In *R v Barton* [1973] 1 WLR 115 and *R v Ataou* [1988] 2 All ER 321 the trial judges suggested that such privilege would end where communications in the lawyers' possession would have acquitted an accused who was actually innocent. The Court of Appeal in *Derby* (above) unequivocally over-ruled this, hence legal professional privilege will continue regardless.

Before we consider third-party communication, the following important points must be noted. First, where privilege is lost or has been waived and there is no injunction restraining use, then the communication can be utilized, subject to the general rules of evidence, ie relevance and admissibility; see *R v Tompkins* (1977) 67 Cr App R 181. Second, in contrast to public interest immunity, privilege only attaches to an original document. However, its contents may be proven by the provision of a copy or the oral testimony of someone who had seen it regardless of the means by which they did, ie improper, see *Calcraft v Guest* [1889] 1 QB 759.

What then of third parties and their communication? Third-party communication is only immune from disclosure by reason of legal professional privilege if the purpose of it, or the dominant purpose of it where there was more than one purpose, was *pending or contemplated*

litigation. Hence no contemplated litigation equals no privilege; see *Wheeler v Le Marchant* (1881) 17 Ch D 675 and *per* Lord Wilberforce in *Waugh v BRB* [1980] AC 521:

J '. . . while privilege may be required in order to induce candour in statements made for the purposes of litigation it is not required in relation to statements whose purpose is different – for example to enable a railway to operate safety. It is clear that the due administration of justice strongly requires disclosure and production of this report: it was contemporary; it contained statements by witnesses on the spot; it would be not merely relevant evidence, but almost certainly the best evidence *of causation* . . . if one accepts that this important public interest can be overridden in order that the defendant may properly prepare his case, how close must the connection be between the preparation of the document and the anticipation of litigation? On principle I would think that the purpose of preparing for litigation ought to be either the sole purpose or at least the dominant purpose of it: to carry the protection further into cases where that purpose was secondary or equal with another purpose would seem to be excessive, and unnecessary in the interest of encouraging truthful revelation. At the lowest such desirability of protection as exists in such cases is not strong enough to outweigh the need for all relevant documents to be made available . . . it appears to me that unless the purpose of submission to the legal adviser in view of litigation is at least the dominant purpose for which the relevant document was prepared, the reasons which require privilege to be extended to it cannot apply. On the other hand to hold that the purpose, as above, must be the sole purpose would, apart from difficulties of proof, in my opinion, be too strict a requirement, and would confine the privilege too narrowly: as to this I agree with Barwick CJ in *Grant v Downs*, 135 CLR 674.'

The rule was further restricted by the Court of Appeal in *Three Rivers District Council v Governor and Company of the Bank of England (No 5)* [2005] EWCA Civ 933; before communications can attract immunity from disclosure by reason of legal professional privilege the following must be satisfied:

- a genuine prospect of litigation
- the purpose, or dominant purpose, must be to obtain legal advice
- the communication must have a relevant legal context.

In this case, the claimants, creditors and liquidators (CCL) of the BCCI bank brought an action against the Bank of England in relation to its supervision of the bank before it collapsed for malfeasance in public office. CCL sought disclosure and inspection of the communications that had taken place during an inquiry into the bank's supervision between the bank's enquiry unit and its solicitors. The bank contended that this information was immune from disclosure by reason of legal professional privilege. The judge ordered disclosure stating that only communications that had as their purpose seeking or obtaining legal advice in respect of legal rights and obligations were protected by legal professional privilege, and not those relating to mere presentation of evidence to the inquiry, ie glossing over the evidence to attract the least criticism. The Court of Appeal dismissed the BCCI's appeal. Lord Scott stated in *Three Rivers* that:

> **J** '. . . advice given by lawyers . . . for the purpose of enhancing the prospects of a successful outcome, from their point of view . . . would be advice given in a relevant legal context and would qualify for legal advice privilege.'

KEY FACTS

Legal professional privilege

This focuses on two issues; the communications between a lawyer and their client in the normal course of legal practice, ie giving or obtaining legal advice and the communications between a lawyer or their client with a third party in contemplation of litigation; for example, expert witnesses.

A claim for legal professional privilege will only be successful if the communication between the lawyer and their client is confidential in nature and, where not made in the course of a lawyer and client relationship, it must have been made with a view to establishing one.

The *general* rule is that communications that are immune from disclosure by reason of privilege will remain so unless it is shown that the communication itself was obtained to further either a crime or a fraud or the privilege is waived.

4.4 Journalistic privilege

The discussion so far has revealed that the English law of evidence does not protect information just because it is confidential. Journalistic privilege, ie freedom from disclosure of the information source, is to some extent considered necessary in any democratic civilization, because the disclosure of such a source could possibly lead to consequences of a serious constitutional nature.

The House of Lords in *British Steel v Granada Corporation* [1981] AC 1096, stated that the court had an inherent jurisdiction to provide journalists with freedom from disclosure. The decision left the law in disarray, and in much need of urgent clarification.

In response, s 10 of the Contempt of Court Act 1981 placed journalistic privilege on a statutory footing stating:

> **S** '... no court may require a person to disclose, nor is any person guilty of contempt of court for refusing to disclose, the source of information contained in a publication for which he is responsible, unless it be established to the satisfaction of the court that disclosure is necessary in the interests of justice or national security or for the prevention of disorder or crime.'

Hence it is clear from this that the person responsible for publication, or the person who is responsible for any means of communicating with the general public or a section thereof, does not have to disclose the source of information, unless of course disclosure is necessary because it is in the interests of justice, national security or to prevent crime and disorder. The party seeking disclosure must prove that one of these reasons applies, ie disclosure is necessary because it is essential and not just relevant, and therefore the court should order disclosure. In *Secretary of State for Defence v Guardian Newspapers* [1989] AC 339 the court held that s 10 should be defined widely so as to include instances in which a source may be indirectly revealed; see *Maxwell v Pressdram* [1987] 1 WLR 298. Further protection is provided to journalistic material under the PACE Act 1984 which prevents seizure of such material without a warrant and court order authorizing the same.

4.5 Negotiations without prejudice

In civil litigation, and some criminal litigation, expediency that results in the early settlement of disputes is much encouraged, for example by the pre-action protocols that accompany the Civil Procedure Rules. On that basis, it makes sense that communications aimed at achieving the resolution of a dispute be protected from disclosure. Such communications, whether oral or in writing, are termed 'without prejudice' communications and cannot be utilized as evidence of guilt. Most such communications, if in writing, will be headed 'without prejudice'. However, it is not this that provides privilege from disclosure – it is in fact the intention of the parties making the communication, ie writing the letter. In *Rush and Tompkins v GLC* [1989] AC 1280 the Court of Appeal clarified the misconceptions that existed in regard to 'without prejudice' negotiations, *per* Balcombe LJ:

J '. . . this case had disclosed what appear to be some widespread misconceptions as to the nature of "without prejudice" privilege. In an attempt to remove those misconceptions, and to give guidance to the profession, we venture to state the following principles. (1) The purpose of "without prejudice" privilege is to enable parties to negotiate without risk of their proposals being used against them if the negotiations fail. If the negotiations succeed and a settlement is concluded, the privilege goes, having served its purpose. This will be the case whether the privilege is claimed as against the other party or parties to the negotiations, or as against some outside party. (2) It is possible for the parties to use a form of words which will enable the "without prejudice" correspondence to be referred to, even though no concluded settlement is reached, for example on the issue of costs . . . (3) In contrast, in our judgment, it might be possible for parties to use a special form of words which, at least as between correspondence even after a settlement has been reached . . . (4) The privilege does not depend on the existence of proceedings. (5) Even while the privilege subsists, ie before any settlement is reached, there are a number of real or apparent exceptions to the privilege. Thus: (a) the court may always look at a document marked "without prejudice" and its contents for the purposes of deciding its admissibility . . . this is not a real exception to the privilege, since the court must always be able to rule on the admissibility of a document, when a claim to privilege is challenged. It is under this head that the court can look at the documents to see, for example if an agreement has been concluded and, if so, to construe its terms. (b) The rule has no application to a document which, by its nature, may prejudice the person to whom it is addressed. (6) The privilege extends to the solicitors of the parties to the "without prejudice" negotiations.'

In addition, 'without prejudice' letters may be written, subject to an express limitation that if a compromise was not made, the letter or offer may be referred to on the issue as to costs. In other words, a party may make an offer to settle proceedings, subject to a 'without prejudice' letter expressing a limitation that if the costs incurred in pursuing the original claim in court proves to be unnecessary or excessive, such party may refer to the relevant offer in an effort to reduce the costs that the court may award against him.

This procedure is called a *Calderbank* limitation derived from the case, *Calderbank v Calderbank* [1976] Fam 93, regarding a matrimonial dispute.

The *Calderbank* limitation has now been extended to all cases; see *Cutts v Head* [1984] Ch 290, where it was confirmed that the parties should be '. . . encouraged [to] fully and frankly put their cards on the table. The public policy justification for the privilege essentially rested on the desirability of preventing statements or offers made in the course of negotiations for settlement

being brought before the court of trial as admissions of liability. Once however, the trial of the issues in an action was at an end and the matter of costs came to be argued, it (the privilege) could have no further application' (Oliver LJ).

This form of privilege continues even when the parties have reached a settlement.

4.6 Public interest immunity

Being adversarial, litigation in the UK is conducted on the basis of bringing before the court all relevant admissible evidence. In criminal cases, the prosecution is under a duty of disclosure with an emphasis on aiding the court to reach its decision promoting fair and efficient administration of justice. In stark contrast, in civil cases both parties have a duty to provide disclosure of evidence that is in documentary form. For example, the early exchange of witness statements has meant that there is now little or no room for those hidden surprises that delay litigation. Occasionally, the public interest may require certain information to be withheld, perhaps because it poses a threat to national security. It may also be that withholding the information promotes the preservation of individual freedom or certain types of privilege, a point discussed later in this chapter.

In some instances the preservation of confidentiality requires access to information to be limited. A claim for *public interest immunity* (PII), where successfully pleaded, permits a party to withhold information on the basis that its disclosure would be prejudicial to the general public good. A claim for PII can be made by private individuals, but, in reality, is normally pleaded by government officials; see *D v NSPCC* [1978] AC 171 or *R v Reading Justices ex parte Berkshire County Council* (1996) 1 Cr App R 239. The justification for establishing 'public interest immunity' is based on the policy that the public interest of protecting specific information or documents outweighs the narrower concept of justice accorded to private individuals in having all relevant evidence available and presented to the court.

Per Lord Pearson in *Rogers v Home Secretary* [1973] AC 388,

> **J** 'The court has to balance the detriment to the public interest on the administrative or executive side which would result from the disclosure of the document against the detriment to the public interest on the judicial side resulting from non-disclosure of a document which is relevant to an issue in legal proceedings.'

Section 21(2) of the Criminal Procedure and Investigations Act 1996 (CPIA) governs the basis of public interest immunity in criminal cases:

S '. . . 21(1) Where this Part applies as regards things failing to be done after the relevant time in relation to an alleged offence, the rules of common law which (a) were effective immediately before the appointed day, and (b) relate to the disclosure of material by the prosecutor, do not apply as regards things failing to be done after that time in relation to the alleged offence . . . 21(2) Subsection (1) does not affect the rules of common law as to whether disclosure is in the public interest.'

The CPIA 1996 normally requires full disclosure by the prosecution unless the common law rules apply. It should be noted that this Act has been amended by the Criminal Justice Act 2003, reference to which will be made in this chapter as and when necessary. In addition, readers should check the website accompanying this book for further up-to-date and crucial amendments.

Historically, the courts decided that a claim for PII by a government minister which sought to prevent disclosure documentary evidence, was conclusive in nature. This meant immunity from disclosure was granted almost automatically; see *Duncan v Cammell Laird & Co Ltd* [1842] AC 624. However, it was not long before the position coveted by this narrow view was challenged for being unreasonable and possibly leading to technical abuse by those in power. PII is normally claimed in cases that involve 'affairs of the state', such as the confidential workings of government or issues relating to national security. In these instances the courts will normally preserve confidentiality but there will be instances in which the public interest requires the evidence to be disclosed. In *Conway v Rimmer* [1968] AC 910 it was stressed by the House of Lords that when dealing with a claim for PII the courts should not grant immunity automatically as the claim is challengeable, *per* Lord Reid:

J '. . . a Minister's certificate may be given on one or other of two grounds: either because it would be against the public interest to disclose the contents of the particular document or documents in question, or because the document belongs to a class of documents which ought to be withheld, whether or not there is anything in the particular document in question disclosure of which would be against the public interest . . . however wide the power of the court may be held to be, cases would be very rare in which it could be proper to question the view of the responsible Minister that it would be contrary to the public interest to make public the contents of a particular document . . . I would therefore propose that the House ought now to decide that courts have and are entitled to exercise a power and duty to hold a balance between the public interest, as expressed by a Minister, to withhold certain documents or other evidence and the public interest in ensuring the proper administration of justice. That does not mean that a court would reject a Minister's view: full weight must be given to it in every case, and if the Minister's

CONTINUED ▸

> reasons are of a character which judicial experience is not competent to weigh, then the Minister's view must prevail. But experience has shown that reasons given for withholding whole classes of documents are often not of that character. For example a court is perfectly well able to assess the likelihood that, if the writer of a certain class of document knew that there was a chance that his report might be produced in legal proceedings, he would make a less full and candid report than he would otherwise have done.'

Lord Morris continued:

> '. . . it has been clearly laid down that the mere fact that a document is private or is confidential does not necessarily produce the result that its production can be withheld.'

The House of Lords has stressed that in some instances it would be right not to preserve confidentiality and to order the disclosure of documents; but in other instances, for example, where the documents are cabinet papers, it would be of utmost importance to preserve confidentiality, *per* Lord Reid in *Conway* (above). In *Burmah Oil v Bank of England* [1980] AC 1090 the House of Lords made it clear that for a successful challenge to a claim for PII a strong counterclaim must be made, *per* Lord Wilberforce:

> '. . . a claim for public interest immunity having been made, on manifestly solid grounds, it is necessary for those who seek to overcome it to demonstrate the existence of a counteracting interest calling for disclosure of particular documents. When this is demonstrated, but only then, may the court proceed to a balancing process.'

Their Lordships made clear in both *Conway* (above) and *Burmah Oil* that even though a Minister claiming PII is in a far better position than the courts to consider the implications that disclosure of the document would have, the courts, nevertheless, have the right to scrutinize the decision of the Minister. Where national security is the basis on which PII is claimed, then it is rare for the courts to scrutinize the Minister's certificate. In *Balfour v Foreign Office* [1994] 1 WLR 681 Mr Balfour was a member of the British diplomatic service which claimed that he had been unfairly dismissed by his former employer, the Foreign and Commonwealth Office. He made an application for discovery of certain documents that were in the possession of the Office.

An order for disclosure was refused by the industrial tribunal on the grounds that the tribunal had no jurisdiction to delve into the certificates issued by two Crown Ministers claiming public interest immunity on the grounds of national security. The Ministers contended that the documents sought concerned the security and intelligence services. An appeal to the Employment Appeal Tribunal was dismissed who interpreted the tribunal's decision as meaning that it was not able to carry out an evaluation of the validity of the national security reasons advanced, *per* Lord Russell LJ:

> **J** '. . . there must always be vigilance by the courts to ensure that public interest immunity of whatever kind is raised only in appropriate circumstances and with appropriate particularity, but once there is an actual or potential risk to national security demonstrated by an appropriate certificate the court should not exercise its right to inspect.'

4.6.1 Requirements on party seeking disclosure

The party seeking disclosure must show that the interests of justice require the document to be disclosed. The disclosure will depend somewhat on the nature of the PII claim, ie a 'class' claim or a 'contents' claim. PII can be claimed where the document belongs to a particular class of documents because it would stifle the candour of those connected to it; basically it may result in such persons refraining from being open, frank and candid in future documents if they believe there is a chance of it being disclosed, ie frank disclosures within a document by Ministers, as Lord Scarman stated in *Burmah Oil* (below):

> **J** '. . . the reasons given for protecting the secrecy of government at the level of policy-making are two . . . first is the need for candour in the advice offered to ministers: the second is that disclosure "would create or fan ill-informed or captious public or political criticism". Lord Reid in *Conway v Rimmer* [1968] AC 910, 952, thought the second "the most important reason".'

Such blanket secrecy is very rarely justified and hence the courts do not place much credence on this argument, especially when it comes to 'generic' or 'routine' documents as in *Science Research Council v Nassé* [1980] AC 1028. Where a claim for PII is made on this basis the presiding judge will decide as to what weight to give to the argument. In contrast, a claim for PII may be made on the basis that the document contains something that, if revealed, gives cause for concern because it would be prejudicial to the general good of the public – this is known as a

contents claim. Claims for immunity on this basis are usually far more successful because it is far more certain, ie it is a specific document that would result in damage.

A court will not, and in most cases cannot, order the disclosure of documents unless it is necessary to save costs, but far more importantly, for the fair disposal of a case. The party seeking disclosure must show that disclosure of the particular document or documents is necessary, which means that without the document the party with a strong claim with good prospects of success will be rendered weak or that the party will definitely lose.

Campbell v Tameside MBC [1982] QB 1065

The claimant was a teacher who was attacked by a student. She sought the disclosure of certain reports produced by the local education authority which showed that the student in question had a known violent past and should therefore have been placed in a special school. Without these reports the teacher had no evidence and therefore was almost certainly going to lose, hence the disclosure of the reports was considered necessary.

There follows two contradicting judgments:

Air Canada v Secretary of State for Trade (No 2) [1983] 2 AC 394

Air Canada sought the disclosure of documents relating to government policy concerning borrowing in the public sector. The Privy Council held that these were not necessary to determine a dispute that concerned landing charges and hence protected from disclosure.

In *Burmah Oil v Bank of England* [1980] AC 1090, the House of Lords held '. . . that, *after inspection*, none of the *documents* . . . contained matter of such evidential value as to make an order for their disclosure, in all the circumstances, necessary for disposing fairly of the case . . . that they were relevant but their significance was not such as to override the public service objections to their production; and that, accordingly, the appeal must be dismissed . . . *and* . . . where the court inspects a document for which Crown privilege is claimed the Crown should have a right to appeal before the document is produced.' The facts of the case are presented *per* Lord Wilberforce:

J

'. . . the appellant the Burmah Oil Co Ltd sued the Governor and Company of the Bank of England for relief in respect of the sale to the Bank by Burmah Oil Co in 1975 of 77,817,507 ordinary stock units of £1 each of the British Petroleum Co Ltd . . . at a price of approximately £179 million.' Burmah Oil Co claimed that the price represented '. . . a substantial undervalue of the stock and that the bargain was unconscionable, inequitable and unreasonable . . . the present appeal arises out of an application by Burmah Oil Co for production of sixty-two documents listed in the list of documents served by the bank. The Bank, on the instructions of the Crown, objected to produce these on the ground that they belong to classes of documents production of which would be injurious to the public interest . . . they have put forward a certificate dated October 18, 1977, signed by the Chief Secretary to the Treasury supporting this objection. On the interlocutory hearing of the objection in the High Court Her Majesty's Attorney-General intervened in order to argue the case in support of it, and it was upheld by Foster J. On appeal by Burmah Oil Co to the Court of Appeal [1979] 1 WLR. 473, the Attorney-General took a similar course, and that court, by majority, affirmed the judge . . . on a further appeal to this House, the Attorney-General was joined as a respondent and as such argued the case against production; the bank, as in the High Court and the Court of Appeal, took no part in the argument. But, I repeat, the only defendant in the action is the bank.'

In summary this case concerned what was a commercial transaction; the company claimed that the government had fixed an unfair price on stock that was sold to the Bank of England – the situation arose in an oil crisis during which the company had to be rescued. The House of Lords held, refusing to order disclosure, that disclosure of the documents was not in fact necessary and that they were high-level policy documents.

4.6.2 Necessity of disclosure

Once the party has done this the court will assess, having looked at the contents of the documents, whether it is actually necessary to order the disclosure of them for the fair determination of the case. The courts will refrain from examining documents that are argued as concerning 'high-level national security' because it would be pointless; such documents are usually automatically immune from disclosure.

Once the necessity requirement has been satisfied, the court will then conduct a weighing exercise which consists of an assessment of the needs of the party seeking disclosure and the interest of the public in preserving confidentiality. Where necessity is shown, then the party seeking immunity will have a hard task of arguing against disclosure and must show that it is really necessary to withhold disclosure for the proper functioning of the public service. The rest

of the discussion will focus on the 'public policy' reasons commonly used to argue against disclosure.

4.6.3 Public policy

There are five main reasons that may be put forward as arguments in applications for PII and these are as follows:

- documents concerning national security or high-level affairs of the state
- national governmental policy documents
- local governmental policy documents
- confidential documents
- documents relating to the detection and prevention of crime.

Let us take a brief look at each of these, starting with national security; this is most commonly pleaded by Crown Ministers. The courts will not usually intervene to order disclosure of a document where immunity is sought on the grounds that it concerns the national security of the state or high-level state affairs.

Most government policy will contain a significant amount of content that is political and therefore a claim for immunity from disclosure may be made on the grounds of public policy as in *Burmah Oil* (above). Other areas of public policy that may result in claims for immunity include documents relating to the police complaints procedure; see *Neilson v Laugharne* [1981] QB 736 and *R v Chief Constable of West Midlands Exp Wiley* [1995] 1 AC 274. Similarly, where delegated legislation provides powers to a local authority or statutory body to formulate and implement policy, then a claim for PII argument may be made because the state is not limited to national government; for an example of an interesting case, see *D v NSPCC* [1978] AC 171.

Another interesting instance in which PII claims may arise is in the prevention and detection of crime; for example, the identity of 'moles' or 'police informants' should not be disclosed because the system requires confidentiality in relation to the identity of such individuals in order to function effectively. Unless of course the identity of the informant is of utmost importance in establishing the defendant's innocence and hence the public interest in not convicting the innocent over-rides immunity; see *Marks v Beyfus* [1980] QB 494. In *R v Rankine* [1986] QB 861, the same principles were applied to surveillance posts, although the Court of Appeal set down guidelines in relation to disclosure for the latter in *R v Johnson* [1968] 1 All ER 121.

Finally, confidential information – this was discussed earlier. In summary, information provided in confidence will be privileged if it qualifies under legal professional or journalistic privilege. There is no automatic preservation of confidentiality as a matter of public policy; each case is decided on its own merits, ie the court will weigh up the public interest in protecting confidential information versus an individual's need for disclosure; see *Alfred Crompton Amusements v Commissioners of Customs and Excise (No 2)* [1974] AC 405 and *Science Research Council v Nassé* [1980] AC 1028.

KEY FACTS

Public interest immunity

A claim for *public interest immunity* permits a party to withhold information on the basis that its disclosure would be prejudicial to the general public good.

Section 21(2) of the Criminal Procedure and Investigations Act 1996 (CPIA) governs the basis of public interest immunity in criminal cases.

There are five main reasons that may be put forward as arguments in applications for PII and these are that the documents concern national security or high-level affairs of the state, national governmental policy documents, local governmental policy, are confidential documents and that they relate to the detection and prevention of crime.

The House of Lords has stressed on many occasions that in some instances it would be right not to preserve confidentiality and to order the disclosure of documents and in others not.

Where a claim is contested, the party seeking disclosure must show that the interests of justice require the document to be disclosed.

4.6.4 Waiver and objection

What if immunity under the public interest exists? Can a party whose documents are protected waive that immunity? There are conflicting authorities on this issue. In *Rogers v Home Secretary* [1973] AC 388 it was suggested that it is not possible to waive immunity; however, in *Alfred Crompton Amusements* (above) it was suggested that it could potentially be waived by the person(s) that were being protected by it. In *Campbell v Tameside MBC* [1982] QB 1065 Lord Denning suggested that waiver should be allowed in cases where the documents were not high but were low-level policy documents where both maker and protected agree:

J
'. . . in these cases the court can and should consider the *significance* of the documents in relation to the decision of the case. If they are of such significance that they may well affect the very decision of the case, then justice may require them to be disclosed. The public interest in justice being done – in the instant

CONTINUED ▸

> **J** case – may well outweigh the public interest in keeping them confidential. But, if they are of little significance, so that they are very unlikely to affect the decision of the case, then the greater public interest may be to keep them confidential. In order to assess their significance, it is open to the court itself to inspect the documents. If disclosure is necessary in the interest of justice in the instant case, the court will order their disclosure but otherwise not.'

Where a party to the proceedings objects to the document being disclosed, then it will be listed as being 'subject to objection' and then the argument for objection will be heard at an alternative hearing or in criminal cases in a *voir dire*. Where a Crown Minister objects, they will normally issue a certificate or affidavit confirming that they have seen the document, detailing any objections they may have to the document being disclosed on public policy grounds. Where an objection is successful, then no reference that tends to reveal the contents either directly or indirectly may be made. Even the European Court of Human Rights has recognized the need to withhold, from disclosure, evidence that would not be in the public interest to disclose; see *Rowe v UK* (2000) 30 EHRR 1.

4.6.5 Contrasting privilege and PII

It is important to understand the differences between privilege and public interest immunity. Privilege may be waived by the party entitled to claim the same. It is doubtful whether PII may be waived and if so, by whom. As a corollary to the first point, no secondary evidence is admissible to prove the relevant document that is subject to PII. In other words, a copy of the prohibited document may not be admitted. In addition, an objection to the admissibility of the evidence may be taken by the judge, if not taken by the parties, witnesses or government department, provided that it is the subject of PII.

This table summarizes the position:

Privilege	Public interest immunity
Privilege can be waived by the party claiming it	In the majority of cases immunity cannot be waived
Secondary evidence is admissible to prove a relevant document	Secondary evidence is not admissible to prove a relevant document
Only the party seeking to assert privilege can take objection to the document being disclosed	A judge, witnesses or a government department may take objection to the document being disclosed

■ Figure 4.3 The difference between privilege and public interest immunity

ACTIVITY

Self-test questions

1. What is disclosure?

2. Are the rules on disclosure in criminal and civil cases the same?

3. On what is standard disclosure in civil cases dependent?

4. Summarize the nature of the privilege against self-incrimination.

5. What changes did s 101 of the CJA 2003 make to the CPIA 1996 in respect of the privilege against self-incrimination?

6. What is the extent of legal professional privilege and does it ever cease?

7. Why was the House of Lords decision in *Three Rivers District Council v Governor and Company of the Bank of England (No 5)* [2005] EWCA Civ 933 of such importance?

8. What assertion does a claim for a public interest immunity make?

9. What is meant by the term 'blanket immunity'?

10. What are the main differences between a claim for privilege and a claim for public interest immunity?

Further reading

Chippindall, A. 'Expert Advice and Legal Professional Privilege', JPI Law (2003) Jan, 61–70.

Brown, S. 'Public Interest Immunity', PL (1994) Win, 579–595.

Ettinger, C. 'Case Comment', JPI Law (2005) 3, C114–117.

Internet links

Part 31 of the CPR: http://www.justice.gov.uk/civil/procrules_fin/contents/parts/part31.htm#IDA4XIR.

Office of Public Sector Information: http://www.opsi.gov.uk/Acts/acts1972/ukpga_19720068_en_1.

European Convention on Human Rights and Fundamental Freedoms: http://www.echr.coe.int/echr/

chapter 5 SILENCE: THE EFFECT ON AN ACCUSATION ■

AIMS AND OBJECTIVES

By the end of this chapter you will learn:

■ About a defendant's right to remain silent

■ How silence can affect an accusation

■ About silence under the common law and statute

■ The instances in which silence can adversely effect an accusation

■ About the inferences that can be drawn from instances in which a defendant remains silent

■ The impact of human rights on any right of the defendant to remain silent.

5.1 Introduction

In this chapter our discussion will focus on the silence of a defendant who is faced with an accusation of committing a crime and its effect on an accusation. We will discuss the common law and statutory rules on this issue and how instances in which the defendant remaining silent can lead to a jury drawing adverse inferences.

5.2 Historical development and the significance of silence

Many legal systems throughout the world recognize that a person may appear, as in the movies or soaps, to be found in the most compromising or incriminating situations and, for reasons unbeknown to those that discover them, still choose to say absolutely nothing. Here is an example that comes to mind from a truly terrible film; A walks in to discover that her husband B has stabbed C, with whom he was having an affair. A sees that C is lying on the floor dying with the dagger still lodged in the chest, whilst attempting to save C, she starts to pull the dagger out. Here is the twist; whilst in the act of pulling the dagger out A is seen by B's husband, D, witnesses what he believes to be A killing C. On seeing D, a startled A says nothing to protect her husband B. The motive behind A's silence is not to expose her husband's crime?

The arguments that centre around silence, and how the right to silence in English law has been eroded, we will discuss later. Focus on the suspiciousness of the defendant saying nothing when instinctively a reaction in protest of innocence would be expected. Let me ask you all a question, for those students amongst you that have rented property with other individuals, or have friends that have done so, you must have heard someone ask 'who drank the last of the milk?' In response most people protest their innocence by retorting 'not me'. Well, an accepted view was that only those individuals that are guilty have something to hide; however, we all know that sometimes the silent and therefore allegedly guilty defendant may have a number of reasons, valid, noble or otherwise for remaining silent.

As we all know, motive can be relevant to mitigation of a crime; however, the law on the issue of silence takes a tougher stance. The general rule is that a jury, when directed, can draw adverse inferences from a defendant's silence during the investigation of a crime or at trial, ie questioning under caution, etc. Before we begin to consider the Criminal Justice and Public Order Act 1994 (CJPOA) in more detail, we must look at the position of English law prior to its introduction. Before the 1994 Act was enacted, the English law of evidence recognized that a defendant had a right to remain silent or a privilege against self-incrimination. These two sets of principles, based on notions of fairness, are somewhat linked and we have covered privilege in Chapter 4. You may want to research *R v Director of the Serious Fraud Office, ex p Smith* [1993] AC 1 which has good reference to that linkage.

When discussing the right to silence, which is a qualified right to silence now, ie it is restricted, a defendant could simply say nothing during interrogation by the police, give a no-comment interview and not even have to give evidence at their own trial. The defendant could in fact stand back and require the prosecution to prove their case.

Lord Runciman chaired the Royal Commission on Criminal Justice and in a report in 1993 stated that high-flying criminals were not abusing the right to silence. In fact the Royal Commission's report stated that removal of the right might result in greater miscarriages of justice. The result of not following the report was the CJPOA 1994. Although a complex piece of legislation it was not long before it ran into problems in regard to fairness under Art 6 of the European Convention on Human Rights and Fundamental Freedoms (ECHR), something we will discuss later. Finally, when reading the rest of this chapter you must keep in mind *Lucas* directions on lies told by a defendant; they too are forms of inferences.

5.3 Silence at common law

The CJPOA 1994 does not affect the common law rules (s 34(5)) on silence.

The accused's silence when confronted about an incident is generally irrelevant. Exceptionally, when an accusation is made in the presence of the accused, his silence may be construed as an adoption of the accusation or charge provided that the circumstances are such that an unequivocal denial or a reasonable explanation could be expected from him.

When would an unequivocal response or explanation be expected from the accused? The solution is when the parties are on equal speaking terms. It is clear that a police officer will not be on equal speaking terms with the accused. In *R v Hall* [1971] 1 WLR 298, the Privy Council decided that the silence of the accused in the face of an accusation put by a police officer as to what an accomplice had said did not amount to an informal admission. *Per* Lord Diplock:

> **J** 'It is clear . . . that a person is entitled to refrain from answering a question put to him for the purpose of discovering whether he has committed a criminal offence. *A fortiori* he is under no obligation to comment when he is informed that someone else had accused him of an offence. It may be that in very exceptional circumstances an inference may be drawn from a failure to give an explanation or a disclaimer, but in their Lordship's view, silence alone on being informed by a police officer that someone else has made an accusation against him cannot give rise to an inference that the person to whom this information is communicated accepts the truth of the accusation . . . The caution merely serves to remind the accused of a right which he already possesses at common law.'

The position may have been different had the accusation been made by the victim or his relation in circumstances requiring an explanation.

To summarize: a defendant has the right to remain silent under the common law; however, it is still difficult to try and reconcile that with the fact that they have stated nothing in response to accusations, made in their presence, that incriminate them.

Can silence, under the common law, ever amount to an acceptance of an allegation from which an adverse inference can be drawn? In most instances silence cannot amount to such an acceptance; see *Hall v R* [1971] 1 WLR 298. In some instances the opposite may be true, where a defendant is faced with an allegation made by a person who stands on an equal footing with the defendant and it is reasonable to expect a reply; then *R v Mitchell* (1982) 17 Cox CC 503 suggests that, at common law, a lack of response may amount to an acceptance of guilt. The real issue is to determine (a) when the parties (accuser and accused) stand on equal speaking terms and (b) whether the circumstances require an unequivocal denial by an innocent person. This is a question of law for the judge to decide.

CASE EXAMPLE

R v Parkes [1976] 1 WLR 1251

A woman whose daughter had been murdered accused the defendant of murdering her. The defendant said nothing; however, when she informed him that she was going to call the police, he tried to stab her. In this case his silence amounted to an acceptance of the accusation.

Lord Diplock:

> **J** 'In the instant case, there is no question of an accusation being made by or in the presence of a police officer or any other person in authority or charged with the investigation of the crime. It was a spontaneous charge made by the mother about an injury done to her daughter. In circumstances such as these their Lordships agree that the direction given by Cave J in *R v Mitchell* is applicable:
>
> > "Now the whole admissibility of statements of this kind rests upon the consideration that if the charge is made against a person in that person's presence it is reasonable to expect that he or she will immediately deny it, and that the absence of such denial is some evidence of an admission on the part of the person charged and of the truth of the charge. Undoubtedly, when persons are speaking on even terms, and a charge is made, and the person charged says nothing, and expresses no indignation, and does nothing to repel the charge, that is some evidence to show that he admits the charge to be true" (Lord Diplock).
>
> Here Mrs Graham and the defendant were on even speaking terms. Furthermore, the defendant's reaction to the accusation was not one of mere silence. He drew a knife and attempted to stab Mrs Graham in order to escape when she threatened to detain him while the police was sent for.'

CASE EXAMPLE

R v Chandler [1976] 1 WLR 585

The Court of Appeal stated that a defendant's silence in the face of an accusation made against him whilst his solicitor was present had amounted to an acceptance of it.

CONTINUED ▸

> **J** '. . . we are of the opinion that the defendant and the detective sergeant were speaking on equal terms since the former had his solicitor present to give him any advice he might have wanted and to testify, if needed, as to what had been said. We do not accept that a police officer always has an advantage over someone he is questioning. Everything depends on the circumstances. A young detective questioning a local dignitary in the course of an inquiry into alleged local government corruption may be very much at a disadvantage. This kind of situation is to be contrasted with that of a tearful housewife accused of shoplifting' (Lawton LJ).

In *R v Jason and Hind* [2005] EWCA Crim 971, the Court of Appeal confirmed that a defendant's right to silence under the common law exists. In fact, in this case, the refusal of the defendant to leave his police cell to answer questions was merely an 'emphatic' way of exercising his right which did not, under the common law, amount to an acceptance of the allegation from which an adverse inference could be drawn.

5.4 Silence under the CJPOA 1994

In addition to the common law rules, the CJPOA 1994 provides specific instances in which a defendant's silence either on being questioned by the police or when reasonably asked to explain themselves may lead to the drawing of adverse inferences under ss 34, 36 and 37.

Under the common law, a defendant's silence when questioned by the police did not in general indicate an acceptance or informal admission incriminating him of the crime of which he had been accused. The position of the CJPOA 1994 is somewhat different. With growing concerns that criminals were using silence as a shield to hinder the prosecution case by depriving it of essential evidence, the government introduced a series of measures, under the 1994 Act, which produced consequences from the defendant taking such a course of action.

The CJPOA 1994 did not abolish the common law rules; it created statutory rules in addition to them. On that basis, a defendant can still exercise the right to silence by refusing to answer questions or give oral evidence. The difference is that the right has become qualified in that the exercise of the right to silence can lead to the trier of fact (the jury) drawing adverse inferences. The rest of the discussion in this chapter will concentrate on the following:

Section 34 – A failure to mention facts, when questioned that are later relied on in defence
Section 35 – A failure to testify
Section 36 – A failure to account for incriminating objects, substances or marks
Section 37 – A failure to account for their presence in an incriminating place

■ Figure 5.1 Silence under the Criminal Justice and Public Order Act 1994

These four sections are the crucial provisions of which you are required to be aware. Remember when assessing evidence that it is not just the defendant's failure you are to look at; you should keep in mind the way in which the evidence was collected, just in case there is a risk that it will be excluded under s 78 of PACE 1984.

Note, however, that ss 34, 36 and 37 have been amended by s 58 of the Youth Justice and Criminal Evidence Act 1999. As a result of the amendment the accused must be in an 'authorized place of detention' when they fail or refuse to do that which is outlined. Authorized places of detention include police stations or anywhere the accused has not been afforded an opportunity to consult their solicitor. This area of the law has been further compromised by the current anti-terrorism legislation, a discussion of which is beyond the scope of this chapter.

Finally, the Criminal Procedure and Investigations Act 1996 (as amended by the Criminal Justice Act 2003) now allows an adverse inference to be drawn where there is a failure to comply with disclosure requirements.

5.4.1 Section 34 – failure to mention facts when questioned

Our discussion begins on the provisions of the CJPOA 1994 with s 34; this provision has caused the courts a considerable amount of difficulty in interpretation of its application, see *R v Bresa* [2005] EWCA Crim 1414. The provision aims to:

- try and discourage an accused from later fabricating a defence
- encourage the accused to disclose any defence or material fact that supports such a defence early on; see *R v Roble* [1997] Crim LR 449.

Section 34(1) states

'where in any proceedings against a person for an offence evidence is given that the accused:

a) at any time before *being* charged with *the commission of* an offence, on being questioned *whilst* under caution by a constable trying to discover whether or by whom an offence had been committed, failed to mention any fact relied on in a defence in those proceedings; or

CONTINUED ▸

b) on being charged with the *Commission of* an offence or officially informed *of the possibility of being* prosecuted for it, failed to mention any such fact, being a fact which in the circumstances existing at the time the accused could reasonably have been expected to mention when being so questioned, charged or informed, as the case may be, subsection (2) applies. Subsection (2) allows the court or jury to "draw such inferences as appear proper".'

The Youth Justice and Criminal Evidence Act 1999 inserted s 34(2A) into the CJPOA 1994; therefore, a jury may only draw an adverse inference under s 34 where an accused has been given the opportunity to receive legal advice. Section 34(2A) states '. . . where an accused was at an authorised place of detention at the time of the failure, subsections (1) and (2) of s 34(1) do not apply if *they* had not been allowed an opportunity to consult a solicitor prior to being questioned, charged or informed as mention in subsection (1) . . .' To clarify, s 38(2A) states that the reference to an authorized place of detention is a reference to a police station.

Let us examine s 34(1) in depth. When dealing with any provision of law, ie a section in an Act, one of the best ways to approach it is by breaking it down into manageable parts. This can be done by first identifying the elements that make up the section itself; here is how it works:

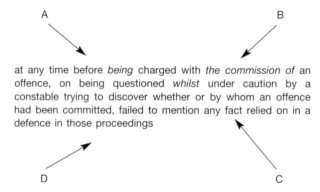

A   B

at any time before *being* charged with *the commission of* an offence, on being questioned *whilst* under caution by a constable trying to discover whether or by whom an offence had been committed, failed to mention any fact relied on in a defence in those proceedings

D   C

■ Figure 5.2 How s 34(1) of the Criminal Justice and Public Order Act 1994 works

When broken down it becomes obvious that the drawing of an adverse inference under s 34 is dependent on the following elements being satisfied:

(a) before charge

(b) questioning, in investigation, under caution

(c) failure to mention any fact

(d) subsequent reliance on the fact that the accused failed to mention in a defence.

This can be re-articulated as: the accused fails to mention any fact, before charge and when questioned under caution, which they subsequently rely on in a defence. The first, element (a), is simple. The investigation and related questioning must take place before the defendant is charged with the commission of the offence. The aim of the provision is effectively to promote a differentiation between honest individuals who usually voluntarily proffer information from those that have something to hide.

Section 34 only applies once the suspect has been cautioned, as that is the point at which they will be made aware of the potential of adverse inferences being drawn from their silence. Under Code C, of the codes that accompany the Police and Criminal Evidence Act 1984, the caution reads as follows: 'You do not have to say anything but it may harm your defence if you do not mention when questioned something that you later rely on in court. Anything you do say may be given in evidence.' Note the following three points:

- The suspect does not have to say anything.

- If the suspect fails to mention anything, when questioned, which they rely on in court it *may* harm their defence.

- Anything the suspect does say *may* be used in evidence.

Moving on to element (b), s 34 requires that the suspect is questioned in investigation; such questioning will normally take place at a police station in an interview room and be recorded. What happens if the suspect issues a significant statement, ie where questioning may be regarded as continuing although not taped, outside of the interview room? Then that must be mentioned at the start of the next recorded interview. The suspect must be asked to confirm or deny, or be asked whether they would like to add anything to it.

The next elements ((c) and (d)) require the defendant (who is no longer a suspect and is now the accused, because he will have been charged) to run a defence based on the facts that he failed to mention at trial. Common examples of this may involve self-defence or perhaps an alibi. If the defence merely deny the prosecution case thereby requiring it to prove it, ie they do not raise a defence based on any fact, then s 34 will not apply, because the defence must be based on the facts that are not mentioned. Furthermore, the facts that the defendant failed to mention must be facts that could reasonably have been mentioned. This means that the defendant must know (a) what allegations are being levied against them, and (b) the significance of the facts to the investigation of the offence.

In *R v Argent* [1997] 2 Cr App R 27 the Court of Appeal outlined the steps that have to be satisfied before an adverse inference can be drawn under s 34. They are:

- The proceedings must be against the defendant for the commission of a criminal offence.

- The defendant must have failed to mention the facts before they were charged.

- The failure must have occurred whilst the defendant was being questioned under caution by a police constable or another person charged with the investigation of criminal offences.

- The aim of the questions should be to ascertain (a) whether an offence has been committed and (b) by whom.

- The defendant must raise the fact or facts that they failed to mention in their defence.
- The fact or facts raised must be issues that could reasonably have been mentioned.

What amounts to a fact that could have been reasonably mentioned? The legal test used to satisfy this is *subjective and objective*, ie what could *that* defendant have reasonably mentioned or what could reasonably have been expected of that defendant. When considering this point it is important to note that the position of the defendant at the time of questioning will be considered. The following factors can be taken into account in determining what could have been expected of a particular defendant at the time of questioning:

- their personality
- the physical and mental state
- age
- intelligence
- any language barriers, ie fluency in spoken English
- experience
- intoxication
- tiredness
- any legal advice received.

CASE EXAMPLE

R v Central Criminal Court, ex parte S and P (1998) 163 JP 776

The court refused to apply s 34 in relation to one of the accused by reason of his low IQ.

What of the instance where a defendant states that they did not mention a fact or facts after having received legal advice to that effect? Section 56 and Code C of the Police and Criminal Evidence Act 1984 entitles an accused to legal advice before and during the interrogation. Although the fact that the accused may have remained silent after having received legal advice is a relevant consideration for the jury when deciding whether or not to draw an adverse inference, it does not in itself prevent the adverse inference from being drawn; see *Argent* (above).

R v Condron [1997] 1 WLR 827

The defendant (a drug addict) was advised by his solicitor to refrain from answering any questions on the basis that he was under the effect of drugs even though the police doctor had deemed him fit for questioning. The court held that the fact that the defendant was acting on the legal advice given to him did not automatically mean that adverse inferences could not be drawn from his silence. If the defendant waived his legal professional privilege and gave evidence on the reasons for the advice, then that may prevent adverse inferences from being drawn. The Court of Appeal decided that the judge's direction that the jury were entitled to draw adverse inferences from his silence was improper.

R v Pointer [1997] Crim LR 676

The court held that an accused's silence would fall outside the provisions of s 34 if, at the time of questioning, the police had enough evidence to levy a charge.

The application of s 34 is dependent on the defendant raising facts in his defence, but not mentioned, in his interview. The Court of Appeal has considered the question 'what is *any fact relied on in defence*', on many occasions concluding that the term should not be construed narrowly. In *R v Milford* [2001] Crim LR 330 the court stated that the term *any fact* means '. . . something that is actually the case . . . a particular truth known by actual observation or authentic testimony, as opposed to what is merely inferred, or to a conjecture or fiction'.

A fact can be raised for the purposes of s 34(1)(a) by the accused in evidence, by a defence witness and even by a prosecution witness whilst giving evidence-in-chief or being cross-examined. Where the defendant puts a fact to a witness in cross-examination, then, so long as the other elements have been satisfied, that is enough for s 34(1) to apply, even if the witness refuses to accept the fact. It is clear from the wording of the provision that it applies to *any fact(s) relied upon* rather than *any fact(s) established*. Procedurally, this had the potential of having some impact on the way in which counsel, instructed by the defendant to act on their behalf, cross-examined witnesses. However, the decision of the courts in cases including *R v Weber* [2004] 1 Crim App R 40 confirm that s 34 will not apply, because no facts will have been relied upon, where counsel's questions are designed to test or probe the prosecution case.

The provision will not apply where the defence offer nothing more than mere theories or speculation (*R v N* [1998] 1 WLR 153); nor will it apply if:

- the matters are too complex
- they had occurred a long time ago so that an immediate response from the accused is not possible
- the police fail to disclose relevant information to the accused's solicitor so that they are unable to appropriately advise the accused.

For a further discussion of these points, you may wish to research the judgment of the court in *R v Roble* [1997] Crim LR 449.

R v McGarry [1999] Cr LR 316

The defendant gave a no-comment interview to the police but later, after having received legal advice, gave a written statement to them. At the trial the defendant was not cross-examined on his statement and the trial judge directed the jury that they could draw an adverse inference from the facts. The Court of Appeal held that the judge had erred in law; the jury should have been directed not to draw an adverse inference.

R v Ali and others [2001] All ER (D) 16 (CA)

The three defendants (1, 2 and 3), who were from family A, had a long-standing feud with another family (B). During an altercation the defendants injured a member of family B and were charged with causing grievous bodily harm contrary to s 18 of the Offences Against the Persons Act 1861. All three gave no comment interviews; however, later on defendants 1 and 2 prepared and gave statements to the police; defendant 1 claimed that he was acting in self-defence. Defendant 3 gave an alibi. All three testified when it came to the trial. Consistently, defendant 3 maintained his alibi but defendant 1 added that he had heard the victim call to his family members for a knife. The trial judge directed the jury that they could draw adverse inferences against all three defendants for a failure to mention facts on which they were now relying. The appeals of defendants 1 and 3 were dismissed; however, defendant 2's appeal was allowed because the facts on which he was relying were disclosed to the police in a

CONTINUED ▶

written statement beforehand. The reason for this was that defendant 3 had made no pre-trial statement and defendant 1 had departed from his by the additional information regarding the knife. Defendant 2 had stuck to his statement.

What happens if the defendant fails to mention a fact when questioned which they later rely on as a sole defence? What if the case depends on the existence or non-existence of that fact? The Court of Appeal has decided that in such an instance, the presiding trial judge should exercise their discretion and refrain from issuing a direction under s 34.

CASE EXAMPLE

R v Mountford [1999] Cr LR 575

The defendant (A) was staying at B's flat which was searched by the police under warrant. During the search A was spotted dropping a package out of the window of the flat, which when recovered the package contained heroin that would have had a street value of £400. After arrest both A and B were taken to the police station. A made a no-comment interview; however, B plea-bargained, offering to testify against A. A was charged with possession of a class A drug with an intention to supply. A testified that B was the dealer and it was he who had thrown the packet out of the window just before the search. Furthermore, he stated that he had not proffered this information at interview because he was unsure what B would have said and therefore did not want to grass on him. The trial judge issued a direction under s 34 and A was convicted. The Court of Appeal allowed the appeal; the trial judge had erred in directing the jury to draw an adverse inference and thereby prejudiced a fair trial. The *fact* that A was to rely on he had not disclosed during questioning, was the sole basis of A's defence and its existence was in question. What the judge should have done is directed the jury to consider the evidence without drawing an adverse inference.

Section 34 – inferences

The CJPOA 1994 provides that the jury may draw 'such inferences *that may* seem proper'. In Northern Ireland, where similar provisions have been running for some years now, the jury can draw the inference that the defence put forward at the trial is a recent fabrication. In England and Wales, the adverse inference simply has the effect of casting doubt on any subsequently raised defence. This may lead to an increased chance of a guilty verdict being returned by the jury. A key point to keep in mind is that no-one can be convicted solely on the basis of an adverse inference and therefore silence alone is not enough from which to infer guilt (s 38(3)). The Court of Appeal confirmed in *R v Daniel* and *R v Montague and Beckles* [1998] Crim LR

148, that the jury is not limited to the drawing, under s 34, of an adverse inference of recent fabrication.

The Judicial Studies Board has issued specimen directions that can be given under s 34 available to download (the latest version, 2007) from their website: www.jsboard.co.uk/index.htm and the actual document from http://www.jsboard.co.uk/downloads/specimendirections_june07%202.doc. Here is a summary of the effect of a direction:

- The legal burden of proof lies with the prosecution.
- The accused has a right to remain silent and can exercise that right.
- The silence of the accused may only be relevant after the prosecution has established a *prima facie* case to the jury's satisfaction.
- Silence alone is not enough to facilitate a guilty verdict.
- The jury may only draw an adverse inference from the accused's silence if they decide that the accused remained silent because of the belief that the story would not stand up when questioned, ie under investigative scrutiny.

When directing the jury the trial judge should also remind them of any reason an accused gives for failing to mention the fact(s) relied upon. Finally, two points to remember:

(a) Section 34(4) applies in those instances where an accused is questioned by the police, or another person who is charged with the investigation of offences.

(b) Section 78 of the PACE Act 1984, discussed later in the book, applies to invest the judge with a discretion to exclude any evidence obtained improperly, ie through breaches of the PACE codes. For an example, see *R v Dervish* [2002] 2 Cr App R 105.

Section 35 – a failure to testify

Let us move on to s 35 of the CJPOA 1994 and the adverse inferences that can be drawn from a defendant's failure to testify at trial.

Section 35 of the CJPOA 1994 '. . . at the trial of any person . . . for an offence, subsections (2) and (3) apply unless (a) the accused's guilt is not in issue; or (b) it appears to the court that the physical or mental condition of the accused makes it undesirable for him to give evidence; but subsection (2) below does not apply if, at the conclusion of the evidence for the prosecution, his legal representative informs the court that the accused will give evidence or, where he is unrepresented, the court ascertains from him that he will give evidence.' Subsection (2) states '. . . where this subsection applies, the court shall, at the conclusion of the evidence for the prosecution, satisfy itself (in the case of proceedings on indictment . . . in the presence of the jury) that the accused is aware that the stage has been reached at which evidence can be given for the defence and that he can, if he wishes, give evidence and that, if he chooses not to give evidence, or having been sworn, without good cause refuses to answer any question, it will be permissible for the court or jury to draw such inferences as appear proper from his failure to give evidence or his refusal, without good cause, to answer any question.' Subsection (3) states '. . . where this subsection applies, the court or jury, in determining whether the accused is guilty of the offence charged, may draw such inferences as appear proper from the failure of the accused to give evidence or his refusal, without good cause, to answer any question.'

CASE EXAMPLE

R v Kavanagh [2005] EWHC 820

The defendant failed to give evidence in his defence. His solicitor had informed the magistrates of this; his mother gave evidence that he was suffering from depression. The magistrates decided that the defendant had no case to answer, they had drawn no adverse inference, because to do so would have been unfair by reason that he had been so depressed.

R v Kavanagh highlights the fact that the court has the discretion under s 35(1)(b) not to draw an adverse inference where it appears to it that the accused's physical or mental condition makes it undesirable for the accused to give evidence. In this case, the Divisional Court highlighted that supporting evidence of the physical or mental state of the accused that makes it *undesirable* to give evidence, other than an assertion to that effect from their advocate, must be provided. This decision reaffirms the Court of Appeal's earlier decision in *R v Friend* [1997] 2 Cr App R 231. An accused that would do more damage to their case by giving evidence will not fall into this category.

The provision does not render the accused compellable to give evidence on their own behalf. This means that they will not be guilty of being in contempt of court by failing to give evidence.

At this point you may wish to refresh your memory on the instances in which a defendant may be competent to give evidence because this provision only applies to defendants who are both competent and mentally capable of giving evidence, ie testifying. Under Practice Direction (Crown Court: Evidence: Advice to a Defendant) [1995] 2 Cr App R 192 the trial judge has to ensure that the defendant is made aware of the consequences that entail in them not testifying. The full text of the Practice Direction is available to download from the Judicial Studies Board website at: http://www.jsboard.co.uk/criminal_law/cbb/mf_05.htm. The Court of Appeal (CA) gave some guidance as to the operation and effect of s 35 in *R v Cowan* [1995] 4 All ER 939. The court stated that the provision only applies once a *prima facie* case has been established by the prosecution. This means that the judge and jury must be satisfied that there is in law and fact a case that the defendant must answer.

At this point the court will also consider whether there is any evidence that shows that the defendant had a good reason for not testifying. The CA stated that the instructed lawyer, a barrister or solicitor, cannot simply speculate as to the reasons why the defendant did not testify. Any reason put forward for not testifying must be supported by relevant and admissible evidence; see *R v Friend* [1997] 1 WLR 1433. Finally, the CA stated that the judge should remind the jury that it is for the prosecution to prove that the defendant is guilty beyond reasonable doubt and that they should remember that silence alone can never amount to an indication of guilt (s 38 CJPOA 1994). The trial judge will then direct the jury that *they can draw such adverse inferences from the defendant's silence that may be proper* if they are satisfied that:

(a) the prosecution has proven that there is a case that the defendant must answer

(b) there is no good reason why the defendant has failed to testify.

The main adverse inference that the jury may draw here is that the defendant does not have an answer to the allegations being levied against them, or that they do not have an answer that would stand up to the scrutiny of counsel's cross-examination. In summary, the effect of s 35 is to confirm (a) that the defendant is competent to give evidence, (b) that the defendant cannot be compelled to testify and (c) that their silence can confirm the case against them.

If the defendant gives evidence, then they must do so from the witness box. The questioning can go to the extent that the defendant may incriminate themselves or others. Prior to the Criminal Justice Act 2003 the defendant could not be questioned as to their previous bad character or convictions (s 1 Criminal Evidence Act 1898). Currently the position depends on whether that evidence is evidence of a type that has already been admitted under the Criminal Justice Act 2003; see Chapter 9.

In this instance any evidence that a defendant gives is evidence for all purposes. This means that it can be used against the defendant even if it incriminates themselves or others; see *R v Paul* [1920] 2 KB 183.

In *R v Rudd* (1948) 32 Cr App Rep 138 it was stated that

> **J** '. . . a statement made in the absence of an accused person by *a* co-defendant cannot be evidence against the accused, *however* if a co-defendant, *in the course of a joint trial*, goes into the witness box and gives evidence, then what *they* say becomes evidence for all the purposes of the case including being evidence against *their* co-defendant.'

Generally, where a defendant elects to testify, then, unless the court directs otherwise, they should do so before any other defence witness (s 79 PACE 1984).

Section 36 – a failure to account for objects, substances or marks that incriminate the accused

Let us move on to those adverse inferences that can be drawn from a defendant's silence in failing to account for incriminating objects, substances or marks. Section 36(1) of the CJPOA 1994 states that

S 'where a person is arrested by a constable, and there is (a) on his person, or (b) in or on his clothing or footwear, or (c) otherwise in his possession, or (d) in any place in which he is at the time of his arrest, any object, substance or mark, or there is a mark on any such object; and that, or another, constable investigating the case reasonably believes that the presence of the object, substance or mark may be attributable to the participation of the person arrested in the commission of the offence specified by the constable; and the constable informs the person arrested that he so believes, and requests him to account for the presence of the object, substance or mark; and the person fails or refuses to do so, then, if in any proceedings against the person for the offence so specified, evidence on those matters is given.'

In summary, s 36 requires the following to be satisfied:

- an arrest
- an object, substance or a mark on any object
- the object, substance or mark or any object with a mark on it must be on their person, in or on their clothing or footwear.

If all three are satisfied, then the constable who is arresting the person or investigating the case must:

- reasonably believe that the object, substance or mark may be attributable to the offence that the person is being arrested or investigated for
- inform the person of this reasonable belief and ask him to account for its presence.

The procedure is as follows: first, the suspect must be arrested and informed in ordinary language by the constable of their belief that the object, substance or mark indicates that the suspect was involved in a specified offence. This latter point is important, the provision will not apply if the constable very generally enquires into the suspect's involvement in *any offences*; it must be specified. The constable must then ask the suspect to account for the object, substance or mark and warn them of the consequences of failing to do so; see Code C paras 10:5 and 10:5B. The constable must ensure that they keep records of the entire process in the case as evidence that can be used in any subsequent trial.

Importantly, s 36 only applies where a suspect fails to account for incriminatory objects, substances or marks that are present at the time the suspect is arrested. Here is a quick example:

> Vanessa is arrested at the scene of a murder. Following her arrest, the constable asks her to account for (a) the blood on her blouse and hands and (b) the fact that she was seen by V's boyfriend with a dagger at the time at which the offence was committed. Section 36 would operate in relation to (a) but not (b) as she did not have the dagger on her person at the time of arrest.

CASE EXAMPLE

R v Compton [2002] EWCA Crim 2835

The accused proffered a bare statement when questioned about a number of drugs offences and a large amount of cash that had been discovered in his safe. The accused had stated that the cash came from a legitimate antiques business but was contaminated with heroin because he was a heroin user. In that instance the judge was entitled to leave the question to the jury whether the accused had failed to account under s 36(1)(c) or (d).

Evidence of the accused's failure to account is admissible against him. The difference between s 36 and ss 34, 35 and 37 (post) become quite obvious: this provision does not need the question requiring the accused to account for the above to be put to them at an authorized place of detention, ie a police station, or after they have had the opportunity of having consulted their lawyer. This is because, referring back to the rules on the *res gestae*, an innocent person would give information regarding the existence of an object, substance or mark or object with any such mark of their own will. No adverse inferences may be drawn where the defendant has consulted his lawyer before a constable has put the question to them (s 36(4A)). Finally, s 36(2) states that a 'court or jury may draw such inferences from the failure or refusal as appear proper'. Once again you should remember that guilt cannot be inferred from silence alone (s 30(3)). A specimen direction (No 41) that the judge should give the jury before they draw such an inference under this provision is available to download free from the Judicial Studies Board website at: http://www.jsboard.co.uk/criminal_law/cbb/mf_05a.htm.

As a quick self-test it is probably a good idea to look at s 36 (above) and try to see if you can identify the elements that have just been outlined.

Section 37 – a failure to account for presence in a place that incriminates the accused

The final provision: s 37 allows for the drawing of an adverse inference for an accused's failure or refusal to account for their presence in an incriminating place. Let us take a closer look, s 37 states, where

(a) a person arrested by a constable was found by *them* at a place at or about the time the offence for which *they* were arrested is alleged to have been committed

(b) that he or another constable investigating the offence reasonably believes that the presence of the suspect at that place and at that time may be attributable to *their* participation in the commission of the offence

(c) the constable must then inform the suspect of their reasonable belief (as *per* s 36).

The suspect's failure or refusal to account will once again lead to the drawing of such adverse inferences as the jury may think proper. The procedure is as follows: s 37 only applies where the suspect is arrested either *at* or *near* a place that incriminates him. This means that the suspect cannot be asked to account for his presence at a particular place on a prior occasion, ie if Marjorie is arrested at the scene of a horrific murder she cannot be asked to account for what she was doing there the previous week. Neither can they be asked to account for their presence at other places, regardless of how much they may incriminate them.

Lastly, two important points: (a) the inferences that are drawn will vary depending on the circumstances of the case; (b) silence alone cannot indicate guilt (s 38(3)), and (c) no adverse inference may be drawn from the silence of an accused where they were not permitted access to legal advice before the constable's request for the suspect to account.

5.5 Human rights: fair trials and adverse inferences

Finally, we must examine the impact of the Human Rights Act 1998 on the inferences drawn from an accused's silence. You will know, from this book and other reading material, that a defendant has the right to a fair trial under Art 6 of the European Convention on Human Rights, you may wish to refresh your memory on the right before continuing to read. A good summary of the rights under the convention is available to download at:
www.echr.coe.int/NR/rdonlyres/D5CC24A7-DC13-4318-B457-
5C9014916D7A/0/EnglishAnglais.pdf.

As the provisions of the CJPOA 1994 have, in effect, undermined the common law in general, the courts have not been shy in stating that the legislation should be interpreted in the manner that was originally intended, ie restrictively. Why? Think about it, silence can never amount to an admission of guilt. Where adverse inferences play a larger part in the prosecution case, then, according to the European Court of Human Rights (ECtHR) in *Murray v UK* (1996) 22 EHRR 29 and *Condron v UK* (2001) 31 EHRR 1, the accused's right to a fair trial may have been undermined.

In *Condron* the ECtHR also state that leaving the issue of silence to a jury does not in itself breach an accused's right to a fair trial under Art 6(1) or (2). For it is a relevant consideration

J '. . . that needs to be weighed when assessing whether or not it is fair to do so in the circumstances'.

The court went further in confirming that the right to remain silent, although regarded as an internationally recognized standard at the heart of the right to a fair trial, was not absolute.

How can the courts ensure that the accused's right is not infringed? You should be aware that a fair trial under Art 6(1) and (2) can be facilitated by the trial judge giving the jury accurate and fair directions to help them. You know that these are standard guidelines which aim to ensure appropriate use of evidence. The direction would include the fact that silence alone can never amount to an admission of guilt. You can freely download specimen directions from the Judicial Studies Board website at: www.jsboard.co.uk/criminal_law/cbb/mf_05a.htm. A failure to direct the jury will most probably result in any resulting conviction being rendered unsafe; see *Beckles v UK* (2002) 13 BHRC 522. In *Bristow v Jones* [2002] EWCA Crim 1571, the defendant, who was being prosecuted for carrying out a contract killing, had his conviction quashed because of a material irregularity in the way in which the judge had delivered the direction.

In summary then, the right to silence has seen many changes and it is likely that it will continue to do so. No doubt the ECtHR and the domestic UK courts will continue to develop the case law in this area of the law of evidence. You can keep up to date with current developments using the online resource that accompanies this book.

KEY FACTS

Silence at common law

The enactment of the CJPOA 1994 did not affect the common law rules (s 34(5)) on silence. Under the common law, the defendant still has the right to remain silent. It is, however, difficult to reconcile that with the fact that they have stated nothing in response to accusations made in their presence that incriminate them. Silence cannot amount to an acceptance of an allegation, unless the defendant is faced with an allegation that is made by a person on an equal footing, and it is reasonable to expect a reply. In these circumstances, a lack of response may amount to an acceptance of guilt.

Silence under the CJPOA 1994

In addition to the common law rules, the CJPOA 1994 provides specific instances in which a defendant's silence either on being questioned by the police or when

CONTINUED ▸

KEY FACTS

reasonably asked to explain themselves, may lead to the drawing of adverse inferences. The CJPOA 1994 did not abolish the common law rules. The effect has been to qualify the right, ie a defendant can still exercise the right to silence. However, exercising it may lead to the trier of fact (the jury) drawing adverse inferences.

Section 34 – Failure to mention facts when questioned

Section 34(1) states:

'where in any proceedings against a person for an offence evidence is given that the accused:

c) at any time before *being* charged with *the commission of* an offence, on being questioned *whilst* under caution by a constable trying to discover whether or by whom an offence had been committed, failed to mention any fact relied on in a defence in those proceedings; or

d) on being charged with the *commission of* an offence or officially informed *of the possibility of being* prosecuted for it, failed to mention any such fact, being a fact which in the circumstances existing at the time the accused could reasonably have been expected to mention when being so questioned, charged or informed, as the case may be, subsection (2) applies. Subsection (2) allows the court or jury to "draw such inferences as appear proper".'

The drawing of an adverse inference under s 34 is conditional upon the accused having received legal advice. The investigation and related questioning must take place before the defendant is charged with the commission of the offence. The provision only applies once the suspect has been cautioned. The jury may draw 'such inferences *that may* seem proper'.

Section 35 – A failure to testify

This provision applies where a defendant fails to give evidence. The Court of Appeal issued guidance in *R v Cowan* [1995] 4 All ER 939 on the operation of the provision; it only applies once the prosecution has established a *prima facie* case; the instructed lawyer cannot speculate as to the reasons why the defendant did not testify. Any reason put forward for not testifying must be supported by relevant and admissible evidence and the trial judge should remind the jury that it is for the prosecution to prove that the defendant is guilty beyond reasonable doubt

CONTINUED ▸

KEY FACTS

and that they should remember that silence alone can never amount to an indication of guilt (s 38 CJPOA 1994). The trial judge will then direct the jury that *they can draw such adverse inferences from the defendant's silence that may be proper* if they are satisfied that the prosecution has proven that there is a case that the defendant must answer and there is no good reason why the defendant has failed to testify.

Section 36 – A failure to account for objects, substances or marks that incriminate the accused

This provision only applies where a suspect fails to account for incriminatory objects, substances or marks that are present at the time the suspect is arrested. Section 36(1) of the CJPOA states that where a person is arrested by a constable, and there is (a) on his person, or (b) in or on his clothing or footwear, or (c) otherwise in his possession, or (d) in any place in which he is at the time of his arrest, any object, substance or mark, or there is a mark on any such object; and that, or another, constable investigating the case reasonably believes that the presence of the object, substance or mark may be attributable to the participation of the person arrested in the commission of the offence specified by the constable; and the constable informs the person arrested that he so believes, and requests him to account for the presence of the object, substance or mark; and the person fails or refuses to do so, then, if in any proceedings against the person for the offence so specified, evidence on those matters is given. The court or jury may draw such inferences from the failure or refusal as appear proper.

Section 37 – A failure to account for presence in a place that incriminates the accused

Section 37 allows for the drawing of an adverse inference for an accused's failure or refusal to account for their presence in an incriminating place. The failure or refusal to account will once again lead to the drawing of such adverse inferences as the jury may think proper.

ACTIVITY

Self-test questions

1. Does an accused have a right to silence?

2. What is the position of the common law in relation to the silence of an accused?

3. What was the effect of the CJPOA 1994 on the common law rules on silence?

4. What were the main reasons for the enactment of the CJPOA 1994?

5. Summarize the common law rules on silence.

6. In what instances can an adverse inference be drawn under s 34?

7. What inference can be drawn under s 34?

8. With reference to current case law, what is the effect of s 35 on an accused's silence?

9. Explain what guidance the Court of Appeal gave in *R v Cowan* [1995] 4 All ER 939 on the drawing of adverse inferences.

10. What will need to be satisfied in order for an adverse inference to be drawn under s 36?

11. Summarize the effect of s 37 on silence.

12. How does Art 6 of the European Convention on Human Rights affect an accused's right to silence?

13. Think of at least one example in which an adverse inference may be drawn under ss 34–37 of the CJPOA 1994.

14. Can you think of any other ways in which evidence that is collected may be excluded?

Further reading

Choo, A. L. T. and Nash, S., 'Evidence law in England and Wales: the impact of the Human Rights Act 1998' (2003) *International Journal of Evidence and Proof*, 7 (1), pp. 31–61.

Redmayne, M., 'Rethinking the privilege against self-incrimination' (2007) OJLS, 27(2), 209–232.

Roberts, P., 'Modernising police powers – again?' (2007) Crim LR, Dec, 934–948.

Internet links

The Judicial Studies Board specimen directions that can be given under s 34:

www.jsboard.co.uk/index.htm and the actual document from

http://www.jsboard.co.uk/downloads/specimendirections_june07%202.doc.

Judicial Studies Board website : http://www.jsboard.co.uk/criminal_law/cbb/mf_05.htm.

http://www.jsboard.co.uk/criminal_law/cbb/mf_05a.htm.

European Convention on Human Rights:

www.echr.coe.int/NR/rdonlyres/D5CC24A7-DC13-4318-B457-5C9014916D7A/0/EnglishAnglais.pdf.

chapter 6 COURSE OF TRIAL ■

By the end of this chapter you should be able to:

- Understand the rules regarding refreshing a witness's memory including the effect of doing so

- Appreciate the distinction and effect between unfavourable and hostile witnesses

- Understand the general rule of evidence concerning previous consistent statements and identify any exceptions to this rule

- Identify the objectives of cross-examination of witnesses

- Understand the rules laid down in ss 41–43 of the Youth Justice and Criminal Evidence Act 1999

- Appreciate the distinction and effect with regard to cross-examination as to issue and credit.

6.1 Introduction

In both civil and criminal cases, proof of a fact through witnesses requires the party calling the witness to present the facts to the court by following a number of strict rules. After the individual has been sworn in or made a solemn affirmation, or exceptionally has been allowed to give unsworn evidence, the witness will be questioned by the party calling him. No leading questions may be asked. This process is known as the evidence-in-chief. The object is to elicit evidence which is favourable to that party, in other words, to elicit from the witness facts that prove or support that party's case. On completion of this process the opposing party(ies) is/are entitled to question the witness. This is the cross-examination and its purpose is (a) to elicit facts that are favourable to the cross-examiner, and (b) to test the veracity of the witness or to discredit the witness. Leading questions may be asked by the cross-examiner. Finally, the witness may be re-questioned by the party calling him in the re-examination. The purpose of the re-examination is to re-establish the credibility of the witness if this was shaken by the cross-examination. The re-examination relates to matters that were raised in the cross-examination. Nothing more need be said about the re-examination. The same restrictions that limit the examiner-in-chief in the questions that he may ask equally apply to the re-examination.

6.2 Examination-in-chief

6.2.1 No leading questions

This process is applicable only with regard to the party calling the witness. As a general rule, the party who calls the witness ought not to ask leading questions. A leading question is one that either assumes the existence of disputed facts or suggests the desired answer. It is also suggested that a leading question is one to which the answer is 'yes' or 'no'. For example, a question such as, 'Did you see Arthur hit the victim, Victor?' The proper course would be to ask Arthur whether he recalls an incident on the relevant date? Where was he? He is then asked to narrate the incident.

If a leading question has been unfairly put by one party, the opposing party ought to intercede and object to the question. In the event of a dispute the judge will be required to make a ruling. However, the answers to leading questions are not inadmissible but relate to the weight of the evidence; see *R v Wilson* 9 (1913) Cr App R 124.

There are a number of situations where, exceptionally, leading questions are permitted. These include formal introductory matters on undisputed issues, such as the name of the witness, occasions when it is necessary to focus the witness's attention on a specific matter and, of course, cases where the opponent has consented to leading questions.

6.2.2 Refreshing the memory of witnesses

Very often a considerable time elapses between the occurrence of an event and the occasion to narrate that event in court proceedings. It would be unrealistic to expect the witness to recall every detail of the event with precision without assistance. Indeed, the process of testifying is not treated as a test of memory but is designed to test the honesty and reliability of the witness. At common law the witness was allowed to refresh his memory with documents, both in court and out of court. Reference to the 'in court' refreshment of the memory of witnesses involves the occasion while the witness testifies from the witness box. The defining moment is the swearing in of the witness. Following this event the strict rules for refreshing the memory of witnesses operate as distinct from the occasion where the witness wishes to refresh his memory prior to testifying in the proceedings.

(a) Refreshing memory in court

Common Law At common law the rule was that a witness was permitted to refresh his memory in the witness box by reference to any document *made* or *verified* by him at a time when the matter was fresh in his mind. The authorship of the document was of immense importance. The requirement here was that the document was created by the witness himself when the facts were fresh in the witness's mind. This is a question of fact. Alternatively, if the document was made by a third party, the onus was on the witness to establish that he had endorsed or verified the

document when the matter was fresh in his mind. Endorsement or verification may involve the process of the witness:

(i) reading the statement in the document at a time when the matter was fresh in his mind and adopting the information as accurate

(ii) having the information read back to the witness who then verifies the statement as accurate. In this event the person reading back the information to the witness is required to testify that the information that he read back was the information that he recorded; see *R v Kelsey* (1981) 74 Cr App R 213.

ASE EXTRACT

R v Kelsey (1981) 74 Cr App R 213

Two men followed a car and one of them (Hill) made a mental note of its registration number. He repeated the number some 20 minutes later to a police officer who wrote it down in his notebook and read it back. The witness (Hill) did not himself see the number that was written by the police officer. At the trial the witness (Hill) testified but could not remember the number. The trial judge allowed the witness to refresh his memory from the officer's note and the officer was called to say that the note produced in court was the one on which he had written the number. On appeal, the court decided that the document was properly used to refresh Hill's memory.

Taylor J:

'In our view there is no magic in verifying by seeing as opposed to verifying by hearing. In the present case, a second witness is required. Hill dictated the number, heard it read back and confirmed its accuracy. But although he saw the note being made, he did not read it, so it was necessary for the officer also to be called to prove that the note he produced was the one Hill saw him making and heard him read back.'

The next requirement was that the document must have been executed at the time of the transaction or so shortly after the event that the facts were fresh in the mind of the maker of the statement. This is essentially a question of fact. An interval of four weeks was considered too long a delay to permit the witness to refresh his memory; see *R v Graham* [1973] Crim LR 628.

It was not essential that the witness should have had any independent recollection of the facts. Indeed, the witness's memory may be at a blank when he sees the document. This is irrelevant because the rule only requires the witness to endorse the document as his own or accept the statement as being accurate. For example, an attesting witness may say that he is sure that he witnessed a document on seeing his signature on the document even though he has no recollection of the event. In *Maugham v Hubbard* (1828) 6 LJKB 299, a witness called to prove the receipt of a sum of money was shown an acknowledgement of the receipt signed by himself. On seeing it, he said that he had no doubt that he had received it, although he had no recollection of the fact. The court held that this was sufficient evidence of the payment. Further, either the original document or a copy may be used by the witness to refresh his memory. Where a copy is used, it needs to have been made when the matter was fresh in the witness's mind.

The *aide memoire* document is required to be produced to the opponent, on request, for inspection. There are no adverse consequences by calling for the documents for inspection. The opponent has a right to cross-examine on the document. If the cross-examiner confines his questioning to the parts of the document used to refresh the witness's memory the document will not be put in evidence. However, if the cross-examiner questions the witness on parts of the document beyond which the witness refreshes his memory, the party calling the witness is entitled to have the document put in evidence. In *Senat v Senat* [1965] P 172, Sir Jocelyn Simon said:

> **J** 'The mere inspection of a document does not render it evidence which counsel inspecting it is bound to put in. Where a document is used to refresh a witness's memory, cross examining counsel may inspect that document in order to check it without making it evidence. Moreover, he may cross examine upon it without making it evidence provided that his cross examination does not go further than the parts which are used for refreshing the memory of the witness.'

At common law, the effect of the note being put in evidence is that the document is treated as evidence of the consistency of the witness, ie the document bolsters up the credibility of the witness's testimony as distinct from being evidence of the truth of the assertions. In short, the document becomes an exhibit; see *R v Virgo* (1978) 67 Cr App R 323.

Civil cases In civil cases, in theory, the common law rules regarding the pre-conditions necessary to be satisfied concerning the refreshing of the memory of witnesses in court continue to apply, subject to two modifications.

1. The effect of the document being put in evidence is now admissible as an exception to the hearsay rule, ie the information is treated as evidence of the truth of the assertion; see s 6(4) of the Civil Evidence Act 1995 which declares as follows: 'Nothing in this Act affects any of

the rules of law as to the circumstances in which, where a person called as a witness in civil proceedings is cross examined on a document used by him to refresh his memory, that document may be made evidence in the proceedings.'

2. The judge has the power to allow the witness to refer to any document which he (the judge) considers reliable enough for such purpose.

Criminal cases. Criminal cases were governed by the common law rules until the enactment of the Criminal Justice Act 2003. Although the 2003 Act does not expressly abolish the common law rules as to the refreshing of memories of witnesses, it is submitted that the purpose of the legislation is that they will supersede the common law.

Section 139 of the 2003 Act provides:

'(1) a person giving oral evidence in criminal proceedings about any matter may, at any stage in the course of doing so, refresh his memory of it from a document made or verified by him at an earlier time if −

(a) he states in his oral evidence that the document records his recollection of the matter at that earlier time, and

(b) his recollection of the matter is likely to have been significantly better at that time than it is at the time of his oral evidence.'

It should be noted that s 139 does not require the judge to consider whether the document (*aide memoire*) was made or verified by the witness when the matter was fresh in his mind. Instead, the statute refers to the dual requirements in s 139 (a) and (b) in that the document records the witness's recollection of the events and his recall of the events is likely to be significantly better at that time as opposed to the current moment in time while he is testifying. However, the judge still has the discretionary power to decide that the document was executed after too long a period of time to permit the witness to refresh his memory with it.

Section 140 defines a document as 'anything in which information of any description is recorded, but not including any recording of sounds or moving images'. The effect is that a record of sounds or images, even in paper form, is not a document for criminal proceedings. In these circumstances s 139(2) permits the witness to refer to the record.

Section 139(2) declares as follows:

'Where −

(a) a person giving oral evidence in criminal proceedings about any matter has previously given an oral account, of which a sound recording was made, and he states in that evidence that the account represented his recollection of the matter at that time,

(b) his recollection of the matter is likely to have been significantly better at the time of the previous account than it is at the time of his oral evidence, and

(c) a transcript has been made of the sound recording,

he may, at any stage in the course of giving his evidence, refresh his memory of the matter from that transcript.'

Thus, a witness may be allowed to refresh his memory from a transcript of a tape-recorded conversation he had with another person; see *R v Mills and Rose* (1962) 46 Cr App R 336. Indeed, Judge LJ in *R v Bailey* [2001] EWCA 733, said, 'We can see no reason why the principle by which a witness is permitted to refresh his memory to the fullest extent should be confined to him looking at a piece of paper with writing on it. Common sense suggests that if modern technology provides a better or different means for the same purpose, it should be available for use in court.'

In conformity with the principle at common law (see above) the *aide memoire* may be surrendered for inspection to the opposing party with impunity. Likewise, the opposing party is entitled to cross-examine the witness on the document without adverse consequences, provided that the cross-examiner restricts his questioning on the parts of the document used to refresh the witness's memory. However, if the cross-examiner questions the witness on parts of the document that were not used to refresh the witness's memory (excessive cross-examination), the party calling the witness is entitled to put the document in evidence, ie the document becomes an exhibit. By statute, the assertions in the document will be admissible as evidence of the truth of such assertions, ie as exceptions to the hearsay rule. Section 120(3) enacts the effect of excessive cross-examination thus:

'A statement made by a witness in a document –

(a) which is used by him to refresh his memory while giving evidence,

(b) on which he is cross examined, and

(c) which as a consequence is received in evidence in the proceedings,

is admissible as evidence of any matter stated of which oral evidence by him would be admissible.'

It should be noted that s 120(3) refers to a 'statement made by a witness' and makes no reference to third-party statements verified by the witness. Assuming that this was not an oversight by Parliament, it would appear that the effect of 'putting the document in evidence' varies with whether the witness refreshes his memory from his document or a third party's document. Where a witness refreshes his memory from a statement made by a third party but verified by the witness, and who is cross-examined excessively, the effect is that the document is evidence of consistency of the witness only, as stated at common law. If there has been excessive cross-examination on that witness's note, the effect is as stated in s 120(3), namely evidence of the truth.

At common law (see above) the courts did not draw a distinction between 'present recollection revived' and 'past recollections recorded'. Both concepts were generously treated as occasions where the witness's memory was refreshed. 'Present recollection revived' refers to occasions where

the witness's memory is genuinely refreshed in the witness box by reference to the note made or verified by the witness, ie the witness recalls the events by referring to the note. On the other hand, the concept of 'past recollections recorded' refers to the situation where the witness's memory is at a blank even after referring to the note. The witness simply does not recall the event in question. This is an occasion where the document allegedly used to refresh the witness's memory will constitute a variety of hearsay evidence; see ss 120(4) and (6) of the 2003 Act.

Section 120(4) enacts as follows:

S 'A previous statement by the witness is admissible as evidence of any matter stated of which oral evidence by him would be admissible, if –
(a) any of the following three conditions is satisfied, and
(b) while giving evidence the witness indicates that to the best of his belief he made the statement, and that to the best of his belief it states the truth.'

Section 120(6) provides as follows:

S 'The second condition is that the statement was made by the witness when the matters stated were fresh in his memory but he does not remember them, and cannot reasonably be expected to remember them well enough to give oral evidence of them in the proceedings.'

It should be noted that these two provisions make no mention of third-party statements verified by the witness. The common law rule will apply in those circumstances. With regard to statements made by the witness in the circumstances laid down in ss 120(4) and (6) the note is admissible as evidence of the facts stated.

Section 122 enacts that when a document becomes an exhibit (excessive cross-examination) it must not accompany the jury when they retire to consider their verdict unless the court considers it appropriate or unless all the parties agree.

(b) Refreshing the memory of witnesses out of court

The rule is that a witness is permitted to refresh his memory out of court by any means that he considers necessary. This may be in the form of the witness's contemporaneous or even non-contemporaneous note of the event, a third party's account of the event, etc. The normal restrictions that are applicable to refreshing memory in court are not extended to this occasion because it is not possible to ensure that any strict rules will apply. In short, any prescriptive rules will be difficult to supervise. In addition, the trial process does not involve a test of memory but is a process of getting at the truth. The effect is that a line is drawn as to when no formal principles concerning the refreshment of the witness's memory applies and this is up to the time that the witness steps into the witness box and takes the oath.

CASE EXTRACT

R v Richardson [1971] 2 QB 484

On a trial for burglary and attempted burglary, four prosecution witnesses were shown statements they had made to the police. The defendant was convicted and appealed on the ground that these witnesses were allowed to refresh their memories before entering the witness box and that their evidence was inadmissible. The court dismissed the appeal. Sachs LJ:

'testimony in the witness box would become more a test of memory than of truthfulness if witnesses are deprived of the opportunity of checking their recollections beforehand by reference to statements or notes made at a time closer to the events in question. In addition, refusal of access to statements would tend to create difficulties for honest witnesses but be likely to do little to hamper dishonest witnesses . . . It is true that by the practice of the courts a line is drawn at the moment when a witness enters the witness box, when giving evidence there he cannot refresh his memory except by a document which must have been written either at the time of the transaction or so shortly afterwards that the facts were still fresh in his memory . . . But there can be no general rule (which incidentally would be unenforceable) that witnesses may not before trial see the statements which they made at some period reasonably close to the time of the event. Indeed, one can imagine many cases particularly those of a complex nature, where such a rule would militate greatly against the interests of justice.'

If a witness, having commenced his testimony, needs to refresh his memory out of court and not from the witness box, it would be for the judge to exercise his discretion to decide whether to allow the witness to refresh his memory and that the document to be used to refresh his memory was made or verified by the witness close to the time of the event. In *R v Da Silva* [1990] 1 WLR 31, the judge exercised his discretion to allow *aide memoire* documents, provided that the following conditions are satisfied:

1. The witness indicates that he cannot recall the details of events because of a lapse of time.

2. The witness had made the statement much nearer to the time of the events and the contents of the statement represented his recollections at the time he made it.

3. The witness had not read the statement shortly before coming into the witness box.

4. The witness wished to have an opportunity to read the statement before continuing his testimony.

This principle was taken one stage further in *R v South Ribble Magistrates ex p Cochrane* [1996] 2 Cr App 544. The court decided that the third condition laid down in *R v Da Silva* was not a requirement to be satisfied. Indeed, the conditions laid down in *Da Silva* were not prerequisites to be fulfilled. The question involved the exercise of discretion and the real test is fairness and justice. In this case the witness had read his witness statement before testifying at the committal proceedings on a charge of conspiracy to pervert the course of justice. He then could not remember details of a conversation included in his statement which was made 12–18 months earlier. The magistrate allowed him to look at the statement before continuing with his testimony. The defendant was convicted and appealed. The Divisional Court dismissed the appeal on the ground that the magistrates (or judge) had a strong discretion to decide whether to allow the witness to refer to the non-contemporaneous note before continuing his testimony. Henry LJ:

> **J** 'I do not understand the court there to be saying, as a matter of law, that once a witness was in the witness box he could only refer to his previous non-contemporaneous statement if all four criteria were satisfied. It was permissive, not expressed by way of invariable limitation. That, it seems to me, is supported from the tenor of the judgment when read as a whole.
>
> For example serious frauds require considerable preparation from witnesses who routinely have their own copies of their statements which may run to hundreds of pages. Clearly they will refer to them in the days or weeks they may spend in the witness box. They will have studied those statements both before and during their time in the witness box, and the course of justice is helped and not hindered by that because in complicated matters it is necessary that witnesses should be properly prepared, otherwise matters are reduced to a memory test and justice is not assisted. What is said there will apply equally to the confused, flustered and nervous old lady. Whether she has read her statement before she goes into the witness box or not, if she was confused and flustered when she first read it before giving evidence, she may very well need to read it again and the discretion should lie in the trial judge to allow her to do so.
>
> Finally, in relation to the relevance as to whether a witness has taken the opportunity to read their statement before going into the witness box, there can be no logical difference between someone who has read the statement and for some reason not taken it in properly and one who has never read it at all. It seems to me

CONTINUED ▶

that the judge has a real discretion as to whether to permit a witness to refresh his memory from a non-contemporaneous document. By 'real discretion' I mean a strong discretion, a choice of alternatives free of binding criteria. I do not mean the so-called weak discretion which is not a true judicial discretion at all, but simply a binding rule of law to be followed by the judge.'

6.2.3 Unfavourable and hostile witnesses

The general rule is that a party calling a witness to testify in proceedings (civil or criminal) guarantees the witness's trustworthiness. The effect is that such a party is not entitled to impeach the witness's credit by questioning the witness as to his previous convictions or otherwise discrediting the witness or bringing out the witness's previous inconsistent statement. In other words, the party calling the witness is not entitled to conduct a cross-examination of his witness. In attempting to prove his case he assumes that the witness would testify on issues relevant to the facts in issue and in his favour.

The witness may disappoint the party in that he fails to prove the relevant issue or proves an issue prejudicial to the party calling him. Such a witness is treated as unfavourable. The witness may not have shown any animosity towards the party calling him but simply that the proof expected from him might have been exaggerated or overstated or the facts were not adequately perceived by him.

At common law, the party was allowed to contradict his witness by adducing contrary evidence in both civil and criminal cases without the leave of the judge. In other words, if W, a witness called by the claimant (in a civil case) or the prosecution (in a criminal case), fails to 'come up to proof', the claimant or prosecution may call another witness, X, to prove the relevant point.

In *Ewer v Ambrose* (1825) 107 ER 910, in an action in quasi contract (*assumpsit*) for money had and received, the defendant called a witness to prove a partnership but he proved the contrary. The defendant called another witness to prove the partnership and on appeal the court decided that he was entitled to do so. Littledale J:

'Where a witness is called by a party to prove his case and he disproves that case, I think the party is still at liberty to prove his case by other witnesses. It would be a great hardship if the rule were otherwise, for if a party had four witnesses upon whom he relied to prove his case, it would be very hard, that by calling first the one who happened to disprove it, he should be deprived of the testimony of the other three. If he had called the three before the other who had disproved the case, it would have been a question for the jury upon the evidence, whether they would give credit to the three or to the one. The order in which the witness happens to be called ought not therefore to make any difference.'

Holroyd J:

> **J** 'If a party calls a witness to prove a fact, he cannot, when he finds the witness proves the contrary, give general evidence to shew that that witness is not to be believed on his oath, but he may shew by other evidence that he is mistaken as to the fact which he is called to prove.'

Hostile witnesses

A 'hostile' witness is one who shows animosity towards the party calling the witness. He is not desirous of speaking the truth or he sets out to sabotage the case of the party calling him. The judge is required to make a ruling as to whether the witness is hostile or not. Once the judge has made the ruling that the witness is hostile, then at common law, in both civil and criminal cases, the party calling the witness is entitled, subject to the discretion of the judge, to conduct a limited form of cross-examination of the witness. Such a party is entitled to ask leading questions and to reduce the impact of the witness's testimony by questioning him with regard to his memory, means of knowledge, etc. The purpose of the line of questioning is twofold:

(a) to persuade the witness to return to the details contained in his witness statement

(b) to highlight inconsistencies between the witness's versions of events.

Whether the witness is merely unfavourable or is to be treated as hostile is a question of law for the judge to decide. Where a witness refuses to co-operate and refuses to answer questions put to him or her, the witness may be treated as hostile.

In *R v Thompson* (1976) 64 Cr App R 96, the defendant was charged and convicted with incest with his daughter (aged 16 at the time of the trial). She had made a statement to the police implicating her father. At the trial, after being sworn in she was asked by counsel for the prosecution about the merits of the case and said, 'I am not saying nothing, I am not going to give evidence.' The judge retorted, 'Oh yes you are'. The witness said, 'I'm not'. The judge said, 'Do you want to spend time in prison yourself?' The witness said, 'no'. The judge continued, 'You wouldn't like it in Holloway, I assure you. You answer these questions and behave yourself, otherwise you will be in serious trouble. Do you understand that?' The witness replied, 'Yes.' She then refused to answer the questions put to her. The judge then gave permission to treat the witness as hostile and she was cross-examined by the prosecution counsel and the accused was convicted and appealed. The Court of Appeal dismissed the appeal because the judge had correctly exercised his discretion to treat the witness as hostile.

It is unclear whether a party may re-examine his witness who was treated as hostile at the examination-in-chief stage. The argument here is that the witness remains the witness of the party calling him and, in theory, ought to be subject to re-examination by such party. However, a witness may be treated as hostile at the stage of the re-examination, see *R v Powell* (1985) Cr LR 592.

At common law, a hostile witness may, in addition to the limited form of cross-examination by the party calling him, be contradicted by the evidence of other witnesses and, with the leave of the judge, be contradicted by the witness's own previous statement.

Section 3 of the Criminal Procedure Act 1865 This provision replaces s 22 of the Common Law Procedure Act 1854. Neither provision replaces the common law which is considered to be broader than these statutory provisions. This was highlighted in *R v Thompson* above where the Court of Appeal decided that the silence of the witness was sufficient to make her hostile at common law but that strictly the witness did not fall within the statutory definition of that term. Lord Widgery CJ:

J   'We think this matter must be dealt with by the provisions of the common law in regard to recalcitrant witnesses. Quite apart from what is said in section 3, the common law did recognise that pressure could be brought to bear upon witnesses who refused to cooperate and perform their duties . . . The short question after all is: was the judge right in allowing counsel to cross examine in the sense of asking leading questions? . . . it seems to us that he was right and there is no reason to suppose that the subsequent statutory intervention into this subject has in any way destroyed or removed the basic common law right of the judge in his discretion to allow cross examination when a witness proves to be hostile.'

Section 3 of the Criminal Procedure Act 1865 provides as follows:

S   'A party producing a witness shall not be allowed to impeach his credit by general evidence of bad character; but he may, in case the witness shall, in the opinion of the judge prove adverse, contradict him by other evidence, or, leave of the judge, prove that he has made at other times a statement inconsistent with his testimony; but before such last mentioned proof can be given the circumstances of the supposed statement sufficient to designate the particular occasion, must be mentioned to the witness, and he must be asked whether or not he has made such statement.'

Points to note with regard to this Act are:

- The 1865 Act, despite its unfortunate name, is applicable to both civil and criminal cases.
- The Act uses the expression 'adverse'. This expression has been construed as meaning 'hostile' only, and does not include 'unfavourable' witnesses.

In *Greenough v Eccles* (1859) 28 LJCP 160, Williams J said:

> **J** 'The section [s 3 of the 1865 Act] lays down three rules as to the power of a party to discredit his own witness, first, he shall not be allowed to impeach his credit by general evidence of bad character, secondly, he may contradict him by other evidence, thirdly, he may prove that he has made at other times a statement inconsistent with his present testimony . . . it is impossible to suppose that the legislature could have really intended to impose any fetter whatever on the right of the party to contradict his own witness by other evidence relevant to the issue – a right not only fully established by authority but founded on the plainest good sense . . . the section requires the judge to form an opinion that the witness is adverse, before the right to contradict or prove that he has made inconsistent statements is to be allowed to operate. This is reasonable and indeed necessary if the word, "adverse" means "hostile" but wholly unreasonable and unnecessary if it means "unfavourable".'

'On these grounds, I think the preferable construction is, that, in case the witness shall, in the opinion of the judge, prove "hostile", the party producing him may not only contradict him by other witnesses, as he might heretofore have done, and may still do, if the witness is unfavourable, but may also, by leave of the judge, prove that he has made inconsistent statements . . .'

- The section lays down the general common law prohibition on the party impeaching his witness.
- The judge in his discretion decides whether the witness is hostile in accordance with the definition as stated earlier, namely that the witness is not desirous of speaking the truth, and shows animosity towards the party calling the witness.
- The hostile witness may be contradicted by other evidence which is inconsistent with his testimony such as the testimony of another witness (similar to an unfavourable witness).
- The hostile witness may be questioned by the party calling him about the inconsistencies in his statement.
- The hostile witness, with the leave of the judge, may be contradicted by his own previous out-of-court statement, but before this is done the circumstances of the statement must be mentioned to the witness and he must be asked whether he made the statement.
- At common law, the evidential value of admitting the out-of-court statement is to establish the inconsistency in the testimony and thereby to discredit the witness. The out-of-court statement was treated as evidence of the inconsistency of the witness. It was a misdirection at common law to direct the jury that they may choose to rely on either the testimony or the statement. In *R v White* (1922) 17 Cr App R 60, on a charge of riotous assembly, a number

of prosecution witnesses who made unsworn statements to the police implicating the defendant, retracted their statements in court and declared that the defendant did not participate in the riot. In his summing up the judge directed the jury to choose between the sworn testimony and the unsworn statements. Following a conviction and an appeal, the Court of Appeal allowed his appeal and quashed his conviction owing to the misdirection.

- In civil cases, s 6(3) and (5) of the Civil Evidence Act 1995 declare that the out-of-court, contradictory statement shall be evidence of any fact stated therein. In other words, both the testimony and the contradictory statement will be put to the tribunal of fact, who will then decide accordingly.

Section 6(3) of the Civil Evidence Act 1995 provides as follows:

'Where in the case of civil proceedings section 3 … of the Criminal Procedure Act 1865 applies, which makes provision as to –
(a) how far a witness may be discredited by the party producing him,
(b) the proof of contradictory statements made by the witness, and
(c) cross examination as to previous statements in writing,
this Act does not authorise the adducing of evidence of a previous inconsistent or contradictory statement otherwise than in accordance with those sections.
This is without prejudice to any provision made by rules of court under s 3 above . . .'
5. 'Nothing in this section shall be construed as preventing a statement of any description referred to above from being admissible by virtue of section 1 as evidence of the matters stated.'

- In criminal cases, s 119 of the Criminal Justice Act 2003 enacts that where the witness testifies and the out-of-court, contradictory statement is admitted in court, the latter will be treated as evidence of the facts stated, ie the effect is similar to civil cases, the statement is treated as an exception to the hearsay rule.

Section 119(1) of the Criminal Evidence Act 2003 provides as follows:

'If in criminal proceedings a person gives oral evidence and –
(a) he admits making a previous inconsistent statement, or
(b) a previous inconsistent statement made by him is proved by virtue of section 3, 4 or 5 of the Criminal Procedure Act 1865
the statement is admissible as evidence of any matter stated of which oral evidence by him would be admissible.'

The effect of s 119(1) is that the jury may choose to rely on either the testimony of the witness or the out-of-court statement. This is a confirmation of the direction in *R v White* (see above).

- Where a party is aware before the witness is called to testify, that his witness wishes to change his testimony or is unwilling to assist the court, but the party nevertheless calls the witness to testify, it is a question of degree as to whether the witness ought to be treated as

hostile if he does not come up to proof. In other words, the question that arises in these cases is whether the twin aims of persuading the witness to return to his original statement and drawing attention to the inconsistencies regarding the witness's version of events can be achieved. This is a question for the judge to exercise at his discretion.

- In *R v Dat* [1998] Crim LR 488, the variation in the witness's version of events was in the detail only and the prosecution witness had merely failed to give evidence supporting the Crown's case.

- On the other hand, in *R v Honeyghon* [1999] Crim LR 221, the Court of Appeal decided that where the prosecution was aware in advance of the trial that there was little hope of the witness returning to his original statement but the witness was called to testify, the judge should not have exercised his discretion to classify the witness as hostile. In a gang fight one person was killed. The defendants were charged with murder. There were a number of witnesses to the fight. Two witnesses agreed to speak to the police but refused to make written statements. A third witness made a written statement to the police implicating the defendant but refused to answer any questions at the committal proceedings. At the Crown Court trial the witness said that she could not remember anything. The prosecution counsel applied to treat these witnesses as hostile, despite defence objection. The witnesses were cross-examined by the Crown about their earlier statements. The defendant was convicted and appealed. The Court of Appeal allowed the appeal and quashed the conviction.

6.2.4 Previous consistent statements (self-serving or narrative statements or the rule against manufactured evidence)

The general rule that is applicable to both civil and criminal cases, is that once the witness called by the party has testified in chief about an assertion,

- that witness may not be asked in chief whether he had made a statement repeating the assertion to another person
- the party calling the witness is not entitled to adduce evidence of the assertion
- the third party recipient of the assertion may not be called to testify that the witness had narrated the assertion to him.

For example, W, an eye witness has testified as to the facts that he perceived. W may not be asked by the party calling him whether he repeated the assertion to X. Likewise, the statement made to X may not be adduced and X may not be called to testify to the effect that W had told him of the relevant facts.

The rationale behind the general rule of the prohibition of such evidence is to avoid the ease with which such evidence may be manufactured by merely repeating the assertion several times in order to admit the evidence several times. In addition, the general bar on the adduction of such evidence saves time and costs by shortening proceedings because such narrative evidence is superfluous in any event. The evidence has already been admitted through the original witness; the repetition of such evidence does not add to the accuracy or reliability of such evidence. Indeed, such narrative evidence has the potential to lead to a multiplicity of collateral issues which are capable of confusing the jury.

The general rule is sometimes referred to as the rule in *Corke v Corke and Cook* [1958] 1 All ER 224. In this case, H, a husband, who was separated from his wife, W, had petitioned for a divorce on the ground of W's adultery with the co-respondent, Mr Cook, a lodger. At about midnight, H and an inquiry agent confronted W in Mr Cook's bedroom and accused her of having recently committed adultery with Mr Cook. W denied this and about 10 minutes later she telephoned her doctor requesting that both she and Mr Cook be examined to ascertain whether they had recently had sexual intercourse. The doctor declined because such an examination could have been inconclusive. W was refused permission to adduce evidence of the request and refusal by the doctor and on appeal the court decided that the evidence was correctly excluded. Sellers LJ:

> **J** 'To what issue does this item of evidence go? It does nothing to prove the condition of either the female or male organ respectively of the parties involved. It does nothing to disprove the intercourse that H alleged. The most that could be said is that W was showing a belief in her story and adding some reason why the court should believe her . . . W's conduct and statement cannot be regarded as revealing consciousness of innocence. They reveal at the most a consciousness that the doctor would not find any physical proof of guilt. I apprehend that the dishonest may be resourceful in giving an air of innocence to their transaction . . . Were it to be held otherwise, one wonders where ingenuity in bolstering up a witness's evidence would stop.'

This general rule is subject to a number of exceptions in both civil and criminal cases.

1. Complaints

The common law that was applicable to criminal cases only was that on charges of sexual offences the terms of a complaint that were made by the victim may be narrated by both the victim and the person to whom the complaint was made. For example, on a charge of a sexual nature, the victim, V, makes a complaint to X to the effect that D, the defendant, was responsible for a sexual assault on her. Obviously V may narrate the events at the time of the assault; V may also testify that she told X about the assault and that D did it, X may testify that she received the complaint from V and repeat the terms of the complaint including the fact that V told her that D did it.

The terms of the complaint were admissible to prove the consistency of the conduct of the complainant with the testimony of the complainant, and where consent is in issue, to negative such consent.

CASE EXTRACT

R v Lillyman [1896] 2 QB 167

The defendant was charged with attempted rape and indecent assault. The employer of the victim (maid) was allowed to narrate the terms of the complaint made to her shortly after the incident. Following a conviction the defendant appealed and the appeal was dismissed on the ground that the complaint was correctly admitted in court. Hawkins J:

> J 'It is necessary in the first place to have a clear understanding as to the principles upon which evidence of such complaint, not on oath, nor made in the presence of the prisoner, nor forming part of the *res gestae* can be admitted. It clearly is not admitted as evidence of the facts complained of; those facts must therefore be established, if at all, on oath by the prosecutrix or other credible witness and strictly speaking evidence of them ought to be given before evidence of the complaint is admitted. The complaint can only be used as evidence of the consistency of the conduct of the prosecutrix with the story told by her in the witness box and as being consistent with her consent to that of which she complains . . . The evidence can be legitimately used only for the purpose of enabling the jury to judge for themselves whether the conduct of the woman was consistent with her testimony on oath given in the witness box . . . we think that it is the duty of the judge to impress upon the jury in every case that they are not entitled to make use of the complaint as any evidence whatever of those facts, or for any other purpose than that we have stated.'

Two conditions are required to be satisfied in order to render the complaint admissible:

(a) The complaint must have been made at the earliest opportunity that reasonably presented itself.

(b) The complaint must not have been made in response to any threat or intimidatory inquiry or leading questions.

CASE EXTRACT

R v Osborne [1905] 1 KB 551

The defendant was charged with indecent assault on a girl aged 12. Evidence was given by another girl, aged 11, to the effect that shortly before the incident, she had left the victim with the defendant, arranging to return soon. On her way back, she met the victim running home and asked her, 'Why are you going home? Why did you not wait until I came back?' The answer from the victim incriminated the defendant. On conviction the appeal was dismissed. Ridley J:

> **J** 'It appears to us that the mere fact that the statement is made in answer to a question in such cases is not of itself sufficient to make it inadmissible as a complaint. Questions of a suggestive or leading character will, indeed, have that effect and will render it inadmissible . . . In each case the decision on the character of the question put, as well as other circumstances, such as the relationship of the question to the complainant must be left to the discretion of the presiding judge. If the circumstances indicate that, but for the questioning there probably would have been no voluntary complaint, the answer is inadmissible. If the question merely anticipates a statement which the complainant was about to make, it is not rendered inadmissible by the fact that the questioner happens to speak first . . . it appears that in accordance with principle such complaints are admissible not merely as negating consent but because they are consistent with the story of the prosecutrix.'

Modern position: Sections 120(4) and (7) of the Criminal Justice Act 2003 Sections 120(4), (7) and (8) supersede the common law in this context and create two radical changes to the law concerning complaints. The first is that the complaint concerns any offence with which the defendant is charged and is no longer restricted to offences of a sexual nature. The second major change is that if the complaint becomes admissible, the complaint shall be treated as evidence of the truth as opposed to merely being evidence of consistency.

Section 120(4) provides as follows:

'A previous statement by a witness is admissible as evidence of any matter stated of which oral evidence by him would be admissible, if –
(a) any of the following three conditions is satisfied, and
(b) while giving evidence the witness indicates that to the best of his belief he made the statement, and to the best of his belief it states the truth.'

Section 120(7) provides as follows:

'The third condition is that –

(a) the witness claims to be a person against whom an offence has been committed,

(b) the offence is one to which the proceedings relate,

(c) the statement consists of a complaint made by the witness (whether to a person in authority or not) about conduct which would, if proved, constitute the offence or part of the offence,

(d) the complaint was made as soon as could reasonably be expected after the alleged conduct,

(e) the complaint was not made as a result of a threat or a promise, and

(f) before the statement is adduced the witness gives oral evidence in connection with its subject matter.'

Section 120(8) enacts:

'For the purposes of subsection (7) the fact that the complaint was elicited (for example, by a leading question) is irrelevant unless a threat or a promise was involved.'

Additional points concerning these statutory provisions are:

- The witness is required to make the declaration laid down in s 120(4)(b).

- The complainant is required to testify in the proceedings. It is immaterial whether the complainant gives sworn or unsworn evidence.

- Section 120(7)(c) enacts that the complaint is required to involve conduct that, if proved, will 'constitute the offence or part of the offence'. The purpose of this provision is to ensure that only relevant complaints that focus on the offence are admissible. On a charge of assault, the fact that the victim states that an unfortunate event occurred to him without indicating that he was assaulted, would not constitute a complaint.

- The complaint is required to be made recently; see s 120(7)(d). The common law adopted a similar principle and this test would involve the discretion of the judge to determine whether there is sufficient evidence that the complaint was made within a reasonable period of time after the event. In *R v O* [2006] Crim EWCA 556, the Court of Appeal decided that the particular circumstances of each case are required to be considered and in particular to whom the complaint was made. In this case the charge was sexual assault by a stepfather over a period of eight years. The victim had first complained to a school friend and that friend's mother and following a period of some four months, she complained to her elder brother during a family row. The Court of Appeal decided that the trial judge had correctly admitted the complaints.

- The condition laid down in s 120(7)(e) is the same as the common law and s 120(7)(f) states the order of events regarding the statement which must follow the testimony of the complainant.

2. Statements forming part of the *res gestae*

The rule is that a witness's testimony may be confirmed by a repetition of the evidence by the same witness or a third party if it forms part of the same transaction or story or the *res gestae* At common law and under s 118(4) of the Criminal Justice Act 2003, such evidence was admissible as an exception to narrative statements and today is admissible as evidence of the facts stated. See later.

Section 118(4) provides:

> **S** 'Any rule of law under which in criminal proceedings a statement is admissible as evidence of any matter stated if –
> (a) the statement was made by a person so emotionally overpowered by an event that the possibility of concoction or distortion can be disregarded,
> (b) the statement accompanied an act which can be properly evaluated as evidence only if considered in conjunction with the statement, or
> (c) the statement relates to a physical sensation or a mental state (such as intention or emotion).'

3. Rebuttal of a suggestion of recent fabrication

At common law, the rule is that, under cross-examination, if it has been suggested that the witness has recently (ie, within a specified period) fabricated his story, the examiner-in-chief, may rebut the suggestion under re-examination of the witness. In other words, in both civil and criminal cases, the party calling the witness is entitled to adduce evidence to rebut a suggestion made by the cross-examiner that the witness has fabricated his story.

But if the witness's testimony is attacked generally by the cross-examiner to show his unreliability as a witness, this exception to the rule against narratives will not entitle the examiner-in-chief to call rebutting evidence. In order to attract this exception, the nature of the cross-examination is required to be equivalent to a submission that the witness's story is a recent invention.

R v Oyesiku (1971) 56 Cr App R 240, in this case the defendant was charged with assaulting an officer in the execution of his duty. The defence was self-defence. The defendant's wife testified to the effect that the police officer was the aggressor. It was put to the defendant's wife that she had prepared her evidence in collusion with her husband (the defendant). The judge had refused to allow defence counsel to adduce evidence to show that the witness had made a consistent statement to her solicitor after her husband's arrest and before she had time to see or contact him. The defendant was convicted and appealed and the appeal was allowed because the judge had ruled incorrectly. Karminski LJ:

J 'Our attention has . . . been drawn to a recent decision in the High Court of Australia, *Nominal Defendant v Clements* (1961) 104 CLR 476. I desire to read only one passage from the full judgment of Dixon CJ. He said this: "The rule of evidence under which it was let in is well recognised and of long standing. If the credit of a witness is impugned as to some material fact to which he deposes upon the ground that his account is a late invention or has been lately devised or reconstructed, even though not with conscious honesty, that makes admissible a statement to the same effect as the account he gave as a witness, if it was made by the witness contemporaneously with the event or at a time sufficiently early to be inconsistent with the suggestion that his account is a late invention or reconstruction. But, inasmuch as the rule forms a definite exception to the general principle excluding statements made out of court and admits a possibly self-serving statement made by the witness, great care is called for in applying it. The judge at the trial must determine for himself upon the conduct of the trial before him whether a case for applying the rule of evidence has arisen and, from the nature of the matter, if there be an appeal, great weight should be given to his opinion by the appellate court. It is evident however that the judge at the trial must exercise care in assuring himself not only that the account given by the witness in his testimony is attacked on the ground of recent invention or reconstruction or that a foundation for such an attack has been laid by the party, but also that the contents of the statement are in fact to the like effect as his account given in his evidence and that having regard to the time and circumstances in which it was made it rationally tends to answer the attack. It is obvious that it may not be easy sometimes to be sure that counsel is laying a foundation for impugning the witness's account of a material incident or fact as a recently invented, devised or reconstructed story. Counsel himself may proceed with a subtlety which is the outcome of caution in pursuing what may prove a dangerous course. That is one reason why the trial judge's opinion has a peculiar importance."

. . . That judgment of the Chief Justice of Australia, although technically not binding upon us, is a decision of the greatest persuasive power, and one which this Court gratefully accepts as a correct statement of the law.'

At common law, the effect of admitting the rebutting evidence was to establish the consistency of the witness; whereas today, in both civil and criminal cases, the effect of admitting the rebutting evidence is to establish the truth of the matters stated. However, in both civil and criminal cases the pre-conditions for admitting the evidence are the same as the common law.

Civil cases. In civil cases where rebutting evidence is admitted, the evidence is admitted under an exception to the hearsay rule.

Section 6(2) of the Civil Evidence Act 1995 provides as follows:

'A party who has called or intends to call a person as a witness in civil proceedings may not in those proceedings adduce evidence of a previous statement made by that person, except –

(a) with the leave of the court, or

(b) for the purpose of rebutting a suggestion that his evidence has been fabricated.

This shall not be construed as preventing a witness statement (that is, a written statement of oral evidence which a party to the proceedings intends to lead) from being adopted by a witness in giving evidence or treated as evidence.'

Criminal case In criminal cases s 120(2) of the Criminal Justice Act 2003 lays down the modern rule.

Section 120(2) provides:

'If a previous statement by the witness is admitted as evidence to rebut a suggestion that his oral evidence has been fabricated, that statement is admissible as evidence of any matter stated of which oral evidence by the witness would be admissible.'

4. Previous statements of identification

The principle of law here at common law is that a prior identification of the defendant after the commission of the crime, but before the trial (perhaps at an identification parade) may be received in evidence either from the witness himself or another person who was present at the time of the identification.

It not infrequently happens that a witness who had made a prior identification of the defendant several months before the trial, may have some doubt at the trial whether the defendant was the same person who was selected at the earlier identification, or the witness may have completely forgotten what took place earlier. In these circumstances, someone present at the prior identification is entitled to testify as to the facts. (It should be noted that this exception is distinct from the identification of the defendant at the time of the alleged commission of the crime, ie the *Turnbull* guidelines; see later.)

ASE EXTRACT

R v Osborne and Virtue [1973] QB 678

The defendants were convicted of robbery. Both defendants had been picked out at an identification parade four days after the robbery. Osborne was identified by Mrs Brookes (Mrs B); Mrs Head (Mrs H) identified Mr Virtue. At the trial some seven-and-a-

CONTINUED ▶

half months later, Mrs B said that she could not remember having picked out anyone at the parade. Mrs H first said that she thought Mr Virtue was the man she had picked out at the parade, but later said that she did not think that he was the same man who was charged. The police inspector in charge of the identification parade then testified that the women had identified the defendants. On conviction the defendants appealed. The Court of Appeal dismissed the appeal on the ground that the police inspector's evidence was admissible. Lawton LJ:

> **J** 'All that Mrs Brookes had said was that she did not remember . . . that is very understandable after a delay of 7½ months . . . One asks oneself as a matter of commonsense why, when a witness has forgotten what she did, evidence should not be given by another witness with a better memory to establish what, in fact she did when the events were fresh in her mind. Much the same situation arises with regard to Mrs Head . . . appearances can change after 7½ months . . . accused persons often look much smarter in the dock than they do when they are first arrested.'

Likewise in *R v McCay* [1990] Crim LR 338, a police officer present at an identification parade was called to testify that a witness had identified the defendant by saying, 'it is number 8' when identifying the defendant at the parade from behind a two-way mirror.

Section 120(4) and (5) of the Criminal Justice Act 2003 enact that such identification is evidence as the facts stated; s 120(4) was mentioned earlier.

Section 120(5) states: 'The first condition is that the statement identifies or describes a person, object or place.'

The effect is that the common law rule has been extended to objects and places. In addition the testimony of the second witness is evidence of the matters stated.

5. Defendant's reaction when first taxed by incriminating material

Evidence of the defendant's reaction when he is arrested or confronted with incriminating material is admissible in evidence as a relevant fact. Accordingly, a denial or exculpatory statement made by the defendant in such circumstances is admissible in order to establish the defendant's consistency; see *R v Storey* (1968) 52 Cr App R 334, below. (It should be noted that this rule exists as part of a wider principle involving the defendant's reaction generally. The defendant's reaction may be incriminating to the defendant in which case the evidence may be admitted as an informal admission. In addition the defendant's reaction may be both exculpatory and incriminating. These are known as mixed statements. Both admissions and mixed statements are admissible as evidence of the facts stated under exceptions to the hearsay rule; see later.)

CASE EXTRACT

R v Storey (1968) 52 Cr App R 334

The defendant was charged with possession of cannabis in her flat. When her premises were searched and the cannabis found, she told the police that it had belonged to a man who brought it there against her will. This evidence was admitted. At the close of the prosecution's case the defence made a no case submission which was rejected and the defendant was convicted. She appealed on the grounds that as her explanation afforded her a complete defence to the charge, the no case submission should not have been rejected. The Court of Appeal decided that the judge was correct in his ruling for the evidence was only as to consistency of the defendant's conduct and not of the facts stated. In short, the statement was admissible as to the credibility of the witness only. Widgery LJ:

> **J** 'A statement made voluntarily by an accused person to the police is evidence in the trial because of its vital relevance as showing the reaction of the accused when first taxed with incriminating facts. If, of course, the accused admits the offence, then as a matter of shorthand one says that the admission is proof of guilt and indeed in the end, it is. But if the accused makes a statement which does not amount to an admission, the statement is not strictly evidence of the truth of what was said but is evidence of the reaction of the accused which forms part of the general picture to be considered by the jury.'

In *R v Pearce* (1979) 69 Cr App R 365, the principle was extended to cover exculpatory statements made to the police on subsequent occasions although such statements may carry less weight compared with a statement made when 'first taxed'. However, it must not be assumed that the time for making the statement does not matter because if a carefully prepared statement is made by the defendant, the statement may lack weight in this context and may be excluded in its entirety. In *R v Newsome* [1980] 71 Cr App R 325, the defendant prior to a third interview with the police had conferred with his solicitor and drafted a statement which he submitted at the third interview. The judge excluded this self-serving statement on the ground that it lacked any weight and the Court of Appeal upheld the decision of the trial judge.

The Criminal Justice Act 2003 does not modify this common law rule with the effect that the principle is governed exclusively by the common law.

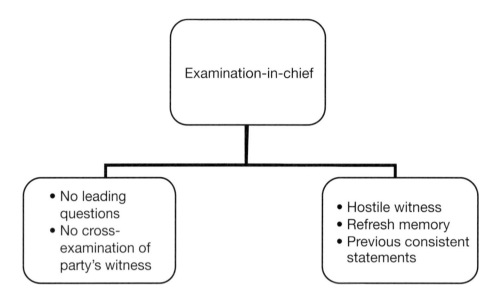

■ Figure 6.1 Rule against previous consistent statements subject to exceptions

6.3 Cross-examination

Cross-examination is the process where the opponent's witness is subjected to questioning. The court may be given a version of facts which support the case of the party calling the witness. It is possible that with clever cross-examination a different version of events may emerge. The cross-examiner will test the accuracy of the events presented to the court. The purpose of the cross-examination is twofold:

(a) to weaken, qualify or destroy the opponent's case, ie the case of the party calling the witness (broadly referred to as cross-examination as to credit)

(b) to elicit, through the opponent's witness, facts that are favourable to the cross-examiner (referred to as cross-examination as to issue).

Leading questions may be asked and the witness is required to answer all questions put to him, except questions related to the following:

(i) where the witness is entitled to claim and does claim a privilege, or the witness is protected by public interest immunity

(ii) where the evidence or information sought by the questioner constitutes inadmissible evidence. Clearly, cross-examination is subject to the rules of admissibility and if the evidence is inadmissible, the need for the witness to answer the question, such as questions concerning the bad character of the witness or the defendant which are not admissible under one of the gateways laid down in the Criminal Justice Act 2003, is dispensed with (see later)

(iii) the judge has a discretion to excuse an answer to a question which he considers is not relevant to the issue or the witness's credit and is oppressive. The scope of this power will depend on the line of cross-examination, the style of questioning, the demeanour of the witness and the extent of repetition. This would vary with the facts of each case.

6.3.1 Sections 41–43 of the Youth Justice and Criminal Evidence Act 1999

A further exception to the requirement that a witness is required to answer questions put in cross-examination, was originally enacted by s 2 of the Sexual Offences (Amendment) Act 1976, which has since been repealed and replaced by Chapter III or ss 41–43 of the Youth Justice and Criminal Evidence Act 1999. The Sexual Offences (Amendment) Act 1976 proved to be too restrictive. The Act was limited to rape charges only and prohibited the cross-examiner from adducing evidence or questioning the complainant in respect of any sexual experience with persons other than the defendant, except with the leave of the judge. The test for granting leave was based on a test of unfairness to the defendant to refuse leave. This was interpreted to mean whether the jury will consider the complainant's testimony in a different light; see *R v Viola* [1982] 1 WLR 1138. Omitted from the protection of the complainant under the 1976 Act was the cross-examination of the complainant regarding sexual experience with the defendant.

Chapter III of the Youth Justice and Criminal Evidence Act 1999 introduced provisions that are much broader and more comprehensive than its predecessor. The principles enacted in the 1999 Act are activated where four conditions are satisfied:

1. The defendant is charged with a 'sexual offence', as defined in s 62 of the Act. Such an offence is broadly defined in the Sexual Offences Act 2003.

2. There is a prohibition on the cross-examiner asking questions or adducing evidence about the 'sexual behaviour' of the complainant, except with the leave of the judge.

The definition of 'sexual behaviour' is laid down in s 42(1)((c) of the Act and means 'any sexual behaviour or other sexual experience whether or not involving the accused or other person . . .' The effect is that any sexual activity of the complainant, either with other persons or on his or her own, will constitute sexual behaviour. But allegations of previous false statements concerning sexual matters, whether against the defendant and/or a third party, are not questions about the sexual behaviour of the complainant and are therefore outside the protection of the 1999 Act. In *R v T* [2002] 1 All ER 683, the defendant was charged with indecent assault and rape on his niece between 1987 and 1989. The complaint was not made until 1999. The defence case was that none of the allegations had taken place. At a preparatory hearing, the defendant applied for leave to cross-examine the complainant about two occasions in 1987 and 1990 when she made

false allegations of a sexual nature against other members of her family but not against the defendant. The judge refused to grant leave and the Court of Appeal reversed the decision on the ground that the questions were not 'about' the sexual behaviour of the complainant but to the veracity of her statements in the past. Keene LJ:

> J 'It seems to this court that normally questions or evidence about false statements in the past by a complainant about sexual assaults or such questions or evidence about the failure to complain about the alleged assault which is the subject matter of the charge, while complaining about other sexual assaults, are not ones 'about' any sexual behaviour of the complainant. They relate not to her sexual behaviour but to her statements in the past or to her failure to complain.'

The court also decided that defence counsel who makes the application for leave to cross-examine the complainant is required to have a proper evidential basis for making the allegation of a false statement and the judge is entitled to seek such assurances. Keene LJ:

> J 'It would be professionally improper for those representing the defendant to put such questions in order to elicit evidence about the complainant's past sexual behaviour as such under the guise of previous false complaints. But in any case the defence must have a proper evidential basis for asserting that any such previous statement was (a) made and (b) untrue ... The judge is entitled to seek assurances from the defence that it has a proper basis for asserting that the statement was made and untrue.'

3. The evidence that the cross-examiner wishes to adduce or the questioning of the cross-examiner relate to a relevant issue in the case. The test regarding a relevant issue is laid down in s 41(4), '. . . if it appears to the court to be reasonable to assume that the purpose (or main purpose) for which it would be adduced or asked is to establish or elicit material for impugning the credibility of the complainant as a witness.' This involves a question of how far the matter is relevant to a fact in issue. This is a question for the judge to decide. The more general the allegation of sexual activity, the more remote the issue is likely to be. In *R v White* [2004] All ER (D) 103, the Court of Appeal decided that a general allegation that the complainant was a prostitute will be too vague to be directly related to the facts in issue of consent to sexual activity, and is more likely to amount to evidence of impugning the credibility of the complainant.

4. The judge is required to grant leave to the cross-examiner only if the tests laid down in s 41(2) have been satisfied. Section 41(2) creates a two-tier test for the granting of leave to cross-examine the complainant about his or her sexual behaviour.

- Section 41(2)(b) enacts that 'a refusal of leave might have the result of rendering unsafe' the verdict of the jury.

- Section 41(2)(a) refers to the relevant issue in subsections (3) and (5) of the Act.

Section 41(3)(a)–(c) of the 1999 Act identifies the tests as to whether the evidence or questions raised by the cross-examiner relate to a relevant issue in the trial.

Section 41(3) enacts as follows:

'This subsection applies if the evidence or question relates to a relevant issue in the case and either –

(a) that issue is not an issue of consent; or

(b) it is an issue of consent and the sexual behaviour of the complainant to which the evidence or question relates is alleged to have taken place at or about the same time as the event which is the subject matter of the charge against the accused; or

(c) it is an issue of consent and the sexual behaviour of the complainant to which the evidence or question relates is alleged to have been, in any respect, so similar –

(i) to any sexual behaviour of the complainant which (according to evidence adduced or to be adduced by or on behalf of the accused) took place as part of the event which is the subject matter of the charge against the accused, or

(ii) to any other sexual behaviour of the complainant which (according to such evidence) took place at or about the same time as the event, that the similarity cannot reasonably be explained as a coincidence.'

Section 41(5) deals with evidence in rebuttal where the prosecution raises evidence of the sexual behaviour of the complainant. The evidence or question 'would go no further than is necessary to enable the evidence adduced by the prosecution to be rebutted or explained by or on behalf of the accused.'

Section 41(3)(a) of the 1999 Act

The test in s 41(3)(a) of the Act (see above) isolates and identifies the relevant issue as one that does not involve 'consent'.

The issue of consent is defined in s 42(1) (b) as 'any issue whether the complainant in fact consented to the conduct constituting the offence with which the accused is charged (and accordingly does not include any issue as to the belief of the accused that the complainant so consented)'. Thus, the 'issue of consent' is distinct from the defendant's mistaken belief that the complainant consented. Thus, an allegation of mistaken identity on the part of the complainant is not an issue of consent. Likewise, an allegation of a false complaint that the defendant had raped the complainant is not an issue of consent. In *R v F* [2005] 1 WLR 2848, on charges of rape of the defendant's stepdaughter between the ages of 7 and 16 years old, the defendant alleged that the complainant fabricated the allegations. The parties lived together as adults and

shared a full consensual sexual relationship. The defendant alleged that the complainant was motivated by a desire for revenge following his decision to end the relationship. The trial judge refused to allow the defendant to adduce evidence, or ask questions about the fact that the complainant had made sexually explicit video recordings during the course of their relationship. The Court of Appeal allowed the appeal on the ground that the evidence was relevant under s 41(3)(a) of the 1999 Act. The court also decided that once the criteria for leave were satisfied the judge does not have a discretion to refuse to admit the evidence. Judge LJ:

> **J** 'If the complainant enjoyed a full and happy adult relationship with the appellant, neither being raped nor dutifully submitting to his dominant control, although not amounting to positive proof that she had not been abused as a child, the relationship would have called into question how she could ever have brought herself into enthusiastic participation for a number of years with her former abuser.'

In *R v Mokrecovas* [2002] 1 Cr App R 20, the charge was rape and the issue was consent, but the defendant wanted to cross-examine the complainant under s 41(3)(a) because she lied as to her allegation that she did not consent in order to mitigate the effects of being drunk and staying out late without permission when she returned to her home and was faced by her angry parents. The defendant wished to adduce evidence that the complainant had twice had intercourse with the defendant's brother within 12 hours of the disputed incident. The Court of Appeal decided that the trial judge had correctly exercised his discretion in refusing leave to cross-examine the complainant as to her sexual behaviour. There was no reason why the complainant could not have been cross-examined as to where she stayed that evening. Lord Woolf CJ:

> **J** 'We ask ourselves to what extent, if at all, is the defendant inhibited in suggesting that there was a motive for the complainant to tell untruths to her parents? How would the ability of the defendant to argue that the complainant had a motive to lie be improved if she were to be allowed to be cross examined to suggest that the brother had had sexual intercourse on two previous occasions? In our judgment, the position of the defendant would not be improved in any way. The refusal of leave to ask the specific questions that Mr Owen wishes to ask will not result in any lack of safety or unfairness in the proceedings or in any relevant issue not being explored.'

Section 41(3)(b) of the 1999 Act

Section 41(3(b) involves two criteria – the issue of *de facto* consent and the contemporaneity of the material ('at or about the same time') which the cross-examiner wishes to bring out and the facts supporting the charge. The explanatory notes accompanying the Act regard the expression 'at or about the same time' as used in the subsection as meaning not much longer than 24 hours before or after the alleged offence. This introduces an informal *res gestae* principle in interpreting the subsection. This subsection may include the complainant initiating consensual sexual activity with the defendant or third parties 24 hours before or after the circumstances constituting the charge in order to support the defence of consent.

Lord Steyn in *R v A* [2001] UKHL 25, said: 'An example covered by this provision would be where it is alleged that the complainant invited the accused to have sexual intercourse with her earlier in the evening . . . Section 41(3)(b) acknowledges by its own terms that previous sexual experience between a complainant and an accused may be relevant but then restricts the admission of such evidence by an extraordinarily narrow temporal restriction.'

Section 41(3)(c) of the 1999 Act

Section 41(3)(c)(i) involves an allegation by the cross-examiner of *de facto* consent on the part of the complainant and a similarity in the sexual behaviour of the complainant as part of the event, the subject-matter of the charge. Section 41(3)(c)(ii) involves consent and the complainant's sexual behaviour was similar to other sexual behaviour 'at or about the same time' (24 hours before or after the event constituting the charge) that the similarity cannot reasonably be explained as coincidence. Lord Steyn in *R v A* [2001] UKHL 25, provides an example, thus:

> **J** 'An example [of the third gateway] would be the case where the complainant says that the accused raped her; the accused says that the complainant consented and then after the act of intercourse tried to blackmail him by alleging rape; and the defence now wishes to ask the complainant whether on a previous occasion she similarly tried to blackmail the accused.'

In *R v T* [2004] EWCA Crim 1220, the defendant was charged with rape that was alleged to have occurred on a triangular climbing frame in the children's play area in a park. The defence was consent. The Court of Appeal decided that the trial judge had erred in failing to allow the defendant to adduce evidence that the same parties had consensual sexual relations on the same triangular climbing frame a few weeks earlier.

In the leading case *R v A* [2001] 3 All ER 1, the House of Lords reviewed the provisions enacted in ss 41–43 of the Youth Justice and Criminal Evidence Act 1999 and considered the extent to which these provisions are consistent with the Human Rights Act 1998. In this case the charge was rape. The accused person's defence was consent, or alternatively, belief in consent. The defendant and the complainant had a consensual sexual relationship about three weeks before the circumstances that constituted the alleged rape. The defendant was prevented from

cross-examining the complainant and adducing evidence as to her sexual behaviour. The House of Lords decided the following:

- The consensual sexual relationship between the defendant and the complainant three weeks before the alleged rape was admissible as to the belief in consent (within s 41(3)(a)) but not relevant as to the issue of consent itself.

- Further, a prior consensual sexual relationship between the defendant and the complainant is not irrelevant to the issue of consent, the subject matter of the proceedings.

- In addition, the test of admissibility under s 41(3)(c) is whether the evidence is so relevant to the issue of consent that to exclude it would endanger the fairness of the trial.

- Finally, the defendant is not allowed to cross-examine the complainant as to his or her sexual behaviour simply by raising the issue of belief in consent and consent as defences. Instead the judge is required to be satisfied that there is a proper foundation for pursuing leave to adduce such evidence or question the complainant.

Lord Steyn:

> **J** 'As a matter of common sense, a prior sexual relationship between the complainant and the accused may, depending on the circumstances, be relevant to the issue of consent. It is a species of prospectant evidence which may throw light on the complainant's state of mind. It cannot, of course, prove that she consented on the occasion in question. Relevance and sufficiency of proof are different things. The fact that the accused a week before the alleged murder threatened to kill the deceased does not prove an intent to kill on the day in question. But it is logically relevant to that issue. After all, to be relevant the evidence need merely have some tendency in logic and common sense to advance the proposition in issue. It is true that each decision to engage in sexual activity is always made afresh. On the other hand, the mind does not usually blot out all memories. What one has been engaged on in the past may influence what choice one makes on a future occasion. Accordingly, a prior relationship between a complainant and an accused may sometimes be relevant to what decision was made on a particular occasion.
>
> In order to assess whether s 41 of the 1999 Act is incompatible with the convention right to a fair trial, it is necessary to consider what evidence it excludes. The mere fact that it excludes some relevant evidence would not by itself amount to a breach of the fair trial guarantee. On the other hand, if the impact of s 41 is to deny the right to the accused in a significant range of cases from putting forward full and complete defences it may amount to a breach.

CONTINUED ▶

> **J** It is possible under s 3 of the [Human Rights] 1998 Act to read s 41 of the 1999 Act, and in particular s 41(3)(c), as subject to the implied provision that evidence or questioning which is required to ensure a fair trial under art 6 of the convention should not be treated as inadmissible. The result of such a reading would be that sometimes logically relevant sexual experiences between a complainant and an accused may be admitted under s 41(3)(c). On the other hand, there will be cases where previous sexual experience between a complainant and an accused will be irrelevant, e.g. an isolated episode distant in time and circumstances. Where the line is to be drawn must be left to the judgment of trial judges. On this basis a declaration on incompatibility can be avoided. If this approach is adopted, s 41 will have achieved a major part of its objective but its excessive reach will have been attenuated in accordance with the will of Parliament as reflected in s 3 of the 1998 Act. That is the approach I will adopt.
>
> It is of supreme importance that the effect of the speeches today should be clear to trial judges who have to deal with problems of the admissibility of questioning and evidence on alleged prior sexual experience between an accused and a complainant. The effect of the decision today is that under s 41(3)(c) of the 1999 Act, construed where necessary by applying the interpretative obligation under s 3 of the 1998 Act, and due regard always being paid to the importance of seeking to protect the complainant from indignity and from humiliating questions, the test of admissibility is whether the evidence (and questioning in relation to it) is nevertheless so relevant to the issue of consent that to exclude it would endanger the fairness of the trial under art 6 of the convention. If this test is satisfied the evidence should not be excluded.'

Section 43 of the 1999 Act provides that where a party wishes to make an application under s 41 for leave to adduce evidence or question the complainant about his or her sexual behaviour, the application is required to be heard in private and in the absence of the complainant.

The court is then required to state in open court, but in the absence of the jury, its reasons for giving or refusing leave. If leave is granted, the court is required to direct the extent to which evidence may be adduced or questions asked.

6.3.2 Chapter II – protection from cross-examination by the accused in person

Sections 34–39 of the Youth Justice and Criminal Evidence Act 1999 introduce a number of provisions designed to ensure that the defendant will not personally cross-examine the witness. In three types of case the defendant is not entitled to cross-examine in person certain witnesses.

Section 34 of the 1999 Act enacts that in respect of sexual offences (as defined in s 62) the defendant is not entitled to cross-examine in person the complainant in respect of that or any other offence. Section 35 prohibits the defendant from cross-examining in person a protected witness (as defined in s 35(2)) on a charge as laid down in s 35(3). Section 36 creates a residual category of cases, namely occasions where the prosecutor makes the application or the court of its own motion raises the issue and makes the direction. The test to be satisfied is laid down in s 36(2) and the factors to be taken into consideration are specified in s 36(3) of the 1999 Act.

Where the accused is prevented from cross-examining a witness in person, the court must (a) invite the accused to arrange for legal representation and notify the court within a specified time. If at the relevant time no legal representation is arranged, the court must consider whether in the interests of justice to appoint a qualified legal representative to act on behalf of the accused to cross-examine the witness; see s 38 of the 1999 Act.

Section 39 of the 1999 Act declares that where the accused is prevented from cross-examining a witness, the judge is required to give the jury a warning to ensure that the accused is not prejudiced by:

- any inferences that might be drawn from the fact that the accused was prevented from cross-examining the witness in person
- the fact that the cross-examination was carried out by a legal representative appointed by the court.

6.3.3 Omission to cross-examine

As a general rule if a party disagrees with, or does not wish to admit, a witness's version of events, he should test the witness's story under cross-examination.

Failure to cross-examine the witness generally will be taken to be acceptance of the witness's account and the party who did not call the witness will not be allowed:

- to attack the witness's testimony in his closing speech
- to put forward explanations of the issue.

In *R v Bircham* [1972] Crim LR 430, defence counsel had failed to cross-examine the co-defendant (who testified) and prosecution witnesses on the issue of whether they were the perpetrators of the crime. He had attempted to make this suggestion in his closing speech when the judge intervened and disallowed him. The Court of Appeal decided that the judge was entitled to intervene in the interests of justice.

Occasionally, situations arise where an omission to cross-examine a witness on an issue was caused by inadvertence on the part of counsel. The advocate simply forgets to raise the issue. This difficulty may be overcome by having the witness recalled to the witness box in the exercise of the judge's discretion and in the interests of justice.

However, in exceptional circumstances a party may consciously refrain from asking a witness questions under cross-examination and, at the same time, dispute or disagree with the assertions made by the witness. These are occasions when the witness's story is incredible in itself and the advocate tactically omits to question the witness; likewise, where counsel indicates that he is refraining from asking questions for the convenience of the witness but does not accept the witness's assertions, for example young children in contentious family matters, a distraught mother testifying as to the achievements of her deceased son.

6.3.4 Distinction between cross-examination as to issue and credit

A distinction is drawn by the courts as to whether a question asked by a cross-examiner relates to a fact in issue or the credit of a witness. The effect of the distinction is that in the former case, ie questions relating to issue, the answers of witnesses are not final and contradictory evidence may be adduced by the cross-examiner. Such contradictory answers are subject to the rules of admissibility. A fact in issue is one which relates directly to the issue of guilt or innocence in criminal cases or to liability in civil cases, whereas the answers to questions related to the credit of the witness are final, subject to a limited number of exceptions. The credibility of a witness's testimony depends on his knowledge of the facts, his intelligence, integrity and veracity. All questions which tend to expose the errors, omissions, inconsistencies and exaggerations of the witness's story relate to his credit.

The question whether or not a fact is relevant to a fact in issue has important implications to the parties in terms of the admissibility of the evidence. Deciding relevance is a difficult question for the judge to decide.

CASE EXTRACT

R v Funderburk [1990] 1 WLR 587

The defendant was charged with unlawful sexual intercourse with a girl under the age of 13. The victim gave a detailed description of the alleged act of intercourse including, during the incident, the loss of her virginity. The trial judge refused to allow the defendant to put questions to the complainant in cross-examination about an allegation that she told a potential witness that she (complainant) had had intercourse with other men. The trial judge also prevented the defendant from calling rebutting evidence, namely, the witness who heard the story. On conviction the defendant appealed claiming that the questions related to the facts in issue and not the credit of the witness. The court allowed the appeal and quashed the conviction. The question was intimately connected with the facts in issue. Henry J:

CONTINUED ▶

'Having heard a graphic account from the child's evidence in chief as to how she had lost her virginity, the jury might reasonably have wished to reappraise her evidence and her credibility if they had heard that on other occasions she had spoken of experiences which, if true, would indicate that she could not have been a virgin at the time of the incident she so vividly described. Her standing as a witness might have been reduced. Unchallenged, the descriptive details could give the account the stamp of truth; detail often adds verisimilitude, and it seems to us that it certainly would have here. If a detail of such significance is successfully challenged it can destroy both the account and the credit of the witness who gave it. Therefore, it is submitted that this is not a challenge which goes merely to credit but that the disputed questions go directly to the issue and not merely to a collateral fact.'

CASE EXTRACT

R v Edwards [1991] 2 All ER 266

The defendant was charged with robbery. The prosecution evidence consisted of police officers who testified that the defendant made oral admissions. The defendant refused to sign the interview notes claiming that the alleged admissions were fabrications. The defendant's counsel was prevented but wished to cross-examine the officers in respect of evidence given in a previous trial where the issue was again alleged fabrication of oral admissions. These defendants were acquitted, suggesting that the jury disbelieved the officers. On conviction the accused appealed. The court dismissed the appeal on the ground that the subject-matter of the cross-examination was not sufficiently relevant to the officers' credibility (collateral issue) to be admitted under an exception. The significant issue was that the court decided that the matter was not directly related to issue but credit. Lord Lane CJ:

'The test is primarily one of relevance, and this is so whether one is considering evidence in chief or questions in cross examination. To be admissible questions must be relevant to the issue before the court. Issues are of varying degrees of relevance or importance. A distinction has to be drawn between, on the one hand, the issue in the case upon which the jury will be pronouncing their verdict and, on the other hand, collateral issues of which the credibility of the witnesses

CONTINUED ▶

J

maybe one. Generally speaking, questions may be put to a witness as to any improper conduct of which he may have been guilty, for the purpose of testing his credit.

The limits to such questioning were defined by Sankey LJ in *Hobbs v Tinling & Co* [1929] 2 KB 1,

> "The court can always exercise its discretion to decide whether a question as to credit is one which the witness should be compelled to answer . . . in the exercise of its discretion the court should have regard to the following considerations: (1) Such questions are proper if they are of such a nature that the truth of the imputation conveyed by them would seriously affect the opinion of the court as to the credibility of the witness on the matter to which he testifies. (2) Such questions are improper if the imputation which they convey relates to matters so remote in time, or of such a character, that the truth of the imputation would not affect, or would affect in a slight degree, the opinion of the court as to the credibility of the witness on the matter to which he testifies. (3) Such questions are improper if there is a great disproportion between the importance of the imputation made against the witness's character and the importance of his evidence."

The distinction between the issue in the case and matters collateral to the issue is often difficult to draw, but it is of considerable importance. Where cross examination is directed at collateral issues such as the credibility of the witness, as a rule the answers of the witness are final and evidence to contradict them will not be permitted.

. . . The acquittal of a defendant in case A, where the prosecution case depended largely or entirely upon the evidence of a police officer, does not normally render that officer liable to cross examination as to credit in case B. But where a police officer who has allegedly fabricated an admission in case B, has also given evidence of an admission in case A, where there was an acquittal by virtue of which his evidence is demonstrated to have been disbelieved, it is proper that the jury in case B should be made aware of that fact. However, where the acquittal in case A does not necessarily indicate that the jury disbelieved the officer, such cross examination should not be allowed. In such a case the verdict of not guilty may mean no more than that the jury entertained some doubt about the prosecution case, not necessarily that they believed any witness was lying.

CONTINUED ▸

> **J** That leaves the second question, namely, whether it would have been proper to allow the defence to call evidence to contradict any answers given by the police officers in cross examination, in the unlikely event of those officers giving answers unfavourable to the defence? In our judgment this questioning would have been as to credit alone, that is to say, on a collateral issue. It would not have fallen within any exception to the general rule.'

CASE EXTRACT

R v Nagrecha [1997] 2 Cr App R 401

The charge was indecent assault. It was alleged that the defendant, the complainant's employer had indecently assaulted her on the first and only occasion that she worked for him. The defendant denied the assault. In cross-examination the complainant denied making unsubstantiated allegations of sexual impropriety against other men (and a previous employer). The trial judge refused to allow defence counsel to call rebutting evidence. On conviction the defendant appealed. The court allowed the appeal and quashed the conviction. The judge had erred in refusing to allow the rebutting evidence for the question related to issue. The jury may well have taken a different view of the complainant's testimony, including the alleged indecent assault. Rose LJ:

> **J** 'In our judgment, the answer to this appeal is, in the light of the authorities to which we have referred, that the judge ought to have permitted the defence to lead evidence from Mr Lee in the light of the complainant's denial in cross examination. Such evidence went not merely to credit, but to the heart of the case, in that it bore on the crucial issue as to whether or not there had been any indecent assault. As to that matter, only the complainant and the appellant were able to give evidence. In our judgment, that being so, the learned judge ought to have permitted the evidence to be called because it might well have led the jury to take a different view of the complainant's evidence.'

6.3.5 Sections 4 and 5 of the Criminal Procedure Act 1865 (previous inconsistent statements)

If a witness is challenged by the cross-examiner on the accuracy of his testimony and the witness repents, agrees with the cross-examiner and changes his testimony, this may constitute evidence on which the tribunal of fact may rely. In other words, the cross-examiner will succeed in getting the witness to testify in a way favourable to such party and the testimony may amount to evidence of the facts stated.

However, where the witness does not repent or does not admit making a contradictory statement, and the cross-examiner wishes to contradict the witness in respect of a matter in issue (as distinct from credit) by the witness's previous statement, he is entitled to utilize the provisions created by ss 4 and 5 of the Criminal Procedure Act 1865. This Act is applicable to both civil and criminal cases.

Section 4 of the Criminal Procedure Act 1865 provides:

'If a witness, upon cross examination as to a former statement made by him relative to the subject matter of the indictment or proceeding, and inconsistent with his testimony, does not distinctly admit that he has made such statement, proof may be given that he did in fact make it; but before such proof can be given the circumstances of the supposed statement, sufficient to designate the particular occasion, must be mentioned to the witness, and he must be asked whether or not he has made such statement.'

It is believed that this section is applicable in respect of an oral previous statement made by the witness and contradictory to his testimony. The subject-matter of contradiction is required to relate to a fact in issue. The section refers to the witness 'not distinctly admitting' the statement. This is a broad expression that covers a variety of situations ranging from a denial of the statement to evasive or vague or equivocal answers, such that the witness does not remember the events or indeed silence. The procedure that has to be adopted by the cross-examiner prior to contradiction, is that the circumstances concerning the particular occasion must be put to the witness.

Section 5 of the Criminal Procedure Act 1865 provides:

'A witness may be cross examined as to previous statements made by him in writing or reduced into writing relative to the subject matter of the indictment or proceeding, without such writing being shown to him; but if it is intended to contradict such witness by the writing, his attention must, before such contradictory proof can be given, be called to those parts of the writing which are to be used for the purpose of so contradicting him; provided always that it shall be competent for the judge at any time during the trial to require production of the writing for his inspection, and he may thereupon make such use of it for the purposes of the trial as he may think fit.'

The section deals with a statement of the witness in writing that is contradictory to his testimony. The section envisages two stages when the cross-examiner may resort to a previous inconsistent statement made by a witness in writing.

First, the cross-examiner may wish to retain the element of surprise, ie he may not wish to show that witness the previous statement. In order to achieve this tactical manoeuvre, he is entitled to

cross-examine the witness about the statement without contradicting the witness. In other words, the cross-examiner will be entitled to ask questions about the authorship of an inconsistent statement and to explore the extent to which the witness is prepared to change his sworn evidence to correspond with his statement. If the witness changes his testimony, this may be relied on by the tribunal of fact.

The second tactical ploy envisaged by s 5 is with regard to the contradiction of the witness's testimony. Before the witness is contradicted, his attention must be drawn to the relevant parts of the document and he is given a last opportunity to explain the discrepancy in his sworn statement and the document.

The proviso to s 5 does not give the judge an absolute discretion to do whatever he likes with the statement, but entitles the judge to call for the document whenever he wishes. Accordingly, the cross-examiner is required to have the document in his possession even though he does not wish to contradict the witness.

At common law the effect of admitting the previous statement under s 4 or 5 is that it is evidence only as to the inconsistency of the witness and was not evidence of the truth. In civil cases, the evidential value of the contradictory statement has been changed by statute and it is now evidence of the truth of the assertion; see s 6(3) and (5) of the Civil Evidence Act 1995.

Civil proceedings

Section 6(3) of the Civil Evidence Act 1995 provides as follows:

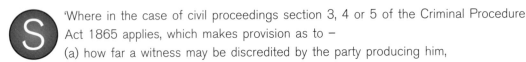

'Where in the case of civil proceedings section 3, 4 or 5 of the Criminal Procedure Act 1865 applies, which makes provision as to –
(a) how far a witness may be discredited by the party producing him,
(b) the proof of contradictory statements made by the witness, and
(c) cross examination as to previous statements in writing,
this Act does not authorise the adducing of evidence of a previous inconsistent or contradictory statement otherwise than in accordance with those sections.
This is without prejudice to any provision made by rules of court under s 3 above . . .'

6. 'Nothing in this section shall be construed as preventing a statement of any description referred to above from being admissible by virtue of section 1 as evidence of the matters stated.'

Criminal proceedings

In criminal proceedings, s 119 of the Criminal Justice Act 2003 has declared that the effect of the prior out-of-court statement contradicting the witness is evidence of the truth of the assertion. Thus, such statement may be put on par with the testimony of the witness.

Section 119 of the Criminal Justice Act 2003 provides as follows:

'If in criminal proceedings a person gives oral evidence and –

(a) he admits making a previous inconsistent statement, or

(b) a previous inconsistent statement made by him is proved by virtue of section 3, 4 or 5 of the Criminal Procedure Act 1865

the statement is admissible as evidence of any matter stated of which oral evidence by him would be admissible.'

R v Hayes [2005] 1 Cr App R 33

The defendant was charged with wounding with intent to commit grievous bodily harm contrary to s 18 of the Offences Against the Person Act 1861. Prior to the trial, the defendant's solicitor, with the permission of the defendant, wrote a letter to the CPS indicating that the defendant was willing to plead guilty to assault occasioning actual bodily harm contrary to s 47 of the 1861 Act. This was consistent with what the defendant said to the police in interview. During cross-examination he denied having injured the victim and the judge allowed the prosecution to cross-examine the defendant regarding the letter. On appeal, the court decided that the judge had correctly exercised his discretion. Such cross-examination did not involve unfairness to the defendant. Scott Baker LJ:

> **J** 'It was relevant to his credibility in just the same way that it may be relevant to a defendant's credibility to cross examine him about details in his alibi notice when his evidence at the trial has turned out to be different. Likewise, there is no objection, in principle, to a defendant being cross examined on what is contained in his defence statement when it becomes relevant to an issue at the trial. We cannot see that there was any unfairness to the defendant in the admission of this evidence.'

6.3.6 Finality of answers to questions in cross-examination as to credit

The general rule is that under cross-examination a witness's answer to questions of a collateral nature or related to the credit of the witness is final. The rationale for this rule is that to allow the cross-examiner to adduce rebutting evidence on matters related to the credit of the witness may lead to a multiplicity of issues and unnecessarily prolong the trial. A collateral issue is one that is not directly related to the question in issue. The test for identifying collateral issues was laid down by Pollock CB in *AG v Hitchcock* (1847) 1 Exch 91, thus:

> **J** '. . . the test whether a matter is collateral or not is this: if the answer of the witness is a matter which you would be allowed on your own part to prove in evidence – if it has such a connection with the issues, that you would be allowed to give it in evidence – then it is a matter on which you may contradict him . . . [and the matter is not collateral].'

CASE EXTRACT

AG v Hitchcock (1847) 1 Exch 91

The defendant was charged with having used a cistern for the making of malt whisky without a licence. A witness for the prosecution, having sworn that the cistern was so used, was asked if he had not said to one Mr Cook, that Excise officers had offered him £20 to say the cistern had been used. The witness denied having made such a statement. The defendant's counsel proposed to call Cook and ask him whether the witness had told him so. The evidence was disallowed. On appeal the court decided that the witness's answer was final because what the witness told Mr Cook was irrelevant to the issue of whether the cistern was used for an illicit purpose. The answer was therefore collateral to the facts in issue. Alderson B:

> **J** '. . . If the witness has spoken falsely he may be indicted for perjury. When the answer given is not material to the issue, public convenience requires that it be taken as decisive and that no contradiction be allowed. In the present case, the witness was asked whether he had been offered a bribe to say that the cistern had been used. This was not material, nor did it qualify what had gone before, for his being offered a bribe did not show that he was not a fair and credible witness.'

6.3.7 Exceptions to the Hitchcock rule

There are a limited number of exceptions to the rule in *Hitchcock*. These are occasions where, despite the questions in cross-examination being related to collateral matters, the party is nevertheless entitled to contradict the witness.

Section 6 of the Criminal Procedure Act 1865

The principle is applicable to both civil and criminal cases. It involves the answers to questions in cross-examination regarding the previous convictions of the witness not being final.

Section 6 of the 1865 Act provides as follows:

S 'A witness may be questioned as to whether he has been convicted [of any offence], and upon being so questioned, if he either denies or does not admit the fact, or refuses to answer, it shall be lawful for the cross examining party to prove such conviction . . .'

The various responses of the witness are included in the broad phrase, 'he either denies or does not admit the fact or refuses to answer' from the equivocal, evasive answer of the witness to a denial or the silence of the witness. Such responses permit the cross-examiner to contradict the witness without the leave of the judge.

In criminal cases, a witness may only be 'lawfully questioned' if the questions are permitted within ss 100 and 101 of the Criminal Justice Act 2003 and in appropriate cases, the discretion of the judge. Assuming the question from the cross-examiner about the witness's previous conviction may be asked, the next hurdle to overcome is to ascertain whether or not the conviction is 'spent' under the Rehabilitation of Offenders Act 1974. Section 4 of the 1974 Act defines 'spent convictions'. Although this Act is applicable to civil cases only, in a Practice Direction issued in 1975 the Attorney General extended the Act to criminal cases.

Section 7(3) of the Rehabilitation of Offenders Act 1974 creates an exception to the non-admissibility of convictions when the judge decides to admit it in the interests of justice.

Section 7(3) declares:

S 'If at any stage in any proceedings before a judicial authority in Great Britain . . . justice cannot be done in the case except by admitting or requiring evidence relating to a person's spent conviction or circumstances ancillary thereto, that authority may admit or, as the case may be, require the evidence in question . . . and may determine any issue to which the evidence relates . . .'

CASE EXTRACT

Thomas v Commissioner of Police [1997] 1 All ER 747

The court decided that the judge has to weigh the degree of relevance of the spent conviction to the issues in question as against the amount of prejudice the admission of the spent conviction may have in respect of a fair trial. This is a balancing exercise that has to be conducted by the judge. Evans LJ:

CONTINUED ▸

> **J** 'Section 7(3) is expressed as a qualification to the general rule of exclusion in s 4(1), and its terms demonstrate that the evidence must be excluded unless judicial authority, ie the trial judge, is "satisfied . . . that justice cannot be done . . . except by admitting [it]." So there is a strong presumption against permitting cross examination or admitting the evidence, but the section also emphasises that the discretion is a broad one. The judge may take into account "any considerations which appear to [him] to be relevant" and the overriding requirement is that "justice shall be done". In the context of civil proceedings, this means taking account of the interests of both parties, and justice requires that there shall be a fair trial between them.'

Bias or partiality

A witness may be cross-examined with a view to showing that he was biased or partial in relation to a party or the relevant cause. If he denies the allegation, the cross-examiner will be allowed to adduce evidence in order to rebut the denial. The effect of admitting such evidence at common law is to discredit the witness. This rule is applicable to both civil and criminal cases.

CASE EXTRACT

Thomas v David (1836) 7 C&P 350

The claimant sued on a promissory note. The defence was that the document was a forgery. An attesting witness to the defendant's purported signature was called by the claimant. This witness was asked in cross-examination whether she was the claimant's mistress. She denied the allegation. The defendant was allowed to rebut the denial. On appeal the court held that the evidence was correctly admitted. Coleridge J:

> **J** 'Is it not material to the issue whether the principal witness who comes to support the Plaintiff's case is his kept mistress? The question is, whether the witness had contracted such a relation with the plaintiff as might induce her the more readily to conspire with him to support a forgery, just in the same way as if she had been asked if she was the sister of the plaintiff and had denied that. I think that the contradiction is admissible.'

It is apparent that this exception is fairly broad based and much depends on the discretion of the judge as to what constitutes bias or partiality.

Another illustration of the principle is *R v Mendy* (1976) 64 Cr App R 4.

CASE EXTRACT

R v Mendy (1976) 64 Cr App R 4

In this case Mrs Mendy was charged with assault. In accordance with the usual practice, all the witnesses were kept out of court prior to giving evidence. While a detective was giving evidence for the prosecution, a constable had noticed a man taking notes from the public gallery. This man was observed by the constable and a court officer leaving the court and discussing the case with the defendant's husband. Mr Mendy gave evidence and in cross-examination denied the incident (collusion). The prosecution was granted leave to call the constable and court officer to rebut the denial. The defendant was convicted and appealed and the appeal was dismissed because the evidence was correctly admitted. Lord Lane CJ:

J '. . . Was the evidence admissible? A party may not impeach the credit of the opponent's witnesses by calling witnesses to contradict him on collateral matters, and his answers thereon will be conclusive . . . Difficulties may sometimes arise in determining what matters are collateral, but no one seriously suggests that the issue in the present case was other than collateral. On the other hand, it seems strange, if it be the case, that the court and jury have to be kept in ignorance of the behaviour of a witness such as that in the present case. The suggestion which lay behind the evidence in question was that Mr Mendy was prepared to lend himself to a scheme designed to defeat the purpose of keeping prospective witnesses out of court . . . The truth of the matter is, as one would expect, that the rule is not all embracing. It has always been permissible to call evidence to contradict a witness's denial of bias or partiality towards one of the parties and to show that he is prejudiced so far as the case being tried is concerned . . . The witness was prepared to cheat in order to deceive the jury and help the defendant. The jury were entitled to be apprised of that fact.'

The issue may arise in connection with contesting police evidence. In *R v Busby* (1981) 75 Cr App R 79, the charges were burglary and handling stolen goods.

ASE EXTRACT

R v Busby (1981) 75 Cr App R 79

Two police officers were called on behalf of the prosecution and were cross-examined by the defendant to establish *inter alia* that they were biased against the defendant. The cross-examiner questioned the witnesses to establish that they fabricated damaging remarks allegedly attributable to the defendant and that one officer, in the presence of the other, threatened a potential witness for the defence in order to stop him testifying. Both officers denied that the potential witness was threatened. The defence was prevented from calling the witness in question. The defendant was convicted and appealed. The Court of Appeal allowed the appeal and quashed the conviction on the ground that the evidence was admissible. Eveleigh LJ:

> J
>
> '. . . It is not always easy to determine when a question relates to facts which are collateral only, and therefore to be treated as final, and when it is relevant to the issue which has to be tried … We are of the opinion that the learned judge was wrong to refuse to admit the evidence. If true, it would have shown that the police were prepared to go to improper lengths in order to secure the accused's conviction. It was the accused's case that the statement attributed to him had been fabricated, a suggestion which could not be accepted by the jury unless they thought that the officers concerned were prepared to go to improper lengths to secure the conviction.'

It must be emphasized that, in this case, the Court of Appeal decided that the questions put to the police officers were related to the facts in issue, and were not concerned with the credibility of the witness. However, in *R v Edwards* [1991] 2 All ER 266 (see earlier), the court came to a different conclusion, deciding that the questions and evidence were related to the credibility of the witnesses and the answers were final in accordance with the general rule.

ASE EXTRACT

R v Edwards (Maxine) [1996] 2 Cr App R 345

The police force featured was the Stoke Newington Drugs Squad. The members of this force had been the subject of an inquiry into planting evidence and perjury. The accused was arrested on suspicion of possessing crack cocaine with intent to supply.

CONTINUED ▸

The police alleged that when they searched the defendant they discovered eight foil wraps containing crack cocaine. They said that the defendant, while in the car on her way to the station, admitted that the wraps contained cocaine. She refused to sign a note of this admission. At her trial she said that she had never been in possession of the foil wraps. She alleged that the police found them in a parked car that she was standing next to. She was convicted. Following an inquiry into the Drug Squad's activities and the acquittal of a number of persons arrested and charged by the Squad, the Home Secretary referred the case back to the Court of Appeal. This court allowed the appeal and quashed the conviction. Beldam LJ:

J 'Once the suspicion of perjury starts to infect the evidence and permeate cases in which the witnesses have been involved, and which are closely similar, the evidence on which such convictions are based becomes as questionable as it was in the cases in which the appeals have already been allowed. It is impossible to be confident that had the jury which convicted this appellant known the facts and circumstances in the other cases in which [the witness] had been involved, that they would have been bound to convict this appellant.'

The Criminal Justice Act 2003 has had the effect of restricting the discretion of the judge in deciding whether the questioning of the cross-examiner relates to credit or issue and involves bias. In criminal cases the issue today may involve an assessment of the admissibility of the bad character of the witness, or more particularly, 'evidence of, or disposition towards, misconduct on his part', within s 98 of the 2003 Act (see later). More specifically, the evidence and questioning may be focused on issues within s 100(1)(b) of the 2003 Act, namely:

'. . . the bad character of a person other than the defendant is admissible if. (b) it has substantial probative value in relation to a matter which –
(i) is a matter in issue in the proceedings, and
(ii) is of substantial importance in the context of the case as a whole'
(see later).

Evidence of reputation for untruthfulness

It has been a long-established practice that a party is entitled to call a witness (A) to testify to the effect that:

(a) from his (witness's) (A) personal knowledge, he is of the opinion that an opponent's witness (B) ought not to be believed on oath

(b) the opponent's witness (B) has a general reputation for untruthfulness. (This aspect of the test need not be based on personal knowledge.)

This is an exceptional and perhaps outdated rule of admissibility, but still has the force of law. This evidence is applicable to both civil and criminal cases and is solely related to the credit of the witness.

R v Brown and Headley (1867) LR 1 CCCR 70. In this case, further to the close of the case for the prosecution, defence counsel applied for leave to call witnesses to prove that specific witnesses who testified for the prosecution had a reputation for untruthfulness. The judge allowed such evidence to be admitted but stated a case for the Court of Crown Cases Reserved. This court held that the evidence was admissible. Kelly CB:

> 'It has been the practice to admit the evidence rejected in this case for centuries without dispute and we have personal knowledge of its existence during our time. So long a practice cannot be altered but by the legislature.'

The rule was considered in a more modern case, *R v Richardson and Longman*, and the court decided that the witness (A) is:

(a) not entitled to testify in chief about his reasons for his opinion

(b) may be entitled to state his reasons for his opinion in cross-examination.

CASE EXTRACT

R v Richardson and Longman [1969] 1 QB 299

The defendants were charged and convicted of conspiring to pervert the course of justice by trying to influence a jury and suborning witnesses at a trial (of the brother of one of the defendants). The chief prosecution witness was Mrs Clemence. The defence called a witness, Dr Hitchens, in order to discredit Mrs Clemence. He was asked whether, in the light of Mrs Clemence's general reputation for veracity, he would be prepared to believe her on oath. He replied that in certain particulars she could not be believed on oath. The judge refused defence counsel to ask the witness further questions which would have been, whether from his personal knowledge of her, he would have believed the prosecution witness? In addition, under examination in chief, the witness was not permitted to qualify his previous answer. The Court of Appeal held that although the judge was incorrect on his first ruling, he was correct on his second

CONTINUED ▶

ruling. The proviso to s 2 of the Criminal Appeal Act 1968 applied and the appeal was dismissed. Edmund Davies LJ:

> J
>
> 'The legal position may be thus summarised:
>
> 6.4.8 A witness may be asked whether he has knowledge of the impugned witness's general reputation for veracity and whether (from such knowledge) he would believe the impugned witness's sworn testimony.
>
> 6.4.9 The witness called to impeach the credibility of a previous witness may also express his individual opinion (based upon his personal knowledge) as to whether the latter is to be believed upon his oath and is not confined to giving evidence merely of general reputation.
>
> 6.4.10 But whether the witness's opinion as to the impugned witness's credibility be based simply upon the latter's general reputation for veracity or upon his personal knowledge, the witness cannot be permitted to indicate during his examination in chief the particular facts, circumstances or incidents which formed the basis of his opinion, although he may be cross examined as to them . . .
>
> It is clear from the transcript that defence counsel also desired to ask another question of Dr Hitchens and we were told (and accept) that it would have been in this form: "From your personal knowledge of Ms Clemence would you believe her on oath? That question, in our judgment, he should have been permitted to put . . . Nevertheless, we are obliged to hold that the trial judge was technically wrong in ruling out that further question. As to whether he was also wrong in cutting short Dr Hitchens's attempt to qualify his earlier answer is far from clear; for it looks very much as though the witness was proceeding to adduce his reasons for qualifying it, and we know of no authority which permits that to be done . . ."'

Evidence of disability of opponent's witness

A party is entitled to call a witness (A) to testify to the effect that from his personal knowledge of a witness called by his opponent (B), such witness (B) was suffering from such a disability (mental or physical) as to militate against the truthfulness of his testimony, ie to discredit the witness. In addition, the witness (A) is entitled in evidence-in-chief to state reasons for his opinion. In a sense this principle of law was created out of the *Brown and Headley* principle. For example, a defence witness may be called to testify to the effect that a prosecution witness who gave evidence of visual identification of the defendant committing the crime from a distance of

200 feet, was so short-sighted that he would have found it difficult to identify anyone from a distance exceeding 50 feet.

The law was settled in *Toohey v Metropolitan Police Commissioner* [1965] AC 595.

CASE EXTRACT

Toohey v Metropolitan Police Commissioner [1965] AC 595

In this case the accused and two others were charged and convicted of assaulting a youth with intent to rob (today robbery). The defence was that they were merely trying to help him, but the youth became hysterical and accused them of hitting him and being after his money. A doctor was prevented from giving evidence for the defence, to the effect that on examination of the victim at the police station, he had formed the opinion that he was suffering from a disease of the mind and was prone to hysteria, and therefore regarded his testimony as unreliable. On conviction, the defendant appealed and the House of Lords allowed the appeal and quashed the conviction on the ground that the evidence was admissible. Lord Pearce:

> **J** 'When a witness through physical (in which I include mental) disease or abnormality is not capable of giving a true or reliable account to the jury, it must surely be allowable for medical science to reveal this vital hidden fact to them. If a witness purported to give evidence of something which he believed that he had seen at a distance of 50 yards, it must surely be possible to call the evidence of an oculist to the effect that the witness could not possibly see anything at a greater distance than 20 yards . . . So too must it be allowable to call medical evidence of mental illness which makes a witness incapable of giving reliable evidence, whether through the existence of delusions or otherwise . . . *R v Gunewardene* [1951] 2 KB 600, was, in my opinion, wrongly decided. Medical evidence is admissible to show that a witness suffers from some disease or defect or abnormality of mind that affects the reliability of his evidence. Such evidence is not confined to a general opinion of the unreliability of the witness but may give all the matters necessary to show, not only the foundation of and reasons for the diagnosis, but also the extent to which the credibility of the witness is affected . . .'

This principle is limited to occasions when the opponent's witness's credibility is attacked by the adduction of expert evidence in order to prove a scientific fact. In other words, expert opinion evidence is inadmissible in order to prove ordinary facts that are within the purview of the jury.

The purpose of the rule is to avoid usurping the function of the jury. Thus, psychiatric evidence is not admissible in order to discredit a witness who is capable of giving reliable evidence. This is a matter for the jury to take into account in observing the demeanour of a witness and the content of his testimony.

CASE EXTRACT

R v MacKenney (1981) 76 Cr App R 271

The defendant and another were charged with murder. A third defendant, Childs, had pleaded guilty and was returning Queen's evidence for the prosecution. The judge had ordered that Childs be examined by a defence psychiatrist, if he so consented. In the circumstances the witness refused to be examined. The defence attempted to secure the nearest alternative to an examination. Mr Irving, who held himself out as a psychologist, prepared a report for the defence after observing Childs testifying from the witness box. Defence counsel sought to call Mr Irving to testify on the basis that he was an expert and to prove that Childs was suffering from a mental illness; one of the characteristics was a tendency to fabrication. The judge after considering the qualifications and experience of Mr Irving and the circumstances supporting his opinion ruled that his report was inadmissible and that he was not allowed to testify. On appeal following a conviction, the Court of Appeal dismissed the appeal on the ground that Mr Irving was not an expert and in any event his report was not compiled after an examination of the witness. Ackner LJ:

J 'Counsel for the defence submitted to us that Mr Irving was qualified to diagnose mental illness. His training, he submitted, as a psychologist enabled him so to do. We do not agree. No doubt his training as a psychologist gave him some insight into the medical science of psychiatry. However, not being a medical man, he had of course no experience of direct personal diagnosis. He was thus not qualified to act as a psychiatrist.

We agree with the learned judge that if a witness is suffering from a mental disability, it may, in a proper case, well be permissible to call psychiatric evidence to show that the witness is incapable of giving reliable evidence. We are prepared to accept that the mental illness need not be such as to make the witness totally incapable of giving reliable evidence, but it must substantially affect the witness's capacity to give reliable evidence. But this is very different from calling psychiatric evidence with a view to warning a jury about a witness

CONTINUED ▸

J who is capable of giving reliable evidence, but who may well choose not to do so. If the witness is mentally capable of giving reliable evidence, it is for the jury, with all the warnings from counsel and the court which the law requires to decide whether or not that witness is giving reliable evidence.'

ACTIVITY

Self-test questions

1. When may a witness refresh his memory (a) in court and (b) out of court and what are the consequences of doing so?

2. What is meant by the expression 'hostile' witness and how does this differ from an 'unfavourable' witness?

3. What exceptions exist in respect of the general rule against the admissibility of previous consistent statements?

4. How has the Criminal Justice Act 2003 improved the exceptions to the rule against narrative statements?

5. What are the traditional purposes of cross-examination?

6. What is the effect of the distinction between cross-examination as to issue and credit?

7. Have the provisions enacted in ss 41–43 of the Youth Justice and Criminal Evidence Act 1999, relating to the cross-examination of the defendant about the sexual behaviour of the complainant, gone too far and have the effect of prejudicing a fair trial?

Further reading

Dein, A. 'Police Misconduct Revisited' [2000] Crim LR 801

Dennis, I. 'Sexual History Evidence: Evaluating Section 41' [2006] Crim LR 869

Durston, G. 'Previous (In) Consistent Statements after the Criminal Justice Act 2003' [2005] Crim LR 206

Ellison, L. 'Cross-examination in rape trials' [1998] Crim LR 605

Kibble, N. 'Judicial Perspectives on the operation of section 41' [2005] Crim LR 190

Kibble, N. 'Judicial discretion and the admissibility of prior sexual history evidence' [2005] Crim LR 263

Munday, R. 'Calling a hostile witness' [1989] Crim LR 866

Temkin, J. 'Sexual history evidence – beware the backlash' [2003] Crim LR 217

chapter 7 HEARSAY: THE EXCLUSIONARY RULE ■

AIMS AND OBJECTIVES

By the end of this chapter you should be able to understand:

- The categories of hearsay evidence

- How the rules operate

- The changes made by the Criminal Justice Act 2003

- How the new rules operate

- The common law exceptions to the rule

- The statutory exceptions in the criminal law

- The exclusion of hearsay evidence.

7.1 Introduction

Hearsay evidence has seen major changes since the introduction of the Criminal Justice Act 2003 (CJA). The general rule in criminal proceedings is that both prosecution and defence witnesses should give oral evidence and be available to be cross-examined on it. Therefore A is, in general, forbidden to give evidence on behalf of B. As evidenced later in our discussion, Article 6(3)(d) of the European Convention on Human Rights and Fundamental Freedoms (ECHR) promotes the general rule by trying to put the accused and accuser on an equal footing.

The changes were introduced because the old law was constantly and considerably criticized with the consequence that in 1997 the Law Commission was instructed to conduct a full consultation on this area of the law of evidence and as a result of which produced its report No 245, entitled 'Evidence in criminal proceedings: Hearsay and related topics'. This paper shows concisely why the law needed the changes later introduced. The protagonists of the changes included the infamous Sir Robin Auld, of the Auld report fame, who concluded that the rules in relation to criminal proceedings, remember the civil rules on the admission of such evidence have always been far more flexible, should be made more flexible and the jury should be allowed to assess the weight of the evidence and not have the decision made for them. This was one of the greatest arguments against its very admission. The Government White Paper entitled 'Justice for All',

which stated that justice could not be served where 'important information is excluded without good reason', further rationalized the changes. Finally, the rule against the admission of hearsay in criminal cases was seen to exemplify the disparity between the civil and the criminal law because the civil law has allowed admission of such evidence since 1968.

Before we begin our discussion of the law, the following point should be noted: the new provisions under the Criminal Justice Act 2003 (CJA) apply equally to the prosecution and defence, with the safeguard that the prosecution must prove the matters beyond reasonable doubt; the criminal standard of proof. The defence, in return, must only prove its matters to the civil standard of proof, on the balance of probabilities. At this point it may be helpful to refer back to the differences between the two standards of proof as discussed in Chapter 2.

Prior to the introduction of the statutory admission of hearsay evidence under the CJA 2003, the rules on the admission of this type of evidence existed in the common law, statute and general practice. The rule against hearsay evidence, and its exceptions, was of great importance in the English Law of evidence. Murphy articulates the rule very well; he defines hearsay as '. . . evidence from any witness which consists of what another person stated (whether verbally, in writing or by any other method of assertion such as a gesture) on any prior occasion, is inadmissible if its only relevant purpose is to prove that any fact so stated by that person on that prior occasion is true. Such a statement may, however, be admitted for any relevant purpose, other than proving the truth of the facts stated in it.' Let us take a closer look at this definition and what it includes. In basic terms the definition has three elements:

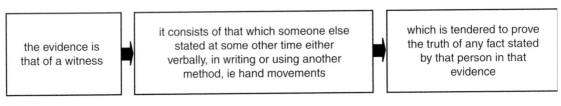

Figure 7.1 Defining hearsay

From this definition we can see that not all statements that were made on prior occasions are excluded; statements tendered to prove anything other than the truth of the facts stated are admissible, ie similar behaviour. Here is an example:

EXAMPLE

Jonathan hears that Mark has beaten Becky again. Jonathan's evidence could not have been admitted to show that Mark had beaten Becky but it could have been admitted to show that Mark had a violent disposition.

In *R v Blastland* [1986] AC 41, Lord Bridge of Harwich stated that the rule is very deeply
rooted in the English common law:

> **J** '. . . hearsay evidence is not excluded because it has no logically probative value.
> Given that the subject-matter of the hearsay is relevant to some issue in the trial, it
> may clearly be potentially probative. The rationale of excluding it as inadmissible,
> rooted as it is in the system of trial by jury, is a recognition of the great difficulty,
> even more acute for a juror than for a trained judicial mind, of assessing what, if
> any, weight can properly be given to a statement by a person whom the jury have
> not seen or heard and which has not been subject to any test of reliability by
> cross-examination. As Lord Normand put it, delivering the judgment of the Privy
> Council in *Teper v R* [1952] AC 480, at page 486: "The rule against admission of
> hearsay evidence is fundamental. It is not the best evidence and it is not delivered
> on oath. The truthfulness and accuracy of the person whose words are spoken by
> another witness cannot be tested by cross-examination and the light which his
> demeanour would throw on his testimony is lost." The danger against which this
> fundamental rule provides a safeguard is that untested hearsay evidence will be
> treated as having a probative force which it does not deserve.'

It applies to all instances of evidence-in-chief, cross-examination and re-examination, and it
cannot be bypassed with questions requiring hearsay inferences or imputations. The rule was
tough because such evidence was considered to be both unreliable and susceptible to risk of
being fabricated if not severely distorted. Technical issues were caused by its inconsistent
application. Other problems lay with the fact that it could not be properly tested using cross-
examination of the prior assertion and juries tended to give such evidence more weight than was
desirable. Although many arguments existed for its exclusion, the rule disadvantaged both the
defendant and prosecution; there was never an argument that it should be included for fairness.

CASE EXAMPLE

Sparks v R [1964] AC 964

The victim, a four-year-old girl, gave her mother a description of her attacker as being a
black male. The girl did not give evidence herself and her mother's statement of that
description was ruled as being inadmissible hearsay evidence, even though it would
have clearly shown the defendant, who was white, to be innocent.

CASE EXAMPLE

R v Turner (1975) 61 Cr App R 67

The issue concerned an admission of guilt in a case involving an armed robbery; the maker of the statement was not called as a witness. The question was whether this admission was hearsay. The Court decided that it was and therefore it could not be admitted as evidence, even though it showed that the defendant might have been innocent.

During years of operation the common law developed a number of exceptions to the rule against the admission of hearsay evidence and this was further strengthened by Parliament with statutory exceptions in both civil and criminal cases. There were many instances where hearsay evidence would have been of crucial importance but it remained inadmissible if it did not fall into any of the exceptions (see *Sparks* above). In summary it should be noted that exceptions to the rule against the admission of hearsay evidence in criminal proceedings developed in the common law and statute. In 1965 the House of Lords in *DPP v Myers* [1965] AC 1001 laid the further expansion of these rules to rest by stating that any future expansion should only be undertaken by statute, *per* Lord Reid:

> **J** '. . . It is difficult to make any general statement about the law of hearsay evidence which is entirely accurate, but I think that the books show that in the seventeenth century the law was fluid and uncertain but that early in the eighteenth century it had become the general rule that hearsay evidence was not admissible. Many reasons for the rule have been put forward, but we do not know which of them directly influenced the judges who established the rule. The rule has never been absolute. By the nineteenth century many exceptions had become well established, but again in most cases we do not know how or when the exception came to be recognised. It does seem, however, that in many cases there was no justification either in principle or logic for carrying the exception just so far and no farther. One might hazard a surmise that when the rule proved highly inconvenient in a particular kind of case it was relaxed just sufficiently far to meet that case, and without regard to any question of principle. But this kind of judicial legislation became less and less acceptable and well over a century ago the patchwork which then existed seems to have become stereotyped. The natural result has been the growth of more and more fine distinctions so that it now takes even so concise an author as Professor Cross over 100 closely packed pages to explain the law of hearsay evidence.'

The reason for this was the problems caused by ad-hoc lawmaking. The result was to make the law uncertain because there was no consistent approach being followed or principle established. One final point to note before we move on to discuss the classification of hearsay evidence is that the old law was contained in a variety of statutes, including the Criminal Justice Act 1988.

KEY FACTS

Hearsay

The definition of hearsay contains three elements:

* it is the evidence of a witness;

* that consists of that which someone else stated at some other time either verbally, in writing or using another method, ie hand movements; and

* it is tendered to prove the truth of any fact stated by that person in that evidence.

The *general rule* in civil cases is that hearsay is admissible. In criminal cases the approach was exclusionary, unless the evidence was admissible by exception. If classifiable as a different type of evidence because it was introduced for different purposes – the enactment of the CJA 2003 has led to an inclusionary approach which means that hearsay is now admissible if it falls under one of the provisions of the 2003 Act.

7.2 Classifying evidence as hearsay evidence

When looking at how evidence is classified as hearsay evidence, the definition of hearsay must be clear; hearsay evidence consists of (1) statements or assertions that are made on previous occasions, and (2) which are tendered as evidence to prove that their contents are true. Under the old rules, determining whether evidence was hearsay evidence and whether it was inadmissible was a two-stage approach; the Court would ask these questions:

a. Does the evidence consist of a previous statement or assertion, which amounts to hearsay?

b. What is the purpose for which it is being tendered?

The court would begin by asking itself whether the statement, assertion or gesture was made outside of court. If it was, then it would ask: is the statement, assertion or gesture being tendered in court to prove the truth of its contents, ie the truth of the statement, assertion or gesture itself?, after which the Court would ask itself a third and final question: does the person

making the statement, assertion or gesture intend that it be either believed or acted upon? Where all of these questions are answered in the affirmative, then the statement, assertion or gesture is hearsay evidence; if not, then the evidence is not hearsay evidence and *may* be admissible as original evidence. The golden rule still applies; only relevant evidence is admissible and there is always a risk that the evidence is not relevant. Furthermore, it could be that the evidence falls under some other category for exclusion, remember judges still have the discretion to exclude at common law.

7.2.1 Rationale for exclusion

The general rule, subject to common law and statutory exceptions, was that hearsay evidence is inadmissible for several reasons, namely:

*   Not the best-evidence rule: When the rules of evidence were going through their formative years, the courts became obsessed with admitting the best evidence available. They considered hearsay evidence as being derived from a secondary source which ought not to be admissible as being untrustworthy.

Per Lord Normand in *Teper v R* [1952] AC 480:

> **J** '. . . hearsay evidence is not the best evidence and it is not delivered on oath. The truthfulness and accuracy of the person whose words are spoken by another witness cannot be tested by cross-examination and the light which his demeanor would throw on his testimony is lost.'

*   Absence of opportunity to cross-examine: As Lord Normand suggested in *Teper* above, the person from whom the source of the relevant fact had derived, by definition, is not available to be cross-examined with a view to testing the accuracy of the testimony.

*   Inaccuracy through repetition: It is a natural phenomenon that issues that are repeated without knowledge of the original facts, are capable of being exaggerated and result in inaccuracy. This accounts for the fear that had been experienced by common law judges in adopting an adversarial procedure of settling disputes.

7.3 The Criminal Justice Act 2003 and its new inclusionary approach to hearsay evidence – in outline

In 2003, the Criminal Justice Act forced an about-turn and introduced a brand new inclusionary approach to hearsay evidence 'modernizing' the law, *per* Rose LJ in *R v Joyce and Joyce* [2005] EWCA Crim 1785. Under the old regime, the accepted rule was that hearsay evidence is inadmissible unless one of the exceptions applied; under the new approach the rule has changed to: hearsay evidence is admissible if it falls under one of the ways outlined in the CJA 2003, each of which is discussed below.

Section 114 of the CJA 2003 provides that hearsay evidence, ie a statement not made in oral evidence in the proceedings, is admissible in criminal trials of any matter stated, if:

- any provision makes it admissible

- any rule of law preserved by s 118 makes it admissible

- all the parties agree to it being admissible

- the court is satisfied that it is in the interest of justice for it to be admissible.

The effect of this about-turn on criminal trials has been profound because more hearsay evidence is now admissible than under the common law. A key point to note is that admission of hearsay evidence in civil cases has been inclusionary and subject to safeguards for a number of years now. The main provisions have been enacted by the Criminal Justice Act 2003, which came into force in April 2005, and apply to all subsequent criminal proceedings. As the provision applies to *criminal proceedings*, we begin with a brief look at what these include. The Court of Appeal in *R v Bradley* [2005] EWCA Crim 20, a case concerning bad character, stated that criminal proceedings in reference to the CJA 2003 mean '. . . criminal proceedings to which the strict rules of evidence apply'. The effect of this is that the new rules apply to all stages in criminal proceedings where the strict evidential rules apply, and that includes trial, *Newton* and now, preparatory hearings; see *R v H* [2006] 1 Cr App R 4. This diagram summarizes the position:

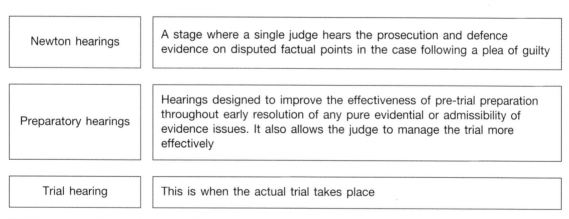

Newton hearings	A stage where a single judge hears the prosecution and defence evidence on disputed factual points in the case following a plea of guilty
Preparatory hearings	Hearings designed to improve the effectiveness of pre-trial preparation throughout early resolution of any pure evidential or admissibility of evidence issues. It also allows the judge to manage the trial more effectively
Trial hearing	This is when the actual trial takes place

■ Figure 7.2 The application of hearsay in all stages of criminal proceedings under the Criminal Justice Act 2003

KEY FACTS

Hearsay under the CJA 2003

The 2003 Act modernized the law, see *R v Joyce and Joyce* [2005] EWCA Crim 1785. Section 114 of the CJA 2003 provides that hearsay evidence is admissible in criminal cases if:

- any provision makes it admissible

- any rule of law preserved by s 118 makes it admissible

- all the parties agree to it being admissible

- the court is satisfied that it is in the interest of justice for it to be admissible.

Criminal proceedings include Newton, preparatory and trial hearings.

7.3.1 Previous statements or assertions – analysis of hearsay

As stated earlier, the rules apply to previous statements, assertions or gestures that are made by any person. This includes any previous statements that may have been made by the witnesses themselves. It should be noted that statements such as these may be admissible as evidence of a previous consistent or inconsistent statement. This is a good example of how a single piece of evidence may not be admissible as one type of evidence, but may be admissible as another. In this part of the chapter we will look at previous inconsistent statements. Previous consistent statements and statements used to refresh the memory of a witness were referred to in Chapter 6.

Before we discuss previous inconsistent statements, the form in which a previous statement, assertion or gesture can take, must be determined. In general, the law accepts that a person may use a variety of methods to communicate information, ie orally, visually, spoken word, in a document or by gestures. Here are some examples of hearsay statements:

CASE EXAMPLE

R v Gibson [1887] 18 QBD 539

The defendant had a quarrel with the prosecutor's son at a public house in Wigan. After the defendant had left the public house the prosecutor along with his son and some others walked home along what happened to be the street where the defendant

CONTINUED ▶

lived. Whilst passing the house the prosecutor was struck on the head by a stone which came from the direction of the defendant's home suffering a serious injury. The defendant was seen entering his house shortly after the stone had been thrown. The prosecutor's son and a police officer broke down the door of the defendant's house finding the defendant with his father who was asleep in a state of intoxication. Shortly before it was thrown, witnesses had seen the defendant come up behind the prosecutor, passing him on the opposite side of the street. At the time the stone was thrown, there was no one except the defendant on the side of the street from where the stone came. The question was whether evidence that A had told B where C, the defendant, who had allegedly thrown a stone at the house, lived by pointing to a particular house was admissible. The court held that the oral statement and the actual gesture of pointing were both hearsay evidence.

CASE EXAMPLE

Chandrasekera v R [1937] AC 200

A woman had suffered a cut throat and was thus unable to speak; however, whilst fully conscious she understood what was said to her and in response to which she was able to make signs and nod her head, after which she was asked whether it was the appellant who had cut her throat. She nodded her head and died shortly afterwards from asphyxia. The court held that the evidence of the signs she made in answer to questions that had been put to her whilst alive was admissible. However, the statements of witnesses as to their interpretation of the signs were not. In addition, the direct question as to whether it was the appellant who had cut her throat and her nod of assent amounted to a verbal statement made by her which fell within the meaning of s 32 of the Ceylon Evidence Ordinance 1895 and was admissible in evidence. Hence, there was proper and sufficient evidence in the form of a verbal statement by the deceased that implicated the appellant. Although this is a case from the Supreme Court of the Island of Ceylon, it is a good example of hearsay statements.

CASE EXAMPLE

Myers v DPP [1965] AC 1001

Myers was charged on indictment on seven counts along with another man; conspiracy to receive stolen cars, conspiracy to defraud purchasers of the stolen cars and receiving five cars knowing them to have been stolen. The prosecution sought to prove

CONTINUED ▸

that for each of the 22 stolen cars that Myers or his accomplice had purchased an identical wrecked car the purpose of which was to transfer the identification and registration numbers from the wrecked to the stolen vehicle. The owners of each of the stolen cars were asked to indentify it. Myers admitted to purchasing 12 of the wrecked cars and selling an equal amount of cars bearing the same registration numbers as the wrecked ones, his contention was that these were cars that had been rebuilt and repaired and thus were not in fact the stolen cars. In addition, he contended that in rebuilding and repairing the cars he had innocently removed the identification marks and plates from the wrecked cars and placed them upon the rebuilt cars so that the numbers corresponded. The prosecution sought to prove that Myers had actually disguised the stolen cars so that he could sell them; in doing so it sought to adduce the evidence of the employees of the car manufacturers who had built the stolen cars and kept detailed records of the engine, chassis, and cylinder block numbers. The cylinder block number had been purposely moulded into a secret part of the block and thus was impossible to remove or replace. Counsel for Myers objected to the admission of this on the grounds that it was hearsay evidence, the evidence was admitted and Myers convicted. He later appealed and lost.

Myers (above) is quite a wide interpretation of a hearsay statement, which led the Courts to seek to reclassify it not as hearsay evidence, but evidence that had a special quality in its own right.

Even though the CJA 2003 covers previous inconsistent statements, they must still be admitted in accordance with the Criminal Procedure Act 1865 which requires the maker of the previous inconsistent statement to be:

(a) mentioned to them

(b) asked whether they made such a statement.

Only then may a previous statement be tendered as proof of an inconsistency. Prior to the enactment of s 119 of the CJA 2003, these statements were only admissible, and usually tendered, to undermine the credibility of the maker of it. Under the current regime once the statement is admitted, it becomes evidence of the truth of all matters that are stated in it, so long as those matters are admissible if the maker were to give oral evidence of them; see Chapter 6.

ASE EXAMPLE

R v Joyce [2005] EWCA Crim 1785

The defendant was identified by many witnesses, all of whom gave detailed statements as to why they were certain that it was he who committed the crime. Once the trial commenced, contrary to their previous statements, they all claimed to be uncertain as to their identifications. This sudden change implied that the witnesses were in some way being forced to change their evidence. The trial judge allowed the admission of the previous statements under s 119, which served as evidence of original identification. The defendant was duly convicted on the basis that the statements were evidence of the truth of the matters which they contained, ie the identification.

What are the conditions for admitting hearsay evidence of a previous inconsistent statement under s 119 CJA 2003? The witness must be called to give oral evidence (s 120(1) CJA 2003).

Let us move on to previous consistent statements (see Chapter 6). What if such a statement is admitted to rebut a suggestion, made by the opposition, that a witness's evidence has been fabricated or concocted? Then, the statement is admissible as evidence of the truth of any matter that it contained in it so long as oral evidence of the matter would have been admissible. That means the admission of such a statement goes to more than just the credibility of the witness (s 120(2) CJA 2003).

Finally, where a witness, whilst in the process of giving oral evidence, uses a statement that he had made on a previous occasion to refresh his memory, and he has been cross-examined on it, that statement becomes admissible as evidence of the truth of the matters that it contains (s 120(3) CJA 2003). Let us summarize this point:

- The witness makes a statement outside of court, ie in a police station.
- The witness uses that statement to refresh his memory whilst giving oral evidence in court.
- The witness is cross-examined on that statement.

When are such statements admissible? The witness can, at any time, whilst giving evidence refresh his memory from a statement that he may have made on a prior occasion. Why would a witness want to do this? How many people could answer the question; what did you have for supper on this day last month? Difficult to remember is it not? Realistically, it can take up to six months before an accused appears in the Crown Court, and that means a similar period of time will have elapsed between the witness making the statement and coming to court to give evidence. Therefore, allowing the witness to refresh his memory avoids oral evidence becoming a test of memory. The American Scholar, Elizabeth Loftus, has carried out extensive research on the fallibilities of evidence that may be of interest. When will a witness be permitted to refresh

his memory from such a statement? The admissibility of the statement and the witness's ability to refresh his memory from it depends on the witness indicating that:

- to the best of his belief, he personally made the statement
- to the best of his belief, it contains the truth
- one of three conditions is satisfied:
  - the statement either identifies or describes a person, place or object (s 120(5) CJA 2003)
  - the statement was made when the matters contained in it were fresh in the witness's memory but he cannot be reasonably expected to sufficiently remember or recall the facts in order to give oral evidence of those facts at the trial (s 120(6) CJA 2003)
  - the witness claims to be the victim against whom the offence was committed, the proceedings relate to it, the statement contains a complaint made by him regarding conduct that constitutes the commission of the offence or a part of it. The complaint was made as soon as was reasonably practicable and was not made because the witness was being threatened or promised something and, before the statement can be adduced in evidence, the witness must give oral evidence in connection with its subject matter (s 120(7)).

This provision restricts the ability of either party automatically to adduce evidence of a previous recent complaint and in the worst-case scenario at all where the delay is substantial.

CASE EXAMPLE

R v Openshaw [2006] 2 Cr App R 27

A complaint was made four months after the commission of the conduct. Evidence of the previous complaint was admitted because the court decided that the concept of what is 'as soon as is reasonably practicable' will depend on the facts of each individual case, and to whom it is made.

7.3.2 The purpose of tendering the evidence

It is quite obvious that not all previous statements, assertions or gestures are admissible. For example, if Margaret was willing to tell the court *what* someone said and her evidence was tendered for that purpose, would it be admissible? The answer is not automatically; the question would now be: does Margaret's evidence fall under any of the provisions of the CJA 2003 or the common law? We can now consider a range of different types of hearsay statements and the position in terms of admissibility.

7.3.3 Statements relevant only to truth

When compared to civil cases, the rule against the admission of hearsay evidence has been strictly applied in criminal cases. The basic position was that a hearsay statement was inadmissible unless it fell within an exception; here are some case examples:

CASE EXAMPLE

R v Attard (1958) 43 Cr App R 90

The witness, a police officer, sought to give evidence of an interview that he had
conducted through an interpreter with a non-English-speaking prisoner. His evidence
consisted of telling the court that which the interpreter had told him; his evidence was
inadmissible hearsay. Note: in such cases it is usual practice to call the interpreter to
give evidence.

CASE EXAMPLE

R v Marshall [1977] Crim LR 106

The defendant (A) confessed that the goods in his possession were stolen. This
confession was inadmissible hearsay evidence because B had told him that they were
stolen. Note: had the confession been tendered to evidence his belief, then it would
have been admissible but because it was tendered to evidence the fact that they were
stolen, it was not.

CASE EXAMPLE

Jones v Metcalfe [1967] 1 WLR 1286

The defendant driver, charged with driving without due care and attention, had only
been traced by reason of an eye witness providing his registration number to the police.
At the trial the eye witness could not remember the number; nor were they allowed to
refresh their memory. Therefore, the officer to whom the information of the registration
number had been provided could not give evidence of that. It was in effect hearsay
being tendered to prove the truth of what had been previously stated.

CASE EXAMPLE

Surujpaul v R [1958] 1 WLR 1050

Surujpaul was tried together with four others on a charge of murder. It was the
prosecution's case that the murder had been committed whilst Surujpaul and his
accomplices were carrying out their plot to steal money. This rested largely on the

CONTINUED ▸

evidence of one of the accomplices, evidence that went to prove the existence of the plot. In addition, there was some material which would have led the jury to believe that the plan had been carried out by all or some of the accused and that it was in the course of carrying out the plot that the murder had been committed. Other than one of the accused who had been discharged, the jury found Surujpaul guilty as an accessory to murder and his co-accused not guilty as either accessories or principals. Surujpaul contended that the verdicts were inconsistent and contradictory because there could be no accessory without a principal. The court of appeal quashed the conviction on the basis that '. . . it was essential to the conviction of the appellant as accessory before the fact for the Crown to prove that he had counselled, procured or commanded one or more of the other accused to commit the murder and that such person or persons had in fact done so'.

Other interesting decisions on this point for research include: *Comptroller of Customs v Western Lectric Co Ltd* [1966] AC 367 and *Wright v Doe d. Tatham* (Exch) (1937) 7 A&E 313. The rule also applies to statements made orally; a good example of this is *Teper v R* [1952] AC 480. In this case the defendant was accused of setting fire to his shop. He produced evidence of an alibi defence. In rebuttal, the prosecution adduced evidence that a woman was heard shouting at a motorist who had passed the shop; she had made a remark that implicated the motorist as the defendant. This evidence ruined his alibi defence and, on conviction, he appealed. The Privy Council allowed the appeal on the ground that the evidence was inadmissible hearsay. Lord Normand:

J '. . . no case is to be found which comes anywhere near this case, suggesting that the statement of this unidentified woman 230 yards away from the fire and 26 or more minutes after it started could be admissible on the authority of any known principle, or be said to be part of the *res gestae*.'

Further, the House of Lords confirmed in *R v Kearley* (discussed later) that implied assertions were subject to the rule against admission of hearsay evidence. This has recently been set aside and in *R v Singh* [2006] 1 WLR 1564; the Court of Appeal has stated that implied assertions no longer fall within the new CJA 2003 rule (see below). See also: *R v N* [2006] EWCA Crim 3303.

7.3.4 Original evidence/non-hearsay statements

Not every statement is classifiable as hearsay evidence. Statements tendered for relevant reasons, other than as proof of the truth of their contents are admissible as original evidence, ie evidence as to the making of the statement itself or evidence of the state of mind of the person making the statement or person hearing it. Let us take a brief look at this point.

Evidence that a statement was made

The discussion in Chapter 1 focused on the fact that only evidence relevant to a fact in issue may be admissible. Occasionally, the fact that a statement was made will be in issue, for example, the existence of a contract, a previous consistent or inconsistent statement or a threat or defamatory remark may not constitute hearsay evidence.

CASE EXAMPLE

Subramaniam v Public Prosecutor [1956] 1 WLR 965

The defendant was charged with the unlawful possession of an offensive weapon and ammunition. He raised the defence of duress on the basis that terrorists had captured him and threatened him. At first instance the trial judge had ruled that this evidence was hearsay and inadmissible. On appeal the Privy Council decided that the court (jury) could receive such evidence so that it could establish (a) that threats had been made, and (b) the effect of them on the defendant.

CASE EXAMPLE

R v Chapman [1965] 2 QB 436

The evidence of a police officer that the police doctor had not objected to a sample being taken from the defendant was not hearsay evidence. It was original evidence by reason of there being consent and no objection. The court went on to state that this evidence would only be hearsay if it were tendered as proof of the defendant's health.

CASE EXAMPLE

Woodhouse v Hall (1980) 72 Cr App R 39

The defendant was prosecuted for acting in the management of a brothel contrary to s 33 of the Sexual Offences Act 1956. Evidence was given by police officers of various conversations they had had, in the absence of the defendant, in which immoral services had been offered to them by two women employed at the premises as masseuses. The

CONTINUED ▸

evidence of the police officers showing that the women at the defendant's premises were offering sexual services for payment was admissible as original evidence. The statements were not being tendered as proof of their contents *per se*. The fact that services were being offered was circumstantial evidence of the point that the defendant's premises was a brothel.

Evidence the state of mind of the maker

Although the exact state of mind of any person can never really be directly established, it can be proved through circumstantial evidence. This means that some statements may amount to original evidence of a person's state of mind and therefore be relevant for reasons other than the truth of its contents.

R v Willis [1960] 1 WLR 55

The court decided that a conversation, between an employer and the defendant, that evidenced the innocent state of the defendant's mind should have been admissible because a statement showing the converse would have been admissible.

Jones v DPP [1962] AC 635

In this case concerning murder, the defendant's false alibis are original evidence of his guilty state of mind.

CASE EXAMPLE

Mawaz Khan and Amasat Khan v R [1967] AC 454

The defendants had suffered injuries which they contended had been sustained in a fight at a nightclub and not as the prosecution case suggested, in the course of a murder. Although their alibis were identical, neither one of the two defendants gave evidence. The trial judge directed the jury that if they felt that any one of the alibis had been fabricated, then that fabrication would incriminate both defendants. The direction,

CONTINUED ▶

on appeal, was held to be correct with the court stating that, *per* Lord Hodson: '. . . a statement is not hearsay and is admissible when it is proposed to establish . . . not the truth of the statement, but the fact that it was made . . .' It went on to state that there would be no breach of the rule against admission of hearsay where it is tendered '. . . not for the purpose of establishing the truth of the assertions contained therein, but for the purpose of asking the jury to hold the assertions false and to draw inferences from their falsity'. The alibi statements showed that they were (a) acting in concert and (b) common guilt.

CASE EXAMPLE

Ratten v R [1972] AC 378

The defendant shot his wife and pleaded accident. At his trial for her murder, evidence of a telephone call made by a hysterical woman five minutes before she was shot was admitted as circumstantial evidence of her terrified state of mind. Her state of mind was an issue before the court. The admission of the call collaterally evidenced whether or not the shooting had been an accident or murder.

CASE EXAMPLE

R v Blastland [1986] AC 41

Ratten should be contrasted with *R v Blastland*, in which the defendant (A) was accused of committing buggery and murdering a boy (C). The defendant admitted that he had committed buggery with C before he had died but denied any involvement in the killing. In his defence he sought to adduce evidence that another man (B) had revealed the fact that the death had occurred well before this information had been made public, and appeared distressed and anxious. In fact, B had admitted to the killing but had later withdrawn his confession. The trial judge refused admission of this evidence on the grounds that it was hearsay. The House of Lords held a contrary view: the evidence was not hearsay as it showed B's state of mind, but because his state of mind was not in issue, it was inadmissible.

In the important decision of *R v Kearley* [1992] 2 All ER 345, the police intercepted calls made by unknown callers to the defendant's premises asking to buy drugs. Some of these unknown callers actually came to the premises in person. The question for the House of Lords was whether the evidence of the calls had been rightly admitted, even though the defendant was not

present at the time they were made. The House decided that evidence of the calls, which was being tendered to show the use of the premises, was inadmissible hearsay, ie the truth of their content. Whether or not the callers thought that they would procure drugs was irrelevant. Therefore, it would be wrong to allow the negative inference that the premises were being used to distribute drugs to be drawn as a result of the assertions of the callers, *per* Lord Bridge of Harwich:

> **J** '. . . I accept the proposition that, if an action is of itself relevant to an issue, the words which accompany and explain the action may be given in evidence, whether or not they would be relevant independently. But here the mere fact of the calls being made to the defendant's house was by itself of no relevance whatever, so we are back to the bare issue as to whether the implied assertion involved in the request for drugs should be excluded as hearsay. As English law presently stands, I am clearly of the opinion that it should.'

In *Kearley* the House distinguished *Woodhouse v Hall* on the basis that in *Woodhouse* the fact of the existence of an offer made on the premises by an employee was sufficient evidence to establish that the premises were being used for the distribution of drugs. Likewise the House distinguished *Ratten v R,* because in that case the hysterical call was made from the premises and could be classed as (a) evidence of the attack on the victim as part of the *res gestae* and (b) relevant to the fabrication of the defence of accident. The House outlined that in *Kearley* it was not the state of the mind of the callers that was relevant to a fact in issue before the jury, *per* Lord Bridge of Harwich:

> **J** '. . . the first question then is whether the fact of the request for drugs having been made is in itself relevant to the issue whether the defendant was a supplier. The fact that words were spoken may be relevant for various purposes, but most commonly they will be so when they reveal the state of mind of either the speaker or the person to whom the words were spoken when that state of mind is itself in issue or is relevant to a matter in issue . . . the state of mind of the person making the request for drugs is of no relevance at all to the question whether the defendant is a supplier. The sole possible relevance of the words spoken is that by manifesting the speaker's belief that the defendant is a supplier they impliedly assert that fact.'

CASE EXAMPLE

R v Gilfoyle [1996] 3 All ER 883

The defendant was accused of murdering his wife, and contended that she had
committed suicide. In furtherance of this he tendered as evidence a note allegedly
written by her of her depressed state of mind. The prosecution, in rebuttal of this,
tendered evidence of remarks made by the wife to her friends in which she had told
them how she had written the note at the request of her husband, and how she had
found the whole thing highly amusing. The conversation was not hearsay evidence when
tendered to show her state of mind, ie that she was not depressed.

Most recently the Court of Appeal has ruled in *R v Singh* (below), that implied assertions are no
longer hearsay and therefore do not fall within the new CJA 2003 rule, because they are
considered to be direct evidence as in *Kearley* (above). Direct evidence that there was a market
for the defendant to supply the drugs from his premises, ie people wanted to buy them from
him.

CASE EXAMPLE

R v Singh [2006] 1 WLR 1564

The defendant was charged on indictment with conspiracy to kidnap. The prosecution
alleged that the defendant had used mobile telephones to make and receive calls to
and from his co-conspirators at the time of the kidnapping. The mobile telephone
memories of the co-conspirators' phones contained the defendant's mobile telephone
numbers. The trial judge ruled that this evidence was admissible to show that the
defendant was a party to the conspiracy. The defendant was convicted and appealed
on the ground that although s 115(3) of the Criminal Justice Act 2003 excluded implied
assertions from the general rule against the admissibility of hearsay under s 114, such
assertions remained inadmissible at common law. His appeal was dismissed, the court
held that '. . . the effect of ss 114 and 118 was to abolish the common law rule
against the admissibility of hearsay and to create a new rule against hearsay which did
not extend to implied assertions . . . that the telephone entries were not "a matter
stated" within the meaning of s 115(3) of the Act but were implied assertions which
were admissible in evidence because they were no longer hearsay . . . that the judge
had been right to allow the Crown to adduce the evidence'.

Evidence of the state of mind of the recipient

Statements may be admitted to prove the state of the mind of the recipient. Is a statement that is tendered to show the effect on someone admissible? Consider the following: Joan receives a telephone call telling her to assault Mark. She is told that if she refuses, her family will be attacked. Two questions arise; first, can Joan admit the evidence of the telephone call as truth of its contents? Second, can she admit it for other purposes? The answer is no to the first question because the call is inadmissible hearsay. However, the answer is yes to the second question. In *Subramaniam v Public Prosecutor* (above) the court admitted evidence of terrorists' threats. These were tendered as evidence relevant to the defendant's defence of duress. They evidenced the effect that such threats had on his mind, and not of the truth of their contents.

Relevant non-hearsay evidence

This is a particularly interesting area of evidence and has had its fair share of difficulties. In *R v Rice and Others* [1963] 1 QB 857, the defendant was accused of conspiracy. It was alleged that he had, on a particular day, taken a flight with his co-defendant to Manchester. In support, the prosecution tendered an airline ticket for a flight to Manchester in the name of each of the defendants. The defence contended that this evidence was inadmissible because it was hearsay, ie the truth of the assertion that the defendants were on the flight. The Court of Appeal decided that the airline ticket was admissible since it was original, circumstantial evidence from which the jury could infer that the defendant had flown to Manchester. Why was this so? In general terms, if production of the ticket by the airline showed compliance with its normal procedures, then the inference that someone with the defendant's name had taken the flight could be drawn. The issue whether or not the defendant had taken the flight was one for the jury to decide. In contrast to the labelling cases it seems that the safeguard in this instance is compliance with the airlines ticket and security procedures.

ASE EXAMPLE

R v Podmore (1930) 22 Cr App R 36

A document found in a particular place, partly written by A, who was deceased by the time of the trial, was admissible as circumstantial evidence of a dishonest relationship between the defendant and the deceased. The contents of the document were hearsay. However, the fact that it was found in a particular place was the relevant non-hearsay element that the party was seeking to adduce.

ASE EXAMPLE

R v Lydon (1986) 85 Cr App R 221

A car was stolen in Neasden, London, and then driven to Oxfordshire where it was used in the robbery of a post office. Both the appellant and his co-accused were charged with taking a conveyance without authority and robbery, charges to which the co-accused pleaded guilty. The issue was whether Lydon was the second person involved in the commission of the offences. Substantial identification evidence incriminated the appellant; a customer who had been in the post office when it was robbed, a part-time assistant who worked there, and the taxi driver who had driven both men to Neasden had accurately described the co-accused and had subsequently picked out the appellant on an identification parade (both of which could be undermined). Additionally, two women had described the car used which was discovered in Nettlebed Road, the place where the taxi driver had picked up the two men. The trial judge allowed the admission of evidence relating to the discovery of a gun on a grass verge on the road the getaway car would have travelled to get to Nettlebed Road. The gun was found in four pieces along with two pieces of paper on which was written 'Sean Rules' and 'Sean Rules 85'. On the gun was a smear in blue ink which forensic evidence showed to be of a similar composition to the ink on the pieces of paper and thus it was likely that both had come from the same pen. The only witness who had seen the gun described it as being brown when in fact the gun that had been found was black and silver. Lydon's only defence was an alibi. The trial judge permitted the prosecution to tender as original circumstantial evidence, the pieces of paper and the gun. He appealed on the ground that the evidence about the gun was hearsay and thus that its prejudicial effect outweighed its probative value. Dismissing his appeal the court decided that the reference to 'Sean' was no more than a statement of fact which involved no assertion as to the truth of the document and if the jury were satisfied that the gun was the same as the one used in the robbery and that the pieces of paper were linked to the gun, then the reference to 'Sean' was but a further fact which would fit with the prosecution's allegation that it was the defendant who was the other person that had committed the robbery. Hence, admission of this evidence was not contrary to the hearsay rule because it was not unduly prejudicial.

Circumstantial evidence: lack of the record

Consider the following: a hearsay statement is tendered to prove the truth of its contents, ie something exists or has happened. What is the position regarding statements that show the negative, ie something does not exist or has not happened; are they hearsay? The answer is *yes*, these statements fall under the same rule. The general rule is that both positive records and

negative records are subject to the rule against the admission of hearsay evidence, and either can be admitted if they fall within any one of the exceptions to it.

The problems associated with negative hearsay still exist. In *R v Patel* [1981] 3 All ER 94, an immigration officer whilst giving evidence for the prosecution, stated that Home Office Records did not show that a person, A, was entitled to enter the UK. The Court of Appeal decided that the records were hearsay, as was any oral evidence based on them. The Court stated that the evidence could have been received by it if the person that had compiled the records had given oral evidence. Although this would not have altered the fact that the records were hearsay, the Court would have been prepared to hear an argument that they were in fact circumstantial evidence. This is a wonderful example of how one type of evidence can be admitted or argued as a different type; the rule is: exhaust all avenues.

ASE EXAMPLE

R v Shone (1983) 76 Cr App R 721

The defendant had been charged with handling stolen motor parts after the goods were found on his premises. It was easily ascertained that manufacturer A had supplied the parts to company B from which they had been stolen. Officials from company B testified as to their record-keeping process, stating that there was no record of these parts being sold or used. The absence of such a record of sale or use did not mean that their evidence was hearsay evidence as it was circumstantial evidence from which the jury was entitled to infer that they had in fact been stolen.

Other evidence: calculators, computers and other devices

The advancement of technology has led to a greater increase in the use of electronic devices, such as computers and other machinery to record or process information. This information is now widely used and presented in court proceedings and therefore the classification or status of such information is important. The categorization of this information depends on the nature and function of the electronic device involved. Let us take a look at this in a little more detail. Where knowledge or discretion is not required to be exercised by a device, ie it performs simple calculations that could be done manually, then that information is classified as *real evidence* and not hearsay evidence, see *R v Woods* (1982) 76 Cr App R 232. Information that is generated by the device, for example a computer, may generate a list after someone inputs information into it. This is classified as hearsay evidence. The general rule is: electronic information that has an element of human involvement in its generation is hearsay evidence.

CASE EXAMPLE

R v Spiby (1990) 91 Cr App R 186

A device had automatically logged all telephone calls at an exchange and was a record. This amounted to real evidence because there had never been any human input into the recording process.

7.4 The common law exceptions to the rule

Our earlier discussion focused on the strictness of the rule against admission of hearsay evidence. It was this strictness that led to the development of exceptions to it in the common law. Each authority that developed an exception overcame the hurdles of the documented unreliability and fabrication of hearsay evidence and judicial reluctance in accepting it as good evidence. In addition, a number of statutory exceptions to the rule developed, thereby curtailing the creation of further common law exceptions; see *Myers v DPP* [1965] AC 1001. Section 114(1)(b) of the Criminal Justice Act 2003 has expressly preserved the common law exceptions to the rule against admission of hearsay in s 118, and s 118(2) has abolished those that are not mentioned. In summary, exceptionally, hearsay assertions that are admissible as evidence of facts stated therein and have been preserved by the Criminal Justice Act 2003 are:

* *res gestae*
* public information
* confessions
* other admissions (agents)
* reputation, ie character (the rule in *Rowton*)
* reputation or familial tradition
* common enterprise
* expert evidence.

Let us take a brief look at the common law exceptions, abolished and preserved; considering the reasons for preservation or abolition, starting with the *res gestae*.

7.4.1 The *res gestae*

Our discussion starts with preservation of the most important common law exception to the rule against admission of hearsay evidence; the *res gestae* rule. Sections 114(1)(d) and 118(1)(4) expressly preserve this exception; such express preservation means that the principles surrounding this concept, including the case law, is also preserved. A quick point to note is that such hearsay

statements may also be admissible under s 116 of the CJA 2003 (see ibid) and that this common law exception applies only to criminal cases. The general rule is that inadmissible hearsay statements are admissible if they form part of the *res gestae*. The term *res gestae* means *state of affairs*. How does a hearsay statement become part of the state of affairs? An otherwise inadmissible hearsay statement will be admissible as evidence of the truth of its contents as part of the *res gestae* where it is *spontaneous* and it is *an integral part of the event*. The statement is so mixed up with the event to which it relates or refers, that it almost becomes part of it. The spontaneity of the statement means that issues of unreliability and fabrication are mitigated, and the risk of the same occurring is reduced. The rationale for this rule may be traced back to *Thompson v Trevanion* (1693) Skin. 402, where, in an action for an assault on the claimant's wife, Holt CJ said that what the wife said immediately on the hurt received, and before she had time to devise or concoct a story to her advantage, might be given in evidence as part of the *res gestae*. The justification, therefore, for admitting this piece of relevant evidence is the spontaneity of such statement.

An example of this: Jonathan is attacked whilst walking home from work at 1 am in Snyde Park. As he flees, he telephones the police in a hysterical state, informing them of what is happening. In this instance, it is likely that the statement will form part of the *res gestae* and be admitted as evidence of the truth of its contents. It may also be tendered to prove Jonathan's state of mind at the time. Evidence of a contemporaneous and spontaneous outburst or statement made by the person doing an act, related to the act, will be admissible as evidence of what occurred, so long as there is no evidence to suggest that it has been calculated or made, knowing the effect that its admission will have; see *R v Bliss* (1837) 7 A&E 500.

ASE EXAMPLE

R v Bliss (1837) 7 A&E 500

Evidence of a comment made casually by a man planting a tree to the effect that it was on the boundary, was inadmissible as evidence of where the boundary was located. The comment would only have been admissible if the purpose of planting it there was to mark the boundary.

Where a statement is made by a bystander, observer or participant to an event, then it will be of utmost importance to assess the facts of the case very carefully. Often an interesting topic to research for comparative purposes is the US version of *res gestae* which is aptly titled the 'excited utterances rule'. What then does spontaneous mean? In evidence the term has a strict accepted meaning, automatically or without an interval of time sufficient to enable the maker of the statement to devise a story; see *Thompson v Trevanion* (1693) Skin. 402. The effect of this test was that over the centuries the courts decided that spontaneity may only exist if the statement was contemporaneous with the event. Spontaneity is certainly included in contemporaneity, but contemporaneity with the event is not the only way of demonstrating spontaneity.

CASE EXAMPLE

R v Bedingfield (1879) 14 Cox CC 341

The utterances of a victim who had just had her throat slit were inadmissible to prove the identity of her attacker because she had stumbled out of the room where the attack had taken place. Therefore her utterance was not spontaneous enough. Not surprisingly, the case was overruled and the butt of many a joke.

The issue of classification came before the Privy Council (PC) in *Ratten v R* [1972] AC 378 (discussed above) which concerned the admission of a hysterical telephone call from the defendant's wife who was shot shortly after making it. The question for the PC was the classification of the statement as hearsay or circumstantial evidence. The PC held that the evidence was admissible as circumstantial evidence. Even if it had been hearsay, it would have been admissible as part of the *res gestae*. The PC criticized the decision on *R v Bedingfield*. Lord Wilberforce stated '. . . *regarding* statements made after the event it must be for the judge . . . to satisfy himself that the statement was so clearly made in circumstances of spontaneity or involvement in the event that the possibility of concoction can be disregarded . . . the same must, in principle, be true of statements made before the event . . . if the drama, leading up to the climax, has commenced and assumed such intensity and pressure that the utterance can be safely regarded as a true reflection of what was unrolling or actually happening, it ought to be received'. The effect of this approach is that the correct test for admission of such evidence was not based on a strict sense of timing or contemporaneity, but the unlikelihood of concoction or fabrication.

The final departure from the decision in *R v Bedingfield* came when it was overruled in *R v Andrews* [1987] AC 251. In this case, the victim of a robbery identified the robbers before lapsing into a coma and dying. It is obvious that this was clearly a hearsay statement, but could not be admitted as a dying declaration (see below). Was it part of the *res gestae*? The defendant argued that the identification was hearsay and it lacked contemporaneous spontaneity. However, the House of Lords restated that the real test for admission involved the lack of opportunity for concoction, and whether there was 'no real opportunity for reasoned reflection', that 'the mind of the *person making the statement* was still dominated by the event'. If there was any doubt as to the admission of the evidence, ie the person making the statement was blind, then it should only be admitted where the possibility or error is excluded. On that basis the House of Lords felt that the admissibility of the telephone call was spontaneous as it was clearly part of the *res gestae*. *Andrews* is a prime example of the restated test from *Ratten* (above) that considered the time the statement was made on a more liberal basis.

In *R v Nye and Loan* (1977) 66 Cr App R 252 the court adopted a far more lenient approach to *res gestae* evidence, by admitting a statement made by a victim of an assault several minutes after it had taken place. In *R v Carnall* (1995) Crim LR 944 the court admitted a statement made one hour after a serious assault, once again as part of the *res gestae*.

CASE EXAMPLE

Tobi v Nicholas (1988) 86 Cr App R 323

A statement made later by A, who had left the scene of the crime to follow the car, identifying B as the defendant in a road accident was inadmissible as it was no longer part of the *res gestae*.

It is therefore important to demonstrate that the individual who made the statement had the state of mind outlined in *Ratten v R* and *R v Andrews* (above). Where the identity of the maker of the statement is unknown, it will not be possible to prove what their state of mind was when they made the statement; see *Teper v R* (above).

7.4.2 Statements evidencing the physical or mental state of the maker

What happens if the maker of a statement refers to a particular state of mind, such as fear or a physical state such as sickness. Can the otherwise hearsay statement be admitted to evidence this? The answer is in the affirmative, the common law facilitated the admission of a statement that evidences either the physical or mental state of the person making it, but not the cause of the physical or mental status; see *Gilbey v Great Western Railway* (1910) 102 LT 202. Furthermore, the statement must refer to the health of the person making it and not another; see *R v Parker* (1960) 45 Cr App R 1. Here is an example: Matthew complains that his partner, Guy, has poisoned him. Matthew's statement will be admissible as evidence showing that he was feeling ill, but not to prove that Guy poisoned him. Two examples of this rule are *R v Conde* (1868) 10 Cox CC 547 in which a child's complaint of hunger was admissible, and *Shephard v US* (1933) 290 US 96, where a wife's statement that her husband had poisoned her was admissible to show that she felt sick, but not admissible to show that he had poisoned her.

7.4.3 Statements by the deceased

Although this sounds like a rather strange category, it does not refer to statements by the dead, but statements made by persons who have died since making them. The general rule states that an assertion that is made by a person that has since died, and cannot therefore give evidence, is admissible in certain instances. The common law recognized the importance of this exception, statute limited it, and the CJA 2003 abolished it. Instead, evidence of this type may be adduced under s 116(2)(a) (supra).

7.4.4 Declarations against an interest

This exception has also been abolished. However, it was an interesting one: where a statement of the maker went against their financial or proprietary interest, it was admissible as evidence.

The requirement was that the statement must have been made against the financial or proprietary interest of the person making it. The fact that the statement incriminated them for the commission of other criminal offences was insufficient.

CASE EXAMPLE

Higham v Ridgeway (1808) 10 East 109

The statement of a midwife, deceased by the time of the trial, indicating that she had been paid for the delivery of a child on a particular date, was admissible hearsay evidence of the date of the child's birth. Two points heavily favoured its admission: (a) the midwife had personal knowledge of the facts, and (b) her statement went against her own interests.

CASE EXAMPLE

R v Roberts [1942] 1 All ER 187

The defendant (A), charged with being involved in drug and gun crime, sought to rely on a statement that had been made by B to his wife that A knew nothing about the drugs or guns which B had intended to use. B died before the trial and his statement was therefore inadmissible under this heading.

7.4.5 Declarations in the course of a duty

This is another exception that has been abolished by the CJA 2003. However, a good appreciation of it is required because it exemplifies why and how the current law operates. Under this exception, hearsay evidence was admissible in certain circumstances where the person making the statement was under either a legal, professional or moral duty to record information relating to the performance of their tasks. The condition was that there was contemporaneity in the creation of the record and the act being recorded. How contemporaneous? This requirement was not strictly interpreted. The courts agreed that it simply meant as soon as it was practicable to do so. This depended on the facts of the case.

211

CASE EXAMPLE

R v Buckley (1873) 13 Cox CC 293

Evidence that a police constable had informed his supervising officer that he was simply going to observe a defendant to gather evidence of what the defendant was doing when he was killed, was admissible.

The condition also required the statement or declaration to be directly related to those matters that the person making the statement was under a duty to record. In *Mercer v Denne* [1905] 2 Ch 538, the records of a surveyor were inadmissible hearsay evidence because he was not under any duty actually to record that information. Contrast this case with *Mellor v Walmesley* [1905] 2 Ch 164, where it was far clearer that the surveyor was under a duty to record the information, and hence was admissible as a declaration (or statement) made in the course of a duty.

7.4.6 Public documents containing facts

At common law the contents of a public document are admissible as evidence of the truth of its contents, even though there is always the risk that the opposition may disprove this. Strangely, this exception was created as a pure matter of convenience; consider this: Jay requests a document and requires the person creating it to verify that it is accurate and true. He telephones the archives department and they tell him that an ex-employee called Mary created the record but she emigrated to somewhere in New Zealand over two years ago and never left a forwarding address. What does Jay do? Given the huge number of public records and innate difficulty in trying to find the actual person who created them and then getting the creator to testify, it was far easier to allow the admittance of such evidence with the knowledge that the contrary could still be proven, ie it was not too onerous to admit it because of the safeguards, scrutiny and processes public records go through. This is still the case today; the exception is preserved under s 118(1)(b) of the CJA 2003, alongside the other statutory exceptions (discussed below) which cover this.

Previously, the common law rules had required the document to satisfy the following before it would become admissible:

- The document must have been created for the public record.
- It must have contained information of public interest.
- It should have been available for public inspection.
- It must have been created in contemporaneity to the events that it sought to record.
- The person creating it has personal knowledge of the events recorded or has enquired into them.

This strict approach did not last long and the rules were relaxed as micro-level knowledge diminished. It should be noted that evidence of this type might also be admissible under s 117 of the CJA 2003 (see ibid).

7.4.7 Informal admissions

Let us now look at an interesting common law exception: admissions. The common law allowed the admission of a hearsay statement that was either entirely or partially adverse to the person making it, as evidence of the facts contained therein, owing to its negative nature. The fact that it may have been incriminating mitigated the likelihood that the assertion may have been fabricated, unreliable or untrue. These assertions can be oral, written or through conduct. However, the weight attached to it will vary according to the facts of the case. Furthermore, the assertion will be read in the light of any other either exculpatory or explanatory remarks that may have accompanied it. Let us take a brief look at admissions in civil and criminal cases:

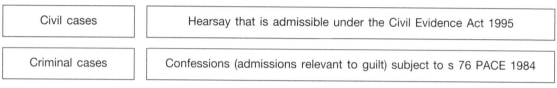

Civil cases	Hearsay that is admissible under the Civil Evidence Act 1995
Criminal cases	Confessions (admissions relevant to guilt) subject to s 76 PACE 1984

■ Figure 7.3 Informal admissions in civil and criminal cases

7.4.8 Binding admissions

An admission by a party either by himself, or someone acting as an agent on his behalf, is admissible under the common law as an exception to the rule against the admission of hearsay evidence. This common law exception has been expressly preserved by s 118(1) of the CJA 2003. Let us take a closer look at these statements. Obviously, a defendant may be bound by an adverse statement that he himself has made in his personal capacity or an admission that he has made whilst acting in a different capacity, ie litigation friend or guardian.

What happens if John makes a confession that adversely implicates him and mentions Mark? The general rule is that an admission only binds the maker of it and not others. In our example, John's confession will implicate only him. In civil cases, such evidence may be adduced by means of a statutory exception under the Civil Evidence Act 1995.

What if a co-defendant makes the adverse statement or confession? Let us say that a case involves two defendants and the allegation is that they jointly committed the offence, ie a common design. Does an admission made by A also bind B? The answer is no, unless the statement was made or words were uttered whilst carrying out the common design. Why? The statement or words becomes circumstantial evidence of a common design, ie non-hearsay. What if the statement or words are uttered after the common design has been carried out? Then that will only bind the maker. This diagram summarizes the position:

| Statement made, words uttered whilst carrying out common design | Bind both defendants |
| Statement made, words uttered after carrying out common design | Bind only the maker |

■ Figure 7.4 Binding admissions

ASE EXAMPLE

R v Blake and Tye (1844) 6 QB 126

A1 and A2 were on trial charged with conspiring to evade customs duty. There were two books in which A1 had written. The first incriminated both of them, because it had been written in the pursuance of a common design, and was admissible against both of them. The second was a personal record by A1 and therefore only admissible against him.

What about statements made by a co-accused outside a police station? These too are outside the common design, therefore are inadmissible as evidence against the co-accused; see *R v Governor of Pentonville Prison, ex p Osman* [1990] 1 WLR 277. Finally, common design can only be evidenced by evidence other than that of a co-accused.

May an accusation that is made by an agent who is acting within the authority given to him by his principal bind the principal? The answer is, yes it can. This raises serious ethical issues for lawyers and the spouse of a defendant. Consider this: Faye is instructed to act as solicitor (agent) on behalf of Sadie (principal) who has been accused of theft. Faye, as Sadie's solicitor, has the right to make admissions on her behalf. Any admissions that Faye makes will bind Sadie, so long as Faye makes the admission:

(a) whilst acting within her instructions

(b) to the opposing party

(c) without any fraud.

If any one of these three factors does not exist, the admission will be rendered void and will not bind Sadie; see *Ellis v Allen* [1914] 1 Ch 904. What about spouses? Unlike competence and compellability and the rules in relation to that within the Police and Criminal Evidence 1984 (PACE), there are no special rules as to statements made by spouses. If spouse A authorizes spouse B to make an admission, then that admission will be binding.

7.4.9 Substance: what can be admitted?

The general rule is as follows; if A makes an admission of fact, then that fact should be within A's knowledge and not be based on hearsay; see *Comptroller of Customs v Western Lectric Co Ltd* [1966] AC 367.

CASE EXAMPLE

R v Chatwood [1980] 1 WLR 874

An admission by a severely addicted drug addict that the substance he was taking was a controlled drug, was admissible as evidence because he had experience in the matter. The nature of the drug was ascertainable from the instruction of expert evidence. However, they were entitled to take the drug addict's admission into account.

7.5 Non-hearsay confessions

Once again the admission of a confession, ie a statement that incriminates the maker of it, tendered as evidence of the truth of their contents, is expressly preserved by s 118(1) of the CJA 2003. Why are confessions admissible against their makers? The law accepts that confessions are reliable and carry more evidential or probative value than other hearsay statements, because they are only likely to be made if they are true. What if that confession mentions or implicates another person? Then that other would have to argue that the confession is inadmissible hearsay evidence. We will consider the extensive rules introduced by s 76 of PACE 1984 later in the book.

7.5.1 Other statements

Finally, what if Jean makes a statement in the presence of Kabir who is a defendant? Then that statement may be admissible as evidence of the truth of its contents by reason that Kabir accepted it as truthful, and as proof of his reaction; see *R v Christie* [1914] AC 545. Such evidence can be admitted through a variety of roots available as a result of the CJA 2003. For example, the statement may be admissible as part of the *res gestae* under s 118(1).

KEY FACTS

Previous statements or assertions

Hearsay includes previous statements, assertions or gestures including information conveyed orally, visually, by spoken word or in a document.

The purpose of tendering hearsay

- statements relevant to truth – the basic position was that the statement was inadmissible unless it fell into an exception.

CONTINUED ▸

KEY FACTS

- original evidence – statements tendered for relevant reasons other than as proof of the truth of its contents are admissible; this includes:
  - evidence that a statement was made
  - evidence of the state of mind of the maker
  - evidence of the state of mind of the recipient.

The common law exceptions to the rule

The rule against the admission of hearsay evidence was strict, hence a number of exceptions developed in the common law which facilitated admissibility. These were expressly preserved by s 114(1)(b) in ss 118 and 118(2) of the CJA 2003 and include:

- public information – s 118(1)(b) preserve this exception – at common law the contents of a public document are admissible as evidence of the truth of its contents

- reputation, ie character (the Rule in *Rowton*)

- reputation or familial tradition

- *res gestae* – ss 114(1)(d) and 118(1)(4) expressly preserve this exception and therefore the case law. The *general rule* is that inadmissible hearsay statements are admissible if they form part of the *res gestae* (state of affairs); spontaneous statements that form an integral part of the event

- confessions – at common law the admission of a hearsay statement that was either entirely or partially adverse to the person making it was allowed

- other admissions (agents) – this common law exception has been expressly preserved by s 118(1); therefore admissions by a party either by themselves or someone acting as an agent on their behalf are still admissible

- common enterprise

- expert opinion evidence.

ACTIVITY

Self-test questions

1. What is the hearsay rule?

2. Define the term hearsay.

3. What do original and direct evidence mean?

4. Define the term *res gestae*.

5. What is relevant non-hearsay?

Further reading

Murphy, P., *Murphy on Evidence* (Oxford University Press, 2007).

Worthern, T., 'Legislative Comment: The Hearsay Provisions of the Criminal Justice Act 2003: So Far,
Not So Good?' (2008) Crim LR, 6, 431–442.

chapter 8 HEARSAY: ADMISSIBILITY IN CRIMINAL CASES ▪

AIMS AND OBJECTIVES

By the end of this chapter you should be able to understand:

- The instances in which hearsay evidence is admissible in criminal cases

- The statutory exceptions in criminal cases

- The statutory safeguards provided by the CJA 2003 in relation to hearsay evidence

- The other exceptions to the hearsay rule

- The impact that the Human Rights Convention has had on the admission of hearsay evidence.

8.1 Introduction

In the previous chapter the discussion focused on the hearsay rule and what is classified as hearsay evidence. In this chapter the discussion will centre on hearsay and its admissibility in criminal cases. Hence, the chapter begins with a brief look at the statutory exceptions providing for admission of hearsay evidence, after which the discussion moves on to the safeguards provided by the Criminal Justice Act 2003 when admitting such evidence, concluding with a look at how human rights has impacted on this area of the law of evidence.

8.2 The statutory exceptions and criminal cases

Let us begin the discussion how the CJA 2003 has, in effect, limited the scope of the rule against the admission of hearsay evidence in criminal cases. Hearsay evidence is now admissible in criminal proceedings by statute under s 114(1) of the 2003 Act. The Act specifically preserves the common law exceptions to admission of such evidence, by mutual agreement and under the safety valve, ie where the interests of justice so require it to be admitted.

Starting with the basics: how is hearsay defined by the CJA 2003? It is defined in ss 114(1), 115(2) and (3) and 134.

Section 114(1) states that

 '. . . in criminal proceedings *any* statement not made in oral evidence *at court* in the proceedings is admissible of any matter stated *if one of the four exceptions applies*'.

What does the CJA 2003 consider to be a hearsay statement? Section 115(2) of the 2003 Act defines a statement as

 '. . . any representation of fact or opinion made by a person by whatever means *including one made in* a sketch, photo-fit or other pictorial form'.

Hence, it is clear that the provision requires the statement to be made by a person. That means the term 'statement' does not cover anything produced by mechanical process, ie audio or video recordings, or photographs. The reason for this is that such evidence is not classified as hearsay evidence and is admissible via other routes. This notion statutorily approves *Taylor v Chief Constable of Cheshire* [1987] 1 All ER 225. Section 115(3) defines the term 'matter stated', which appears in s 114(1) as '. . . a matter stated is one . . . the purpose, or one of the purposes, of the person making the statement appears to the court to have been . . . to cause another to believe *it* or act or a machine to operate on the basis that the matter is as stated'. Section 134 of the Act defines 'oral evidence' as including 'evidence *that* by reason on any disability, disorder or other impairment *that* a person called as witness gives in writing, by signs or *through* any device'. Here is a summary diagram of the definition:

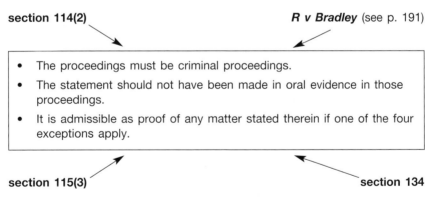

■ Figure 8.1 Definition of hearsay

The new definition has caused some problems. In *R v Isichei* (2006) 170 JP 759, A and B, two female students, along with C, whom they did not know, were being ferried around Manchester late one night, looking for an open nightclub. Whilst at the club they came across C and D. A and B were robbed and assaulted and identified D as one of the two assailants. The prosecution sought to adduce hearsay evidence that whilst in the taxi, C had stated that he was going to call Marvin (D). The word 'Marvin', which happened to be the defendant's first name, was not a

matter stated within the definition of hearsay in s 114(1). It was not made with the purpose of causing A or B to believe anything; therefore, evidence of the telephone call was admissible. On appeal Auld LJ stated that the judge may have erred. The evidence was admissible nonetheless under s 114(1)(d) (see below).

Interests of justice

Sections 114(1)(d) and 114(2) are two important provisions knowledge of which is required for assessment purposes. Our discussion will begin with the first of these. Under s 114(1)(d) of the 2003 Act, the court may admit hearsay evidence if, and only if, it is satisfied that it is in the interests of justice to do so. This provision is very wide and has resulted in the admission of hearsay evidence where none of the other exceptions to the rule is applicable; see *R v Xhabri* [2006] 1 Cr App R 26. This provision is supported by a *safety valve*, ie factors that the court must consider before it can exercise its discretion. These are outlined in s 114(2) and are:

- its probative value
- the existence and availability of any other relevant evidence
- the importance of the evidence in the entirety of the circumstances, ie considering the case as a whole
- how the statement was made, ie circumstances
- the reliability of the maker of the statement
- how reliable the evidence of the making of the statement is
- can oral evidence of the matter be given and if not, why not?
- any difficulties the opposition would face in challenging it
- prejudice to any party resulting from its admission or facing a party challenging it.

Does the judge have to make a decision on each of these? No, as Rose LJ stated in *R v Taylor* [2006] 2 Cr App R 14 '. . . what is required is *that the judge* give consideration to those factors . . . nothing in the wording of the statute requires *the judge* to reach a specific conclusion in relation to each or any of them . . .' Therefore, the trial judge is not under an obligation to reach a conclusion on each or any of these. The duty extends to considering them and stops there. Why? How long and to what extent would enquiries have to be made? Another key point to note is that both the prosecution and defence can apply to have the evidence admitted. The court will always exercise its discretion cautiously to avoid potential miscarriages of justice; see *Sparks v R* [1964] AC 964.

KEY FACTS

The statutory exceptions to the rule

The CJA 2003 has had the effect of limiting the scope of the hearsay rule and the admission of such evidence in criminal cases.

Definition of hearsay under the CJA 2003

- Section 114(1) defines hearsay as any statement that is not made in oral evidence, at court and in criminal proceedings is admissible of any matter stated if one of four exceptions applies.

- Section 115(2) defines a statement as any representation of fact or opinion made by a person by whatever means, including one made in a sketch, photo-fit or other pictorial form.

- Section 134 defines oral evidence as evidence, including that by reason of any disability, disorder or other impairment, that a person called as a witness gives in writing, by signs or through any device.

The admission of hearsay evidence

Section 114(1)(d) allows the court to admit hearsay evidence if it is satisfied that it is in the interests of justice to do so. This provision allows the admission of hearsay evidence where none of the other exceptions is applicable and is therefore supported by a *safety valve* under s 114(2), which outlines the following factors that the court must consider before it can exercise its discretion:

- the probative value of the evidence

- the existence and availability of any other relevant evidence

- the importance of the evidence in the entirety of the circumstances, ie considering the case as a whole

- how the statement was made, ie circumstances

- the reliability of the maker of the statement

- how reliable the evidence of the making of the statement is

- can oral evidence of the matter be given and if not, why not?

- any difficulties the opposition would face in challenging it

- prejudice to any party resulting from its admission or facing a party challenging it.

8.3 Statutory exceptions and documentary hearsay

Let us move on to another interesting type of hearsay statement: documentary hearsay, ie statements where any representation of fact, whether by words or otherwise (schedule 2 of the CJA 1988 which is replaced by s 115(2) of the CJA 2003 as above). Prior to the CJA 2003, ss 23–24 of the Criminal Justice Act 1988 provided that documentary hearsay evidence was admissible in limited instances, in criminal cases. The condition was that it was either impossible or impracticable to call the witness to give oral evidence. Both ss 23 and 24 only applied to documentary hearsay and not oral evidence. These provisions were respectively replaced by ss 116 and 117 of the CJA 2003; the first of these now provides for the admission of first-hand documentary and oral hearsay statements; this was a major turn-around for the statute books. The old case law has been used to interpret s 116 of the 2003 Act. Before we begin to discuss s 116, it is salient to note that neither s 23 or s 24 of the CJA 1988 applied to confessions.

Section 116 replaced s 23(1) of the CJA 1988 which made first-hand documentary hearsay evidence admissible in criminal proceedings, so long as it is a '. . . statement made by a person in a document . . . as evidence of any fact of which direct oral evidence by *them* would be admissible if:

- the person was dead, unfit due to mental or physical condition and thus unable to attend court (s 23(2)(a))

- was outside the UK and his attendance could not be reasonably and practicably secured (s 23(2)(b)) or

- could not be found where reasonable steps to find him had been undertaken (s 23(2)(c)).

This was complemented by s 23(3) which provided for the admission of a hearsay statement made to a police officer or another person charged with either the duty of investigating offences or charging offenders where the person making the statement would not give oral evidence through fear or because they were kept out of the way, ie security issues. Therefore, the main effect of s 23 was to facilitate the admission of documentary hearsay evidence where the maker of such a statement was unable to give oral evidence.

The law changed, in that s 116(1) of the CJA 2003 allows the admission of first-hand hearsay statements where the witness is not available whether they are in documentary or oral forms. It is not as simple as it sounds. Before admission, the following criteria must be satisfied:

- The evidence of the witness should have been admissible if they had been available to give evidence.

- The court is satisfied as to the identity of the maker of the statement.

- The unavailability of the maker must be due to any one of the conditions in s 116(2).

Before moving on to discuss s 116(2), let us consider the first two of these conditions. Only relevant admissible evidence can be admitted. What does that mean? It means that the maker should be competent to give evidence. The evidence should be relevant to a fact in issue and it should be generally admissible, barring the fact that it is excluded by reason of it being hearsay evidence.

ASE EXAMPLE

Sparks v R [1964] AC 964

The court held that a three-year-old child was incompetent to testify. Her evidence was inadmissible because her oral evidence was also inadmissible.

CASE EXAMPLE

R v Macgillvray [1993] Crim LR 530

The victim, who had been set on fire, made a statement to a policeman whilst a nurse was present in which he implicated the defendant. However, he was too seriously injured to sign the statement that had been made. It was read back to him and he agreed its contents were true. The defendant contended that the statement was not made by the victim, but was made by the police officer. The Court of Appeal held that the victim had made the statement since he had clearly indicated that the record was true when read back to him.

Second, the court must be satisfied as to the identity of the maker of the statement. For example, in *R v Teper* [1952] AC 480, a statement by an unidentifiable passer-by who suggested that the defendant was the arsonist was inadmissible. Why does the court need to be satisfied of the maker's identity? Consider this: the person against whom the statement is being adduced will not have the opportunity to have their barrister test or contradict the statement through cross-examination. Does this result in an unfair advantage to the party adducing such evidence? Contrary to what many may think, it does. Hence, the promotion of fairness in the proceedings requires satisfaction of the maker's identity. Finally, the unavailability of the maker of the statement must be due to one of the following factors outlined in s 116(2):

- The witness is dead (s 116(2)(a)).

- The mental or physical state of the witness means that they are unfit to testify (s 116(2)(b)).

- The attendance of the witness cannot be reasonably or practically secured because the witness is not in the UK (s 116(1)(c)).

- After taking all reasonable and practicable steps, the maker of the statement cannot be found (s 116(2)(d)).

- The witness will not give oral evidence or continue to give oral evidence in respect of their statement due to fear and on that basis the court gives permission for the hearsay statement to be given in evidence (s 116(2)(e)).

It will become obvious that these conditions are very similar to their predecessor s 23(2) of the CJA 1988. If any of the conditions (barring the final one, which we have just discussed) applies, the admission of hearsay evidence will be automatic. Let us examine each of these in a little more depth. What is the use of the old case law? Where the hearsay statement is admissible under s 116(2)(a) or (b), but the witness does not testify by reason of mental or physical unfitness or death, then the old case law helps to determine that which is required to be proven if the statement is to be admissible. The requirement in this instance is similar to that in civil proceedings. He who asserts must prove. The onus to prove the condition is on the party seeking to admit the evidence. On that basis, the prosecution must prove beyond all reasonable doubt that the maker of the statement is either dead or unfit, etc, and the defence has to satisfy the same on the civil standard of proof; the balance of probabilities; see *R v Minors* [1989] 1 WLR 441 or *R (Meredith) v Harwich Justices* [2006] EWHC 3336.

Let us now address the conditions outlined in s 116(2)(c) and (d). It is not reasonably practicable to secure the attendance of the witness because the maker of the statement is outside the UK. What are the requirements? The party seeking to have the statement admitted must prove that the maker of the statement is outside the UK by reason of their geographical location, ie they are in Canada. It is very clear that the practicalities in securing the attendance of the statement maker will depend on the facts of the individual case; see *R v Jiminez Paez* (1994) or *R v Radak* [1999] 1 Cr App R 187, where the court has confirmed that attendance includes physical attendance and evidence by live link.

How far must the party seeking to adduce the evidence go? This is a case of simple maths. The more important the witness, the greater the number of steps that should be taken to secure his attendance; see *R v Castillo* (1996) 1 Cr App R 438. The party must evidence the steps that they have taken whilst acting diligently (*R v Bray* (1988) 88 Cr App R 354) in trying to secure the witness's attendance (*R v Case* (1991) or *R v Henry* [2003] EWCA Crim 1296) *but* have failed to do so. Finally, consider the condition outlined in s 116(2)(e), where a witness does not give oral evidence in respect of their statement due to fear. Then the court has the discretion to allow the hearsay statement to be admitted, but only where the interests of justice so require. Section 116(2)(e) of the CJA 2003 is far wider than its predecessor s 23(3) of the CJA 1988. How? The current provision does not require the statement to have been made to an officer of the police service. What are the implications of the change? If Damien makes a statement to his barrister, Michael, then Michael can apply to the court for leave to adduce the statement, a situation that was not covered by s 23(3).

Has the law become clearer as a result? Arguably, yes it has; s 116(3) of the CJA 2003 acts to clarify and widen the definition of fear by including within its definition the personal or collateral fear of death, injury and financial loss; see *R v Davies (Anita)* [2006] EWCA Crim

2643. This means that the definition includes fear of injury to oneself and even to a relative, for example, Aunt Jemima. Thus, the fear experienced does not have to be wholly personal. Furthermore, like its predecessor and barring a few exceptions, there is no requirement for the fear to be caused by any particular person. If, however, the prosecution causes the fear, then the trial Judge may exclude the evidence under s 78 of PACE 1984.

ASE EXAMPLE

R v O'Loughlin [1988] 3 All ER 431

The court decided that the very fact that the witness is absent through fear of some sort must be proven through means of admissible evidence. In this instance threats and pressure by terrorists was enough.

It was argued that it was not good enough for an individual to state that they had feared something. The fact that the person had feared something should only be accepted if it could be objectively justified, ie that a reasonable person would also have apprehended such fear as a result of the threat that was made to his pet cat. In *Acton JJ ex p McMullen* (1991) 92 Cr App R 98, the court refused to accept that it did, but stated that the party seeking to prove that the witness was in fear as '. . . a consequence of the commission of the material offence or of something said or done subsequently in relation to that offence and the possibility of the witness testifying as to it'.

CASE EXAMPLE

R v H, W and M (2001) *The Times* 6th July

The statement of a witness who was absent through the fear of death was admitted even where no one connected with the case had actually made contact with him. The admission was technically incorrect and the conviction quashed.

CASE EXAMPLE

R v Martin (1996) Crim LR 589

The court suggested that there was no need to limit the fear to that which arises from the crime or the defendant.

Neill v N. Acton Magistrates Court [1992] 1 WLR 1221

Two boys made statements after having witnessed an offence take place. After this, their mother informed the police that the boys were frightened to give evidence. At the trial the officer was called by the prosecution to give evidence of what the mother had said to him. His evidence was not admissible in order to establish the fear that the children felt. It was in effect hearsay because it came through their mother. The officer should have interviewed the boys so that he could then have presented evidence of their state of mind. Rule: evidence of fear, ie the state of mind must be established through admissible evidence.

The other major point that should be noted is that the provision applies equally to those witnesses who begin to give evidence but do not continue to do so through fear; see *R v Ashford Mags exp Hilden* [1993] QB 555.

What are the formalities for admission under s 116(2)(e)? The party seeking to adduce the evidence must obtain leave from the court to do so, persuading it that it is in the interests of justice to admit the evidence. The court must be satisfied of this and consider the factors outlined in s 116(4) of the CJA 2003. The court must consider:

* the contents of the statement
* the risk of any unfairness to the party seeking to adduce the evidence if it is excluded
* the risk of any unfairness to the party against whom the evidence is being admitted
* the fact that the evidence cannot be challenged through cross-examination
* the availability of special measures under ss 17 and 19 of the Youth Justice and Criminal Evidence Act 1999.

For good examples on this, see *R v Doherty* [2006] EWCA Crim 2716. Let us take a look at the special measures under ss 117 and 119 of the CJA 2003, starting with s 117. This provides for the admissibility of a hearsay statement that is contained in a document so long as:

(a) oral evidence of the information contained in the statement would have been admissible

(b) the conditions outlined in s 117(2) of the CJA 2003 are satisfied.

The conditions outlined in s 117 are very similar to those in s 24 of the CJA 1988, which permitted the use of documentary hearsay in a range of circumstances, including those instances in which the document itself was created or received in the course of a trade or business; and where the maker of the statement could be assumed to have had personal knowledge of the facts contained in it. What did s 24 provide? It stated that '. . . any statement in a document shall be admissible in criminal proceedings as evidence of any fact of which direct oral evidence would be admissible if . . . (i) the document was created or received by a person in the course of a trade, business, profession or other occupation, or as the holder of a paid or unpaid office and (ii) the information contained in the document was supplied by a person (whether or not the maker of the statement) who had, or may reasonably be supposed to have had, personal knowledge of the matters dealt with'.

Subsections 117(2)(a) and (b) mimic those previously contained in s 24(1)(i) and (ii). What is the effect of this on the law? It is positive. The case law that went with s 24 remains relevant. In the greater context it is clear that s 117(2) no longer requires the document to form part of a record. However, it still needs to be created or received in a business or professional context. Why? The latter ensures that the document still has some degree of reliability because of the supposed business checks it would go through, ie accuracy. Furthermore, no longer is the maker of the statement required to be under a duty of any sort. He simply needs to create or receive the document in a business or professional context.

Much of the criticism of this provision centres on the fact that although satisfaction of business or professional requirements means the document is more likely to be reliable, these requirements may also act as safeguards where the information is being created or simply compiled. However, this is not really adequate where the information is merely received in such a context. The fact that some personal knowledge is required mitigates the potential inaccuracy or unreliability of such a document. An interesting fact about this provision is that the person supplying the information and creating or compiling the record can be the same as the party seeking to adduce such evidence. Such party still does not need to show that the supplier of the information is unable to give evidence; see *R v Foxley* [1995] 2 Cr App R 523.

Once the conditions in s 117(2)(a) and (b) are satisfied, the final consideration is s 117(2)(c). Only if all three conditions are satisfied can evidence under this provision be admitted. Once again this subsection is similar to its predecessor, s 24(2) of the CJA 1988. What did s 24(2) provide? It stated that where the information was indirectly supplied, then '. . . each person, through whom the information was supplied, who received it must act . . . (a) in the course of a trade, business, profession or other occupation, or (b) as the holder of a paid or unpaid office'. What did that mean? It meant that every person that received the information should have done so in either a business or professional context. It did not state whether or not the person was required to communicate it in that context too.

Statements prepared for the purpose of pending or contemplated litigation, ie criminal proceedings or investigation, s 117(4) of the CJA 2003 replaced s 24(3) of the CJA 1988, which provided that such evidence could not be admitted unless the maker of the statement:

- was dead or not fit enough to attend
- was outside the UK and it was not reasonably practicable to secure their attendance
- could not be found after all reasonable steps had been taken to trace them

- was in fear or being kept away and it was made to an officer of the police service.

Students of the law of evidence often wonder why this provision was revoked and an almost identical one re-enacted. The problem with this provision was that it was inherently unclear whether it applied to the original eyewitness of a crime or to the actual person who incorporates the information in the document; s 117(4) albeit in an almost similar provision rectifies this issue. For an example of the functioning of the old law, see *R v Bedi* (1992) Crim LR 299, *R v Carrington* (1994) 99 Cr App R 376 which should be contrasted with *R v Derodra* [2000] 1 Cr App R 41.

Finally, s 117(5) requires the party seeking to adduce the evidence to provide a statutory reason (see s 116(2) CJA 2003) as to why the supplier of the information cannot or does not attend to give evidence. This provision also allows for an additional reason for non-attendance; it states that such evidence will be admissible where the supplier cannot reasonably be expected to have any recollection of the matters in the statement due to the time that has elapsed, taking into account all the circumstances, including the interval of time between the making of the statement (supply) and now (trial).

In support of these changes s 117(7) of the CJA 2003 has given the court the discretion to exclude evidence it believes to be unreliable. What does that mean? It may mean that the contents or source of the information is unreliable or the method by which it was created, supplied or received rendered it so.

8.4 The safeguards: ss 124–126

Consider this: in adversarial proceedings, like those in England and Wales, the method used rigorously to test any evidence in court is cross-examination, the purpose of which is to ensure that a miscarriage of justice does not occur, ie no one is convicted on a weak evidential basis. What happens to that opportunity where the evidence of an absent witness is admitted? It is tragically lost and sometimes at the expense of the opposing party. This fact is considered very seriously because of the resultant unfairness that could arise, giving rise to grounds for an appeal.

Let us begin our discussion with s 124 of the CJA 2003. This provision allows the admission of evidence that relates to the credibility of the witness that is absent. What does that include? It includes any issue or relevant matter that could have been put to the witness in cross-examination. It also includes evidence of a previous inconsistent statement tendered as proof of any contradiction (s 124(2)). In addition, the opposition may adduce additional evidence in rebuttal of any allegation made in the absent witness's statement (s 124(3)). This allows the evidence of an absent witness to be rigorously tested in balancing fairness to the defendant.

S 125 gives the court a discretion to direct an acquittal or discharge the jury after the close of the prosecution case. Why would the court be minded to that? Consider this; what if the whole or a substantial part of the evidence against a defendant was purely hearsay evidence? Remember, it is still important that the prosecution secure a case against the defendant that is based on relevant and admissible evidence, that is, not purely hearsay or circumstantial in nature. Why? The securing of a conviction on the basis of such potentially unreliable evidence would result in an unsafe conviction that would eventually be quashed, because the evidence is not considered, in essence, to be strong enough. The increased risk of unfairness and a miscarriage of justice outweighs the need to secure a conviction. Section 125 of the CJA 2003 only applies to jury trials, because on summary trial in the magistrates' court the magistrates would direct themselves to acquit the defendant.

Under s 126 of the CJA 2003, the court can also exclude hearsay evidence if it is satisfied that the case for excluding it substantially outweighs the case for admitting it. This may be done after considering the danger that to admit it would result in undue waste of time and the value of the evidence to the entire case. This means that the court, after assessing the value of the evidence in relation to the case as a whole, can exclude hearsay evidence where it considers that its admission would result in a waste of time. The discretion is a broad one and the consideration of the value of the evidence to the case as a whole is not usually the only factor taken into account. Finally, the court retains the discretion to exclude any prosecution evidence, including hearsay evidence, where its admission would adversely affect the fairness of the proceedings under s 78(1) of PACE 1984. An equal discretion to exclude defence evidence now, arguably, exists under s 126(1) of the CJA 2003.

KEY FACTS

Statutory exceptions and documentary hearsay

Documentary hearsay is a statement containing any representation of fact whether by words or otherwise. Prior to ss 116 and 117 of the CJA 2003 ss 23–24 of the CJA 1988 provided that documentary hearsay was admissible in criminal cases in limited instances.

- Section 23 is superseded by s 116 which allows the admission of first-hand hearsay statements where the witness is not available whether they are in documentary or oral forms if:
  - the evidence of the witness should have been admissible if they had been available to give evidence
  - the court is satisfied of the statement makers identity
  - the unavailability of the maker must be due to any one of the conditions in s 116(2) which require that:

CONTINUED ▸

KEY FACTS

> - the witness is dead (s 116(2)(a))
> - the mental or physical state of the witness means that they are unfit to testify (s 116(2)(b))
> - the attendance of the witness cannot be reasonably or practically secured because the witness is not in the UK (s 116(1)(c))
> - after taking all reasonable and practicable steps, the maker of the statement cannot be found (s 116(2)(d))
> - the witness will not give oral evidence or continue to give oral evidence in respect of their statement due to fear and on that basis the court gives permission for the hearsay statement to be given in evidence (s 116(2)(e)).

- Section 24 is superseded by s 117 which allows the admission of a hearsay statement that is contained in a document so long as:
  - oral evidence of the information contained in the statement would have been admissible
  - the conditions outlined in s 117(2) of the CJA 2003 are satisfied.

Sections 124–126 safeguards

To prevent miscarriages of justice these provisions provide safeguards where the evidence of an absent witness is admitted.

- Section 124 allows the admission of evidence that relates to the credibility of the witness that is absent.

- Section 125 gives the court discretion to direct an acquittal or discharge the jury after the close of the prosecution case.

- Section 126 allows the court to exclude hearsay evidence if it is satisfied that the case for excluding it, after considering the danger that to admit it would result in undue waste of time and the value of the evidence to the entire case, substantially outweighs the case for admitting it.

8.5 Further exceptions to the hearsay rule

In addition to the exceptions outlined in the CJA 2003, there are a series of exceptions to the rule against the admission of hearsay evidence in other statutes. Let us take a brief look at the status of some of these, they include:

- Children and Young Persons Act 1933
- Criminal Justice Act 1967
- Criminal Justice Act 1988
- Bankers Books Evidence Act 1879
- Youth Justice and Criminal Evidence Act 1999.

Sections 42 and 43 of the Children and Young Persons Act 1933 provide for the admission of statements made by child witnesses in cases concerning sexual offences, assaults and murder. The condition is that the court must be satisfied that if the child was forced to give oral testimony in court, then there would be serious danger to his or her health. In practice, it can be difficult to argue admission under these provisions by reason of the fact that the Youth Justice and Criminal Evidence Act 1999 (YJCEA) facilitates the presentation of such evidence. The court may permit such a child witness to give evidence by means of a video recording or a television live-link. A good point to note here is that s 30 of the YJCEA 1999 repealed s 69 of PACE 1984 which provided for the admission of computerized documentary evidence. This is now subject to the CJA 2003.

Section 9 of the Criminal Justice Act 1967 provides for the admission of depositions, ie hearsay statements, with the consent of the parties. Section 30 of the Criminal Justice Act 1988 provides for the admission of expert reports but only where the evidence was admissible and the expert would have been competent to give it. We will discuss this in more detail later in the book. Finally, ss 3 and 4 of the Bankers Books Evidence Act 1879 provide for the admission of any entry in a banker's book of any matter that is recorded in it.

8.6 Other issues

Our final topic of discussion in relation to hearsay evidence in criminal cases, concerns hearsay evidence in retrials and multiple hearsay. Let us start with hearsay at a retrial. In summary, a retrial occurs when an appeal against conviction is successful and, in the interests of justice, the appeal court orders the case to be retried. Section 131 of the Criminal Justice Act 2003 amends the Criminal Appeal Act 1968 which means that any oral evidence that was given at the original trial must also be given orally at the retrial. Consider this; if oral evidence was given in the original trial, and then that evidence was tendered as a written statement in the retrial, it would be hearsay and therefore potentially inadmissible. Section 131 allows such evidence from the original trial to be tendered in a way, other than orally, where all the parties to the case agree or it falls under ss 114(1)(d) or 116; see *R v Lang* [2004] EWCA Crim 1701, where the transcript of evidence given by A at the original trial was admitted, under s 116, as evidence in the new trial.

A question: ever played the game 'Chinese whispers'? The whole purpose of the game is to get one set of information from person A through to person Z without it being altered. What normally happens is that when the information has reached person Z, it has gone from being 'I like eating jelly babies' to 'John's dog has rabies'. The same can happen to evidence when it is

shunted from pillar to post; consider this: Sheetal witnesses a robbery; she tells her brother, A, who tells his friend, B, who finally tells a police officer, C. How can evidence of this sort be classified? When evidence, such as that of Sheetal's, filters through more than one individual before it is recorded, it is referred to as multiple hearsay. This type of hearsay is only admissible in the following instances:

- under s 117 of the CJA 2003 as a business document
- under s 119 of the CJA 2003 as a previous inconsistent statement
- under s 120 of the CJA 2003 as another previous statement
- where all parties to the case agree to it being admissible
- the court decides to exercise its discretion, under s 121 of the CJA 2003, to admit the evidence on the basis that the interests of justice require it to be admitted. This may be due to its value and reliability in the context of the overall case.

The test under s 121 of the CJA 2003 is more stringent that under s 114(1)(d) of the CJA 2003 because multiple hearsay is more likely to be infected and unreliable than first-hand hearsay evidence.

8.7 The impact of human rights on the admission of hearsay evidence

Students, practitioners and researchers of the law, more specifically for current purposes the law of evidence, soon realize that human rights law is a pervasive topic, ie it crops up everywhere. This section of the chapter will take a brief look at the human rights issues that have arisen, and those likely to arise as a result of the changes brought about by the Criminal Justice Act 2003. Whether or not the admission of the hearsay evidence of an absent witness breaches the right to a fair trial provided by Art 6 of the European Convention on Human Rights and Fundamental Freedoms (ECHR) is questionable. The current concern is whether or not the admission of such evidence breaches the right of the defence to cross-examine prosecution witness evidence provided by Art 6(3)(d). It is clear that the safeguards provided by ss 124–126 of the CJA 2003 mitigate the issue of unreliability.

What does the European Court of Human Rights (ECtHR) have to say on the matter? According to the case law that is coming out of the court it seems that no consistent approach is being taken. For example, in *Kostovski v The Netherlands* (1990) 12 EHRR 434, the court decided that a defendant is entitled to an 'adequate and proper' opportunity to 'challenge and question' any witness that is giving evidence against them. In contrast, in *Asch v Austria* (1993) 15 EHRR 597, the court stated that the right provided by the ECHR is only breached if the prosecution case is substantially based on the evidence of a witness that is absent. Another useful example is *R v Thomas and Flannagan* [1998] Crim LR 887. The problem with these judgments is twofold; a case-by-case approach, albeit desirable because each is decided on its own merits, results in inconsistency of application, and as a result, there is no guidance or standard on which to base any practical reality. What is clear from the judgments is the following:

- The defendant has the right to examine or have examined the evidence of a witness that stands against them.

- Where a case is not solely based on the hearsay evidence of an absent witness, ie evidence other than that of the absent witness, then the requirement that the defendant be given an 'adequate and proper' opportunity to 'challenge and question' it will be satisfied.

- Where a case is wholly or substantially based on the hearsay evidence of an absent witness, ie there is not any other or much other evidence apart from that of the absent witness, then the defendant will have grounds on which to lodge an appeal, ie the trial was unfair and the conviction unsafe.

Other issues in relation to this are more than likely to crop up, and I recommend frequent visits to the website that accompanies this book at www.unlockingthelaw.co.uk for updates.

Here is a summary diagram of the ways in which hearsay evidence may be admitted:

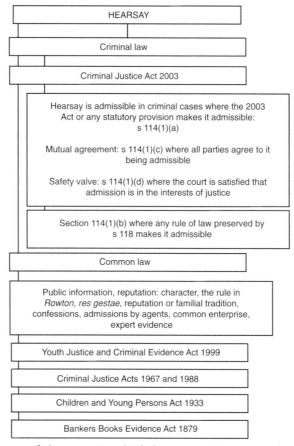

■ Figure 8.2 Summary diagram of the ways in which hearsay evidence may be admitted

8.8 Summary

Classifying evidence as hearsay evidence

Hearsay evidence consists of statements or assertions that are made on previous occasions, which are tendered as evidence to prove that their contents are true. Under the *old* rules determining whether evidence was hearsay evidence and whether it was inadmissible was a two-stage approach, the Court would ask: does the evidence consist of a previous statement or assertion, which amounts to hearsay, and what is the purpose for which it is being tendered?

The CJA 2003 and a new approach to hearsay evidence

The Criminal Justice Act 2003 introduced a brand new inclusionary approach to hearsay evidence modernizing the law. Under the new approach the rule s 114 of the CJA 2003 provides that hearsay evidence, ie a statement not made in oral evidence in the proceedings, is admissible in criminal trials of any matter stated. The occasions are when any provision makes it admissible, any rule of law preserved by s 118 makes it admissible, all the parties agree to it being admissible, or, the court is satisfied that it is in the interests of justice for it to be admissible.

Previous statements or assertions

The hearsay rule applies to previous statements, assertions or gestures that are made by any person; this includes a previous statement that may have been made by the witness themselves. It is accepted by the law that a person may use a variety of methods to communicate information, ie orally, visually, spoken word, in a document or by gestures. The CJA 2003 covers previous inconsistent statements which are admitted in accordance with the Criminal Procedure Investigations Act 1865 (CPIA).

Statements relevant only to truth

In criminal cases the rule against the admission of hearsay evidence has been strictly applied; the basic position was that a hearsay statement is inadmissible unless it falls within an exception.

Original evidence/non-hearsay statements

Statements tendered for relevant reasons other than as proof of the truth of their contents are admissible as evidence, ie to evidence the making of the statement itself, or to evidence the state of mind of the person making the statement, or person hearing it.

Circumstantial evidence: lack of the record

Normally a statement will amount to a hearsay statement if it is tendered to prove the truth of its contents, ie something exists or has happened. If tendered to show the opposite, the statement still falls under the same rule.

The common law exceptions to the rule

Section 114(1)(b) of the Criminal Justice Act 2003 (CJA) expressly preserves the common law exceptions to the rule against hearsay in s 118, and s 118(2) has abolished those not mentioned. In summary, documents admissible as evidence of facts stated therein, that have been preserved are:

- public information
- reputation, ie character (the Rule in *Rowton*)
- reputation or familial tradition
- *res gestae*
- confessions
- other admissions (agents)
- common enterprise
- expert evidence.

Further exceptions to the hearsay rule

In addition to the exceptions outlined in the CJA 2003 there are a series of exceptions to the rule against the admission of hearsay evidence in other statutes including:

- Children and Young Persons Act 1933
- Criminal Justice Act 1967
- Criminal Justice Act 1988
- Bankers Books Evidence Act 1879
- Youth Justice and Criminal Evidence Act 1999.

Other issues

Section 131 of the Criminal Justice Act 2003 amends the Criminal Appeal Act 1968 which means that any oral evidence that was given at the original trial must also be given orally at the retrial. In addition, multiple hearsay is only admissible in the following instances:

- under s 117 as a business document
- under s 119 as a previous inconsistent statement
- under s 120 as another previous statement
- where all parties to the case agree to it being admissible
- the court decides to exercise its discretion, under s 121, to admit the evidence on the basis that the interests of justice require it to be admitted because of its value and reliability in the context of the overall case.

ACTIVITY

Self-test questions

1. Outline the four exceptions in which hearsay is admissible under the CJA 2003?

2. Explain the purpose of the safety valve.

3. Are there any other statutes under which hearsay evidence is also admissible barring the CEA 1995 and the CJA 2003?

4. What is multiple hearsay? Provide at least one example.

5. Are there any human rights issues that affect the use of hearsay evidence?

Further reading

Ormerod, D., 'Case comment: Ali v Revenue and Customs Prosecutions Office [2008] EWCA Crim 1466; (2008) 172 J.P. 516 (CA (Crim Div)) – Criminal Justice Act 2003 s 114 – judge's refusal to admit document based on information as to its contents derived from PII hearing', (2009) Crim LR, 2, 106–109.

Choo, A. L. T. and Nash, S., 'Evidence Law in England and Wales: The Impact of the Human Rights Act 1998', (2003) International Journal of Evidence and Proof, 7 (1), pp. 31–61.

Worthern, T., 'Legislative Comment: The Hearsay Provisions of the Criminal Justice Act 2003: So Far, Not So Good?' (2008) Crim LR, 6, 431–442.

HEARSAY: CIVIL CASES ■

AIMS AND OBJECTIVES

By the end of this chapter you should be able to understand:

- The reasons behind the inclusionary approach to hearsay in civil cases

- The instances in which hearsay evidence is admissible under the Civil Evidence Act 1995

- Issues of the competence, compellability or witnesses and weight that is attached to hearsay

- The relative procedural requirements.

9.1 Introduction

In the previous chapter the discussion focused on the hearsay rule in criminal cases. In this chapter the discussion will centre on hearsay and its admissibility in civil cases. Hence, the chapter begins with a brief look at the use of hearsay evidence in civil cases and its admission according to the Civil Evidence Act 1995.

9.2 The use of hearsay evidence in civil cases

This is the final chapter on hearsay evidence and we begin with a brief discussion of the rules on hearsay evidence in civil cases. In basic terms, because civil cases tend rarely to involve juries, in that they are tried by a judge sitting alone, the attitude towards the admission of hearsay as evidence is far more relaxed than its counterpart in criminal proceedings. Why? Think back; we discussed earlier how lawyers, judges and politicians all believed that juries were not necessarily able to assess hearsay appropriately, and how there remained a danger that they may attribute more weight to the hearsay evidence than should have been attributed. This is avoided in civil cases because of the lack of jury trial. Finally, it should be noted that the definition of hearsay in relation to civil cases and criminal cases is slightly different. Hence, the realignment of the rules in these two separate areas of law is not exact.

9.2.1 The Civil Evidence Act 1995

The very first set of statutory exceptions to the rule against the admission of hearsay evidence in civil cases was formulated in the Civil Evidence Act 1968. These were not without their critics.

The provisions were very far-reaching and unduly complex. The Civil Evidence Act 1995 (CEA) sought to rectify these complexities, with the effect that hearsay evidence is generally admissible in civil cases. The general rule is that hearsay in civil cases is admissible under the CEA 1995, the Children Act 1989 and the Child Support Act 1991.

9.2.2 Section 1 CEA 1995

Section 1(1) of the CEA 1995 states that in civil proceedings '. . . evidence shall not be excluded on the ground that it is hearsay'. That means that evidence cannot be excluded simply because it is hearsay but suggests that procedural requirements must be satisfied. We will deal with these s 2 requirements in a moment. What are civil proceedings? They are defined in ss 11 and 12 of the CEA 1995 as any proceedings in a court or tribunal, or in arbitration, where strict rules of evidence apply.

What are hearsay statements? Are they the same as those in criminal proceedings? The answer is no; statements in this instance include any representation of fact or opinion, regardless of how it is made (s 13 CEA 1995). The definition of hearsay is outlined in s 1(2)(a) of the CEA 1995 as 'a statement made otherwise than by a person *whilst* giving oral evidence in the proceedings which is tendered as evidence of the matters stated *therein*'. The CEA 1995 applies to all types of hearsay evidence (s 1(2)(b)).

9.2.3 Section 2 CEA 1995

Any party wishing to rely on hearsay evidence must comply with the requirements of s 2 of the CEA 1995, that is, to give notice of their intention to rely on such evidence. In addition, the opposition must be provided with, if they request it, details of the hearsay evidence so that they may overcome any practical difficulties that arise from the admission of it (s 2(1)). In support of the admission of such evidence, s 2(2) gives power, usually to the relevant Minister, to make rules of court, ie what hearsay issues are excluded from the notice requirement and any time limits for the serving of notice on the opposition, etc. This allows the functioning of the law. Think about this; Sachin gives notice to the opposition barrister, Sheetal, of his intention to rely on hearsay at trial on 25th July 2009. However, he gives Sheetal that notice on 24th July 2009. Would that situation be absurd? It would lead to increased expenses and a waste of court time where proceedings are subsequently delayed. The overriding objective is contained within the Civil Procedure Rules 1998, which are readily available to freely download at www.justice.gov.uk/civil/procrules_fin/contents/parts/part01.htm. These lay down the considerations that are taken into account in the conduct of civil proceedings.

What if a party fails to comply with either s 2(1) or (2)? Section 2(4) of the 1995 Act makes it clear that any such failure, does not render the evidence inadmissible, but affects the weight that will be given to it, with potential costs penalties for the party in default. The general study of Civil Litigation and Practice, if it forms part of your LLB Honours degree, shows that the general rule in civil proceedings is that costs follow the event, ie the loser pays the other side's

costs. Are there any instances in which no notice is required? Yes, where the evidence is given by affidavit, ie sworn, or the maker of the statement is dead and his estate is subject to probate, then no notice is required to be given.

9.2.4 Section 3 CEA 1995

The provision under s 3 of the CEA 1995 is peculiar to civil cases; no equivalent exists in relation to criminal proceedings. Where party A proposes to tender hearsay evidence against party B, without calling the maker of the statement as a witness, then party B may, under s 3, be allowed to call the maker of the statement to give evidence. Let us look at this in slightly more detail. Sarah, acting on behalf of Ben, gives notice to Jay, who acts on behalf of Chanelle, of her intention to tender the hearsay evidence of Daniel at the trial. Jay can, under s 3, apply to the court for leave to call Daniel to give oral evidence. The purpose of this is so that Jay may cross-examine Daniel on his hearsay statement, even though Daniel has not given any evidence-in-chief. This is because his hearsay statement will stand as evidence-in-chief.

9.2.5 Section 4 CEA 1995: weight

In civil cases the court has the discretion to allocate appropriate weight to hearsay evidence; s 4(1) sets out the criteria the court can use to assess the weight of such evidence, including any circumstances that may reasonably lead the court to infer that the evidence is unreliable or reliable. Within this, there is a possibility that absolutely no weight will be attached to it. Section 4(2) states that the court may have regard to the following:

- how reasonable and practicable it was for the party tendering the evidence to produce the maker of the statement at court as a witness
- whether the statement was made contemporaneously in relation to the occurrence or matters stated
- whether the evidence is multiple hearsay
- whether anyone involved has a motive to either hide or conceal the matters contained in the evidence
- whether the hearsay statement is a first-hand hearsay or an edited account
- whether the statement was made jointly with another person
- whether the statement was made for a particular purpose
- whether the evidence is presented as hearsay to prevent the court apportioning the appropriate weight to it.

Hence, where a witness can easily give oral evidence at trial but fails to do so, then the weight attached to the hearsay statement can be substantially reduced. Once again reliability is dealt with by a requirement that the statement be produced as close as possible in time to the event occurring.

9.2.6 Section 5 CEA 1995: competence and credibility

Think back to Chapter 3 and our discussion on competence and compellability. In civil proceedings, hearsay statements made by anyone considered to be incompetent as a witness cannot be admitted (s 5(1)). That includes anyone who is mentally ill or those who do not understand the nature of the proceedings and children that do not satisfy the test under s 96(1) of the Children Act 1989.

In addition to this, the credibility of the maker of the statement can be attacked under s 5(2). What does the attack include? It only includes the use of any evidence that would have been admissible had the witness given oral evidence, ie previous inconsistent statements. Why is this restrictive approach taken? It prevents the issues being bogged down by collateral issues, ie things not relevant to the facts in issue. Any party wishing to attack the credibility of the statement maker must give notice of the intention to do so within 28 days of receiving the s 2 notice from the party intending to use the statement.

9.2.7 Section 6 CEA 1995: previous statements

Section 6(1) allows, with the leave of the court, the admission of the previous statements of any witness called to give evidence. Where a party is seeking to adduce a previous statement to rebut an allegation of fabrication, then they can do so without first obtaining the leave of the court. Both previous consistent and inconsistent statements are evidence of the matters stated therein. For purposes of further reading, reference should be made to ss 3–5 of the Criminal Procedure Act 1865 and to Chapter 6.

Finally, it should be noted that s 6(4) and (5) preserves the instances in which memory-refreshing documents become evidence; see Chapter 6 for further discussion.

9.2.8 Section 7 CEA 1995: common law

Let us look very briefly at the preservation of some of the common law rules of civil evidence under s 7(1) of the 1995 Act. Section 7(2) provides that the following documents are admissible as evidence of facts stated therein:

- published works, ie histories, dictionaries or maps
- public documents, ie registers
- records, ie court records, treaties and crown pardons.

Section 7(3) preserves the common law rules that allow the court to find certain evidence as proving or disproving matters where:

- evidence of reputation is admissible to prove good or bad character
- evidence of reputation or familial tradition is admissible
- the purpose is to prove or disprove pedigree

- the purpose is to prove or disprove the existence any person or thing
- the purpose is to prove or disprove the existence of a marriage
- the purpose is to prove or disprove that any public or general right exists.

It should be noted that notice under s 2 is not required where any of these common law exceptions apply.

9.2.9 Section 8 CEA 1995

In civil cases, any statement that is contained in a document can be proven using either an original or authenticated document (s 8(1)), or even a copy of a copy of a copy (s 8(2)). It becomes quickly obvious how laid back these rules are in comparison to those in the criminal law.

9.2.10 Sections 9 and 10 CEA 1995

Sections 9 and 10 of the 1995 Act makes admissible any records that are shown to form part of either a business or public authority record. What normally happens is that an officer from the business or public authority will give a signed certificate confirming that they are part of the records (s 9(2)). What is a record? Section 9(4) defines a record as including records in any form, ie paper or electronic. The same provision also defines business and public authority. What happens if there is an entry missing from the record? These are known as instances of negative hearsay, which can be rectified by the officer producing an affidavit to establish its absence. Finally, it should be noted that the court could dispense with any formalities that are required under s 9.

Section 10 of the 1995 Act states that the Ogden tables are admissible for the calculation of future financial loss based on actuarial sciences. A useful discussion on these tables is available to download freely from the Government Actuary's Department Internet website at www.gad.gov.uk/Services/Other_Services/Compensation_for_injury_and_death.asp.

KEY FACTS

Hearsay in civil cases

The *general rule* in civil cases is far more relaxed than in criminal cases because of the lack of jury; trial lawyers are far more competent to assess appropriately for purposes of weight this type of evidence.

The law is contained in the CEA 1995:

CONTINUED ▸

KEY FACTS

- **Section 1** states that evidence in civil proceedings shall not be excluded on the ground that it is hearsay.

- **Section 2** requires the party intending on relying on the statement to give notice of its use.

- **Section 3** allows the party against whom the hearsay was adduced to call the maker of the statement to give evidence.

- **Section 4(2)** sets out the criteria the court must use to assess the weight and reliability of the hearsay, this includes:
  - how reasonable and practicable it was for the party tendering the evidence to produce the maker of the statement at court as a witness
  - how contemporaneously the statement was made in relation to the occurrence or matters stated
  - whether the evidence is multiple hearsay
  - whether anyone involved has a motive to either hide or conceal the matters contained in the evidence
  - whether the hearsay statement is a first-hand hearsay or an edited account
  - whether the statement was made for a particular purpose
  - whether the statement was made jointly with another person
  - whether the evidence is presented as hearsay to prevent the court apportioning the appropriate weight to it.

- **Section 5** provides that the hearsay evidence of a legally incompetent witness is not admissible.

- **Section 6** allows, with the leave of the court, the admission of the previous statements of any witness called to give evidence.

- **Section 7(1)** makes admissions admissible; s 7(2) provides that the following documents are admissible as evidence of facts stated therein:
  - published works, for example histories, dictionaries or maps
  - public documents including registers
  - records such as court records, treaties and crown pardons.

Here is a summary diagram of the ways in which hearsay evidence may be admitted:

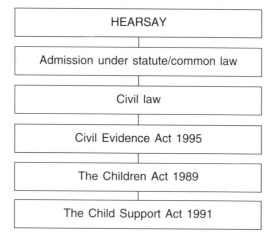

■ Figure 9.1 Summary diagram of the ways in which hearsay evidence may be admitted

9.3 Summary

The use of hearsay evidence in civil cases

In civil cases the attitude towards the admission of hearsay as evidence is far more relaxed than in criminal proceedings.

The Civil Evidence Act 1995 – section 1 CEA 1995

Section 1(1) of the CEA 1995 states that in civil proceedings '. . . evidence shall not be excluded on the ground that it is hearsay'. This means that evidence cannot simply be excluded because it is hearsay but suggests that procedural requirements set out in s 2 must be satisfied.

Section 2 CEA 1995

Any party wishing to rely on hearsay evidence must comply with the requirements of s 2 of the CEA 1995; that is, to give notice of their intention to rely on such evidence and provide them with, if requested, details of the hearsay evidence so that they may overcome any practical difficulties that arise from the admission of it.

Section 3 CEA 1995

Section 3 allows the party against whom the hearsay evidence is tendered to call the witness to give evidence.

Section 4 CEA 1995

This provision allows the court to use its discretion to allocate appropriate weight to hearsay evidence, after considering any circumstances that may reasonably lead the court to infer that the

evidence is unreliable or reliable. In doing so, the court will, under s 4(2), have regard to the following:

- how reasonable and practicable it was for the party tendering the evidence to produce the maker of the statement at court as a witness
- how contemporaneously the statement was made in relation to the occurrence or matters stated
- whether the evidence is multiple hearsay
- whether anyone involved has a motive either to hide or conceal the matters contained in the evidence
- whether the hearsay statement is a first-hand hearsay or an edited account
- whether the statement was made jointly with another person
- whether the statement was made for a particular purpose
- whether the evidence is presented as hearsay to prevent the court apportioning the appropriate weight to it.

Section 5 CEA 1995

In civil proceedings, a hearsay statement made by anyone considered to be incompetent as a witness cannot be admitted.

ACTIVITY

Self-test questions

1. What is the difference between the definitions of hearsay in the Civil Evidence Act 1995 and the CJA 2003?

2. When seeking to adduce hearsay evidence the party seeking admission of it must comply with the requirements of s 2 of the CEA 1995. What are these?

3. Does the CEA 1995 allow the party against whom hearsay evidence is tendered to call the witness to give evidence?

4. Summarize the effect of s 4 of the CEA 1995.

5. Which, if any, rules of the common law rules relating to the admission of hearsay evidence does the CEA 1995 preserve?

Further reading

Keane, A., *The Modern Law of Evidence* (Oxford University Press, 2008).
Murphy, P., HHJ, *Murphy on Evidence* (Oxford University Press, 2007).

Internet links

Civil Procedure Rules 1998: www.justice.gov.uk/civil/procrules_fin/contents/parts/part01.htm

Government Actuary's Department
www.gad.gov.uk/Services/Other_Services/Compensation_for_injury_and_death.asp

chapter 10 CONFESSIONS AND OTHER ILLEGALLY OBTAINED EVIDENCE ■

AIMS AND OBJECTIVES

By the end of this chapter you should be able to understand:

■ The nature of confession evidence

■ The definition of confession evidence and its use

■ The law regarding the admissibility and exclusion of confession evidence

■ The rules regarding illegally obtained evidence.

10.1 Introduction

In this chapter the discussion will focus on confession and other illegally obtained evidence. The discussion will look at how a confession is defined, then progress to its uses and possible issues of admissibility. We finish with a debate on other illegally obtained evidence, such as that obtained through the *agent provocateur*, or through breach of the Codes of Practice, that accompany the Police and Criminal Evidence Act 1984.

10.2 The common law development of confession evidence

The criminal law regards an informal admission that is relevant to guilt of the accused as a confession. For example, Alexandra admits that she murdered her husband, Simon. Confessions are important evidence, being exceptions to the hearsay rule in criminal cases. Once again, this area of the law of evidence developed in the common law through concepts such as voluntariness. Decisions of admissibility were aided by the obsolete Judge Rules. The current position is regulated by s 76 of the Police and Criminal Evidence Act 1984 (PACE) and Codes C and E of the Codes of Practice that accompany the Act. It should be noted that as a result of s 67(9) of the Act, the Codes apply to all organs of the State charged with investigating or charging offenders. This ranges from the police, customs officers and more recently Inland Revenue Special Compliance Officers; see *R v Gill* [2004] 1 WLR 469. The *general rule* is that a confession obtained in breach of Code C will not automatically be rendered inadmissible. However, the breach will most definitely make it more difficult for the prosecution to argue for its admission. Code of Practice C lays down detailed procedural requirements that must be observed when interrogating suspects. For example, alongside s 58 of the Act, para 6 of Code of Practice C confers extensive rights to legal advice (see also Guidance note 6D on the role of solicitors advancing the rights of the client). Section 60 regulated by Code of Practice E advances the authenticity of interviews through the requirement of tape recording. The most up-to-date versions of all PACE Act 1984 Codes of Practice are available to download freely at http://police.homeoffice.gov.uk/operational-policing/powers-pace-codes/pace-code-intro/.

10.2.1 Definition of a confession

A partial statutory definition of a confession is provided by s 82(1) of the PACE 1984 which states:

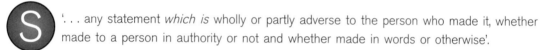

'. . . any statement *which is* wholly or partly adverse to the person who made it, whether made to a person in authority or not and whether made in words or otherwise'.

The definition seems straightforward; however, it caused many interpretational problems; see *R v Ward, Andrews and Broadley* [2001] Crim LR 316. Let us take a brief look at the requirements; first, s 82(1) clearly states that the statement may be wholly or partly adverse to the maker. This means that it does not have to wholly incriminate a defendant. It is enough that some of it does so. Such statements are also referred to as 'mixed statements'. What then is adverse? The Court of Appeal in *R v Sat-Bhambra* (1988) 88 Cr App R 55, decided that the test to determine adversity should be applied to the time when the confession was made. This means that a defendant's favourable statement at the time it was made cannot become a confession when it later becomes incriminatory. In *Sat-Bhambra,* the court were of the opinion, although it did not form part of the judgment or ruling, that purely exculpatory statements did not fall within the meaning of s 82(1), per Lord Lane CJ:

> '. . . the section is aimed at excluding confessions obtained by words or deeds that render them unreliable . . . *not at* statements containing nothing which the interrogator wished the defendant to say and nothing apparently adverse to the defendants interests'.

This approach was confirmed in *Park* [1993] 99 Cr App R 270. Second, the incriminatory content in the confession must be unambiguous. In *R v Schofield* (1917) 12 Cr App R 191, the

247

defendant on arrest shouted, 'just my luck'. The court decided that this statement could not amount to a confession because it was too ambiguous. Third, the statement does not have to be made to a person in an authoritative position. It can be made to a police officer or a friend. For example, Barry confesses to John that he murdered his gay lover, Graeme. Finally, the statement does not have to be in a particular form. This means that almost any method that is used to communicate adverse information is capable of establishing a confession.

What if the suspect remains completely silent – can such a situation amount to a statement? This situation obviously falls outside of the ambit of s 82(1) and may be indicative of guilt. The position is covered by the Criminal Justice and Public Order Act 1994, which provides for the drawing, in some instances, of adverse inferences from silence.

So far, it seems that the law readily accepts confession evidence; what, then, are the restrictions? Confessions are normally obtained as the result of suspect interrogation, either by the police or the authority that is charged with the investigation of an offence. Thus, the Codes of Practice that accompany the PACE Act 1984 must be adhered to, so that the rights of the suspect are not infringed and are safeguarded. The main Code of Practice on this issue is Code C, but further protection is provided by Code E which requires all interviews to be recorded, whether by tape or digital instrument. On occasion this may not be possible because the confession was made outside the interview room. In that instance, non-recording does not render the confession inadmissible. It may still be admissible (discussed later).

The procedural safeguards provided by Code E ensure that the tape is an accurate reflection of what actually occurred in the interview, with a transcript being agreed between the parties, which will undoubtedly be used in court. The cases of *R v Riaz, R v Burke* [1992] Crim LR 366, are authorities for the proposition that even if a transcript has been agreed, the tapes themselves can still be used. This may be a strategic ploy by the prosecution – it is far more powerful hearing a

KEY FACTS

Confessions

A *partial* definition is outlined in s 82(1) of the PACE 1984; the following four points are important:

- The statement must be a wholly or partly adverse statement that incriminates the suspect.
- The incriminatory content must be unambiguous.
- The statement can be made to anyone, even those not in an authoritative position.
- No particular form is required for purposes of admissibility.

confession in contrast to listening to one being read out. Where the prosecution wishes to rely on either the accused's significant statement or silence which had occurred outside of the interview, such as the accused's response when the tape is switched off, in these circumstances the police are required to mention the significant statement or silence to the accused in the next taped interview that they conduct and to invite a response.

10.2.2 Admissibility

At this point it may be a useful reminder to restate the *general rule* on the admissibility of evidence. Evidence must be *relevant evidence* if it is to be *admissible*. As discussed earlier the common law provided for the admission of confession evidence. Currently, s 76(1) of the PACE Act 1984 provides the same, but in a more regulated manner. Under this provision the court has the power to exclude such evidence. Sections 76(1) and 76(7) provide that where confession evidence is admitted, it is only admissible against the maker. For example, if Heather confesses to killing her husband James, her confession, if admitted, is only evidence against her.

An interesting question arises: does confession evidence need to be supported or corroborated by other evidence? The answer to this question is simply, no, it does not; the confession will stand as evidence in its own right and evidence that does not require corroboration. Furthermore, it is for the jury to determine how much weight they may attribute to the confession, ie how believable is it in the circumstances. Thus, where a confession has been ruled admissible by the trial judge, it is the role of the defendant's counsel to raise such arguments before the jury. That may have the effect of reducing the weight that the jury may attach to the confession, even if the same arguments failed to convince the trial judge from excluding it in the first place. The arguments that the defendant can put forward include:

- a challenge to the factual basis of the confession
- a dispute as to whether a confession was ever made
- a dispute as to what is being represented as being a misrepresentation of what was said.

The effect of this will be to undermine the confession evidence, and the matter will then fall for the jury to decide what weight they should attribute to it. Remember, where a tape-recording of the confession exists, the latter of these will be very difficult to prove. No grounds of appeal will lie where a conviction is based on a jury's view of an admissible confession, unless the confession evidence was ambiguous, or where it could not have been reasonably taken to indicate that the defendant was guilty.

10.2.3 Exclusion: *general*

Let us move on now to exclusion of confession evidence; s 76(2) of the PACE Act 1984 provides:

'. . . if, in any proceedings where the Prosecution proposes to give in evidence a confession made by an accused person, it is represented to the court that the confession was or may have been obtained: (a) by oppression of the person who made it; or (b) in consequence of anything said or done which was likely, in the circumstances existing at the time, to render unreliable any confession which might be made by him in consequence thereof, the court shall not allow the confession to be given in evidence against him except in so far as the prosecution proves to the court beyond reasonable doubt that the confession (notwithstanding that it may be true) was not obtained as aforesaid'.

This means that confession evidence that is obtained by oppression or is rendered unreliable by things said or done, is excluded. In addition, where the defence does not do so of its own volition, s 76(3) of the PACE Act 1984 allows the court to require the prosecution to prove that the confession evidence was not obtained by oppressive means or in circumstances which render it unreliable. Note: s 78 of the PACE Act 1984 also provides for a mechanism to exclude such evidence, this provides:

'. . . In any proceedings the court may refuse to allow evidence on which the prosecution proposes to rely to be given if it appears to the court that, having regard to all the circumstances, including the circumstances in which the evidence was obtained, the admission of the evidence would have such an adverse effect on the fairness of proceedings that the court ought not to admit it'.

CASE EXAMPLE

R v Mason [1988] 1 WLR 139

The defendant was tricked by the police into making a confession. There existed no oppression and thus the confession was reliable. The court excluded the evidence on the basis of s 78 (above).

10.3 Exclusion: *specific*

Let us take a look at exclusion under ss 76 and 78 in more detail, beginning with s 76. Where a defendant contends, or the court suggests under the power invested in it under s 76(3), that a confession was obtained in circumstances of oppression or unreliability, then the prosecution will bear the legal burden of disproving this allegation. This means that the prosecution is required to prove beyond reasonable doubt that the confession was obtained without oppression and that it is reliable.

10.3.1 Section 76 and exclusion by reason of oppression

The interpretation of the term 'oppression' has been the subject of much debate. Where oppression is alleged, then the law requires that the oppression *causes* the making of the confession. What then is oppression? Section 76(8) of the PACE Act 1984 states that oppression:

 '. . . includes torture, inhuman or degrading treatment, and the use or threat of violence'.

It could be that a variety of behaviour is oppressive. However, the key factor of it is impropriety on the part of someone in an authoritative position. Deliberate and harsh ill-treatment or behaviour that falls short of that but would have affected the suspect, would still fall under s 76(2)(b).

CASE EXAMPLE

R v Fulling [1987] QB 426

A female suspect was informed that her partner was having an affair. This information caused her much distress and she made a confession to the police.

The Court of Appeal held that this was not in fact oppression, it was the

 '. . . exercise of power in a burdensome, harsh or wrongful manner . . . unjust or cruel treatment of subjects . . . the imposition of unreasonable or unjust burdens'. The court also stated that the word oppression meant '. . . something above and beyond that which is inherently oppressive in police custody, and must import some impropriety, some oppression actively applied in an improper manner by the police'.

CASE EXAMPLE

R v Emmerson (1990) 92 Cr App R 284

The court decided that a police officer losing his temper and swearing at a suspect whilst questioning him, did not amount to oppression.

CASE EXAMPLE

R v Miller, Paris and Others (1993) 97 Cr App R 99

The defendants, accused of murdering a prostitute, were interviewed by the police for long periods of time. Mr Miller, who had a very low mental age, was interviewed for over 13 hours, during this period he denied his involvement over 300 times. Apart from this fact, the tape-recordings showed that he was subject to verbal bullying by the initial team of investigators. The subsequent team refused him access to legal advice, distorted the evidence they had against him and consistently pushed him to accept the police version of events. Mr Miller finally confessed; however, the court ruled the confession inadmissible, because it was unreliable and obtained by oppression.

Let us take a look at the decision in *Paris* in slightly more detail. The factors the court considered in ruling that the confession was inadmissible were:

- the suspect's mental capacity
- the length of the interviews being over 13 hours long
- over 300 denials
- the verbal bullying
- the refusal of access to legal advice
- the distortion of the evidence
- the badgering of the suspect with the police version of events.

The Court of Appeal made the point that it would still have considered the tactics of the police to be oppressive if Mr Miller had had a normal mental capacity. *Miller* adopts a far more lenient approach than that adopted in *Fulling,* and it is therefore unclear how far police questioning may go before it becomes oppressive.

10.3.2 Section 76 and exclusion by reason of unreliability

Section 76(2)(b) of the PACE Act 1984 provides for the exclusion of confession evidence, if anything said or done is likely in the circumstances existing at the time, to render it unreliable. Therefore, under this provision the court will consider two points; first, *things said or done* and second, those things within the context of the *circumstances that existed at the time*; see *R v Wahab* [2003] 1 Cr App R 232. The effect of this provision is to render unreliable a confession that was obtained by means falling short of oppression.

CASE EXAMPLE

R v Harvey [1988] Crim LR 241

H confessed to murdering someone in order to protect the other suspect who happened to be her lesbian lover. The court confirmed that the test was whether a *confession that was made in the circumstances that existed was likely therefore to be unreliable.* H was, however, mentally retarded and the court excluded her confession by reason of its unreliability.

A confession will be excluded if it was made as a consequence of things said or done which are likely to render it unreliable. In *R v McGovern* (1990) 92 Cr App R 228, the Court of Appeal held that the confession evidence of a defendant who had confessed to being involved in a murder to be inadmissible as being unreliable. At the time of making the confession, she was,

1. denied access to legal advice, contrary to s 58 of the PACE Act 1984

2. of a low IQ level

3. six months pregnant and in a highly distressed and emotional state.

The police had also failed to keep written notes of her initial interview, *per* Farquharson LJ:

> **J** '. . . this Court is clearly of the view that even if the confession given at the first interview was true, as it was later admitted to be, it was made in consequence of her being denied access to a solicitor and is for that reason in the circumstances likely to be unreliable. It follows that the prosecution has not in our judgment proved otherwise . . . if a solicitor had been present at the time this mentally backward and emotionally upset young woman was being questioned, the interview would have been halted on the very basis that her responses would be unreliable. It seems that the interview was held quickly and without the formalities prescribed by the Code of Conduct because the police were anxious to discover the missing girl, but this heightened the risk of the confession being unreliable.'

McGovern is evidence that an initial interview that does not comply with the PACE Act 1984 or its Codes of Practice will mean any subsequent interview will be tainted, even though it may be compliant with the law, *per* Farquharson LJ:

> 'J ... we are of the view that the earlier breaches of the Act and of the Code renders the contents of the second interview inadmissible also. One cannot refrain from emphasising that when an accused person has made a series of admissions as to his or her complicity in a crime at a first interview, the very fact that those admissions have been made are likely to have an effect upon her during the course of the second interview. If, accordingly, it be held, as it is held here, that the first interview was in breach of the rules and in breach of section 58, it seems to us that the subsequent interview must be similarly tainted.'

In *McGovern,* the court was unequivocal in excluding the confession. In *Fulling* (above), the court confirmed that unlike s 76(2)(a), exclusion of a confession under s 76(2)(b) of the PACE Act 1984 does not require impropriety on the part of the investigative questioner to be shown, ie by police officers; see *R v Walker* [1998] Crim LR 211.

In considering the *circumstances existing at the time* under s 76(2)(b), the Act sets an objective test. For example, the question in Mr Everett's case would have been, did the defendant have a mental impairment? Consider the following scenario: Maggie is interviewed on the charge of low value robbery. Unbeknown to the police, she is a heroin addict. Maggie confesses to the crime, thinking that she will be quickly released on bail, and will then be able to satisfy her need. In *R v Goldenberg* (1989) 88 Cr App R 285 a case involving a similar situation, the court stated that s 76(2) does not apply where the *only* cause of the confession being unreliable is the suspect themselves. The decision in *Goldberg* was followed in *R v Crampton* (1991) 92 Cr App R 369. This decision should be distinguished from those where the court has taken into account individual characteristics, such as mental capacity; see *R v Blackburn* [2005] EWCA Crim 1349.

CASE EXAMPLE

R v Everett [1988] Crim LR 826

Mr Everett, although aged 42, had a mental age of eight. On appeal it was held that the circumstance of his existing mental condition should have been taken into account when considering whether his confession to the commission of the offence was to be admitted.

The individual characteristics of a suspect may mean that certain behaviour will give rise to concern in relation to the suspect's vulnerability, even though the same behaviour may not have that effect in relation to another suspect, for example, mental ability, threats or inducements. Section 76(2)(b) is wide enough to cover such situations, even those where it is the personal circumstances of the suspect that have led to unreliability. Finally, those things said or done, considered in the light of the circumstances existing at the time, must result in a confession being made.

10.3.3 Causation

In order for confession evidence to be excluded, there must be a causal link between either the oppression or unreliability, and the making of the confession. This means that in instances where the effects of either the oppression or unreliability have worn off at the point when the confession is made, then oppression or unreliability can be no ground to exclude the evidence. This diagram summarizes the point:

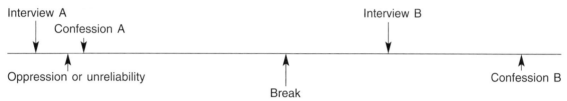

Figure 10.1 The exclusion of a confession: causation, unreliability and oppression

The diagram is purely for the illustration of a causal link; contemporaneity between the oppression or unreliability and the making of a confession, will undoubtedly indicate that a causal link exists.

CASE EXAMPLE

R v Smith [1959] 2 QB 35

The court decided that Mr Smith's confession, following threats from his commanding officer, was inadmissible. However, his confessions to investigating officers whilst in custody, were admissible as the effects of the oppression/unreliability had worn off.

KEY FACTS

Admissibility

The *general rule* is that only relevant evidence is admissible:

* The common law provided admissibility of confession evidence, now s 76 of the PACE Act 1984 regulates their admission.

CONTINUED ▶

KEY FACTS

- Sections 76(1) and (7) provide that admissible confession evidence is only admissible as evidence against its maker.

- Confession evidence does not require to be corroborated or supported by other evidence.

- It is for the trier of fact (jury or magistrates) to decide how much weight to attach to a confession.

Exclusion

Section 76(2) of the PACE Act 1984 provides that confessions obtained through oppression or rendered unreliable because of things said or done are inadmissible:

- Section 76(2)(a) provides for the exclusion of confession evidence obtained by oppressive means, s 76(8) defines oppression as including treatment that is torturous, inhumane or degrading and the use or threat of violence.

- Section 76(2)(b) provides for the exclusion of confession evidence obtained as a consequence of something 'said or done' which is likely in the circumstances existing at the time to render it unreliable, impropriety on the part of the police is not required.

Causation

For exclusion under s 76 of the PACE Act 1984, there must be a causal link between the oppression or unreliability and the making of the confession.

10.4 Exclusion of evidence under s 78 of the Police and Criminal Evidence Act 1984

In addition to exclusion of confession evidence, and in spite of all the changes made to the law of evidence, judges have retained the general discretion to exclude any evidence, including a confession: s 78 of the PACE Act 1984 states that a court may exclude evidence where:

'it appears to *it* that, having regard to all the circumstances in which the confession was obtained, that the admission of the *evidence* would have an adverse effect on the fairness of the proceedings *and therefore it should be excluded*'.

Section 67(11) of the PACE Act 1984 states that if any of the PACE Codes of Practice:

'. . . appears to the court to be relevant to any question arising in proceedings, *then the Code should* be taken into account in determining it'.

There are a number of circumstances that fall within this provision. Therefore, the PACE Act 1984 and its accompanying Codes of Practice give guidance on the treatment, detention and interrogation of suspects for fear of exclusion under s 78. The adherence to Codes C and E are of particular importance when it comes to s 78. The effect of this provision is not automatically to exclude evidence in the event of a breach of the Act or its Codes as the Court of Appeal clearly stated in *R v Delaney* (1988) 88 Cr App Rep 338, per the Lord Chief Justice:

> J '. . . the flagrant breach of the Code, as the judge correctly described it, was the starting point of the submission made to the judge by counsel for the appellant that the confessions should be rejected . . . the mere fact that there has been a breach of the Codes of Practice does not of itself mean that evidence has to be rejected.'

In *Delaney* the Lord Chief Justice also thought it necessary to confirm that s 78 is not a disciplinary section, which means that it was not intended to be used as a method of disciplining the police for not following procedure:

> J '. . . It is no part of the duty of the court to rule a statement inadmissible, simply in order to punish the police for failure to observe the Codes of Practice.'

It is, however, intended to promote the pursuance of the correct procedure. Non-compliance with the provisions, for example serious and substantial breaches of the Act or Codes, will result in the court exercising its discretion and thereby excluding the evidence. The practical importance of s 78 may in effect be the difference between a successful conviction and no conviction by reason of exclusion of the main evidence. For current examples, see *R v Keenan* [1989] 3 All ER 609, *R v Mason* [1988] 1 WLR 139, a case concerning trickery, and *R v Kwabena Poku* [1978] Crim LR 488, a case involving the innocent misleading of a defendant.

It would be correct to say that s 78 has caused a great deal of problems for the police and exists as a bright beacon of hope for an accused who has been treated unfairly. Section 58 of the PACE Act 1984 provides the suspect with the right to access legal advice, ie privately to consult with a solicitor, if they so wish. The only restriction on this right arises if the offence is a serious arrestable one and a police officer with the rank of at least superintendent, authorizes its suspension on the grounds under s 58(8).

Section 58(8) of the PACE Act 1984 states that:

'. . . refusal of the suspect's right can be made on the basis that there exist reasonable grounds for believing that exercise of the suspect's right will (a) lead to interference with or harm to evidence connected with a serious arrestable offence or interference with or physical injury to other persons; or (b) will lead to the alerting of other persons suspected of having committed such an offence but not yet arrested for it; or (c) will hinder the recovery of any property obtained as a result of such an offence'.

In the case of *R v Samuel* [1988] 2 WLR 920, the Court of Appeal thought a refusal under s 58 would only be very exceptionally justified because solicitors are professionals, and therefore it is unlikely that their advice would give rise to the conditions of this provision being satisfied. The right to advice is considered to be a fundamental legal right and on many occasions its refusal has led to confession evidence being excluded. There are, however, some contradictory cases, such as *R v Alladice* (1988) 87 Cr App R 380, where a refusal to allow a suspect access to legal advice was unreasonable. However, the suspect's confession was not excluded, because he was an occasioned criminal who knew very well what his rights were, and would therefore have been in a position to protect himself.

10.5 The effect of exclusion

Let us move on to discuss the consequences of such evidence being excluded. The *general rule* is as follows: excluded confession evidence cannot be used by the prosecution as part of their case against the defendant; see *R v Treacy* [1944] 2 All ER 229. What use, if any, can be made of an excluded confession; does it fall by the way? No. Section 76(4)–(5) allows the prosecution to extract certain evidence from the excluded confession. Section 76(4) of the PACE Act 1984 states that evidence is admissible if it relates to:

'. . . any facts discovered as a result of the confession; or . . . where the confession is relevant as showing that the accused speaks, writes or expresses *themselves* in a particular way'.

This is often referred to metaphorically, as the 'fruit of the poisoned tree'. Let us look at the effect of this provision. For example, Alley Lillen is charged with assault occasioning actual bodily harm. After a lengthy 15 hours of interviews without comfort breaks and with persistent threats, she confesses and in her confession, informs the police that the weapon is hidden in her friend, Harris Pilton's lavatory cistern. Surely if her confession is excluded by reason of oppression, so should any evidence obtained as a result of it? Section 76(4)(a) allows for the admission of *any facts discovered as a result of the confession*. Such evidence is admissible, even where the actual confession from which it was derived is not. Can the prosecution refer to how the evidence was discovered? No. Section 76(5) prohibits the prosecution from referring to the fact that the evidence was discovered as a result of what the suspect said in their confession unless the defence refers to it. In this case, the prosecution are then free to make such reference. This diagram summarizes the position:

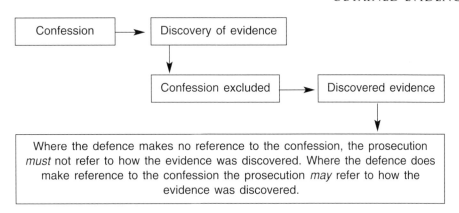

Figure 10.2 Using an excluded confession: s 74 Police and Criminal Evidence Act 1984

Section 76(4)(b) of the PACE Act 1984, allows the prosecution to use an excluded confession to prove something other than the truth of its contents, perhaps to prove that the defendant speaks or writes in a particular way. A good example of this is mis-spelling. For example, in a very popular television drama, an excluded confession was used to show that a murderer continuously mis-spelt the term murderer as 'murderrerr'.

Finally, it should be noted that a co-defendant may cross-examine the maker of an excluded confession on an inconsistency relevant to their own guilt; see *R v Rowson* [1986] QB 174. In *R v Myers* [1997] 3 WLR 552, (HL) (below) counsel argued that such cross-examination was not permitted where the confession was excluded by reason of oppression.

KEY FACTS

Exclusion of evidence under s 78

The court may in the interests of justice exclude evidence that would have an adverse effect on the fairness of the proceedings.

The effect of exclusion

The *general rule* is that excluded confession evidence cannot be used by the prosecution as part of its case against the defendant, however, s 76(4)–(5) allows the prosecution to use any facts discovered as a result of the confession or to use it for a purpose other than to prove the truth of its contents, ie it may be relevant to show that the accused speaks, writes or expresses *themselves* in a particular way.

10.6 Presentation of confession evidence

Even where a confession is admissible, it will not usually be presented to the court in its 'raw' form. In effect, this means that not every word uttered by the defendant will be presented to the court. The most likely statement presented will consist of a mixture of incriminatory and exculpatory remarks. These will be remarks that point to the defendant's guilt or that are prejudicial to their case.

10.6.1 Remarks that are prejudicial to a defendant

Even though a confession represents an accurate reflection of what a defendant says, and the way in which it is said, it may be edited to remove remarks that are either inadmissible or prejudicial. Editing of this sort only takes place if, after the removal of the offending remarks, the remainder of the confession makes sense. An example of such editing is a reference in a confession to a defendant's previous antecedent history (prior convictions). This will be removed as in *R v Knight* (1946) 31 Cr App R 52, unless one of the provisions of the CJA 2003 apply. If prejudicial remarks are put before the jury, then the only likely outcome is that the conviction will be rendered unsafe and therefore may be quashed on appeal.

10.6.2 Remarks that exculpate or incriminate a defendant

Remarks may be incriminatory or exculpatory and the distinction is of vital importance. It makes sense then that any incriminatory remarks in a confession are put to a jury, thereby providing a complete picture. What of exculpatory remarks, ie how a defendant has responded to exculpate or explain themselves? In the case of *R v Storey* (1968) 52 Cr App R 334, the court decided that such exculpatory remarks, made by a defendant to the police in a confession, were inadmissible because they amounted to proof of the truth of their contents. Although, the same exculpatory remarks were admissible as part of the *res gestae* evidencing the defendant's reaction when accused. This approach was confirmed in *R v Donaldson* (1976) 64 Cr App R 65. The distinction that incriminatory remarks can be used as evidence of the truth of their contents and exculpatory remarks as evidence of reaction is often unclear. In *R v Duncan* (1981) 73 Cr App R 359, the court stated that the interests of fairness dictated that an entire response should be put to the jury with a direction from the trial judge to the effect that, whilst the incriminatory remarks are likely to be true, the remarks that exculpate the defendant are less likely to be so.

10.6.3 Remarks that incriminate a co-accused

The *general rule* is that a confession is admissible only against its maker and not anyone else that it may incriminate. The reasoning is simple, such evidence amounts to hearsay evidence of the guilt of the person implicated and is therefore inadmissible as against a person other than the maker of the statement; see *R v Spinks* [1982] 1 All ER 587. Editing such a reference is possible, but not usual in practice. Alternatively, it may be that the reference has little or no relevance to the allegations being made against the defendant, and therefore can be easily excluded.

Remember, only relevant evidence is admissible; see *R v Rogers* [1971] Crim LR 413. What, then, of prejudicial remarks that damage the case of a co-accused? Such remarks can be edited out so long as they do not disadvantage the defendant; see *R v Lobban* [1995] 1 WLR 877. Where a confession made by defendant A is too prejudicial and results in unfairness to co-defendant B, but that unfairness is helpful to A's case, then, as is quite common, the confession will be used in its fuller form and a joint trial will be avoided – the indictment will be severed so that each defendant can be tried separately.

KEY FACTS

Remarks that are prejudicial to a defendant

Most confessions will be edited to remove remarks that are inadmissible or prejudicial.

Remarks that exculpate or incriminate a defendant

Incriminatory remarks will be put to a jury providing a fuller picture, even though these are tendered as proof of the truth of their contents. Exculpatory remarks cannot be tendered as proof of the truth of their contents but will normally be admissible because they are part of the *res gestae* – an exception to the rule against the admission of hearsay; see now the CJA 2003.

Remarks that incriminate a co-accused

The *general rule* is that a confession is admissible only against its maker and not anyone that it may incriminate.

10.7 Challenging and using confession evidence

There are two main points that need discussion at this stage. First, how confession evidence can be challenged to exclude it, and second, how an accused can use the confession of a co-accused? Let us begin with the former. Any challenges to the admissibility of confession evidence under s 76 or 78 of the PACE Act 1984 are undertaken in a *voir dire* the nature of which was discussed in Chapter 1; see *R v Oxford City Justices ex p Berry* [1988] QB 507 and *R v Manji* [1990] Crim LR 512. If a challenge arises, then it is usual for a *voir dire* to be held in Crown Court cases. Whether or not it is practical in a magistrates' court case depends on whether the issue of admissibility can be dealt with at the time.

Where an accused completely denies ever making a confession, that the prosecution attributes to the accused, this does not involve the reliability of a confession. No *voir dire* will be held in

these circumstances. This is because the issue is a factual one of the credibility of the witness and therefore one for the jury; see *Ajodha v The State* [1982] AC 204.

A defendant can choose to give evidence in the *voir dire*. If he does so, then he does not have to give evidence at the trial. Where a defendant gives evidence at the *voir dire,* an important issue arises. What, if at all, is the extent to which those answers can be used at the trial? The *general rule* is that any evidence that emerges as a result of the *voir dire* may not be used by the prosecution at the trial, provided that the judge rules that the confession is inadmissible.

Wong Kam Ming v R [1980] AC 247

The defendant Mr W confessed to (a) being present at the scene of a crime and (b) attacking someone with a knife. Counsel on his behalf challenged the admissibility of the confession in a *voir dire* at which Mr W admitted that he was both present and had participated. The trial judge ruled the confession inadmissible. Subsequently, at trial, the prosecution cross-examined Mr W on the differences between his evidence to the jury and that which he had stated in the *voir dire*. The Privy Council (PC), on public policy grounds, held that it was inappropriate for the prosecution to have questioned Mr W in the *voir dire* on the truthfulness of his statement and then use this incriminating evidence that had emerged in the *voir dire* at the trial before the jury. The PC also confirmed that such evidence could only have been used if the result of the *voir dire* was to include the confession; the prosecution would then have been free to cross-examine Mr W on his inconsistencies.

A similar approach to *Wong* was adopted by the House of Lords in *R v Brophy* [1982] AC 476. The case concerned questioning in a *voir dire* which resulted in evidence of Mr Brophy admitted that he was a member of the Irish Republican Army (IRA), the offence with which he was charged. The confession that was being challenged was ruled inadmissible by the trial judge. At the trial the prosecution was allowed to use evidence of his admission, which resulted in the defendant being convicted. The House of Lords held that this was wrong. Evidence relevant to an issue in a *voir dire* could not later be the subject of cross-examination if the outcome of the *voir dire* is to result in the non-admission of a confession.

Can an accused make use of the confession of a co-accused? This diagram summarizes the position:

Where a co-accused's confession is inadmissible *only* under s 78	Where a co-accused's confession is inadmissible under *either* s 76 or s 78

The prosecution can cross-examine the co-accused on the confession or adduce it as evidence in defence	The prosecution cannot adduce evidence of the confession

The accused has an absolute right to present relevant and admissible evidence, the trial judge has no discretion to exclude the evidence or disallow cross-examination

 Figure 10.3 The accused's and their use of the confession of a co-accused

CASE EXTRACT

R v Myers [1997] 3 WLR 552 (HL)

Myers and her co-defendant were charged with the murder of a taxi driver. Both ran cut-throat defences, ie each blamed the other. Myers, whilst not under caution, made two confessions to the police to the effect that she had stabbed the taxi driver in order to rob and not to kill him. At the trial, the prosecution did not adduce evidence of these confessions and Myers denied ever making them. Her co-defendant was eligible to adduce evidence of the confessions in defence and Myers was convicted. The House of Lords dismissed her appeal; her confession was relevant to the defence of her co-accused and therefore admissible, *per* Lord Slynn of Hadley:

> J '. . . It seems to me that there is force in that comment despite Lord Bridge's anxiety that if confessions by third parties were admitted it would only be too easy for fabricated confessions to produce unjustified acquittals. Accepting Lord Bridge's view in *Blastland* that statements by third persons are not admissible there is a long line of authority showing that a defendant must be allowed to cross-examine a co-accused as to a previous inconsistent confession so long as the material is relevant to the defendant's own defence. In my opinion a defendant should also be allowed to put a co-defendant's confession to witnesses to whom the confession was made so long as the confession is relevant to the defendant's defence and so long as it appears that the

CONTINUED ▸

<table>
<tr><td>J</td><td>confession was not obtained in a manner which would have made it inadmissible at the instance of the Crown under s 76(2) of the Act of 1984. There may be doubt as to whether the co-accused will be called (so that it may not be possible to put the confession to the co-accused directly) and not to allow the defendant to introduce it by way of cross-examination of prosecution witnesses could lead to great unfairness.'</td></tr>
</table>

10.8 Confessions made by mentally handicapped persons

Section 77 of the PACE Act 1984 provides additional protection for people who are mentally handicapped. Where the prosecution case against such a person relies wholly or substantively on a confession that was not made in the presence of an independent person, who then is an independent person? Section 77(3) of the Police Act 1996 specifically excludes police officers or those employed for police purposes, but includes lawyers, ie solicitors. If such an instance arises, the court will direct the jury of the special need for caution before they decide to convict a mentally handicapped person on the basis of such a confession. Failure to comply with the provision will result in a conviction being quashed, as in *R v J* [2003] EWCA Crim 3309.

10.9 Other illegally obtained evidence

Section 78 of the PACE Act 1984 also applies to exclude prosecution evidence, the admission of which may have such an adverse effect on the fairness of the proceedings that it ought not to be admitted. The courts retained, as they do today, discretion under the common law to exclude confession evidence that was either illegally, improperly or unfairly obtained where it considered that the prejudicial effect of the evidence outweighed its probative value; see *R v Sang* [1980] AC 402. An example of a situation that would fall under the common law discretion would be a confession obtained in breach of the PACE codes. The discretion is now preserved in s 82(3) of the PACE Act 1984 which states:

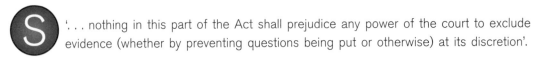

'. . . nothing in this part of the Act shall prejudice any power of the court to exclude evidence (whether by preventing questions being put or otherwise) at its discretion'.

The discretion to exclude under s 78 is far wider than that under the common law. In contrast, this provision applies to all types of evidence on which the 'prosecution proposes to rely', and the court will consider all the circumstances, including the manner in which it was obtained. Section

78 applies prospectively and not retrospectively. For example, it cannot be used to withdraw evidence that has already been adduced in court. Three important points should be noted:

- The statutory power to exclude confession evidence is preferred over the common law discretion in practice.

- Section 78 only provides the trial judge with the power to exclude prosecution evidence and not relevant admissible evidence for a co-accused.

- The common law discretion allows a trial judge to direct a jury to disregard confession evidence if, after allowing its admission following a *voir dire* they subsequently decide, having heard all the evidence, that it should have been excluded.

Whether or not s 78 applies is a matter for the trial judge to decide, having considered the circumstances of the particular case. What is obvious is that its use is very much based on policy considerations. Strangely, the rules of evidence in jurisdictions such as the USA or India operate to exclude evidence that is in breach of the law. In contrast, the rules of evidence in the UK only render evidence inadmissible on the basis of relevance and even then without the need to prove bad faith or deception.

CASE EXAMPLE

R v Mason [1988] 1 WLR 139

The police when investigating the commission of a minor offence blatantly lied and tricked both the defendant and his solicitor a number of times. Those lies and that deception was such that it had an adverse effect on the fairness of the proceedings and hence the evidence was excluded.

Although Mason (above) was a fairly straightforward case, it is obvious that investigators have problems where they act as agents provocateurs. The House of Lords in *Sang* (above) doubted that evidence obtained as a result of an agent provocateur instigated crime, would be excluded. This rather oblique reasoning was challenged in *R v Edwards* [1991] Crim LR 45. In *R v Christou and Wright* [1992] 4 All ER 559 the police set up fake jewellers and the defendants were arrested trying to sell stolen jewellery. Counsel for the defendants argued for the exclusion of this evidence by reason of the manner in which it had been obtained. The court decided that the evidence was relevant and therefore chose not to exercise its discretion to exclude it under s 78. In *Williams v DPP* [1993] 3 All ER 365, the police had loaded a 'bait' van with fake cigarette cartons and placed it in a vulnerable place. The defendants were arrested attempting to steal the cigarettes. In this case, the evidence was still admitted, even though no offence had been committed before the police had tricked the defendants – the evidence was lacking in assertions that pressure was brought to bear on the defendants to participate in an offence.

The Court of Appeal laid down much-needed guidelines in *R v Smurthwaite* [1994] 1 All ER 898. In this case, the defendant was convicted of soliciting a murder when he sought a contract killer, and unbeknown to him, in arranging it he had met with an undercover policeman and another, merely posing as a contract killer. Smurthwaite sought to have the evidence excluded on the basis that it had been improperly obtained by an undercover police officer. The court held that as the PACE Act 1984 required it to consider the circumstances in which the evidence was obtained, s 78 could operate to exclude evidence in cases of entrapment. The court stated that in such cases, when considering exclusion the court should have regard to the following:

- whether the agent provocateur was encouraging the commission of a criminal offence that the defendant may not have otherwise committed
- the means that the agent had used to entrap the defendant
- the role the agent had played in entrapping the defendant
- the strength of the evidence on what had actually occurred.

In *R v Latif* [1996] 1 All ER 353, a customs officer posed as a drug runner thereby obtaining evidence which incriminated the defendant, Mr Latif, who was convicted. In this case, counsel argued that where the agent provocateur plays an active and therefore arguably improper role, any evidence obtained thereby should be excluded, or the proceedings against the defendant stayed for an abuse of the courts' process – this latter claim may be the basis of future claims; see *R v Loosely* [2001] 1 Cr App R 29. Unfortunately for Mr Latif his conviction was upheld. In doing so, the court stated that it will take into account the public interest.

In *R v Hall* [2002] EWCA Crim 1881, the police suspected that Mr Hall had murdered his wife and in investigating the offence, a policewoman, to whom he later confessed, initiated a romantic relationship with the defendant. In trying to ascertain whether he had in fact killed his wife, the policewoman asked him questions designed to elicit incriminatory information. This the trial judge held to be improper. In contrast, information obtained by the police through discreet surveillance will not necessarily be excluded; for example, evidence obtained through bugging a defendant's cell, as in *R v Bailey* [1993] 3 All ER 513 or bugging the home of the defendant's brother, as in *R v Khan* [1995] QB 27, even though the latter was done by trespassing.

In *Texeira de Castro v Portugal* (1999) EHRR 101 the European Court of Human Rights stated that:

> '. . . the general requirements of fairness embodied in Article 6 *of the European Convention on Human Rights* apply to proceedings *that concern* all types of criminal offences . . . the public interest cannot justify the use of evidence *that was* obtained as a result of *incitement by the police*'.

Finally, the court confirmed in *Nottingham County Council v Amin* [2001] 1 WLR 1071 that the mere giving of an opportunity to break the law is not entrapment, and therefore evidence obtained as a result, should not necessarily be excluded.

KEY FACTS

Other illegally obtained evidence

Section 78 of the PACE Act 1984 applies to exclude prosecution evidence the admission of which may have such an adverse effect on the fairness of the proceedings. The courts also retain a common law discretion to exclude confession evidence if obtained illegally, improperly or unfairly where its prejudicial effect outweighs its probative value. Exclusion under s 78 is wider than under the common law because it applies to *all* types of evidence on which the 'prosecution proposes to rely' and the court will consider all the circumstances, including the manner in which it was obtained.

ACTIVITY

Self-test questions

1. What is a confession?

2. When is a confession admissible?

3. Against whom is it admissible?

4. In what circumstances may a confession be excluded under s 76 of the PACE Act 1984?

5. What is oppression under s 76?

6. What is unreliability under s 76?

7. Can an excluded confession be used for another purpose?

8. What is the status of evidence discovered as a result of a subsequently excluded confession?

9. Summarize the effect of s 78 of the PACE Act 1984.

10. What is the position of the law on evidence obtained by reason of an investigator acting as an agent provocateur?

Further reading

Birch, D., 'Criminal Justice Act 2003: (4) Hearsay – Same Old Story, Same Old Song?' (2004) Crim LR, Jul, 556–573.

Mirfield, P., *Silence, Confessions and Improperly Obtained Evidence*, Oxford Monographs on Criminal Law and Justice (Oxford University Press, 1998).

Munday, R., 'Convicting on Confessional Evidence in the Complete Absence of a Corpus Delicti' (1993) 157 JPJo 275.

Munday, R., 'Adverse Denial and Purposive Confession' (2003) Crim LR, Dec, 850–864.

R v Delaney (1989) 88 Cr App R 338 – 'Case Comment: Evidence and the Admissibility of a Confession' (1989) Crim LR, Feb, 139–140.

R v Goldenberg (1989) 88 Cr App R 285 – 'Case Comment: Admissions and Confessions: words or acts of person making confession not included in matters affecting reliability' (1988) Crim LR, Oct, 678–679.

Internet links

PACE Act 1984 Codes of Practice:

http://police.homeoffice.gov.uk/operational-policing/powers-pace-codes/pace-code-intro/

chapter 11 EVIDENCE OF BAD CHARACTER IN CRIMINAL PROCEEDINGS ■

AIMS AND OBJECTIVES

By the end of this chapter you should be able to understand:

■ The various meanings of character at common law

■ The modes of proving character, both good and bad

■ The effect of adducing evidence of good character

■ The meaning of bad character under the Criminal Justice Act 2003.

11.1 Introduction

In this chapter we will be dealing with the definition of the expression 'character' in criminal proceedings. The common law definition of the term will be considered as well as the modes of adducing evidence of the defendant's character. Directions by the judge as to the proper treatment by the jury of the defendant's good character are of enormous importance, and to that end, the *Vye* directions will be considered. The common law notion of similar fact evidence will be analysed by reference to a number of illustrations. Finally, the definition of 'bad character' as laid down in the Criminal Justice Act 2003 will be explored.

11.2 Meaning of character evidence prior to the Criminal Justice Act 2003

There are two significant questions relating to character in a trial. These are:

(a) the meaning of the expression 'character evidence'

(b) the admissibility of character evidence in the proceedings.

The expression 'character evidence' has distinct connotations in criminal proceedings, depending on the context in which it is used. This varies with whether character is directly in issue or relates to credit of the relevant individual (defendant or witness) and whether we are dealing with good or bad character.

There were three meanings that were attached to the expression 'character' in criminal proceedings. These were reputation, disposition or either disposition or reputation evidence. Reputation evidence involves the general opinion of society concerning the witness. Indeed, the more popular the witness, the more likely that society will have an opinion of the witness. Disposition evidence involves specific incidents or separate acts of the witness, such as specific donations to charitable organizations, the previous convictions of the witness (including the accused) or background evidence. In other words, the expression means a tendency, propensity or inclination to do or omit from doing something connected to the proceedings.

At common law the meaning of character in criminal proceedings was restricted to the reputation of the witness. This rule was applicable to the admissibility of the accused's good character. In other words, prior to the Criminal Evidence Act 1898, a rule of law was developed to the effect that although the good character evidence of the accused was strictly irrelevant to the issue of guilt, he was nevertheless entitled to prove that, as a man of impeccable reputation, he was less likely to have committed the offence charged. The approach was based on a concession granted to accused persons who, at the time, did not have the capacity to testify. Such character witnesses called by the defendant were not allowed to testify as to specific acts of good conduct, but only as to the reputation of the defendant. Likewise, the prosecution was entitled to call rebutting evidence to challenge or dispute the good character of the accused. Again, such evidence was restricted to evidence of 'general reputation' only. This is known as the *Rowton* rule derived from the case *R v Rowton* (1865) 11 LT 745.

CASE EXAMPLE

R v Rowton (1865) 11 LT 745

The accused, a headmaster of a boys' school was charged with indecent assault on one of his pupils. The defence called character witnesses to testify on his behalf. The prosecution called rebutting evidence and such witness was asked the question, 'What is the defendant's general character for decency and morality of conduct?' The witness said, 'I know nothing of the neighbourhood's opinion, because I was only a boy at school when I knew him; but my own opinion, and the opinion of my brothers, who were also pupils of his, is that his character is that of a man capable of the grossest indecency and the most flagrant immorality.' It was held that this answer was inadmissible as it was a statement of disposition, not reputation.

Cockburn J:

CONTINUED ▶

J 'I am clearly of the opinion that when evidence in favour of the character of the prisoner has been given on his behalf, evidence of his bad character can be adduced upon the part of the prosecution to rebut the evidence so given . . . What is the meaning of evidence of character? It is laid down in the books that a prisoner is entitled to give evidence as to his general character. What does that mean? Does it mean evidence as to his "reputation" amongst those to whom his conduct and position are known? Or does it mean evidence of "disposition"? I think it means evidence of reputation only . . . The truth is, this part of our law is an anomaly. Although, logically speaking, it is quite clear that an antecedent bad character would form quite as reasonable a ground for the probability of guilt, as previous good character lays the foundation for the presumption of innocence, yet the prosecution cannot go into evidence as to the prisoner's bad character. The allowing of evidence of a prisoner's good character to be given has grown from a desire to administer the law with mercy as far as possible . . . I think that rebutting evidence must be of the same character and kept within the same limits; that while the prisoner can give evidence of general good character, so the evidence called to rebut it must be evidence of the same general description showing that the evidence which has been given to establish good reputation on the one hand is not true, because the man's general reputation is bad.'

This principle was affirmed by the Court of Appeal in *R v Redgrave* (1982) 74 Cr App R 10. The charge was importuning men for immoral purposes contrary to s 32 of the Sexual Offences Act 1956, in that he noisily and violently performed acts of gross indecency in the presence of plain clothes police officers at a urinal. The accused had wished to produce five bundles of love letters written to his girlfriends, and photographs, not being indecent, but of a heterosexual nature in order to rebut the inference of being of a homosexual disposition. The judge disallowed such evidence and the accused was convicted and appealed. The court dismissed the appeal and decided that the evidence was of disposition and inadmissible.

Lawton LJ:

J '. . . although disposition to commit the kind of offence charged was relevant, the law is as decided in *Rowton* (1865), viz., that the defendant could do no more than say, or call witnesses to prove, that he was not by general repute the kind of young man who would have behaved in the kind of way that the Crown alleged.'

271

The learned Lord Justice of Appeal continued by referring to the practice of the court to suspend or relax this rule in certain circumstances. Lawton LJ:

> **J** 'It has long been the practice of judges to allow some relaxation of the law of evidence on behalf of defendants. Had this young man been a married man, or alternatively had he confined his relationship to one girl, it might not have been all that objectionable for him to have given evidence in general terms that his relationship with his wife or the girl was satisfactory. That would have been an indulgence on the part of the court.'

11.3 Good character

Before the Criminal Evidence Act 1898, evidence of the defendant's good character took the form of evidence of witnesses called by the defendant, as well as the cross-examination of witnesses on behalf of the defendant to bring out the good character of the defendant. Such evidence was restricted to the reputation of the defendant. Likewise, rebutting evidence adduced by the prosecution was restricted to evidence of the defendant's reputation in the community; see *R v Rowton* (above). Following the introduction of the 1898 Act, the defendant was allowed to testify on his own behalf and the court allowed the practice of permitting the defendant to testify as to his disposition, such as having done a number of good deeds or stressing the fact that he has led a good life. This remains the position today although the 1898 Act has been replaced by the Criminal Justice Act 2003.

11.3.1 Directions as to good character

The courts have issued guidelines in *R v Vye* [1993] 3 All ER 241, as to the relevance of the good character of a defendant. The judge is required to consider whether to issue directions to the jury as to the use they may make of the evidence of the good character of the defendant and, if so, the contents of the direction.

- Good character may be relevant to the credibility of the defendant's testimony or pre-trial statements, ie whether the defendant is the sort of person who would tell the truth (first limb direction), ie a credibility direction.

- In addition, the judge is required to direct the jury as to whether the defendant is a person likely to have committed the offence charged (second limb direction), ie a propensity direction.

- The 'two limb' direction is required to be given even where the defendant does not testify, provided that he had made pre-trial statements to the investigating authorities or other persons.

- Such directions are to be given even where the defendant of good character is jointly tried with a defendant of bad character.

- The judge is entitled to tailor his directions to the particular circumstances of each case.
- There is no rule in favour of separate trials for defendants of good and bad character.

Lord Taylor CJ:

J

'It is now an established principle that, where a defendant of good character has given evidence, it is no longer sufficient for the judge to comment in general terms. He is required to direct the jury about the relevance of good character to the credibility of the defendant. Conventionally, this has come to be described as the "first limb" of the character direction. In our judgment, when the defendant has not given evidence at the trial but relies on exculpatory statements made to the police or others, the judge should direct the jury to have regard to the defendant's good character when considering the credibility of those statements . . . Clearly, if a defendant of good character does not give evidence and has given no pre-trial answers or statements, no issue as to his credibility arises and a first limb direction is not required.'

[As to the 'second limb' direction, Lord Taylor CJ considered the leading authorities and continued] 'We have reached the conclusion that the time has come to give some clear guidance to trial judges as to how they should approach this matter. It cannot be satisfactory for uncertainty to persist so that judges do not know whether this court, proceeding on a case-by-case basis, will hold that a 'second limb' direction should or need not have been given. Our conclusion is that such a direction should be given where a defendant is of good character.

Does the need for a second limb direction still exist when the defendant has not given evidence? We can see no logical ground for distinguishing in regard to a "second limb" direction between cases where the defendant has given evidence and cases where he has not.

Having stated the general rule, however, we recognise it must be for the trial judge in each case to decide how he tailors his direction to the particular circumstances. He would probably wish to indicate, as is commonly done, that good character cannot amount to a defence. Provided that the judge indicates to the jury the two respects in which good character may be relevant, ie credibility and propensity, this court will be slow to criticise any qualifying remarks he may make based on the facts of the individual case.

In our judgment, a defendant A of good character is entitled to have the judge direct the jury as to its relevance in his case even if he is jointly tried with a defendant B of bad character.

CONTINUED ▸

> **J** To summarise, in our judgment the following principles are to be applied. (1) A direction as to relevance of his good character to a defendant's credibility is to be given where he has testified or made pre-trial answers or statements. (2) A direction as to the relevance of his good character to the likelihood of his having committed the offence charged is to be given, whether or not he has testified, or made pre-trial answers or statements. (3) Where defendant A of good character is jointly tried with defendant B of bad character, (1) and (2) still apply.'

In *R v Aziz* [1995] 3 All ER 149, the House of Lords approved of the approach in *Vye* regarding the two-limb direction. In addition, the court decided that the judge has a residual discretion to add words of qualification concerning other proved or possible criminal conduct of the defendant which had emerged during the trial, so as to place a fair and balanced picture before the jury. In the limited case where the defendant's claim to good character, other than his lack of previous convictions, was so spurious that it would make no sense to give the general character direction, the judge could dispense with the direction in its entirety, for example where the defendant has been guilty of dishonesty concerning his employer but has not been charged with an offence.

In this case, A, Y and T were jointly charged with income tax and VAT frauds. A had no relevant previous convictions and Y and T had no previous convictions. A did not testify but relied on self-serving exculpatory statements made during interviews with customs officers. Y and T testified and denied committing the offences. The judge directed the jury to the effect that Y and T were entitled to be treated as persons of good character for the purpose of deciding whether their evidence was to be believed and A was to be treated as a person of good character for the purpose of considering whether he had the propensity to commit the offence. All three defendants were convicted and successfully appealed to the Court of Appeal. The House dismissed the prosecutor's appeal on the ground that all three defendants were entitled to full, good character directions (both limbs) notwithstanding that Y admitted to making a false mortgage application and to having lied to Customs officers during interview. T admitted to not having declared his full income to the Inland Revenue.

Lord Steyn:

> **J** 'The certified question, although phrased in very general terms, was intended to raise the problem whether a defendant without any previous convictions may "lose" his good character by reason of other criminal behaviour. It is a question which was not directly before the court in *Vye*. It is a complex problem. It is also an area in which generalisations are hazardous. Acknowledging that a wide spectrum of cases must

CONTINUED ▶

J be kept in mind, the problem can be illustrated with a commonplace example. A middle-aged man is charged with theft from his employers. He has no previous convictions. But during the trial it emerges, through cross-examination on behalf of a co-defendant, that the defendant has made dishonest claims on insurance companies over a number of years. What directions about good character, if any, must the judge give? A good starting point is that a judge should never be compelled to give meaningless or absurd directions. And cases occur from time to time where a defendant, who has no previous convictions, is shown beyond doubt to have been guilty of serious criminal behaviour similar to the offence charged in the indictment. A sensible criminal justice system should not compel a judge to go through the charade of giving directions in accordance with *Vye* in a case where the defendant's claim to good character is spurious. I would therefore hold that a trial judge has a residual discretion to decline to give any character directions in the case of a defendant without previous convictions if the judge considers it an insult to common sense to give directions in accordance with *Vye*.

The residual discretion of a trial judge to dispense with character directions in respect of a defendant of good character is of a limited variety. Prima facie the directions must be given. And the judge will often be able to place a fair and balanced picture before the jury by giving directions in accordance with *Vye* and then adding words of qualification concerning other proved or possible criminal conduct of the defendant which emerged during the trial. On the other hand, if it would make no sense to give character directions in accordance with *Vye*, the judge may in his discretion dispense with them.

Subject to these views, I do not believe that it is desirable to generalise about this essentially practical subject which must be left to the good sense of trial judges. It is worth adding, however, that whenever a trial judge proposes to give a direction, which is not likely to be anticipated by counsel, the judge should follow the commendable practice of inviting submissions on his proposed directions.'

11.4 Disposition evidence of bad character of the defendant at common law (similar fact evidence)

As distinct from reputation evidence, the prosecution was allowed to adduce evidence of the disposition of the accused in order to prove that he committed the offence with which he had been charged. This is known as evidence of the propensity of the defendant to commit crimes of a similar nature. This is the position even though the evidence will have the incidental effect of

presenting the accused in a bad light. In other words, where the specific acts of the accused are admissible to prove his guilt, the ancillary effect of admitting such circumstantial evidence may involve bringing out the accused's bad character. Such evidence was loosely called similar fact evidence. The test of admissibility involved eschewing a chain of forbidden reasoning to the effect that the evidence establishes only that the accused is a person likely to have committed the offence charged. Indeed, the prosecution is required to go further and establish that the prejudicial evidence manifests a high degree of relevance.

The classic test of admissibility was stated by Lord Herschell in *Makin v AG for New South Wales* [1894] AC 57, thus:

> J 'It is undoubtedly not competent for the prosecution to adduce evidence tending to show that the accused has been guilty of criminal acts other than those covered by the indictment, for the purpose of leading to the conclusion that the accused is a person likely from his criminal conduct or character to have committed the offence for which he is being tried. On the other hand, the mere fact that the evidence adduced tends to show the commission of other crimes does not render it inadmissible if it be relevant to an issue before the jury, and it may be so relevant if it bears upon the question whether the acts alleged to constitute the crime charged in the indictment were designed or accidental, or to rebut a defence which would otherwise be open to the accused.'

In this case, the two accused persons, husband and wife, were charged with the murder of a baby which they had in care for adoption. They were paid an inadequate amount for its maintenance. The child had died and its corpse was found buried in the garden of their home. Their defence was that the child died from natural causes or died accidentally. The prosecution was allowed to adduce evidence that the remains of a total of 12 other babies were found buried in gardens of houses occupied by the Makins over the years; these children were in the care of the Makins at the time of their deaths. The purpose for admitting the evidence was to rebut the defence of death from natural causes or accident.

In *Boardman v DPP* [1975] AC 421, Lord Hailsham explained the approach laid down by Lord Herschell in *Makin* thus:

> J 'It is perhaps helpful to remind oneself that what is not to be admitted is a chain of reasoning and not necessarily a state of facts. If the inadmissible chain of reasoning is the only purpose for which the evidence is adduced as a matter of law, the evidence itself is not admissible. If there is some other relevant, probative purpose than the forbidden type of reasoning, the evidence is admitted, but should be made the subject of a warning from the judge that the jury must eschew the forbidden reasoning.'

In *R v P* [1991] 3 All ER 337, the House of Lords reiterated the *Makin/Boardman* principle and declared that an essential feature of the evidence requires that its probative force is sufficiently great to make it just to admit the evidence despite its prejudicial effect on the accused.

Lord Mackay:

> **J** '. . . what has to be assessed is the probative force of the evidence in question, the infinite variety of circumstances in which the question arises demonstrates that there is no single manner in which this can be achieved. Whether the evidence has sufficient probative value to outweigh its prejudicial effect must in each case be a question of degree.'

The Criminal Evidence Act 1898 made the accused a competent witness in his defence for the first time. It was clear that if the accused had testified and was treated as an ordinary witness, he would have been unduly favoured on the one hand and unfairly disadvantaged on the other. The accused would have been unduly favoured in the sense that he would have been entitled to claim a privilege against self-incrimination and would have been entitled in cross-examination to refuse to answer questions relating to the facts in issue. This potential privilege was withdrawn by s 1(2) of the Criminal Evidence Act 1898. On the other hand, but for s 1(3), the accused would have been unduly prejudiced had he been subject to cross-examination like any ordinary witness. His previous convictions or bad character would have been admissible in order to discredit him as a witness. Undoubtedly, this would have had a discouraging effect on an accused with a criminal record. Accordingly, a compromise was reached in s 1(3). The accused was afforded protection from undue prejudice by being granted a 'conditional shield'. The shield involves a prohibition on the questioning of the accused to show that he 'had committed or been convicted of or been charged with' an offence other than the subject of the charge or is of 'bad character'. Subject to the discretion of the judge, this 'shield' or protection will be lost under one or more of the provisos laid down in s 1(3). This view was expressed by Lord Sankey in *Maxwell v DPP* [1935] AC 309:

> **J** 'When Parliament by the Act of 1898 effected a change in the general law and made the prisoner in every case a competent witness, it was in an evident difficulty, and it pursued the familiar English system of compromise. It was clear that if you allowed a prisoner to go into the witness box, it was impossible to allow him to be treated as an ordinary witness. Had that been permitted, a prisoner who went into the box to give evidence on oath could have been asked about any previous convictions with the result that an old offender would seldom, if ever, have been

CONTINUED ▸

> **J** acquitted. This would have offended against one of the most deeply rooted and jealously guarded principles of our criminal law . . . Some middle way, therefore, had to be discovered, and the result was that a certain amount of protection was accorded to a prisoner who gave evidence on his own behalf. As it has been expressed, he was presented with a shield and it was provided that he was not to be asked, and that if he was asked he should not be required to answer, any question tending to show that he had committed or been convicted of or been charged with any offence, other than that wherewith he was then charged, or was of bad character. Apart, however, from this protection he was placed in the position of an ordinary witness . . .'

The Act contains no definition of 'character' but its meaning has been treated as including both 'reputation' and 'disposition' evidence. Indeed, in *R v Dunkley* [1927] 1 KB 323, the Court of Appeal decided that it was much too late in the day to change the meaning of character under the 1898 Act to accord to the common law meaning of reputation. The practice of the court is to accord to the expression, character, a wide meaning including both reputation and disposition. Lord Hewart:

> **J** 'It is apparent that within the space of a very few lines [of the Act] the word "character" is used in this part of the section no fewer than four times . . . Nevertheless, when one looks at the long line of cases beginning very shortly after the passing of the Criminal Evidence Act 1898, it does not appear that the argument has ever been so much as formulated that the "character" which is spoken of is the character which is so well known in the vocabulary of the criminal law – namely general reputation of the person referred to. The argument was formulated yesterday. One can only say that it is now much too late in the day even to consider that argument, because it could not now prevail without the revision, and indeed to a great extent the overthrow of a very long series of decisions.'

11.5 Abolition of the common law rules and the Criminal Evidence Act 1898

The Law Commission in its report on 'Evidence of Bad Character in Criminal Proceedings', No 273, October 2001 stated:

C   'The present law suffers from a number of defects . . . In summary, however, they
     constitute a haphazard mixture of statute and common law rules which produce
     inconsistent and unpredictable results, in crucial respects distort the trial process,
make tactical considerations paramount and inhibit the defence in presenting its true case
to the fact-finder whilst often exposing witnesses to gratuitous and humiliating exposure of
long forgotten misconduct.'

The Government's White Paper, 'Justice for All' published in 2002 summarized the current rules
and indicated its preference in this area:

C   'The current rules of evidence . . . are difficult to understand and complex to apply in
     practice. There has been growing public concern that evidence relevant to the search
     for truth is being wrongly excluded . . . We favour an approach that entrusts relevant
information to those determining the case as far as possible. It should be for the judge to
decide whether previous convictions are sufficiently relevant to the case, bearing in mind the
prejudicial effect, to be heard by the jury and for the jury to decide what weight should be
given to that information in all the circumstances of the case . . . Under this approach,
where a defendant's previous convictions, or other misconduct, are relevant to an issue in
the case, then, unless the court considers that the information will have a disproportionate
effect, they should be allowed to know about it. It will be for the judge to decide whether
the probative value of introducing this information is outweighed by its prejudicial effect.'

Section 99(1) of the CJA 2003 abolishes the common law definition of character, save for one
exception, the *Rowton* rule retained in s 118(1) (see above). In addition, several statutory
provisions which permitted the use of bad character evidence, including s 1(3) of the Criminal
Evidence Act 1898, were repealed (see sched 37 of the 2003 Act). The Criminal Justice Act 2003
introduces an all-encompassing definition of bad character in s 98 (see below).

Section 99 of the 2003 Act provides that:

S   1. 'The common law rules governing the admissibility of evidence of bad character in
        criminal proceedings are abolished.
     2. Subsection (1) is subject to s 118(1) in so far as it preserves the rule under which
     . . . a person's reputation is admissible for the purposes of proving his bad character.'

11.6 Definition of bad character

Section 98 of the Criminal Justice Act 2003 identifies the type of evidence the admissibility of
which will be determined by the new statutory regime. The issue concerns the 'bad character' of
the accused and other persons. The 2003 Act completely reverses the pre-existing general rule
that existed at common law and specific statutory provisions such as the Criminal Evidence Act
1898. Evidence of bad character is now admissible if it satisfies certain criteria (see s 101(1)),
and the approach is no longer one of inadmissibility, subject to exceptions.

The explanatory note to the Criminal Justice Act 2003 declares:

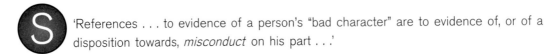

'The intention is that this Part of the Act will provide a new basis for the admissibility of previous convictions and other misconduct. Accordingly, s 99 abolishes the common law rules governing the admissibility of such evidence. This abolition does not extend to the rule that allows a person's bad character to be proved by reputation . . .'

Section 98 of the Criminal Justice Act 2003 (CJA) enacts as follows:

'References . . . to evidence of a person's "bad character" are to evidence of, or of a disposition towards, *misconduct* on his part . . .'

This definition is applicable to all aspects of bad character evidence governed by the CJA 2003. Thus, the definition is applicable to the admissibility of evidence of the bad character of non-defendants as well as the accused in criminal trials. The section also applies to misconduct both before and after the offence with which the accused is charged, but obviously does not include the facts concerning the commission of the offence charged. This last point is dealt with below; see s 98 (a) and (b).

'Misconduct' as defined by s 112(1) of the CJA 2003, 'means the commission of an offence or other reprehensible behaviour'. The subsection includes the commission of an offence but implicitly excludes the subject-matter of the charge. Thus, the expression 'commission' must be taken to mean the commission of other offences which are not currently before the court. At the same time there is no requirement that the accused must have been convicted of the offence. If there is a conviction of the offence, then by virtue of s 6 of the Criminal Procedure Act 1865 and s 74 of the Police and Criminal Evidence Act 1984, the convicted person is treated as having committed the offence, until the contrary is proved. However, if a conviction does not exist, it does not follow that no inference could be drawn that he committed the offence. At common law the fact that the accused was charged with an offence and was acquitted did not preclude the prosecution from establishing that he committed those offences. The test, however, is based on relevance of the facts surrounding the charges that led to the acquittal and the facts underpinning the current charge, ie the defendant's guilt of the current charge may be overwhelming by virtue of the evidence of a number of similar incidents. This would be the position where a number of witnesses are willing to come forward and, without collusion, give a similar account of the defendant's behaviour which was denied by the defendant. In *R v Z* [2000] 2 AC 483, the defendant was charged with the rape of a young woman, C, in 1998. The defendant did not dispute that he had had sexual intercourse with the complainant, but his defence was that she consented, or that he believed she had consented to intercourse. Prior to this charge, the defendant had faced four separate allegations of rape of different young women which resulted in four separate trials. In three of these trials the defendant was acquitted. In the fourth trial he was convicted. In each of the trials the defendant did not dispute that sexual intercourse had taken place, but alleged that each complainant had consented, or that he believed that each complainant had consented to intercourse with him. In the current trial, the House of Lords ruled that the Crown was allowed to call the four complainants involved in the previous trials in order to testify against the defendant on the issue of consent or to negate the defendant's claim that he believed the victims had consented. There was a considerable degree of striking similarity between the defendant's conduct, as alleged by C, and the other four complainants.

The concept of reprehensible behaviour has not been defined by the Act and has been kept vague to avoid collateral arguments about whether conduct that does not result in a charge or conviction should be treated as misconduct. Undoubtedly, the concepts of 'misconduct' and 'reprehensible behaviour' are required to be judged objectively. This would include activities that are contrary to the criminal law (convictions) and other immoral conduct, whether or not resulting in a charge, prosecution or conviction. Pre-2003 examples are *R v Marsh* [1994] Crim LR 52, cross-examination of a rugby player on his bad disciplinary record, or a warning to or dismissal of an employee for misconduct at work. Likewise, an acquittal of an offence may amount to reprehensible behaviour; see *R v Z* above. Difficulties with the definition might arise in cases where there is no definitive measure for judging a person's conduct such as lack of courtesy, drunkenness or excessive swearing. May such conduct be treated as reprehensible? In *R v Renda* [2005] EWCA Crim 2826, the Court of Appeal stated that there must be some element of culpability or blameworthiness before conduct could be treated as reprehensible.

An analogy may be drawn between 'reprehensible behaviour' under the Criminal Justice Act 2003 and 'imputations' on the character of prosecution witnesses within s 1(3)(ii) of the Criminal Evidence Act 1898 (now repealed). There have been many decisions concerning the interpretation of the expression 'imputations', and not all of these decisions are consistent. In *R v Rouse* [1904] 1 KB 184, it was decided that calling the prosecutor a liar from the witness box was not an imputation on the character of the prosecutor. It was decided that the statement amounted to no more than a plea of not guilty put in emphatic language. However, someone charged with receiving stolen goods may cast imputations if he makes allegations as to the morality of the prosecutrix; see *R v Jenkins* (1945) 31 Cr App R 1. Similarly, on a charge of burglary, an allegation by the accused that the complainant had a homosexual relationship with him amounted to casting imputations; see *R v Bishop* [1975] QB 274. Likewise, imputations were cast when the defence suggested that a confession was obtained by threats or bribes; see *R v Wright* (1910) 5 Cr App R 131; and that successive remands were obtained by the police to enable them to fabricate evidence; see *R v Jones* (1923) 17 Cr App R 117. On the other hand, on a charge of robbery the allegation that the prosecutor was a habitual drunkard did not amount to casting imputations on the character of the prosecutor; see *R v Westfall* (1912) 7 Cr App R 176.

In *R v Edwards* [2006] 2 Cr App R 4, it was decided that in a drugs case, the judge was wrong to allow a defendant to be cross-examined about his legal possession of an antique, but functional, Derringer firearm. Such legitimate possession of the gun could not be treated as evidence of misconduct.

Scott Baker LJ:

> **J** 'It is difficult to see how evidence of lawful possession of an antique firearm can amount to evidence of, or a disposition towards, misconduct. The judge did not prevent questioning on it, but doubted its relevance. In our view it was not evidence of bad character and therefore no question of admissibility under s 101 arose.'

In *R v Weir* [2006] 2 All ER 570, in a consolidated appeal, the Court of Appeal decided that on a charge of a sexual offence on a 13-year-old girl, a 39-year-old defendant who had a three-year consensual sexual relationship with a girl (B) who had been 16 at the commencement of the relationship, and a suggestive remark made to the 15-year-old sister of the complainant did not, *per se*, constitute evidence of 'misconduct'. The position may have been different had there been some peculiar feature in the case, such as grooming, parental disapproval or particular immaturity of the complainant, but the contraction of an odd but lawful relationship by the defendant was insufficient to make it reprehensible, and was not evidence of bad character.

Kennedy LJ:

> **J** 'In our combined view, the judge was wrong to conclude that the sexual relationship between the appellant and B, without more, amounted to "evidence of, or a disposition towards, misconduct on his part" and therefore evidence of "bad character" for the purposes of s 98 . . . of the 2003 Act. The definition of "misconduct" is very wide. It makes it clear that behaviour may be reprehensible, and therefore misconduct, though not amounting to the commission of an offence. The appellant was significantly older than B. But there was no evidence . . . of grooming of B by the appellant before she was 16, or that the parents disapproved and communicated their disapproval to the appellant, or that B was intellectually, emotionally or physically immature for her age, or that there was some other feature of the lawful relationship which might make it "reprehensible".'

The court decided that the evidence was nevertheless relevant and admissible at common law to demonstrate that the defendant had a sexual interest in girls of the complainant's age.

Kennedy LJ:

> **J** '. . . once it is decided that evidence of the appellant's sexual relationship with B did not amount to "evidence of bad character", the abolition of the common law rules governing the admissibility of "evidence of bad character" by s 99(1) did not apply. We have no doubt that evidence of the relationship was admissible at common law, in particular circumstances of this case, because it was relevant to the issue of whether the appellant had a sexual interest in A [the victim]. It was capable of demonstrating a sexual interest in early- or mid-teenage girls, much younger than the appellant, and therefore bore on the truth of his case of a purely supportive, asexual interest in A. It was not in our judgment unfair to admit the evidence (see s 78 of PACE 1984).'

In *R v Osbourne* [2007] EWCA Crim 481, it was decided that on a charge of murder the fact that the defendant became verbally aggressive if he failed to take his medication for schizophrenia was not reprehensible behaviour.

11.6.1 Exclusion from the definition of bad character

Section 98 of the CJA 2003 creates two exceptions to the definition of bad character. These exclusions or exceptions to bad character evidence are outside the new statutory rules and when they apply, the evidence will be admissible because of its obvious relevance. The Law Commission identified the reasoning behind the exclusions enacted in s 98. These are occasions when the Crown may wish to adduce evidence of the defendant's misconduct, not in respect of the offence charged, but as part of the transaction connected with the offence. In short, evidence that may be intimately connected with the commission or investigation of the offence, if admissible prior to the introduction of the 2003 Act, will continue to be admissible.

These occasions are

'evidence which
(a) has to do with the alleged facts of the offence with which the defendant is charged, or
(b) is evidence of misconduct in connection with the investigation or prosecution of that offence.'

Section 98(a) relates to facts or matters that are directly relevant to the offence. These are facts which, at common law, would have been admissible to prove the prosecution's case, such as similar fact and background evidence, for example evidence of an assault that had been committed in the course of a burglary as evidence to do with the facts of the offence. The effect is that under the statutory regime introduced by the Criminal Justice Act 2003, such evidence within s 98(a) does not have to pass through any of the gateways in s 100 (non-defendants) or s 101 (defendants). The phrase, 'has to do with' is not the clearest that Parliament could have selected but the policy behind the subsection involves the situation where the charge against the defendant

cannot be proved without establishing the additional prejudicial evidence of the defendant, for example on a charge of driving whilst disqualified, proof of the defendant's prior conviction and disqualification is not within the bad character definition but admissible within s 98(a).

In *R v Edwards* [2006] 3 All ER 882, Scott Baker LJ said:

> **J** 'Often the first inquiry is whether it is necessary to go through the "bad character" gateways at all. In this regard, s 98 is not to be overlooked. It excludes from the definition of bad character evidence which "has to do with the alleged facts of the offence or evidence of misconduct in connection with the investigation or prosecution of that offence". While difficult questions can arise as to whether evidence of background or motive falls to be admitted under those exclusions in s 98 or requires consideration under s 101(1)(c), it does not follow that merely because the evidence fails to come within the s 101 gateways it will be inadmissible. Where the exclusions in s 98 are applicable the evidence will be admissible without more ado.'

Likewise, in *R v Machado* [2006] All ER (D) 28, the prosecution alleged that the defendant had engaged in a conversation with the victim and then robbed him, but the defendant denied this allegation and contended that the victim had offered to supply drugs to him and had said that he (victim) had taken an Ecstasy tablet before. The Court of Appeal decided that this was not evidence of the victim's bad character governed by s 100 of the Criminal Justice Act 2003. The disputed evidence related to the very circumstances in which the offence had allegedly occurred. The evidence was contemporaneous with, and closely associated with the alleged facts of the offence. It was therefore not bad character evidence.

Similarly, in *R v Malone* [2006] All ER (D) 321, the Court of Appeal decided that on a charge of murder, evidence of a private investigator's report that was forged by the defendant as part of his plot to prove that the victim, his wife, was unfaithful was properly admitted to establish evidence of a matrimonial dispute and a build-up of hostility. The evidence could also have been admitted under s 101(1)(d) of the Criminal Evidence Act 2003.

Gage LJ:

> **J** 'There is no dispute that the document constituted evidence of bad character. It was, at the least, reprehensible behaviour (see s 112(1)). In our judgment, evidence of this sort was capable of being admitted under s 98(a). The prosecution case was based on circumstantial evidence. Its case was that the matrimonial difficulties between the appellant and his wife caused him to flare up and kill her . . . As such evidence of matrimonial difficulties, the intensity and effect of these difficulties on the appellant and how he dealt with them before she disappeared could, in our judgment, have been admissible as evidence going directly to show with other circumstantial evidence

CONTINUED ▸

J that he had committed the offence. As such it was capable of being evidence "to do with the alleged facts of the case" in the same way as evidence to show a conspiracy or a joint venture would be admissible under s 98(a).'

Section 98(b) concerns evidence that exist after the alleged commission of the offence such as evidence that the defendant tried to intimidate a prosecution witness or lied during the interrogation by police officers. Likewise, evidence of misconduct by a police officer in attempting to extract a confession from the accused would not constitute evidence of bad character but would be subject to the common law rules.

A further exception is enacted in s 99(2) of the CJA 2003, which preserves the common law in criminal proceedings concerning a person's reputation being admissible to prove his bad character. This is the *R v Rowton* exception; see above.

ACTIVITY

Self-test questions

1.   What meanings were attached to character evidence in criminal proceedings at common law?

2.   What forms did good character evidence take in criminal proceedings, prior to the introduction of the Criminal Justice Act 2003?

3.   What directions must the judge give in respect of the good character of a defendant in criminal proceedings?

4.   What was meant by 'similar fact evidence' before the introduction of the Criminal Justice Act 2003?

5.   What is meant by 'bad character' under the Criminal Justice Act 2003?

Further reading

Hoffman, L. 'Similar Facts after *Boardman*' (1975) 91 LQR 193

Law Commission Report, Law Com No 273 (2001) 'Evidence in Criminal Proceedings: Previous Misconduct of a Defendant'

Munday, R. 'What constitutes a good character?' [1997] Crim LR 247

Munday, R. 'What constitutes "Other Reprehensible Behaviour" under the Bad Character Provisions of he Criminal Justice Act 2003?' [2005] Crim LR 24

Munday, R. 'Cut-Throat Defences and the "Propensity to be Untruthful" under Section 104 of the Criminal Justice Act 2003" [2005] Crim LR 624

Redmayne, M. 'The Relevance of Bad Character' (2002) CLJ 684

Stone, J. 'The Rule of Exclusion of Similar Fact Evidence: England' (1932) 46 Harvard LR 954

Tapper, C. 'The Criminal Evidence Act 2003: Evidence of Bad Character' [2004] Crim LR 533

chapter 12 ADMISSIBILITY OF BAD CHARACTER EVIDENCE OF DEFENDANTS ▪

AIMS AND OBJECTIVES

By the end of this chapter you should be able to understand:

■ The occasions under s 100 of the Criminal Justice Act 2003 when bad character evidence of persons, other than the defendant, is admissible

■ The various gateways for admitting the bad character evidence of the defendant in criminal proceedings

■ The contents of the directions that are required to be given by the judge

■ The notion and significance of contaminated evidence

■ The procedure concerning the adduction of bad character evidence by the prosecution

■ Miscellaneous statutory provisions authorizing the admissibility of bad character evidence of the defendant

■ Bad character evidence in civil cases.

12.1 Introduction and outline of the scheme of the Act

The statutory regime for the admissibility of evidence of bad character is laid down in s 100 for non-defendants and s 101 for defendants. These provisions have been qualified by ss 102–106 of the 2003 Act. Safeguards and the procedure governing the admissibility of bad character evidence are laid down in ss 107–111 of the Act.

12.2 Grounds for admitting bad character evidence – non-defendant's bad character

At common law, a witness other than the accused could be cross-examined on matters related to facts in issue as well as credit. As far as facts in issue are concerned, the witness's answer is not final but the cross-examiner is entitled to contradict the witness's answer. On matters related to credit the witness's answer is final, subject to a number of exceptions (see earlier). This rule was applicable to prosecution and defence witnesses, other than the accused. There were few restrictions on the nature of the questions relating to credit that could be asked of such witnesses. Important restrictions included the discretion of the judge to intervene on grounds of oppression as well as ss 41–43 of the Youth Justice and Criminal Evidence Act 1999. The Law Commission was of the view that a more structured approach ought to be introduced with regard to the bad character of persons other than the defendant, in order to encourage such persons testifying and to restrict offensive cross-examination. The effect was the introduction of s 100 of the 2003 Act.

Section 100 is expressed in exclusionary language in the sense that such evidence is admissible 'if and only if'. The section is also referable to 'evidence . . . of persons other than the defendant'. This is taken to mean witnesses and non-witnesses. Non-witnesses may include a third party who is alleged to have committed the offence. In addition, non-witnesses may possibly include deceased persons, such as the deceased victim of the offence. Witnesses include those called for the prosecution as well as the defence, other than the defendant.

Section 100(1) enacts three alternative criteria for the admissibility of the evidence, as follows:

'In criminal proceedings evidence of the bad character of a person other than the defendant is admissible if and only if –

(a) it is important explanatory evidence,

(b) it has substantial probative value in relation to a matter which –

(i) is a matter in issue in the proceedings, and

(ii) is of substantial importance in the context of the case as a whole,

or

(c) all the parties to the proceedings agree to the evidence being admissible.'

Section 100(1)(a) is identical to s 101(1)(c) that is applicable to the accused and will be discussed later.

Section 100(1)(b) enacts a number of pre-conditions for the admissibility of the evidence. These are:

(a) that the evidence has 'substantial probative value', and

(b) relates to a 'matter in issue' in the proceedings, and

(c) 'is of substantial importance in the context of the case as a whole'.

The notion of 'substantive probative value' relates to the enhanced quality that the evidence is required to possess. Ordinary relevance of the non-defendant's bad character to a matter in issue may not be sufficient, for the evidence is required to meet an 'enhanced relevance' test to be determined by the judge. Thus, evidence that is only marginally relevant to an issue will not be

admissible. Section 100(3) lays down a number of factors that the judge is required to take into account when evaluating the 'probative value' of the evidence. These factors are by no means comprehensive or exclusive.

The expression 'matter in issue' has not been defined by the statute and despite the sharp distinction at common law between facts in issue and credit, there is some evidence that the expression is taken to mean matters directly in issue and the creditworthiness of a witness.

In *R v Weir* [2006] 2 All ER 570, Kennedy LJ said:

> **J** 'Although couched in different terms from the provisions relating to the introduction of the defendant's bad character, in our view, s 100(1) does cover matters of credibility. To find otherwise would mean that there was a significant lacuna in the legislation with the potential for unfairness. In any event, it is clear from the explanatory notes that the issue of credibility falls within the section.'

Para 362 of the Explanatory notes to the Criminal Justice Act 2003 declares as follows:

> **C** 'Evidence is of probative value to a matter in issue where it helps to prove that issue one way or the other. In respect of non-defendants, evidence of bad character is most likely to be probative where the question is raised about the credibility of a witness (as this is likely to affect the court's assessment of the issue on which the witness is giving evidence). The evidence might, however be probative in other ways. One example would be to support a suggestion by the defendant that another person was responsible for the offence.'

In addition, the expression 'matter in issue' is required to be of 'substantial importance' in the case. Thus, the issue for the judge to decide, on an application to cross-examine a witness on his previous convictions, will be whether the matter is one of 'substantial importance in the case as a whole'.

In cross-examining a police officer in respect of alleged improper conduct, the issue may be governed by s 100 of the Criminal Justice Act 2003 and some guidance may be discerned from pre-2003 decisions.

CASE EXAMPLE

R v Busby (1981) 75 Cr App R 79

The defendant was charged with burglary and handling stolen goods. He was alleged to have made certain damaging remarks to the police when interviewed. He alleged that these were fabricated by the police. At his trial, two police officers were cross-examined to establish that the defendant did not make the remarks and also that one officer, in the presence of the other, had intimidated a potential witness for the defence to stop him testifying. Both officers denied that they threatened the potential witness for the defence. The defence was not allowed to call the defence witness and following conviction, the defendant appealed. The Court of Appeal allowed the appeal on the ground that the evidence was admissible to show that, if true, the prosecution was prepared to go to improper lengths to secure a conviction.

Eveleigh LJ:

'It is not always easy to determine when a question relates to facts which are collateral only, and therefore to be treated as final, and when it is relevant to the issue which has to be tried . . . We are of the opinion that the learned judge was wrong to refuse to admit the evidence. If true, it would have shown that the police were prepared to go to improper lengths in order to secure the accused's conviction. It was the accused's case that the statement attributed to him had been fabricated, a suggestion which could not be accepted by the jury unless they thought that the officers concerned were prepared to go to improper lengths to secure a conviction.'

CASE EXAMPLE

R v Edwards [1991] 1 WLR 207

It was held that a police officer could be questioned as to any relevant criminal offences or disciplinary charges found proved against him. However, charges which had not yet been adjudicated on should not be put to the officer in cross-examination. Such question would have no probative value. Where a police officer had allegedly fabricated an admission attributed to a different defendant in a different trial and who was acquitted, he may be cross-examined to make the jury aware that the officer's evidence in the previous case was disbelieved. Where, however, the previous acquittal did not

CONTINUED ▸

necessarily indicate that the officer had been disbelieved, such cross-examination was not allowed.

Lord Lane CJ:

J

'The test is primarily one of relevance, and this is so whether one is considering evidence in chief or questions in cross examination. To be admissible questions must be relevant to the issue before the court.

Issues are of varying degrees of relevance or importance. A distinction has to be drawn between, on the one hand, the issue in the case upon which the jury will be pronouncing their verdict and, on the other hand, collateral issues of which the credibility of the witnesses may be one. Generally speaking, questions may be put to a witness as to any improper conduct of which he may have been guilty, for the purpose of testing his credit.

The limits to such questioning were defined by Sankey LJ in *Hobbs v Tinling & Co* [1929] 2 KB 1:

"The court can always exercise its discretion to decide whether a question as to credit is one which the witness should be compelled to answer . . . in the exercise of its discretion the court should have regard to the following considerations: (1) Such questions are proper if they are of such a nature that the truth of the imputation conveyed by them would seriously affect the opinion of the court as to the credibility of the witness on the matter to which he testifies. (2) Such questions are improper if the imputation which they convey relates to matters so remote in time, or of such a character, that the truth of the imputation would not affect, or would affect in a slight degree, the opinion of the court as to the credibility of the witness on the matter to which he testifies. (3) Such questions are improper if there is a great disproportion between the importance of the imputation made against the witness's character and the importance of his evidence."

[After referring to two decisions, namely, *Harris v Tippett* (1811) 2 Camp 637, and *R v Shaw* (1888) 6 Cox CC 503, his Lordship continued] The result of those two decisions seems to be this. The acquittal of a defendant in case A, where the prosecution case depended largely or entirely upon the evidence of a police officer, does not normally render that officer liable to cross examination as to credit in case B. But where a police officer who has allegedly fabricated an admission in case B, has also given evidence of an admission in case A, where

CONTINUED ▸

J there was an acquittal by virtue of which his evidence is demonstrated to have been disbelieved, it is proper that the jury in case B should be made aware of that fact. However, where the acquittal in case A does not necessarily indicate that the jury disbelieved the officer, such cross examination should not be allowed. In such a case the verdict of not guilty may mean no more than that the jury entertained some doubt about the prosecution case, not necessarily that they any witness was lying.'

If the evidence of misconduct of the person other than the defendant 'has to do with the alleged offence with which the defendant is charged' within s 98(a), the evidence will not be subject to the requirements of s 100. Instead, the evidence will be subject to the common law test of admissibility based on relevance to facts in issue. Accordingly, where it is alleged that in order to prove the defendant's guilt of the offence charged, it is necessary to prove that a person other than the accused was guilty of an offence, the application will be made under s 98(a), for example in *R v Pigram* [1995] Crim LR 808, on a charge of handling it is essential for the prosecution to prove that the goods were stolen. Thus, it would be admissible to prove the commission of the theft by another.

On the other hand, the defendant may wish to elicit evidence of the bad character of a witness or non-witness for a variety of reasons. This may be to suggest that someone else committed the offence with which the defendant is charged; see *R v Blastland* [1986] AC 41, or to bolster up a defence such as self-defence or duress; see *R v Randall* [2004] 1 Cr App R 375.

12.3 Requirement of leave

The leave requirement is a pre-condition to admissibility of the bad character of a person other than the defendant.

Section 100(4) of the 2003 Act enacts as follows:

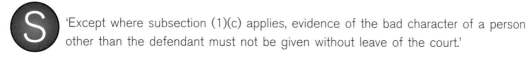

'Except where subsection (1)(c) applies, evidence of the bad character of a person other than the defendant must not be given without leave of the court.'

The exclusion of the leave requirement from s 100(1)(c) is self-explicit in the sense that all the parties had agreed to the admissibility of the evidence.

The subsection does not indicate the grounds on which the judge is entitled to grant leave, but s 100(3) identifies some of the factors the judge is required to take into account in deciding on the 'probative value of the evidence' when the application is made under s 100(1)(b). These

factors may act as guidance to the judge in deciding whether leave may be granted. Of course, if the allegation is that the evidence of misconduct has to do with the facts of the offence or the investigation or prosecution of that offence within s 98(a) or (b), the bad character provisions or gateways are not relevant and the leave of the judge is not required, for example an allegation by the defendant that a prosecution witness or another person committed the offence or that the police fabricated a material part of the evidence of the prosecution does not fall within s 100.

The requirement of leave to cross-examine a witness other than the defendant on his bad character has the effect of modifying the common law, subject to the restrictions imposed by ss 41–43 of the Youth Justice and Criminal Evidence Act 1999, concerning cross-examination of the complainant on his or her sexual behaviour. It is believed that when the cross-examination is permitted under s 41, the leave requirement under s 100(4) would automatically be satisfied.

12.4 Bad character evidence of the defendant

The common law rules and the principles laid down in the Criminal Evidence Act 1898 governing the admissibility of evidence of the bad character of the defendant have been repealed and replaced by the provisions enacted in s 101 as supplemented by other provisions. The grounds on which bad character evidence of the defendant may be admitted in a trial are today laid down in s 101 of the Criminal Justice Act 2003. There are seven 'gateways' enacted in s 101(1) which declares as follows:

S 'In criminal proceedings evidence of the defendant's bad character is admissible if, but only if –
(a) all the parties to the proceedings agree to the evidence being admissible,
(b) the evidence is adduced by the defendant himself or is given in answer to a question asked by him in cross examination and intended to elicit it,
(c) it is important explanatory evidence,
(d) it is relevant to an important matter in issue between the defendant and the prosecution,
(e) it has substantial probative value in relation to an important matter between the defendant and a co-defendant,
(f) it is evidence to correct a false impression given by the defendant, or
(g) the defendant has made an attack on another person's character.'

12.4.1 Gateway (a) – s 101(1)(a) 'agreement between parties'

Very little may be said of the subsection for it is the subject of an agreement between the parties. The purpose for which the evidence may be used would be identified by the terms of the agreement and may be the subject-matter of a formal admission.

12.4.2 Gateway (b) – s 101(1)(b) 'evidence added by the defendant'

This gateway may be non-contentious and may be resorted to for tactical reasons. The subsection involves the defendant testifying and declaring his bad character in the witness box or/and cross-examining witnesses with a view to bringing out the defendant's bad character. The leave of the judge is not required, for the admissibility of the evidence concerns a waiver by the defendant and a conscious decision to admit the evidence. This may be the case where the prosecution has been allowed to adduce evidence of the defendant's bad character and such evidence has already be admitted in the trial. In addition, the defendant may feel that for tactical reasons he ought to 'come clean' with his bad character and volunteer the information to the court, rather than allow it to be 'dragged' out of him. In *Jones v DPP* [1962] AC 635, on a charge of murder, the defendant, having given a false alibi, explained at the trial why he lied as to his whereabouts at the time of the murder. The explanation involved the defendant 'being in trouble with the police before'.

If, alternatively, the defendant's bad character is revealed unintentionally through witnesses under cross-examination, perhaps because the witness volunteers the information without being asked, the evidence is inadmissible. Accordingly, the judge is required to direct the jury to ignore the evidence or, exceptionally, discharge the jury and order a retrial.

12.4.3 Gateway (c) – s 101(1)(c) – 'important explanatory evidence'

Section 102 of the 2003 Act defines 'important explanatory evidence' thus:

'(a) without it, the court or jury would find it impossible or difficult properly to understand other evidence in the case, and
(b) its value for understanding the case as a whole is substantial.'

The test of important explanatory evidence is this 'double-barrelled' requirement which involves highly relevant, but prejudicial evidence, not of the facts in issue but significant in understanding the background evidence. If the facts of the case or evidence is understandable on its own without recourse to other material, then the evidence is not admissible under this head. Para 360 of the explanatory note accompanying the Act declares as follows:

'The term "explanatory evidence" is used to describe evidence which, whilst not going to the question of whether the defendant is guilty, is necessary for the jury to have a proper understanding of other evidence being given in the case by putting it in its proper context. An example might be a case involving the abuse of one person of another over a long period of time. For the jury to understand properly the victim's account of the offending and why they did not seek help from, for example, a parent or other guardian, it might be necessary for evidence to be given of a wider pattern of abuse involving that other person.'

Such background evidence existed at common law and includes in exceptional circumstance the motive of the accused, *per* Atkinson J in *R v Ball* [1911] AC 47.

'Evidence of motive necessarily goes to prove the fact of the homicide by the accused, as well as his "malice aforethought" in as much as it is more probable that men are killed by those that have some motive for killing them than by those who have not.'

In *R v Fulcher* [1995] 2 Cr App R 251, the defendant was charged with the murder of his infant son. The issue was the identity of the assailant. There were three possible suspects, the defendant, the defendant's wife or the defendant's mother-in-law with whom the family was living. In order to prove that the defendant committed the crime, the prosecution was allowed to adduce evidence that the child had suffered injuries which were likely to cause the child to cry. The defendant became extremely irritable when the child cried. The defendant was found guilty and appealed. The Court of Appeal dismissed the appeal and decided that the evidence was admissible to show 'motive'. In view of the fact that the defendant was one of only three potential killers of the child, the evidence was highly probative of the identity of the offender.

Similarly, in *R v Phillips (Alun)* [2003] 2 Cr App R 35, the defendant was charged with the murder of his wife. It was held that the judge had correctly admitted evidence that the marriage had broken down to rebut his claim of a happy marriage and to demonstrate a motive for killing her.

The test of background evidence at common law was that, without the evidence, the account to be placed before the court would be incomplete and incomprehensible. This would be the position even though the evidence may have established that the defendant was guilty of an offence of which he was not charged.

In *R v Sawoniuk* [2000] 2 Cr App R 220, the defendant was convicted on two counts of the murder of Jews in Belarus in 1942 contrary to the War Crimes Act 1991. Two witnesses testified that they saw the defendant commit the offences charged. In addition, the court allowed two other witnesses to testify as to the defendant's participation in a 'search and kill' operation against Jewish survivors of an earlier massacre for which the defendant was not charged. On conviction the defendant appealed. The Court of Appeal dismissed the appeal on the ground that the evidence was important explanatory material. Lord Bingham CJ:

'Criminal charges cannot fairly be judged in a factual vacuum. In order to make a rational assessment of evidence directly relating to a charge it may often be necessary for a jury to receive evidence describing, perhaps in some detail, the

CONTINUED ▶

> **J** context and circumstances in which the offences are said to have been committed. This, as we understand, is the approach indicated by this court in *R v Pettman*, May 2, 1985 (unreported): "Where it is necessary to place before the jury evidence of part of a continual background of history relevant to the offence charged in the indictment and without the totality of which the account placed before the jury would be incomplete or incomprehensible, then the fact that the whole account involves including evidence establishing the commission of an offence with which the accused is not charged is not of itself a ground for excluding the evidence." This approach seems to us of particular significance in an exceptional case such as the present, in which a London jury was asked to assess the significance of evidence relating to events in a country quite unlike our own, taking place a very long time ago in the extraordinary conditions prevailing in 1941 to 1942. It was necessary and appropriate for the Crown to prove that it was the policy of Nazi Germany first to oppress and then to exterminate the Jewish population of its conquered territories in Eastern Europe . . . It seems to us that evidence relevant to . . . these matters was probative and admissible, even if it disclosed the commission of criminal offences, other than those charged.'

Similarly, in *TM et al* [2000] 2 Cr App R 266, the Court of Appeal relied on the approach advocated by Lord Bingham CJ and upheld the trial judge's admission in a case of horrific sexual abuses by TM of his sister, the fact that TM had been forced at an earlier time to watch and then take part in other acts of sexual abuse committed by older members of the family. Without this information concerning the way that TM and the other children were groomed, the jury could not have properly appreciated the significance of the other evidence in the case, in particular why the victim did not feel able to seek protection against her brother from the rest of the family.

It is imperative that the courts are alert to the notion that 'background' evidence does not comprise a magnet to allow in otherwise inadmissible evidence under a broad heading. This caution was heeded by the Court of Appeal in *R v Dolan* [2003] 1 Cr App R 18, on a charge of murder of his child by forceful shaking. The issue was the identity of the killer. There were two suspects, namely the parents. It was held that the fact that the defendant (father) had in the past vented his fury on inanimate objects was not admissible as background evidence. Tuckey LJ:

> **J** 'The fact that a man who is not shown to have a tendency to lose his temper and react violently towards human beings becomes frustrated with and violent towards inanimate objects is, we think, irrelevant.'

Likewise, in *R v Beverley* [2006] EWCA Crim 1287, the Court of Appeal ruled that the application to admit the previous convictions of the defendant under s 101(1)(c) was unfounded. In this case the charge was conspiracy to import more than 1kg of cocaine from Jamaica. It was held that the judge had wrongly admitted previous convictions of possession with intent to supply cannabis and possession of cannabis. Laws LJ:

> **J** '[The Crown's] submission ignores the provisions of s 102, whose two parts at (a) and (b) are cumulative. We are entirely unable to see how the jury would have been disabled or disadvantaged in understanding any of the evidence allegedly connecting the appellant with the crime without having these convictions before them. The evidence was perfectly clear. It required no footnote or lexicon . . . There should never have been an application under s 101(1)(c) in this case nor should it have been supported here. The gateway at s 101(1)(c) was entirely unavailable.'

In *R v Osbourne* [2007] Crim LR 712, on a charge of murder of a close friend, the judge allowed evidence to be given from a former partner of the defendant that when he failed to take medication that controlled his schizophrenia, he was capable of snapping and verbally abusing her. At the time of the incident the defendant did not take his medication. The judge ruled that the evidence was admissible under s 101(1)(c) of the 2003 Act. On appeal, it was decided that the earlier verbal abuse did not amount to 'reprehensible behaviour' and, in any event, did not amount to 'important explanatory evidence' within s 101(1)(c).

12.4.4 Gateway (d) – s 101(1)(d) – 'relevant to an important matter in issue between the defendant and the prosecution'

Section 101(1)(d) of the 2003 Act has introduced a self-contained code of what used to be called 'similar fact evidence' (see earlier) prior to the introduction of the Act. The gateway under s 101(1)(d) is only applicable to prosecution evidence of bad character; see s 103(6) and makes provision for the admissibility of evidence going towards the guilt of the defendant as well as his credibility. To this extent the provision is much wider than the common law rules of similar fact evidence.

Under this gateway the prosecution is required to establish the following requirements:

1. that the bad character of the defendant is relevant

2. that it satisfies the test of 'important matter in issue' between the defendant and the prosecution (as defined in s 103)

3. the judge is satisfied that the admissibility of the evidence would not have an adverse effect on the fairness of the trial (s 101(3)). In determining 'fairness', the judge is required to have

regard to the length of time between the matters concerning the bad character of the defendant and the matters which form the subject of the offence charged; see s 101(4). In addition, the judge is required to consider exercising his discretion generally under s 78 of PACE 1984 and the common law.

In assessing 'relevance', s 109 enacts that the evidence is assumed to be true, unless the judge decides that no reasonable jury may so regard the evidence. Thus, an element of credibility is written in to the notion of relevance except where the evidence is incredulous in the first place.

An issue is 'important' if it is of 'substantial importance in the context of the case as a whole', s 112(1). A 'matter in issue between the defendant and the prosecution' has been defined in s 103 as including the defendant's 'propensity to commit offences of the kind with which he is charged' or the defendant's 'propensity to be untruthful', ie facts in issue or credibility; see s 103(1)(a) and (b). The effect is that the matters in issue between the defendant and the prosecution are (1) whether the defendant committed the *actus reus* of the offence, (2) with the appropriate *mens rea* and (3) the relevance of any subsidiary issues related to defences raised by the defendant, such as provocation, self-defence, etc.

Propensity to commit offences – s 103(1)(a) The expression 'propensity' has not been defined by the Act and an aspect of the test involves a propensity to commit offences of the kind with which the defendant is charged, *provided* that the admissibility of the evidence leads to the conclusion that the defendant had, more than likely, committed the offence charged. If the prosecution evidence establishes only that the defendant is *likely to have committed* the offence charged, this inference will be insufficient to establish the degree of relevance envisaged by the subsection, see s 103(1)(a). Such evidence may shed more heat and light.

Proof A defendant's propensity to commit offences of the kind charged may be established ('without prejudice to any other way of doing so') by evidence that he has been *convicted* of an offence of the 'same description' or an offence of the 'same category' as the one charged, s 103(2). Section 103(4)(a) defines offences of the same description as offences with the same statements of offences as in the charges or indictments. Thus, on a charge of assault contrary to s 47 of the Offences Against the Person Act 1861, the fact that the defendant has a conviction for a s 47 assault is evidence within s 103(2)(a) that the defendant has a propensity to commit offences of the same description. The age of the conviction is required to be considered by the judge to determine whether it is sufficiently relevant to the charge; see s 101(4). In addition, two offences are the 'same category' if they belong to the same category of offences prescribed by the Secretary of State, s 103(4). Since October 2004, there are currently two types of offence that, by order, have been made the subject of offences of the same category. These are offences within the 'theft category' and 'sexual offences'. In deciding on the admissibility of the conviction, the judge is required to consider whether it would be 'unjust' to admit the evidence by reason of the length of time since the defendant was convicted or for any other reason.

In *R v Hanson, Gilmore and Pickering* [2005] EWCA Crim 824, Rose LJ said:

> **J** 'Where propensity to commit the offence is relied upon there are . . . three questions to be considered:
> (i) Does the history of conviction(s) establish a propensity to commit offences of the kind charged?
> (ii) Does that propensity make it more likely that the defendant committed the offence?
> (iii) Is it unjust to rely on the conviction(s) of the same description or category; and, in any event, will the proceedings be unfair if they are admitted?'

Accordingly, the first question for the court to decide under this gateway is whether the proposed bad character evidence goes to propensity to commit offences of the kind charged. Having done so, the court is required to identify the specific matter in issue between the parties to which the evidence of misconduct is relevant. Finally, the judge is required to consider whether the admissibility of the evidence may have an adverse effect on a fair trial.

In *R v Hanson, Gilmore and Pickering* [2005] EWCA Crim 824, the Court of Appeal issued guidelines as to the principles of admissibility under this gateway. Rose LJ:

> **J** 'A single previous conviction for an offence of the same description or category will often not show propensity. But it may do so where, for example, it shows a tendency to unusual behaviour or where its circumstances demonstrate probative force in relation to the offence charged.'

Thus, in *R v M* [2007] Crim LR 637, the Court of Appeal allowed an appeal on a charge of possessing a firearm with intent to cause fear and violence contrary to s 16A of the Firearms Act 1968. The trial judge had admitted a previous conviction of 20 years old of possessing a firearm without a licence. The court decided that the single conviction was too old and with insufficient unique qualities to justify its admissibility under s 101(1)(d).

By contrast, in *Pickering*, on charges of rape and indecent assault on one of his daughters, the court admitted a conviction that was about a decade old for indecent assault on an 11-year-old girl. The court decided that this was an 'unusual' type of offence and even a single, old conviction for an offence of the same category was highly probative of the charge.

The court in *R v Hanson, Gilmore and Pickering* also gave an indication of some of the factors the judge is required to consider in determining whether it would be 'just' to admit the previous convictions of the defendant under s 101(1)(d). Rose LJ:

J

'When considering what is just under s 103(3), and the fairness of the proceedings under s 101(3), the judge may, among other factors, take into consideration the degree of similarity between the previous conviction and the offence charged, albeit they are both within the same description or prescribed category. For example, theft and assault occasioning actual bodily harm each embrace a wide spectrum of conduct. This does not however mean that what used to be referred as striking similarity must be shown before convictions become admissible. The judge may also take into consideration the respective gravity of the past and present offences. He or she must always consider the strength of the prosecution case. If there is no or very little other evidence against a defendant, it is unlikely to be just to admit his previous convictions, whatever they are . . . Old convictions, with no special feature shared with the offence charged, are likely seriously to affect the fairness of proceedings adversely, unless despite their age, it can properly be said that they show a continuing propensity. It will often be necessary, before determining admissibility and even when considering offences of the same description or category, to examine each individual conviction rather than merely to look at the name of the offence or at the defendant's record as a whole.'

In *R v Beverley* [2006] Crim LR 1065, see above, the Court of Appeal decided that two convictions for possession of cannabis with intent to supply (five years before the current charge) and simple possession of cannabis (two years prior to the current charge) were wrongly admitted under s 101(1)(d) to prove the guilt of the defendant on a charge of conspiracy to import cocaine. The previous convictions were too old, were of a different character, involved a different type of drug and were less serious than the current charge.

The extent of the similarity of the circumstances shared by the conviction and the charge may establish a high degree of probative value to justify the admissibility of the conviction. In *R v Smith* [2006] EWCA Crim 1355, the defendant was charged with domestic burglary, having tricked an elderly woman into letting him into her home by telling her that he was from the water company. The defendant's previous convictions for burglary and attempted burglary in entering houses of elderly people by deception and then stealing or attempting to steal from them were admitted under s 101(1)(d). The probative value of the convictions were found in the rather similar details of the circumstances surrounding the convictions.

Section 103(2) enacts that 'without prejudice to any other way' of proving the bad character of the defendant concerning his propensity to commit offences of the kind with which the defendant is charged. Other methods of proof of misconduct other than by way of conviction include:

- previous acquittals in the exceptional circumstances decided in *R v Z* (see ante)

- other counts in the indictment where these are cross-admissible; see *DPP v P* (1991) 93 Cr App R 267

- an offence where the defendant received a caution or was taken into consideration, *R v Nicholson* (1948) 32 Cr App R 98

- previous, similar acts even though the defendant was not charged, *R v Smith* (1916) 11 Cr App R 229 ('brides in the bath' case).

Propensity to be untruthful – s 103(1)(b) The principle here is that the defendant's bad character is relevant and admissible as part of the prosecution case to prove that the defendant has a propensity to be untruthful. Although this is a departure from the common law, the justification for the provision is that in some trials the accuracy or truth of the defendant's version of events is in itself an important issue. This is likely to be the case where the defendant's explanation of the events in the current trial is not dissimilar to the explanation that was not believed by the jury on a different occasion; see *Jones v DPP* [1962] AC 635.

The explanation for this provision was expressed in the Explanatory Notes accompanying the Act in para 374:

'Section 103(1)(b) makes it clear that evidence relating to whether the defendant has a propensity to be untruthful (in other words, is not to be regarded as a credible witness) can be admitted. This is intended to enable the admission of *a limited range of evidence such as convictions for perjury or other offences involving deception*... as opposed to the wider range of evidence that will be admissible where the defendant puts his character in issue by for example, attacking the character of another person. *Evidence will not be admissible under this head where it is not suggested that the defendant's case is untruthful in any respect*, for example, where the defendant and prosecution are agreed on the facts of the alleged offence and the question is whether all the elements of the offence have been made out.'

In *R v Hanson, Gilmore and Pickering*, Rose LJ explained the operation of this provision, thus:

'As to propensity to untruthfulness, this, as it seems to us, is not the same as propensity to be dishonest. It is to be assumed, bearing in mind the frequency with which the words honest and dishonest appear in the criminal law, that Parliament deliberately chose the word "untruthful" to convey a different meaning, reflecting a defendant's account of his behaviour, or lies told when committing an offence. Previous convictions, whether for offences of dishonesty or otherwise, are therefore only likely to be capable of showing a propensity to be untruthful where, in the present case, truthfulness is an issue and, in the earlier case, either there was a

CONTINUED ▸

plea of not guilty and the defendant gave an account, on arrest, in interview, or in evidence, which the jury must have disbelieved, or the way in which the offence was committed shows a propensity for untruthfulness, for example, by the making of false representations.'

Additional ways of establishing relevance

The matters in issue relating to bad character evidence of the accused within the gateway enacted in s 101(1)(d) are not restricted to those laid down in s 103 (concerning propensity to commit offences and be untruthful). Section 103(1) uses the expression 'include' to refer to propensity evidence. This does not exclude the common law that preceded the introduction of the Criminal Justice Act 2003, *per* Lord Woolf CJ in *R v Highton* [2005] 1 WLR 3472, HL.

'Section 103(1) prefaces s 103(1)(a) and (b) with the word, "include". This indicates that the matters in issue may extend beyond the two areas mentioned in the subsection.'

In *R v Barrington,* the Court of Appeal decided that under the pre-2003 law, the evidence need not be in respect of a conviction provided that it exhibited high probative value.

CASE EXTRACT

R v Barrington [1981] 1 All ER 1132

The charge was indecent assault on three young girls at his mistress's (accomplice) house. The prosecution alleged that he had lured the girls to the house on the pretext that they were required as babysitters. In reality he needed them for his own sexual purposes. Once the girls arrived at the house he showed them pornographic pictures, asked them to pose for photographs in the nude and then indecently assaulted them. The victims gave evidence to this effect. The defendant contended that the evidence was a tissue of lies and each victim had her own private motive for concocting a story. In order to show that the girls were telling the truth, the prosecution applied for and was granted leave to call three other young ladies to show that they too had been lured to the house, had been shown pornographic pictures and asked to pose in the nude. None of them alleged that she had been assaulted by the defendant. The defendant appealed against his conviction. The Court of Appeal dismissed the appeal on the

CONTINUED ▸

ground that the evidence had a high degree of probative value in proving the guilt of the defendant. Dunn LJ:

> '. . . the judge had taken into account the following six factors which he left to the jury as capable of constituting similar fact evidence. First, the baby sitting proposition. Second, the boasting claims to the girls about his position as a scriptwriter of well known television programmes and a friend of stars. Third, his mistress and accomplice was described as a professional photographer. Fourth, the evidence of the £200 prize for nude photographs. Fifth, the evidence that all the girls were shown pornographic pictures and sixth, the technique that was employed to try to get the girls to strip eventually for nude photographs . . .
>
> That the evidence of the three girls did not include evidence of the commission of offences similar to those with which the appellant was charged does not mean that they are not logically probative in determining the guilt of the appellant. Indeed, we are of the opinion that taken as a whole they are inexplicable on the basis of co-incidence and that they are of positive probative value in assisting to determine the truth of the charges, in that they tended to show that he was guilty of the offences with which he was charged.'

A similar result was reached under the 2003 Act in *R v Saleem* [2007] EWCA Crim 1923. On a charge of assault, the court admitted evidence that the defendant had violent rap lyrics and photographs stored on his computer, not to demonstrate a propensity to commit serious offences of violence, but because such evidence undermined his defence that he had been an innocent bystander with no prior knowledge of the attack. His store of photographic images of victims of violent assaults, accessed a few days before the attack, demonstrated an interest in such images. This supported the prosecution's allegation that the defendant had recorded the attack with the camera attached to his mobile phone. Moreover, the alteration of a number of rap lyrics by the defendant was suggestive of his knowledge of a plan to commit the assault on the defendant's birthday.

Directions by the judge

The judge is required to direct the jury as to the use it may make of the bad character of the defendant. The issues to be included in a direction were considered by the Court of Appeal in *R v Hanson, Gilmore and Pickering*, by Rose LJ. These issues are:

1. The judge should warn the jury against placing undue reliance on previous convictions.

2. The jury should not conclude that the defendant was guilty or untruthful merely because he had the convictions.

3. Although the convictions might show propensity, that did not mean that the defendant committed the offences of being untruthful in respect of the current charge.

4. Whether the convictions, in fact, show a propensity was for the jury to decide.

5. The jury is required to take into account what the defendant said about his previous convictions.

6. Propensity may be only one relevant factor and the jury should assess its significance in the light of all the other evidence in the case.

12.4.5 Gateway (e) – s 101(1)(e) – 'important matter in issue between the defendant and the co-defendant'

The policy regarding the admissibility of bad character evidence of an accused under gateway (e) is that it has 'substantial probative value' in respect of an 'important matter' in issue between the defendant and the 'co-defendant'. The expression 'probative value' is determined on the assumption that *prima facie* the evidence is true; see s 109(1) and an 'important matter' is defined in s 112(1) as a matter of substantial importance in the case. Thus, trivial or insignificant issues would not activate the subsection. The expression 'co-defendant' is defined in s 112(1) as a person charged in the same proceedings as the defendant. The co-defendant need not be charged with the same offence but is required to be jointly tried on the same indictment. In this respect the judge retains a discretion to decide whether the indictment ought to be severed; the test was considered in *Ludlow v MPC* [1970] 2 WLR 521. The House of Lords decided that for counts to be joined on an indictment, in addition to expediency, a loose nexus between the offences sufficient to constitute a series of offences would be sufficient; see also s 4 of the Indictment Act 1915 and r 14.2(3) of the Criminal Procedure Rules 2005.

The underlying issue under this gateway is that the defendant alleges that the co-defendant's bad character is relevant to an important matter in issue between the defendant and the co-defendant. When may this arise? There are two occasions when this gateway may be activated.

- The first is when the bad character of the co-defendant is relevant to establish that he (co-defendant) is more likely, as compared with the defendant, to have committed the offence, ie propensity to commit offences. This involves the defendant running a 'cut-throat' defence, blaming the co-defendant for the commission of the crime, for example on a charge of murder committed after a violent struggle, the defendant, A, alleges that his co-defendant, B, has several convictions for violent assault and is more likely to have committed the offence on his own.

- The second occasion involves the credibility of the co-defendant, ie the bad character of the co-defendant relates to his propensity to be untruthful and the co-defendant has attempted to undermine the nature or conduct of the defence of the defendant; see s 104(1), for example on a charge of burglary the defendant (A) raises the defence of duress held out by the co-defendant (B). The co-defendant (B) alleges that the defendant (A) is a liar and that B did

not make any threats to A. A alleges that B has a number of previous convictions for dishonesty, perjury and assault.

Section 104(1) enacts as follows:

'Evidence which is relevant to the question whether the defendant has a propensity to be untruthful is admissible on that basis under section 101(1)(e) only if the nature or conduct of his defence is such as to *undermine the co-defendant's defence*.'

The expression 'undermine' has not been defined by statute, but the expression had been referred to under the pre-2003 law in interpreting s 1(3)(iii) of the Criminal Evidence Act 1898. The expression 'giving evidence against' the co-defendant in s 1(3)(iii) of the 1898 Act means evidence 'which supports the prosecution's case in a material respect or undermines the defence of the co-accused'. This test was applied objectively and not simply subjectively in accordance with a hostile intent, for it was the effect of the evidence upon the minds of the jury that matters and not the state of mind of the defendant. The pre-2003 test was whether the defence of the co-defendant would, if believed, leave the defendant without an effective defence or increase the risks of the defendant being found guilty of the offence. A mere denial by the co-defendant may be insufficient to have this effect. In *R v Varley* (1982) 75 Cr App Rep 242, the defendant was jointly charged with the co-defendant, X, on two counts of robbery and one count of possession of a firearm at the time of the robbery. Both defendants had previous convictions. At the trial, X said that they had both taken part in the robbery but that he acted under duress imposed by the defendant. The defendant testified to the effect that he was not there at all and that X was lying. X's evidence was clearly against the defendant and X was cross-examined by the defendant's counsel. The judge allowed the defendant to be cross-examined as to his previous convictions under s 1(3)(iii). The defendant was convicted and appealed. The court dismissed his appeal and decided that the defendant had given evidence against the co-defendant on the ground that if the defendant's evidence was believed, X would have been left as a participant on his own volition and not acting under duress. Perhaps the provision under the 2003 Act may be interpreted in the same way as before the passing of the 2003 Act.

In addition, this gateway may only be utilized by the defendant and not by the prosecution, and the methods of raising the issue are through testimony of the co-defendant or a witness cross-examined by the co-defendant; see s 104(2).

Section 104(2) enacts:

'Only evidence –
(a) which is to be (or has been) adduced by the co-defendant, or
(b) which a witness is to be invited to give (or has given) in cross-examination by the co-defendant,
is admissible under s 101(1)(e).'

CASE EXTRACT

Lowery v R [1974] AC 85

Two defendants (L and K) were charged with a vicious and sadistic murder. It was clear from the evidence that only one of them committed the crime. Each blamed the other for the commission of the crime. L testified to the effect that he was not the sort of man to commit such a brutal crime and claimed that he had tried his best to stop K from committing the crime. K denied committing the offence and alleged that at the time he was under the influence of drugs and incapable of carrying out the deed and to prevent L from committing the offence. K was allowed to call a psychologist to testify that, having examined the two defendants, K was immature and easily led, but L was aggressive and sadistic. His view was that K was less likely to have committed the offence. L was convicted and appealed. The Privy Council dismissed the appeal and decided that since the issue was which one of the defendants committed the crime, K was entitled to call rebutting evidence to determine that L was more likely to have committed the offence.

Lord Morris:

J 'Lowery and King were each asserting that the other was the completely dominating person at the time Rosalyn Nolte was killed: each claimed to have been in fear of the other. In these circumstances it was most relevant for King to be able to show, if he could, that Lowery had a personality marked by aggressiveness, whereas he, King, had a personality which suggested that he would be led and dominated by someone who was dominant and aggressive. In support of King's case, *the evidence of Professor Cox was relevant if it tended to show that the version of the facts put forward by King were more probable than put forward by Lowery.* Not only, however, was the evidence which King called relevant to this case: its admissibility was placed beyond doubt by the whole substance of Lowery's case. Not only did Lowery assert that the killing was done by King and not only did he say that he had been in fear of King, but . . . he set himself up as one who had no motive whatsoever in killing the girl and as one who would not have been interested in the sort of behaviour manifested by the killer. While ascribing the sole responsibility to King he was also in effect saying that he himself was not the sort of man to have committed the offence. The only question now arising is whether in the special circumstances above referred to, it was open to King in defending himself to call Professor Cox to give evidence that he gave. The evidence was relevant to and necessary for this case which involved negativing what Lowery had said and put forward: in their Lordships' view . . . the evidence was admissible.'

In this case the two tests for admissibility under this gateway would have been satisfied. King's testimony that L was aggressive, sadistic and that he was in fear of L was relevant to the issue of propensity to commit the offence. The italicized words, concerning the testimony of Professor Cox, indicate that the test laid down in s 104(1) – propensity to be untruthful – would also be satisfied today.

No discretion to exclude bad character evidence under gateway (e) Prior to the introduction of the 2003 Act, the judge did not have a discretion to exclude 'evidence given against' the co-defendant under s 1(3)(iii) of the Criminal Evidence Act 1898, the reason being that the court has always been reluctant to interfere with a case presented by the defendant, including the co-defendant. In short, fairness to one defendant may be perceived as unfairness to another defendant in the same trial, *per* Lord Donovan in *Murdoch v Taylor* [1965] AC 574:

'. . . a trial judge has no discretion whether to allow an accused person to be cross examined as to his past criminal offences once he has given evidence against his co accused. [Section 1(3)] in terms confers no such discretion and in my opinion, none can be implied.'

Likewise, in *R v Randall* [2004] 1 Cr App R 375, Lord Steyn repeated the view of Lord Donovan.

'The discretionary power to exclude relevant evidence which is tendered by the prosecution if its prejudicial effect outweighs its probative value, does not apply to the position as between co-accused. In a joint criminal trial a judge has no discretionary power at the request of one accused to exclude relevant evidence tending to support the defence of another.'

Under similar provisions enacted in s 101(1)(e) of the Criminal Justice Act 2003, the courts have affirmed that there is no judicial discretion to prevent one defendant from adducing evidence of the co-defendant's bad character whenever such evidence has substantial probative value, *per* Moses LJ in *R v Musone* [2007] 2 Cr App R 29.

12.4.6 Gateway (f) – s 101(1)(f) – 'correct a false impression given by the defendant'

This provision was introduced by s 101(1)(f) of the Criminal Justice Act 2003 with the object of admitting the bad character evidence of the defendant in order to correct a false impression given by the defendant. Thus, it is the defendant's action in creating a false impression that entitles the prosecution to adduce the bad character evidence. There is some similarity between this provision and the repealed s 1(3)(b) of the Criminal Evidence Act 1898 that involved the defendant putting his character in issue and thereby subjecting him to cross-examination on his bad character. Of course, s 101(1)(f) is much broader than its predecessor in that the admissibility of bad character evidence under the 2003 Act is not restricted to the defendant testifying at the trial.

Modes of creating a false impression Section 105(1) defines when the defendant may create a false impression. This would be the position if the defendant is:

Section 105(1)(a):

'responsible for the making of an express or implied assertion which is apt to give the court or jury a false or misleading impression.'

Only the prosecution is entitled to utilize this gateway in order to admit evidence of the defendant's bad character; see s 105(7). Thus, in joint trials with more than one defendant and where a co-defendant has given evidence creating a false or misleading impression, the defendant is not entitled to adduce bad character evidence under s 101(1)(f), but may do so if the circumstances warrant the admissibility of such evidence under s 101(1)(e); see earlier.

An express assertion that is false may be made by the defendant if he alleges that he is a man of 'good character' when in reality there are several previous convictions recorded against the defendant; see *R v Ullah* [2006] EWCA Crim 2003. However, the subsection endorses 'implied assertions' made by the defendant. This will include assertions made from the defendant's conduct or behaviour to the extent that it may be implied that the defendant is a person of good character. In this respect, s 105(4) declares that:

 'where . . . a defendant, by means of his conduct (other than the giving of evidence) in the proceedings, is seeking to give the court or jury an impression about himself that is false or misleading, the court may, if it appears just to do so, treat the defendant as being responsible for the making of an assertion which is apt to give that impression.'

Section 105(5) declares that:

 'conduct includes appearance or dress'.

Illustrations of this principle include on a charge for theft an assertion by the defendant that in the past he had restored lost property to their owners; see *R v Samuel* (1956) 40 Cr App R 8. In *R v Robinson* [2001] Crim LR 478, the Court of Appeal doubted whether the defendant holding of a copy of the Bible in his hands whilst testifying amounted to an assertion of good character. Today, it is arguable that it is the impression that is required to be misleading, not the assertion, and Mr Robinson may reasonably be treated as attempting to convey the image of an honest and truthful individual whilst testifying. At the same time, it is obvious that some limit will be imposed on this provision for it would be unjust for the judge to allow in bad character evidence on the ground that the defendant had recently changed his appearance by growing a beard or shaving his head at the time of the trial.

In effect, the following methods have been envisaged by the provisions for making assertions, by or on behalf of the defendant:

- the testimony of the defendant, s 105(2)(a)

- an assertion made on behalf of the defendant who does not testify, s 105(2)(a)

- an assertion made by the defendant on being questioned under caution, before charge and admitted in court, s 105(2)(b)(i)

- an assertion made by the defendant on being charged with the offence or officially informed that he might be prosecuted and admitted in court, s 105(2)(b)(ii)

- an assertion made by a witness called by the defendant, s 105(2)(c)

- in response to any answer given by any witness in cross-examination on behalf of the defendant and intended to elicit the assertion, s 105(2)(d)

- the assertion was made by any person out of court and endorsed and admitted by the defendant, s 105(2)(e).

Withdrawal of assertion Section 105(3) of the 2003 Act enacts that a defendant may be allowed to 'withdraw or disassociate' himself from an assertion with the effect that he will not be treated as making the assertion. There are a number of issues with this provision, first, whether the withdrawal/disassociation will be sufficiently clear to convince the court that the defendant has made a genuine withdrawal. Second, what constitutes the court for these purposes – the judge or the judge and jury? It is not clear from the Act what method(s) of withdrawal or disassociation will be effective for this purpose. At the same time, the defendant is a competent but not compellable witness for himself; it would be against his constitutional rights to require him to testify in order to disassociate himself from an assertion. It would appear that the defendant's legal representative may be entitled to communicate the defendant's withdrawal from the assertion in the presence of the judge on a *voir dire*. Indeed, s 105(3) permits a partial withdrawal and to that extent is treated as not making an assertion. In this respect it is important that the court is clear as to the assertions that are still being made by the defendant. In *R v Renda* [2006] 1 WLR 2948, Judge LJ issued a note of caution thus:

> J 'There is a significant difference between the defendant who makes a specific and positive decision to correct a false impression for which he is responsible, or to disassociate himself from false impressions conveyed by the assertions of others, and the defendant who in the process of cross examination is obliged to concede that he has been misleading the jury. A concession extracted in cross examination that the defendant was not telling the truth in part of his examination-in-chief will not normally amount to a withdrawal or disassociation from the original assertion for the purposes of section 105(3).'

Rebuttal evidence Section 105(6) enacts that the rebutting evidence may not be excessive but is restricted to the specific issue of rebutting the assertion creating the false impression. Section 105(6) declares as follows:

'Evidence is admissible under section 101(1)(f) *only if* it goes no further than is necessary to correct the false impression.'

Thus, the prosecution is only entitled to adduce evidence of the defendant's misconduct that has probative value in correcting the false impression for which the defendant was responsible.

As distinct from the pre-2003 law (see *R v Winfield* [1939] 4 All ER 164), bad character evidence is not indivisible but is required to deal with the specific assertion for which the defendant is responsible. This involves a specific test of relevance in that the evidence deals with only the assertion that creates the false impression. This may require a certain amount of editing of the evidence by the judge.

In addition, s 105(1)(b) declares that the rebutting evidence is required to be of probative value. Thus, the quality of the evidence will be determined by the judge. Section 105(1)(b) enacts as follows:

'Evidence to correct such an impression is evidence which has probative value in correcting it.'

Discretion to exclude Since the prosecution alone is allowed to adduce rebutting evidence to correct a false impression created by the defendant, the judge has a discretion under s 78 of the Police and Criminal Evidence Act 1984 to refuse to admit evidence which would otherwise have 'an adverse effect on the fairness of the trial'. This approach is encouraged under s 112(3)(c).

In *R v Weir* [2006] 1 Cr App R 303, Kennedy LJ said:

> 'We note that the provisions of section 101(3) do not apply to subsection (1)(f), and we see no reason to doubt that section 78 of the 1984 Act should be considered where section 101(1)(f) is relied upon.'

12.4.7 Gateway (g) – s 101(1)(g) – 'attack on another person's character'

The principle under this gateway bears a similarity with the old 'tit-for-tat' principle enacted in s 1(3)(b)(ii) of the Criminal Evidence Act 1898 ('the nature or conduct of the defence is such as to involve imputations on the character of the prosecutor or witnesses for the prosecution or the deceased victim of the offence'). Under the new provision enacted in s 101(1)(g) of the 2003 Act the prosecution will be entitled to adduce evidence of the defendant's bad character if he (defendant) has made an attack on any other person's character, and it is irrelevant that the defendant has chosen to give or not to give evidence. The rationale of the provision is not to protect the character of others but to provide evidence to the jury to balance any attack which the defendant has made. Lord Pearce in *Selvey v DPP* [1970] AC 304, stated the rationale for the repealed s 1(3)(b) thus:

> '. . . The practical justification for [s 1(3)(b)] is the 'tit-for-tat' argument. If the accused is seeking to cast discredit on the prosecutor, then the prosecution should be allowed to do likewise. If the accused is seeking to persuade the jury that the prosecutor behaved like a knave, then the jury should know the character of the man who makes these accusations, so that it may judge fairly between them instead of being in the dark as to one of them . . .'

The old law involved the concept of casting 'imputations', whereas the new provision introduced the new concept, 'attack on another person's character'. While many of the cases decided under the 1898 Act may be relevant in interpreting this provision, it is clear that the provisions under the 2003 Act are much broader than its nineteenth-century equivalent. When does a defendant make an attack? Section 106(2) enacts as follows:

'. . . evidence attacking the other person's character means evidence to the effect
that the other person –

(a) has committed an offence (whether a different offence from the one with which
the defendant is charged or the same one), or

(b) has behaved, or is disposed to behave, in a reprehensible way;

and "imputation about the other person" means an assertion to that effect.'

There are a number of points that need clarification. First, the provision is not restricted to persons
who testify in the trial; indeed, the person attacked need not be named. It may involve the
defendant alleging that such a person committed the offence charged or a different offence or in
some way misconducted himself. In *R v Bishop* [1975] QB 274, it was decided that under the pre-
2003 law, suggesting that a prosecution witness had a homosexual relationship with the defendant
was treated as casting imputations on the character of the witness, whereas in *R v Westfall* (1912) 7
Cr App R 176, calling the prosecutor an habitual drunkard did not have this effect. Likewise, in *R
v McClean* [1978] Crim LR 430, an allegation that the complainant was intoxicated and swearing
did not justify adducing evidence of the defendant's bad character. In *R v Weir* [2006] 1 Cr App R
303, on a charge of rape, an allegation by a Hindu priest that the complainant conspired with
others to fabricate the complaint was treated as an attack. Similarly, in *R v Renda* [2006] 1 WLR
2948, comments by the defendant that suggested that the complainant would consent to sexual
intercourse with anyone amounted to an attack. In *R v Nelson* [2006] EWCA Crim 3412, a
suggestion that a neighbour and the victim conspired to fabricate evidence against the defendant
amounted to an attack on the character of a non-witness. Second, there is no requirement that the
attack should be untrue or unfounded. Accordingly, if the attack is an integral part of the defence,
in theory the defendant's bad character may be admitted. Of course this is subject to the discretion
of the judge to disallow the defendant's bad character evidence within s 101(3) of the 2003 Act or
s 78 of the Police and Criminal Evidence Act 1984, where the admissibility of the evidence may
have an adverse effect on the fairness of the trial. In *R v Singh (James Paul)* [2007] EWCA 2140,
on a charge of robbery an allegation by the defendant that the complainant was smoking crack
cocaine and had fabricated his evidence amounted to an attack on the character of the
complainant. Hughes LJ explained the discretion of the judge thus:

J

'. . . it may be relevant to the exercise of discretion if an attack on the complainant is
an entirely gratuitous one. Gateway G is, however, not limited to such cases and the
question is not relevant to whether the gateway is passed. The purpose of gateway
G is to enable the jury to know from what sort of source allegations against a
witness (especially a complainant but not only a complainant) have come . . . This
court will not interfere with the exercise of the judge's discretion under s 101(3) any
more than it would under section 78 of the Police and Criminal Evidence Act 1984
or similar provisions unless the judge has either misdirected himself or had arrived at
a conclusion which is outside the legitimate band of decisions available to him.'

A similar view was expressed by Keene LJ in the earlier case, *R v Nelson* [2006] EWCA Crim 3412.

> J
>
> '. . . we must emphasise that the trial judge still has a discretion as to whether the jury should hear about a defendant's bad character when he has merely made imputations about the character of a non-witness. Not only does he have such a general discretion under s 78 of the Police and Criminal Evidence Act 1984, but section 101(3) of the 2003 Act specifically provides that: "the court must not admit evidence under subsection (1) (d) or (g) if on an application by the defendant to exclude it it appears to the court that the admission of the evidence would have such an adverse effect on the fairness of the proceedings that the court ought not to admit it".
>
> How the trial judge exercises that discretion is a matter for him or her, but it seems to this court that it would be unusual for evidence of a defendant's bad character to be admitted when the only basis for so doing was an attack on the character of a non-witness who is also a non-victim. The fairness of the proceedings would normally be materially damaged by so doing.'

In *R v Rouse* [1904] 1 KB 184, a plea of not guilty, even in forcible language, did not involve casting imputations; but if the defendant, in his defence, makes an allegation which goes beyond a mere denial of the charge, his bad character may become admissible. This would be the position where the defence alleges that the police had fabricated evidence attributed to the defendant, see *R v Britzmann and Hall* [1983] 1 All ER 369. In *Selvey v DPP* [1970] AC 304, the defendant alleged that the complainant had committed buggery earlier on the same day of the incident and had been refused £1 when he offered himself to the defendant amounted to imputations. Viscount Dilhorne postulated four guidelines relevant to s 1(3)(ii), thus:

> J
>
> '1. the words of the statute must be given their ordinary meaning.
> 2. The section permits cross examination of the accused as to character both when imputations on the character of the prosecutor and his witness are cast to show their unreliability as witnesses independently of the evidence given by them and also when the casting of such imputations is necessary to enable the accused to establish his defence.
> 3. In rape cases, the accused can allege consent without placing himself in peril of such cross examination.
> 4. If what is said amounts in reality to no more than a denial of the charge, expressed, it may be, in emphatic language, it should not be regarded as coming within the section.'

The methods by which the defendant may make an attack on another person's character are both in and out of court, and are stated in s 106(1) as follows:

S '(a) he adduces evidence attacking the other person's character,

(b) he (or any legal representative appointed under s 38(4) of the Youth Justice and Criminal Evidence Act 1999 to cross examine a witness in his interests) asks questions in cross examination that are intended to elicit such evidence, or are likely to do so, or

(c) evidence is given of an imputation about the other person made by the defendant –

   (i) on being questioned under caution, before charge, about the offence with which he is charged, or

   (ii) on being charged with the offence or officially informed that he might be prosecuted for it.'

Thus, the definition of attacking a person's character under gateway 'g' is similar to the general definition of 'bad character' in s 98 and includes facts relating to the offence charged as well as the investigation and prosecution of the offence. These allegations or attacks may be made by the defendant in person, or through defence witnesses or by cross-examination of witnesses.

Evidential value of the bad character evidence Once evidence of the defendant's bad character has been admitted in court, the judge is required to direct the jury as to the value of such evidence. The Act does not give an indication, but the courts have declared that such evidence is admissible as to credibility of the defendant and his propensity to commit the offence. In *R v Highton* [2006] 1 Cr App R 125, *per* Lord Woolf CJ said:

J 'Once the evidence is admitted, it may, depending on the particular facts, be relevant not only to credibility but also to propensity to commit offences of the kind with which the defendant is charged.'

A similar view was expressed by Hughes LJ in *R v Singh (James Paul)* [2007] EWCA Crim 2140.

J 'We think that it is perfectly plain that, once admitted under gateway G, bad character evidence does go to the credibility of the witness in question. That accords with common experience. It is, among other things, the obverse of the reason why a defendant is entitled to plead his own good character in support of his claim that he should be believed. The reason why he is entitled to do that is because ordinary human experience is that people of proven respectability and

CONTINUED ▸

> **J** good character are, other things being equal, more worthy of belief than those who are not. Conversely, persons of bad character may of course tell the truth and often do, but it is ordinary human experience that their word may be worth less than that of those who have led exemplary lives. Once gateway G is passed the consequence of the defendant's bad character falls to be weighed with all the other evidence when the jury decides whether or not he has been proved to be guilty, and in doing so it may think him less worthy of belief because of his history.'

12.5 Warning by judge

Although there is no legal requirement for the judge to issue a warning to the defendant (in the absence of the jury) that his defence or allegation may expose him to a risk of revealing his bad character, it is submitted that it is good legal practice to issue such a warning in appropriate cases. Failure to issue such a warning may not be fatal to a conviction but involves the exercise of judicial discretion to disallow evidence in order to ensure a fair trial. A similar principle existed before the 2003 Act was passed; see Viscount Dilhorne in *Selvey v DPP* [1970] AC 304.

> **J** 'It is desirable that a warning should be given when it becomes apparent that the defence is taking a course which may expose the accused to cross examination [as to his bad character]. That was not given in this case but the failure to give such a warning would not, in my opinion, justify in this case the allowing of the appeal.'

12.6 Contaminated evidence

Section 107 introduces a special principle to protect a defendant whose bad character may be admitted under s 101(1)(c) to (g) and who may be prejudiced where such evidence has been contaminated to the extent that a conviction may be unsafe; see s 107(1). This power of the court is additional to the court's power to order an acquittal or to discharge the jury; see s 107(4). But in *R v Renda* [2006] 1 WLR 2948, Judge LJ declared that the power of the trial judge to stop the case within s 107 will not be construed generously for this function is reserved for the Appeal Courts.

J 'Section 107 deals with a particular situation where the evidence of "bad character" has been admitted and proves to be false or misleading in the circumstances described in s 107(5). Unless the case falls squarely within that statutory provision, the Court of Appeal, Criminal Division is the appropriate court in which the correctness of the judge's decision should be questioned.'

The expression 'contamination' has been defined in s 107(5) as follows:

'... a person's evidence is contaminated where –
(a) as a result of an agreement or understanding between the person and one or more others, or
(b) as a result of the person being aware of anything alleged by one or more others whose evidence may be, or has been, given in the proceedings,
the evidence is false or misleading in any respect, or is different from what it would otherwise have been.'

The contamination may originate from bribery of or threats to a witness, potential or otherwise, to adjust or colour his evidence or the modification may have been brought about inadvertently. If the judge rules that the evidence has been contaminated as enacted in s 107(1), then s 107(2) and (3) specify what orders the judge is required to issue – this may amount to an acquittal of the charge or any alternative charges or a discharge of the jury and a retrial.

In *R v C* [2006] 3 All ER 689, the Court of Appeal made the following observations:

1. Contamination may arise from deliberate collusion, the exercise of improper pressure, through inadvertence or innocently.

2. The section required the judge to make what was in effect a finding of fact after the admission of the evidence (based on an assessment as to whether the evidence of a witness was false or misleading, or different from what it would have been, had it not been contaminated).

3. The purpose of the section is to reduce the risk of conviction based on over-reliance on evidence of bad character and the provision acknowledges the potential danger that, where evidence is contaminated, the evidence of bad character may have a disproportionate impact on the evaluation of the case by the jury.

4. Although the duty to stop the case does not arise unless the judge is satisfied that there has been an important contamination of the evidence, if he is so satisfied, he has no discretion and he must stop the case (whether or not there would, on a conventional approach, be a case to answer).

5. An order for retrial, rather than a direction to acquit, would not normally be susceptible to a subsequent application based on an asserted abuse of process since, without something fresh emerging, that would amount to an appeal of the order for a retrial.

6. Where the prosecution make an application to adduce evidence of the defendant's bad character at the start of the trial and the defence make a responsible submission that there is material in the prosecution case to suggest that there was or may have been witness contamination, it would normally be sensible for the judge to postpone a decision on the application until the allegedly contaminated evidence has been examined in the trial; by doing so, the judge will have well in mind the precise details of the evidence actually given, rather than anticipated, with such weaknesses and problems as may have emerged.

In this case, the charge was sexual assault on a child under the age of 13. There was evidence that the complainant's mother had told the complainant what to say and had told the complainant that she (mother) had suffered sexual abuse. The trial judge ruled that the defendant's previous convictions for sexual offences with children were admissible. The defendant was convicted and his appeal was allowed under s 107 and conviction quashed. At some stage before the complaint the child had acquired more information from another source which suggested that the child's evidence was different from what it would otherwise have been.

In the pre-2003 case, *R v H* [1995] 2 AC 596, the House of Lords decided that where there is an issue of contamination raised by the defence, and the trial judge leaves the issue with the jury, the judge is required to issue a direction to the jury not to accept the allegedly contaminated evidence, unless they are satisfied that it is reliable and true.

12.7 Duty to give reasons

Section 110 enacts that on certain occasions called 'relevant rulings', the judge is required to state in open court, in the absence of the jury, its reasons for relevant rulings. In the magistrates' court, relevant rulings and reasons are required to be entered on the register of court proceedings. The relevant rulings to which this provision applies are identified in s 110(2) of the Act as follows:

> '(a) a ruling on whether an item of evidence is evidence of a person's bad character;
> (b) a ruling on whether an item of such evidence is admissible under section 100 or 101 (including a ruling on an application under section 101(3));
> (c) a ruling under section 107.'

Thus, the trial judge is required to make rulings, giving reasons, on whether an item of evidence is within the definition of bad character, rulings on questions of admissibility of the bad character of non-defendants and defendants and decisions to withdraw a case from the jury on grounds of contamination.

12.8 Rules of court

Section 111 authorizes the making of rules for the prosecution to give notice (14 days after committal) and particulars to the defendants if it proposes to adduce evidence of the defendant's bad character or to elicit evidence from a witness in cross-examination; see s 111(2). These rules have been made and are referred to as the Criminal Procedure Rules 2005, Part 35. Similar rules may be made where a party wishing to raise bad character evidence is the co-defendant. The rules may also prescribe the circumstances when the notice requirements may be dispensed with; see s 111(3).

In *R (on the application of Robinson) v Sutton Coldfield Magistrates Court* [2006] 2 Cr App R 13, the Divisional Court considered the policy behind the notice procedure and the approach of the courts towards applications for extensions. In this case the charge was assault and was tried summarily. At the pre-trial hearing the prosecution orally indicated that it would seek to introduce the defendant's bad character. However, written notice was not served on the defendant until the eve of the trial. This was well out of the time limit and the prosecution applied for leave to introduce the defendant's previous convictions. The defence objections were rejected by the magistrates and the defendant was convicted and appealed. The Divisional Court dismissed the appeal and decided that in the circumstances there was no prejudice to the defendant, *per* Owen J:

> **J** 'The first point to be made is that the time limits must be observed. The objective of the Criminal Procedure Rules "to deal with all cases efficiently and expeditiously" depends upon adherence to the timetable set out in the rules. Secondly, Parliament has given the court a discretionary power to shorten a time limit or to extend it even after it has expired. In the exercise of that discretion the court will take account of all the relevant considerations, including the furtherance of the overriding objective . . . In my view a court would ordinarily wish to know when the relevant enquiries had been initiated, and in broad terms why they have not been completed within the time allowed. Any application for an extension will be closely scrutinised by the court. A party seeking an extension cannot expect the indulgence of the court unless it clearly sets out the reasons why it is seeking that indulgence. But importantly, I am entirely satisfied that there was no conceivable prejudice to the claimant, bearing in mind that he would have been well aware of the facts of his earlier convictions; secondly, that he was on notice on April 14 [date of the pre-trial hearing] that there could be such an application; and thirdly there was no application [from the defendant's legal adviser] for an adjournment on June 16 [eve of the trial] from which it is to be inferred that the claimant and his legal advisers did not consider their position to be prejudiced by the short notice.'

12.9 Other statutes admitting evidence of the bad character of the defendant

A miscellaneous number of other statutory provisions have allowed the defendant's previous convictions to become facts in issue admissible by the prosecution as part of its case. In other words, specific statutory provisions have created specific instances of the defendant's character as constituent elements of the relevant offence or the means of proving an element of the offence, such as *mens rea*.

Section 21 of the Firearms Act 1968:

 'It is an offence for a person who has been sentenced to imprisonment for a term of three years or more, to have a firearm or ammunition in his possession.'

The effect of s 21 is that a sentence of imprisonment of at least three years following a conviction for an offence is an essential prerequisite to the commission of the offence. The judge is required to direct the jury that the conviction is an essential part of the crime and has no probative value in respect of the charge under the Firearms Act.

Section 27(3) of the Theft Act 1968:

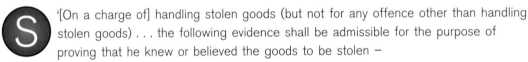 '[On a charge of] handling stolen goods (but not for any offence other than handling stolen goods) . . . the following evidence shall be admissible for the purpose of proving that he knew or believed the goods to be stolen –

(a) evidence that he has had in his possession, or has undertaken or assisted in the retention, removal, disposal or realisation of stolen goods from any theft taking place not earlier than 12 months before the offence charged; and

(b) (provided that 7 days notice in writing has been given to him of the intention to prove the conviction) evidence that he has within the five years preceding the date of the offence charged been convicted of theft or of handling stolen goods.'

The policy of s 27(3) was designed to assist the prosecution in discharging the legal burden of proof that the defendant had the relevant *mens rea* in relation to the handling charge. This may be done by showing that the defendant had goods in his possession (the subject of a different charge) which were stolen 12 months before the offence charged (s 27(3)(a)) or that he was convicted of theft or handling stolen goods within five years preceding the date of the offence charged. In other words, Parliament was of the view that the bad character evidence, in the circumstances specified by the Act, has a tendency to show that the defendant knew that the goods (the subject of the current charge) were stolen. The cogency of such evidence will depend on the frequency of such occurrence and the circumstances surrounding the event, including the similarity between the previous occasions and the current charge. Merely adducing evidence of the 'fact' of possession without considering the circumstances surrounding the previous occasion has the effect of reducing the impact of the section; see *R v Bradley* [1980] Crim LR 173.

In *R v Bradley*, the defendant was charged with handling stolen goods contrary to s 21(1) of the Theft Act 1968 in that it was alleged that he received a diamond ring knowing or believing it to be stolen. The prosecution relied on s 27(3)(a) and adduced evidence that the defendant on another occasion had handled another ring within 12 months preceding the offence. The thief was called and gave detailed evidence of the theft and transactions with the defendant. The summing up of the judge included a direction on the doctrine of recent possession, but following defence objection, the direction was withdrawn tersely. The defendant was convicted and appealed. The Court of Appeal allowed the appeal and quashed the conviction on the ground that s 27(3)(a) ought to be construed strictly and did not allow the prosecution to render details of the possession or theft on the earlier occasion which is not the subject-matter of the present charge.

If the defendant does not admit the conviction, the prosecution may prove the same under s 73 of the Police and Criminal Evidence Act 1984. This may allow in court some of the details of the offence such as the substance, etc of the charge and the conviction; see s 73(2) of the 1984 Act. In *R v Hacker* [1995] 1 All ER 45, the defendant was charged with handling stolen goods – the body shell of a Ford Escort RS turbo motor car. The prosecution was allowed to adduce evidence of the defendant's previous conviction for handling a Ford RS turbo motor car by reference to a certificate of conviction under s 73 of the Police and Criminal Evidence Act 1984. Thus, the substance of the previous conviction was revealed and this related to similar goods as those involved in the charge. The stated purpose of admitting the evidence was to determine whether the defendant knew or believed that the goods (the subject-matter of the current charge) were stolen, the subject of a direction by the judge, and not that the defendant had a propensity to commit this sort of crime.

In addition, the judge has a discretion, under s 78 of the Police and Criminal Evidence Act 1984, to refuse to admit evidence under s 27(3) of the Theft Act 1968, if the adduction of such evidence would be of minimal probative value in relation to the charge. In short, the judge is required to consider whether the probative value of admitting the evidence would outweigh the prejudicial effect of admitting the evidence; see *R v Perry* [1984] Crim LR 680.

12.10 Bad character of defendants in civil cases

The rule in civil cases is that disposition evidence of the bad character of a party is admissible provided that it is relevant to a fact in issue. There are no special rules that are peculiar to parties in civil proceedings. Such parties are treated like any other witness. Thus, a defendant with a previous conviction, like an ordinary witness, may be subjected to cross-examination about his record, subject to the provisions within the Rehabilitation of Offenders Act 1974.

Likewise, other occasions of misconduct may be admitted in court if they are relevant to an issue in the case. In *Mood Music Publishing Co Ltd v De Wolfe Publishing Ltd* [1976] 1 All ER 463, the claimants and defendants were both music publishers. The claimants brought an action for

alleged infringement of copyright. The defendants admitted the similarity of the musical work owned by the claimants but contended that the similarity stemmed from sheer coincidence. To rebut this contention, the claimants were allowed by the trial judge to adduce evidence of other works ostensibly produced by the defendants but bearing a marked similarity to works in which other persons owned the copyright. The defendants appealed to the Court of Appeal against the judge's ruling. The Court of Appeal dismissed the appeal on the ground that the evidence was relevant to an issue in the case and was not oppressive or unfair. Lord Denning MR:

> **J** 'In civil cases, the courts will admit evidence of similar facts if it is logically probative, that is, if it is logically relevant in determining the matter which is in issue: provided that it is not oppressive or unfair to the other side: and also that the other side has fair notice of it and is able to deal with it.'

In *Berger v Raymond & Son Ltd* [1984] 1 WLR 625, a case involving allegedly fraudulent share transfers, Warner J amplified the principle in *Mood Music*, by referring to the burden on the defendant of adducing evidence, the possibility of lengthening the trial, and the undesirability of re-litigating issues disposed of in previous proceedings, as factors militating against admission.

The leading authority today is the House of Lords decision in *O'Brien v Chief Constable of the South of Wales Police* [2005] 2 WLR 1038, the claim for damages was against the defendants' officers for malicious prosecution for murder and misfeasance in public office by putting pressure on the claimant to make false admissions. He wished to adduce evidence that the same officers had been involved in similar misconduct on two other occasions. The claimant had spent 11 years in prison before his conviction was quashed. His claim was allowed at a case management hearing prior to trial. The House of Lords decided that the evidence was properly allowed in the trial. The court advocated a two-stage test for the admissibility of the evidence. The first stage involved satisfying the test of relevance and the second stage involved considering factors that are significant in maintaining a fair balance between the parties. Lord Bingham:

> **J** 'In a civil case such as this the question of admissibility turns, and turns only, on whether the evidence which it is sought to adduce, assuming it (provisionally) to be true, is in Lord Simon's sense probative. If so, the evidence is legally admissible. That is the first stage of the inquiry. The second stage of the inquiry requires the case management judge or the trial judge to make what will often be a very difficult and sometimes a finely balanced judgment: whether evidence or some of it . . . which *ex hypothesi* is legally admissible, should be admitted. For the party seeking admission, the argument will always be that justice requires the evidence to be

CONTINUED ▶

J

admitted; if it is excluded, a wrong result may be reached. In some cases, as in the present, the argument will be fortified by reference to wider considerations: the public interest in exposing official misfeasance and protecting the integrity of the criminal process; vindication of reputation; the public righting of public wrongs. These are important considerations to which weight must be given. But even without them, the importance of doing justice in the particular case is a factor the judge will always respect. The strength of the argument for admitting the evidence will always depend primarily on the judge's assessment of the potential significance of the evidence, assuming it to be true, in the context of the case as a whole.'

ACTIVITY

Self-test questions

1. How many gateways exist to adduce evidence of the bad character of a person other than the defendant in criminal proceedings?

2. What is meant by 'important explanatory evidence' under s 100(1)(a) of the CJA 2003?

3. What factors determine whether evidence has reached the test of 'substantial probative value' under s 100(1)(b) of the CJA 2003?

4. How many gateways exist to admit the bad character evidence of the defendant under s 101 of CJA 2003?

5. What safeguards exist to ensure that no miscarriages of justice take place as a result of admitting the bad character evidence of the defendant?

Further reading

Munday, R., 'What Constitutes 'Other Reprehensible Behaviour' under the Bad Character Provisions of the Criminal Justice Act 2003?' [2005] Crim LR 24.

Munday, R., 'Cut-throat Defences and the "Propensity to be Untruthful" under section 104 of the Criminal Justice Act 2003' [2005] Crim LR 625.

Munday, R., 'The Purposes of Gateway (g)' [2006] Crim LR 300.

Tapper, C., 'Criminal Justice Act 2003: Evidence of Bad Character' [2004] Crim LR 533.

Waterman, A. and Dempster, T., 'Bad Character: Feeling our Way One Year On' [2006] Crim LR 614.

chapter 13 CORROBORATION, LIES, CARE WARNINGS AND IDENTIFICATION EVIDENCE ■

AIMS AND OBJECTIVES

By the end of this chapter you should be able to understand:

■ How the courts handle suspicious evidence

■ The nature and purpose of corroboration evidence

■ The use of corroboration and care warnings

■ The significance of *Turnbull* warnings

■ The importance of *Lucas* directions and *Turnbull* warnings.

13.1 Introduction

In this chapter we will discuss care warnings, namely, directions by the judge for the jury to take care when dealing with certain pieces of evidence: corroboration evidence, that is, supporting evidence and finally, identification evidence (including lies told by the accused). These three topics refer to the rules that relate to what can be referred to as 'suspicious evidence'. The discussion begins with corroboration, then moves on to care warnings and finishes with identification evidence.

13.2 Corroboration

What then is corroboration evidence? In *R v Baskerville* [1916] 2 KB 658, Lord Reading CJ stated that '. . . It would be in high degree dangerous to attempt to formulate the kind of evidence which would be regarded as corroboration, except to say that corroborative evidence is evidence which shows or tends to show that the story of the accomplice that the accused committed the crime is true, not merely that the crime has been committed, but that it was committed by the accused'. Thus, it can be stated that corroboration evidence is admissible and independent evidence that supports or confirms that a defendant committed the offence with which he is charged. In short, three elements must be satisfied:

- The evidence must be admissible.

- It must be independent.

- It must support or confirm that the defendant committed the offence.

In *DPP v Hester* [1973] AC 296 Lord Morris said:

> **J** '. . . The essence of corroborative evidence is that one creditworthy witness confirms what another creditworthy witness has said. Any risk of the conviction of an innocent person is lessened if conviction is based upon the testimony of more than one acceptable witness. Corroborative evidence in the sense of some other material evidence in support, implicating the accused, furnishes a safeguard which makes a conclusion more sure than it would be without such evidence . . . The purpose of corroboration is not to give validity or credence to evidence which is deficient or suspect or incredible but only to confirm and support that which as evidence is sufficient and satisfactory and credible: and corroborative evidence will only fill its role if it itself is completely credible evidence . . .'

In *DPP v Kilbourne* [1973] AC 729, Lord Reid echoed this view:

> **J** '. . . There is nothing technical in the idea of corroboration. When in the ordinary affairs of life one is doubtful whether or not to believe a particular statement one naturally looks to see whether it fits in with other statements or circumstances relating to the particular matter; the better it fits in the more one is inclined to believe it. The doubted statement is corroborated to a greater or lesser extent by the other statements or circumstances with which it fits in . . .'

Hence, the more corroborative evidence that is available, the better the chances of success, ie more weight will be attached to the case. Interestingly, the English law of evidence is not known for its concern for corroboration and many disputes are determined without it. However, convictions without corroboration evidence were considered of greater risk and thus, there exist a number of criminal offences that actively require it. This is discussed in Section 13.3. Let us take a look at the three elements in a little more detail.

323

KEY FACTS

Corroboration

This can be defined as evidence that is admissible and independent and supports or confirms that a defendant committed the offence with which he is charged. See *R v Baskerville* [1916] 2 KB 658.

- The general rules on relevance and therefore admissibility apply.

- The evidence must be admissible.

- It must be independent.

- It must support or confirm that the defendant committed the offence.

13.2.1 Admissible and independent evidence

All evidence, if it is to be tendered, must satisfy the general rules on relevance and therefore admissibility. The position is the same in respect of corroboration evidence. Thus, where the evidence is admissible, it must also be shown to have come from a source independent of the evidence which it is to corroborate. Statements made by the victim to other witnesses and then repeated by the witnesses, although often admissible in criminal cases as previous consistent statements cannot amount to such corroboration evidence. In the case of *R v Whitehead* [1929] 1 KB 99, a young girl was the victim of sexual assault by Whitehead. She complained of this to her mother a few months later. It was held that evidence from the mother of what the girl had said could not amount to corroboration evidence, because it had come from the witness, ie the girl herself.

Lord Hewart CJ confirmed the need for the corroboration to be independent of the witness stating in *Whitehead* (above) that:

> **J** '. . . any such inference as to what the girl had told her mother could not amount to corroboration of the girl's story, because it proceeded from the girl herself; it was merely the girl's story at second hand. In order that evidence may amount to corroboration it must be extraneous to the witness who is to be corroborated. A girl cannot corroborate herself; otherwise it is only necessary for her to repeat her story some twenty-five times in order to get twenty-five corroborations of it'.

What, then, is the status of the complaint that was made by person A to person B? Although the complaint itself cannot amount to corroboration evidence, evidence of the complainant's distress may be given by the person to whom the complaint is made. Thus, if a situation as the one in *Whitehead* was to arise again, then the girl's mother could give evidence of her daughter's distress as an independent observation (percipient evidence) which is in itself capable of amounting to corroboration.

CASE EXAMPLE

R v Redpath (1962) 46 Cr App R 319

The defendant was charged with indecently assaulting a 7-year-old girl. The girl stated that whilst playing on the moor with her two friends, Redpath pulled her to the ground and indecently assaulted her. The girl's mother stated in her evidence that the girl had come home in a terrible state and had immediately complained of the indecent assault to her. This was a case in which corroboration evidence was required, albeit, the story that the girl had told her mother was a consistent one. At the time of the indecent assault a Mr and Mrs Hall were near the edge of the moor and witnessed two important things; first, a parked car and second, a man whom they claimed was Redpath walking towards the girl. The same couple witnessed the man return and drive off. Mr Hall gave evidence that the little girl was terribly white and almost on the brink of tears, at which point, the little girl burst into tears and thus they accompanied her home. The defendant was convicted and appealed. In dismissing his appeal, the Court of Appeal stressed that in order for distress to amount to corroboration, it must not be faked. Lord Parker CJ:

J '. . . So far as any question of indecent assault is concerned, the learned judge told the jury that her distressed condition observed by Mr Hall and spoken to by Mr Hall was capable of being corroboration. The point in this appeal is whether that is so. Counsel for the defence has argued that the distressed condition of the complainant is no more corroboration than the complaint, if any, that the complainant makes, and that while the latter merely shows that the story is consistent and is not corroborative, so the distressed condition is not corroborative. This Court is quite unable to accept that argument. It seems to this Court that the distressed condition of a complainant is quite clearly capable of amounting to corroboration. Of course, the circumstances will vary enormously, and in some circumstances quite clearly no weight, or little weight, could be attached to such evidence as corroboration. Thus, if a girl goes in a distressed condition to her mother and makes a complaint, while the mother's evidence as to the girl's condition may in law be capable of amounting to corroboration, quite clearly the jury should be told that they should attach little, if any, weight to that evidence, because it is all part and parcel of the complaint. The girl making the complaint might well put on an act and simulate distress. But in the present case, the circumstances are entirely different . . .'

CASE EXAMPLE

R v Chauhan (Ramesh) (1981) Cr App R 232

Chauhan was accused of indecently assaulting a woman with whom he had been left in a room. The woman had managed to get away and had run off to the company lavatory in tears. When asked by a fellow employee what had happened she complained that Chauhan had assaulted her. At the trial, the judge directed the jury that evidence of her distress could amount to corroboration evidence, if tendered through an independent witness. The defendant was convicted and appealed. In upholding his conviction the Court of Appeal confirmed this principle. The Court of Appeal confirmed that '. . . there may be cases (eg *Redpath* (1962) 46 Cr App R 319) where there can be no suggestion that the distress was feigned. In normal cases, however, the weight to be given to distress varies infinitely, and juries should be warned that, although it may amount to corroboration they must be fully satisfied that there is no question of it having been feigned.'

Per Lord Widgery CJ:

> **J** '. . . In the present case there is no doubt, whatever view one may take of the correctness of the trial judge's direction to the jury, that it was extremely carefully prepared; it was beautifully phrased and it was of outstanding clarity. It starts, after he has given a very full and accurate warning, yet nevertheless concise, on the dangers inherent in this type of allegation of indecent assault, and a very clear direction on the reasons for the desirability of corroboration . . .'

In summary, it would appear that:

(a) provided that there is sufficient evidence of identity, ie that the accused has been shown to have been implicated in the alleged crime

(b) The 'distressed condition' of the complainant may be capable of corroborating her testimony if it is proved not to have been simulated, ie if it is proved that her condition was genuine.

13.2.3 Supporting or confirming the commission of the criminal offence by the defendant

The corroboration evidence *must* either directly or circumstantially support or confirm that it was the accused who committed the offence alleged. Hence, the corroboration evidence must be such that it implicates the defendant.

CASE EXAMPLE

James v R (1970) 55 CR App R 299

The defendant, a Mr James, was charged on indictment of having sexual intercourse with a woman without consent. The allegation was that he did so whilst armed with a gun and knife. He was convicted and sentenced to 10 years' imprisonment and 12 strokes to be given by an approved instrument (lashes). He appealed on the grounds that the trial judge had misdirected the jury by telling them that medical evidence of recent sexual intercourse was corroborative evidence that the defendant had raped the woman. The Privy Council agreed. Such medical evidence proved nothing more than the fact that sexual intercourse had occurred. It also stated that in order for such evidence to amount to corroboration evidence, it must confirm two things; first, that sexual intercourse with the defendant had taken place, and second, that it had taken place without the woman's consent.

KEY FACTS

Independence

Where the evidence is admissible, it must also be shown to have had an independent source for it to be classed as corroboration evidence. Statements by witnesses, although admissible in criminal cases, cannot amount to such corroboration evidence.

Support or confirmation

The corroboration evidence *must* either directly or circumstantially support or confirm that it was the accused who committed the offence alleged. Hence, the corroboration evidence must be such that it implicates the defendant.

13.3 Instances in which corroboration evidence is required by statute

Where a statute requires corroboration evidence, then it must be provided by the prosecution. A failure to do so will result in the trial judge having to direct the trier of fact, ie the jury, to acquit the defendant of the charge. Let us take a look at some of the criminal offences that require corroboration evidence. The two most commonly cited are:

- perjury

- speeding.

Other offences requiring corroboration, many of which have now been abolished, include those relating to corrupt electoral practices or sexual offences. Let us take a look at the offences listed above in a little more detail. Prior to being abolished by the Statute Law Revision Act 1875, s 1 of the Treason Act 1848 only permitted a conviction where the oaths of two lawful and credible witnesses corroborated the act of treason.

Section 13 of the Perjury Act 1911 states:

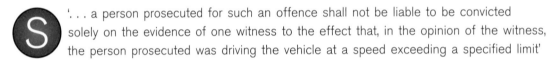

'. . . a person shall not be liable to be convicted of any offence against this Act, or of any offence declared by any other Act to be perjury or subornation of perjury, or to be punishable as perjury or subornation of perjury, solely upon the evidence of one witness as to the falsity of any statement alleged to be false'.

Hence, a conviction under this Act still requires corroboration evidence. Finally, s 89(2) of the Road Traffic Regulation Act 1984 states:

'. . . a person prosecuted for such an offence shall not be liable to be convicted solely on the evidence of one witness to the effect that, in the opinion of the witness, the person prosecuted was driving the vehicle at a speed exceeding a specified limit'

– once again requiring corroboration evidence.

13.4 Other types of corroboration evidence

There are a number of other types of evidence that can amount to corroboration evidence of which an appreciation is required; these include:

- collective corroboration

- mutual corroboration.

In short, the latter of these simply refers to the instance in which the evidence of witness A is corroborated by the corroboration evidence of witness B whose evidence may require corroboration itself. Hence, the corroboration evidence of witness B will still be valid corroboration evidence, even though it itself requires corroboration, so long as it satisfies the rules discussed earlier.

In contrast, collective corroboration is where the evidence of witness A is corroborated by a number of independent pieces of evidence. Each of those pieces of evidence must satisfy the rules discussed earlier. Although the trial judge will direct the jury as to what is corroboration, it is still down to the jury to attach relevant weight to each of those pieces of evidence. The Court of Appeal has recognized that there may be cases where a number of independent pieces of evidence that do not satisfy the criteria for corroboration evidence when assessed individually, may do so when assessed collectively. Thus, it may be possible for a range of independent pieces of evidence to amount collectively to corroboration.

CASE EXAMPLE

R v Hills (1988) 86 Cr App R 26

The defendant was charged with being knowingly concerned in the fraudulent evasion of the prohibition on the importation of a Class A controlled drug. Mr Hills was accused of organizing the collection of four kilograms of heroin from Bombay (now Mumbai). The courier that he had enlisted to carry the drugs, had pleaded guilty and turned Queens Evidence stating that Hills had arranged for him to travel to Mumbai to pick up what he thought were suitcases containing illegal snakeskins that were not to be declared. The trial judge summed up listing 13 points that contained circumstances and facts which had been admitted or proven by independent evidence. The trial judge directed the jury that these facts were not capable of amounting to corroborative evidence when considered alone, but may do so when considered collectively. The jury convicted the defendant, who appealed. In allowing his appeal, the Court held that:

> J '. . . there had been a material misdirection for some of the circumstances listed by the trial judge were themselves dependent on [the evidence of the courier] and did not without regard to that evidence sufficiently go towards proving the appellant's guilt'.

KEY FACTS

Corroboration required by statute
Where a statute requires corroboration evidence, then it must be provided. A failure to do so will result in the trial judge having to direct the trier of fact to acquit the defendant of the charge. Current examples are perjury and speeding.

Other types of corroboration
There are a number of other types of evidence that can amount to corroboration. These include collective corroboration and mutual corroboration.

CONTINUED ▸

KEY FACTS

- Mutual corroboration refers to the instance in which the evidence of witness A is corroborated by the corroboration evidence of witness B, whose evidence may require corroboration itself.

- Collective corroboration occurs where the evidence of witness A is corroborated by a number of independent pieces of evidence.

13.5 Corroboration warnings

Although it was considered dangerous to convict a defendant without corroboration evidence, as far as certain types of offence are concerned, the discussion so far has revealed that by its very nature, corroboration evidence was also considered to be fraught with issues concerning fabrication, and thus validity. Thus, where corroboration evidence was tendered in the commission of certain offences, the law required the trial judge to give the jury a corroboration warning, rather than a general care warning. Care warnings are discussed later in this chapter, but for current purposes, they are simply warnings from the judge to the jury advising them to exercise care when considering convicting on the basis of particular evidence, either because the witness is potentially unreliable, ie an accomplice, or it is generally accepted that such evidence requires care by reason of the expertise of the court. Corroboration warnings were used to direct the jury's attention to the need for them to look for some corroboration evidence. Hence, the discussion in this part of the chapter will focus on corroboration warnings in three categories of case, those involving the evidence of an accomplice, a child and sexual offences.

KEY FACTS

Corroboration warnings

Corroboration warnings were used to direct the jury's attention to the need for them to look for some corroboratory evidence, these were given in three categories of case:

- the evidence of accomplices

- the evidence of complainants in cases of sexual offences

- children.

13.5.1 Does the evidence of an accomplice require corroboration?

Does the evidence of an accomplice require corroboration or at least a care warning to be given? Consider this scenario: Judy Smith and Maggie Dench conspire to attack and murder Helen Murrin, which they duly carry out one night in August. They now stand charged with murder and thus turn on one another, each running cut-throat defences. Righty, the evidence of an accomplice is considered with care and suspicion for they may have a vested interest in proving that they were least involved in the commission of the offence, and possibly even arguing that the other committed it. Furthermore, as cases such as *Hills* (above) and *R v Barnes* [1940] 2 All ER 229 exemplify the definition of accomplice, the rule only applies to witnesses giving evidence for the prosecution, and does not apply where a defendant gives evidence that may implicate a co-defendant.

 ASE EXAMPLE

Davies v DPP [1954] AC 378

Davies, along with a number of other young men, attacked a second group of young men. During the fist fight one of the young men from the second group was stabbed and subsequently died. Davies and five other men from his group, including one known as 'L', were charged with murder. At the trial, no evidence was offered against L and three others and not guilty verdicts were entered for the remaining two. At Davies's trial, L gave evidence against him, which resulted in Davies being convicted. Davies appealed on the basis that L and one of the other witnesses were his accomplices and thus, the judge failed to give the jury a warning as to the risk of accepting their evidence without corroboration. Davies's appeal was dismissed. The House of Lords confirmed that L was not an accomplice, because at the time he gave evidence he had been acquitted. Just because the group had attacked with their fists, did not mean that the rest of the men became associated when one used a knife and the others had no knowledge of this.

Hence, in Davies 'L' was unaware of the knife and thus could not be considered to be an accomplice. Should, then, the trial judge give the jury a warning to take care when handling this evidence? Prior to the enactment of s 32 of the Criminal Justice and Public Order Act 1994, this would have been standard procedure – the provision abolished this requirement. Let us take a look at the provision itself in s 32(1) of the Criminal Justice and Public Order Act 1994:

'. . . any requirement whereby at a trial on indictment it is obligatory for the court to give the jury a warning about convicting the accused on the uncorroborated evidence of a person merely because that person is: (a) an alleged accomplice of the accused, or (b) where the offence charged is a sexual offence, the person in respect of whom it is alleged to have been committed, is hereby abrogated. [Subsection] . . . (2) In section 34(2) of the [1988 c 33.] Criminal Justice Act 1988 (abolition of requirement of corroboration warning in respect of evidence of a child) the words from "in relation to" to the end shall be omitted. [Subsection] . . . (3) Any requirement that (a) is applicable at the summary trial of a person for an offence, and (b) corresponds to the requirement mentioned in subsection (1) above or that mentioned in section 34(2) of the Criminal Justice Act 1988, is hereby abrogated'.

It should be noted that the term 'abrogation' here means to repeal or abolish.

13.5.2 Does the evidence of children require a corroboration warning?

Prior to the enactment of the Criminal Justice Act 1988 (CJA), corroboration warnings, where sworn or unsworn evidence of a child was tendered, were routine occurrences – this requirement was also abolished by the CJA 1988.

13.5.3 Does the evidence of a victim of a sexual offence require corroboration warning?

This is an interesting and sensitive topic in the English law of evidence. At this point, it will begin to become clear that the requirements for corroboration evidence have diminished substantially over time. The alleged victim of a crime of a sexual nature will in most cases make allegations against the person he or she alleges has committed the offence, rebuttal of which can be a difficult task. In addition, allegations may be fabricated for a number of reasons including anger, jealousy or shame. Hence, the law previously required a corroboration warning to be given to the jury. The case of *Burgess* highlights this.

CASE EXAMPLE

R v Burgess (Bertram Fraser) (1956) 40 Cr App R 144

The defendant was convicted of indecent assault on an adult male in a cinema. Unbeknown to Burgess, the male was a police officer. Burgess appealed. No corroboration evidence of the police officer's evidence had been tendered, and the jury had not received a care warning. In addition, Burgess contended that the officer was a willing participant in the acts. His conviction was quashed; the case concerned an indecent assault by one adult male upon another, and thus, the jury should have been

CONTINUED ▶

warned of the desirability of having some corroboration evidence in a case such as this. The position was also altered by s 32 of the Criminal Justice and Public Order Act 1994, which abolished this requirement.

CASE EXAMPLE

R v Makanjuola (Oluwanfunso) [1995] 2 Cr App R 469

Both Makanjuola and another were convicted of indecent assault. They made an application to appeal on the ground that, although s 32 of the Criminal Justice and Public Order Act 1994 had removed the requirement that the judge give a corroboration warning, the trial judge had failed to exercise his discretion to warn the jury about the dangers of convicting the defendants, in the case of a sexual offence, on evidence that was not corroborated. The defendants argued that the judge had, in his failure, given retrospective effect to the provision which had only come into force after they had been charged and committed for trial on indictment but before the trial. Dismissing the applications, the Court held that following the repeal of s 32 the judge could choose to exercise, or not, their discretion to give a warning that they considered appropriate in respect of such a witness. The Court stressed that the decision to give the warning and the terms in which the warning would be given were matters for the judge to decide on the basis of the circumstances of the case, the issues raised and the quality of the witness's evidence.

The effect of the Court's decision in *Makanjuola* is to confirm that s 32 of the CJPOA 1994 abolished the need for corroboration warnings as a routine operation, where a witness is considered to be within a particular category, ie one of the three outlined above. In addition, the Court gave guidance as to when such a warning should be issued, stating that the trial judge:

- has the discretion as to whether or not to issue a warning
- in considering whether or not to exercise the discretion, should:
  - take into account the entire facts of the case
  - decide whether any witness gives cause for concern.

If a witness has given cause for concern, then the judge should warn the jury to exercise care when looking for supporting evidence, rather than a technical corroboration warning.

13.6 Care warnings

The discussion has shown that the law no longer requires the trial judge to give a corroboration warning. However, the judge may prefer to give a care warning instead. A judge may consider

giving such a warning where the evidence tendered is that of an accomplice, a child, a complainant in a case involving a sexual offence or a witness who may have a grudge against the defendant, ie malicious fabrication, or suffers from mental illness or he is handicapped. Let us take a look at some of these categories in a little more detail.

Although the evidence of children over the age of 14 is given under oath, ie it is sworn evidence, the evidence of a child under that age may be given unsworn. Where the evidence of children is involved, the trial judge may consider that the evidence tendered gives cause for concern in relation to the ability of the child to differentiate between what is fact and what is fiction. In such a case, the judge should consider exercising his discretion and issue a care warning.

ASE EXAMPLE

DPP v Hester [1973] AC 296

Hester was charged with indecently assaulting a 12-year-old girl, contrary to s 14(1) of the Sexual Offences Act 1956. Although the complainant (A) gave evidence on oath, her 9-year-old sister (B) was permitted to give unsworn evidence under s 38 of the Children and Young Persons Act 1933. The trial judge directed the jury that the unsworn evidence of B could amount to corroboration of the sworn evidence of A. Hester was convicted and appealed. Quashing the conviction, the Court of Appeal stated that the unsworn evidence of B could corroborate the sworn evidence of A only if it satisfied the proviso that '. . . in the present case the complainant's sworn evidence could corroborate that of her sister and the sister's evidence that of the complainant provided that the jury after suitable adequate guidance and warning were satisfied that each child was a truthful and satisfactory witness . . . but that the appeal should be dismissed on the ground that the conviction was unsafe and unsatisfactory'.

Although the evidence of children was considered to be unreliable in the past, the contemporary approach is different. These days, such evidence is considered more reliable, and thus, relevant statutory assistance exists to facilitate the court in receiving it; see s 55(2) of the Youth Justice and Criminal Evidence Act 1999.

What of the evidence of those witnesses who have a grudge of sorts against the defendant? Once again it is within the discretion of the trial judge as to whether or not to give a care warning, where the evidence that gives concern is that of an accomplice. On occasion, the judge may feel it proper to direct the jury that the evidence of an accomplice should be treated carefully, because accomplices may have an agenda of their own, ie to reduce the case against themselves. In the case of *R v Knowlden* (1981) 77 Cr App R 94, the trial judge considered it unnecessary to give the jury a warning where the defendant's family members tendered evidence that implicated one another. Even where a co-defendant turns Queen's Evidence, there is no requirement that a care warning be given. However, the trial judge will be obliged to direct the jury to take care when handling such potentially unreliable evidence, as the witness may have an ulterior motive.

What, then, of the mentally ill or handicapped? Section 77 of the Police and Criminal Evidence Act 1984 requires a trial judge to give a care warning in relation to a mentally handicapped defendant who has confessed to the commission of a crime without the presence of an appropriate adult. In most other cases, the trial judge retains the discretion as to whether or not to give the jury such a warning; see *R v Bagshaw* [1948] 1 WLR 477 and *R v Spencer* [1987] AC 128. Generally, a warning will be given by reason of the dangers that exist in manipulation of witnesses with such disabilities, manipulation that could lead to unsafe convictions that are later quashed. What if the prosecution's case depends wholly or in part on the identification evidence of a witness? In that instance, what is known as a *Turnbull* warning will be given to the jury.

KEY FACTS

Care warnings

The law no longer requires the trial judge to give a corroboration warning. However, the judge may prefer to give a care warning instead, where the evidence tendered is that of an accomplice, a child, a complainant in a case involving a sexual offence or a witness who may have a grudge against the defendant, ie malicious fabrication, or be mentally ill or handicapped.

13.7 *R v Turnbull* guidelines

Owing to the public outcry that greeted several convictions based on miscarriages of justice in reliance on visual identification evidence, the Devlin Committee made a number of strong recommendations in 1976 to the Home Secretary.

Shortly after the report, the Court of Appeal took the opportunity to refine the laws on identification evidence to such a degree that it became unnecessary for Parliament to adopt the recommendations of the Committee. Guidelines were issued by the Court of Appeal in *R v Turnbull* [1977] 3 All ER 549 (CA).

CASE EXAMPLE

R v Turnbull [1977] 3 All ER 549 (CA)

Turnbull and others were convicted on conspiracy to burgle. Their defence was based on mistaken identification evidence. Four separate appeals were made from separate trials and dealt with by the court. They all appealed on the quality of the identification evidence.

The court held that two of the appeals would be allowed and the remaining two dismissed.

The *Turnbull* case (largely reflecting the Devlin Committee's recommendations) established guidelines for courts in how to handle evidence of witnesses purporting to identify the defendant as the perpetrator of the crime. The reasoning behind the need for such dogmatic guidance to be given by the judge to the jury is due to the generally unreliable nature of identification evidence.

13.8 Guideline 1

Whenever the prosecution's case is based wholly or substantially on identification evidence which the defence claims to be mistaken, the jury should be warned of the need for caution and the reasons for such caution (factors taken into account).

Lord Widgery CJ in *R v Turnbull*:

> J '. . . The judge should direct the jury to examine closely the circumstances in which the identification by each witness came to be made. How long did the witness have the accused under observation? At what distance? In what light? Was the observation impeded in any way, as for example by passing traffic or people? Had the witness ever seen the accused before? How often? If only occasionally, had he any special reason for remembering the accused? How long elapsed between the original observation and the subsequent identification to the police? Was there any material discrepancy between the description of the accused given to the police by the witness when first seen by them and his actual appearance? ...'

13.9 Guideline 2

'Recognition, on the other hand, is potentially more reliable than identification of a stranger for the first time, but even when the witness is purporting to recognise someone whom he knows, the jury should be reminded that mistakes in recognition of close relatives and friends are sometimes made . . .' (*per* Widgery CJ in *R v Turnbull* (above)).

'Recognition' evidence involves identifying a person who has previously been known to the witness. In short, an acquaintance of the witness, whereas 'identification' evidence involves selecting an individual from features which had been observed previously. The length and clarity of the observation will vary with the facts of each case. The point is that recognition evidence may potentially carry more weight than identification evidence. At the same time, the witness may be mistaken in his recognition of a person known to him.

ASE EXAMPLE

R v Walshe (1982) 74 Cr App R 85 (CA)

The defendant was charged and convicted of obtaining property on forged prescriptions. Two of the prescriptions were presented to the same chemist on two separate occasions. At an identification parade, the shop's proprietor and his daughter both identified the defendant as the person who presented the prescription. The proprietor had served the man four times previously and his daughter had twice. Each time, the man had waited in the well-lit shop for about 10 minutes for the prescription to be filled. The prosecution's case depended on the identification. The defendant claimed that the identification was mistaken. An application was made to the judge to hold a trial-within-a-trial to determine whether the evidence was admissible. The judge granted the application and ruled that the evidence was admissible. (From the report, it was not clear whether a warning was given by the judge. Presumably there was.)

On appeal, the Court of Appeal held that:

1. The *voir dire* was an inappropriate procedure to hear such evidence, as the Crown did not have a specific legal burden on this issue.

2. In the circumstances, the evidence was admissible – identifications were made on more than one occasion in circumstances well suited for identification.

Boreham J:

'. . . It is unnecessary to go through the catalogue of the matters which will be relevant when considering the quality of the identification. Here there could be no basis for stopping the case on the ground that the quality was inferior. The identifying witnesses had seen the man on more than one occasion in circumstances well suited to accurate observation and identification and for a period of time which put this case well outside those where the identification depended on but a fleeting glance which was made in difficult conditions . . .'

CASE EXTRACT

R v Bentley (1994) 99 Cr App R 342

Lord Taylor CJ explained the need for caution even in respect of recognition evidence:

> **J** 'The recognition type of identification . . . [cannot] be treated as straightforward or trouble-free . . . Each of us, and no doubt everyone sitting in this court, has had the experience of seeing someone in the street whom we know, only to discover later that it was not that person at all. The expression, "I could have sworn it was you" indicates the sort of warning which the judge should give, because that is exactly what the witness does. He swears that it was the person he thinks it was.'

13.10 Guideline 3

When the identification evidence is poor, the judge should withdraw the case from the jury unless there is other evidence which supports the identification – not necessarily in the strict sense of corroboration but any evidence which may make the jury feel sure that there has been no mistaken identification.

Lord Widgery in *R v Turnbull*:

> **J** '. . . When, in the judgement of the trial judge, the quality of the identifying evidence is poor, as for example when it depends solely on a fleeting glance or on a longer observation made in difficult conditions, the situation is very different. The judge should then withdraw the case from the jury and direct an acquittal unless there is other evidence which goes to support the correctness of the identification. This may be corroboration in the sense lawyers use that word; but it need not be so if its effect is to make the jury sure that there has been no mistaken identification . . .'

13.11 Guideline 4

Where the quality of the identification is good, the jury may be left to assess the weight of the evidence but should be given a warning of the need for caution. If there is any supporting evidence of identification, the judge should say so (tell this to the jury).

Lord Widgery CJ in *R v Turnbull*:

> **J** '. . . The trial judge should identify to the jury the evidence which he adjudges is capable of supporting the evidence of identification. If there is any evidence or circumstances which the jury might think was supporting when it did not have this quality, the judge should say so. A jury, for example, might think that support for identification evidence could be found in the fact that the accused had not given evidence before them. An accused's absence from the witness box cannot provide evidence of anything and the judge should tell the jury so. But he would be entitled to tell them that when assessing the quality of the identification evidence they could take into consideration the fact that it was uncontradicted by any evidence coming from the accused himself . . .'

13.12 Voice identification

The jury may be asked to compare a recording of the offender's voice with the voice of the accused. If there is a dispute as to whether the offender's voice is that of the defendant, expert evidence may be admissible to assist the jury. In *R v Roberts* [2000] Crim LR 183, the court received expert evidence to the effect that voice recognition is more likely to be mistaken compared with visual identification evidence. Thus, it is appropriate for a judge to issue a warning to the jury analogous to a visual identification warning but adapted to the circumstances; see *R v Hersey* [1998] Crim LR 281 and *R v Gummerson* [1999] Crim LR 680.

13.13 Failure to follow guidelines

Failure to follow the guidelines would invariably lead to a conviction being quashed; see *R v Hunjen* (1979) 68 Cr App R 99. However, each case is decided on its own facts and, in particular, on the strength of the evidence.

In exceptional circumstances, a failure to issue a *Turnbull* warning concerning identification evidence may not lead to the conviction being quashed. In *R v Shand* [1996] 1 WLR 67, the Privy Council decided that despite a failure on the part of the judge to issue a *Turnbull* warning, the conviction was safe. Two eyewitnesses recognized the defendant in daylight from 4 to 300 feet away, respectively. There was nothing to suggest that the witnesses were mistaken and the recognition evidence was very good. In addition, there was evidence before the jury that the defendant had confessed his guilt.

In addition, it would appear that the evidence of more than one independent and credible identification witnesses would have the effect of supporting each other. It is the duty of the

judge to point this out to the jury subject to the appropriate warning. In *R v Weeder* [1980] Crim LR 645 (CA), the defendant was charged with wounding with intent contrary to s 18 OAPA 1861, following a street attack on the victim. He was struck from behind on the back of the head and fell to the ground under a lamp-post. The street lamp provided a bright light and he had a good look at W, the defendant. Another witness, Miss X, looked out of the window during the attack and saw W's face. She was acquainted with him. The victim identified W at an identification parade. The judge in his summing up, *inter alia*, told the jury that one identification witness may support the identification of the other or another and issued a clear warning that even honest witnesses could be mistaken. On appeal the Court of Appeal dismissed the appeal and held that there was no misdirection.

CASE EXAMPLE

R v Shelton & Carter [1981] Crim LR 776 (CA)

S and C were convicted of robbery in that S drove a 'Triumph' motor car and they both robbed A. The evidence in dispute was of identification. A detective constable, Hodgson, had seen a 'Triumph' motor car half-an-hour before the incident and had recognized both S and C in it. A week earlier another police officer, Bennett, had seen the same car and had recognized S in it. Both S and C denied having any connection with the car. The judge allowed the evidence to be put to the jury subject to a warning of the danger of relying on inaccurate identification evidence. Both the defendants were convicted and appealed.

The Court of Appeal held that the evidence was correctly admitted on the grounds that (i) the evidence of the officers was of 'recognition' rather than 'identification', which was potentially more reliable; (ii) in the alternative, relying on *R v Weeder*, even if the evidence of each officer taken separately was not very strong, as a matter of common sense and taken collectively, the evidence of two credible witnesses who identified the accused on independent and separate occasions was sufficient to rebut the suggestion that the accused persons were victims of an incorrect identification.

The *voir dire* is an inappropriate procedure to deal with disputed identification evidence; see *R v Flemming* (1988) 86 Cr App R 32 (CA). Woolf LJ:

> J '. . . It is quite unnecessary to hold a trial within a trial for this purpose. The normal procedure in identification cases is clearly laid down in *Turnbull* . . . In the normal way, the trial judge will make his assessment either at the end of the prosecution case or after all the evidence has been called. There may be exceptional circumstances where the position is so clear on the depositions . . .'

In *R v Willoughby* (1989) Cr App R 91 (CA), the victim of a sexual assault testified that her attacker, whom she saw briefly, had spots on his face and identified him on this basis. At the trial the accused had spots on his face, which he developed while waiting for trial and was convicted. The Court of Appeal quashed the conviction on the basis that the identification was poor and was inadmissible.

In *R v McInnes* (1989) 90 Cr App R 99, on a kidnapping charge the victim gave a detailed, accurate description of the inside of the defendant's car, including sweet papers and a rip in the upholstery of the car. It was decided that such knowledge was independent corroborative identification evidence.

13.14 Dispensation with a warning

If the judge is in doubt as to whether he should issue a *Turnbull* warning, he should proceed prudently and err on the side of caution and issue the warning. In certain exceptional circumstances, a *Turnbull* warning is unnecessary. These are, first, where the defendant admits his presence at the scene of the crime and there is no possibility of mistaken identity, because of the distinctive quality of the defendant. In *R v Slater* [1995] 1 Cr App R 584, on a charge of assault in a nightclub, the defendant admitted that he was present in the club. He was six feet six inches tall and extremely large and there was evidence that no one else with his height was in the club. The trial judge did not issue a warning and the Court of Appeal dismissed his appeal against conviction. There was no possibility of a mistaken identity.

Second, a *Turnbull* warning is not necessary where the issue is not whether there is a possibility of mistaken identity, but whether the witness is telling the truth. In short, the issue involves the veracity of the witness. In *R v Courtnell* [1990] Crim LR 115, the defence was alibi. It was alleged that the witness had known the defendant for a week and claimed to recognize the defendant was fabricating the evidence. No warning was issued by the judge and, following a conviction, the Court of Appeal dismissed the appeal and decided that a *Turnbull* direction would have confused the jury.

Third, where the witnesses merely provide a description of the defendant which matches his appearance, there is no need to issue a *Turnbull* direction. Thus, in *R v Constantinou* (1989) 91 Cr App R 74, the witness provided a description of the defendant and a photofit picture was admitted to the court and was consistent with the appearance of the defendant; a warning was not required to be issued. In *R v Gayle* [1999] 2 Cr App R 130, following the theft of a handbag, a caretaker at a school described seeing a man on the premises. The description was that the man was stocky, black and wearing a bomber jacket with a distinctive logo. The defendant matched the description, was acting suspiciously and was discovered near the stolen item. The trial judge did not issue a warning and the Court of Appeal dismissed the appeal.

Fourth, a *Turnbull* direction is unnecessary with regard to the identification of motor vehicles; see *R v Browning* (1991) 94 Cr App R 109. The reason is that motor vehicles, unlike

individuals, do not change their shape in the sense that each is not unique in appearance. The judge, however, is duty bound to direct the jury on the witness's ability to distinguish makes of cars and their characteristics.

Fifth, a *Turnbull* direction is unnecessary where the jury is asked to make an identification from photographs or video recordings, etc. In *R v Blenkinsop* [1995] 1 Cr App R 7, photographs and video footage were taken at the scene of a violent demonstration. The question was whether the photographic evidence was of the defendant taking part in the demonstration. The court held that it was not necessary for a *Turnbull* warning to be issued.

13.15 Accused conduct: lies told by the accused (in or out of court)

The law in this respect was clarified by the Court of Appeal in 1981. The rule is that lies told by the accused, generally, are incapable of corroborating the evidence of a prosecution witness. However, if the lie was

(a) deliberate, and

(b) relates to a material issue, and

(c) the motive for the lie had been the realization of guilt, and

(d) the statement of the accused is clearly shown to be a lie by the evidence from an independent witness (other than the accomplice who required corroboration). These are complementary (not competitive) criteria

it is capable of being corroborative evidence and the judge is required to direct the jury accordingly.

CASE EXTRACT

R v Lucas [1981] 2 All ER 1008 CA

The accused, Ruth Lucas and A were charged and convicted on two counts of importing cannabis contrary to the Misuse of Drugs Act 1971 – count (1) related to an offence committed at Heathrow and count (2) took place at Gatwick airport. A pleaded guilty on both counts. The accused pleaded 'guilty' to the Heathrow count but 'not guilty' on count (2).

The main prosecution witness, B, had pleaded guilty and was sentenced, and testified, implicating both accused. It was proved by B that the accused, A, had lied out of court

CONTINUED ▸

about the events and the judge told the jury that this was capable of amounting to corroboration. The defendant appealed to the Court of Appeal.

It was held that since the accused's lies were only proved by an accomplice, the lies did not corroborate the prosecution witness's testimony. In this respect, there is no distinction between lies told out of court and in court. The appeal was allowed and the conviction was quashed. Lord Lane CJ:

J

'. . . Statements made out of court, eg statements to the police which are proved or admitted to be false may in certain circumstances amount to corroboration . . . It accords with good sense that a lie told by a def. about a material issue may show that the liar knew that if he told the truth he would be sealing his fate . . . To be capable of amounting to corroboration the lie told out of court must first of all be deliberate. Secondly, it must relate to a material issue. Thirdly, the motive for the lie must be a realisation of guilt or fear of the truth. The jury should in appropriate cases be reminded that people sometimes lie, eg in an attempt to bolster up a just cause, or out of shame or out of a wish to conceal disgraceful behaviour from their family. Fourthly, the statement must be clearly shown to be a lie by evidence other than that of the accomplice who is to be corroborated, ie by admission or by evidence from an independent witness . . . Providing that the lies told in court fulfil the 4 criteria we are unable to see why they should not be available for the jury to consider in just the same way as lies told out of court . . .'

This test is known as a Lucas direction was approved by the Court of Appeal in *R v Burge and Pegg* [1996] 1 Cr App R 163. In this case, the accused were charged with murder. They burgled the 74-year-old victim's flat, having forced their way into the flat, wearing masks and carrying sticky tape and cord. They gagged and bound the victim and stole from his flat. The left the victim tied up and he died from asphyxia. In interview, each blamed the other. At the trial they claimed that a neighbour of the deceased who lived upstairs had killed the deceased after they had left the flat. The judge gave the jury a warning as to the significance of lies told to the police. The accused were convicted and appealed. The Court of Appeal dismissed the appeal and decided that the direction was correct. The jury was told of the proper significance of the lies. Kennedy LJ:

J '. . . it may be helpful if we conclude by summarising the circumstances in which, in our judgment, a *Lucas* direction is usually required. There are four such circumstances, but they may overlap:

1. Where the defence relies on alibi.
2. Where the judge considers it desirable or necessary to suggest that the jury should look for support or corroboration of one piece of evidence from other evidence in the case, and amongst that other evidence draws attention to lies told, or allegedly told, by the defendant.
3. Where the prosecution seek to show that something said, either in or out of the court, in relation to a separate and distinct issue was a lie, and to rely on that lie as evidence of guilt in relation to the charge which is sought to be proved.
4. Where although the prosecution have not adopted the approach to which we have just referred, the judge reasonably envisages that there is a real danger that the jury may do so.

If a *Lucas* direction is given where there is no need for such a direction (as in the normal case where there is a straight conflict of evidence), it will add complexity and do more harm than good. Therefore, in our judgment, a judge would be wise always, before speeches and summing up in circumstance number four, and perhaps also in other circumstances, to consider with counsel whether, in the instant case, such a direction is in fact required, and, if so, how it should be formulated. If the matter is dealt with in that way, this court will be very slow to interfere with the exercise of the judge's discretion . . .

. . . The direction should, if given, so far as possible, be tailored to the circumstances of the case, but it will normally be sufficient if it makes the two basic points:

1. that the lie must be admitted or proved beyond reasonable doubt, and;
2. that the mere fact that the defendant lied is not in itself evidence of guilt since defendants may lie for innocent reasons, so only if the jury is sure that the defendant did not lie for an innocent reason can a lie support the prosecution case.'

It follows that a *Lucas* direction is not appropriate where the lie told by the defendant related to the central issue in the trial – whether the defendant is guilty of the crime or not; see *R v Ball* [2001] Lawtel, 5th January 2001.

ACTIVITY

Self-test questions

1. What is the corroboration evidence?

2. What criteria must be satisfied for evidence to amount to corroboration evidence?

3. Explain what is meant by the term 'collective corroboration evidence'.

4. Define the term 'mutual corroboration' with an example.

5. Who is an accomplice?

6. Is the judge required to give a corroboration warning where an accomplice has given evidence against a defendant?

7. Why is there a need for the judge to issue a care warning to a jury when considering visual identification evidence?

8. When is a *Turnbull* warning required to be issued to the jury and what is the effect of failure to issue such a warning?

9. When may a *Turnbull* warning be dispensed with concerning identification evidence?

10. Is disputed voice identification evidence subject to a warning?

11. When would the judge be required to issue a *Lucas* direction?

12. Historically, what categories of case required a corroboration warning to be given?

13. What is the effect of s 32 of the Criminal Justice and Public Order Act 1994?

14. What is the effect of *R v Makanjuola*?

15. Summarize the extent of the discretion a judge has when deciding whether or not to give a corroboration or care warning?

Further reading

Birch, D., 'Corroboration: Goodbye to All That? [1995] Crim LR 524.

E and P, Corroboration and Care Warnings after *Makanjuola* (1998) 2(1), 1–12.

Jackson, J., 'Insufficiency of Identification Evidence based on Personal Impression [1986] Crim LR 203.

Mirfield, P., 'Corroboration after the 1994 Act' [1995] Crim LR 448.

Murphy, P., HHJ *Murphy on Evidence* (Oxford University Press, 2007).

Ormerod, D., 'Sounds Familiar? Voice Identification Evidence' [2001] Crim LR 595.

chapter 14 OPINION, DOCUMENTARY AND REAL EVIDENCE ■

AIMS AND OBJECTIVES

In this chapter you will learn:

- What the different types of opinion evidence are

- About expert and non-expert opinion evidence

- Who qualifies as an expert

- The status of opinion evidence in the criminal and civil cases

- About real and documentary evidence

- About the forms of documentary evidence, ie primary and secondary

14.1 Introduction

The aim of this chapter is to provide an overview of three categories of evidence; opinion, real and documentary evidence. The discussion begins with a brief introduction to the background to opinion evidence and then more specifically in relation to expert and non-expert opinion evidence, its importance and the rules governing its admission, after which the discussion focuses on real and documentary evidence and the rules on relevancy and admission.

14.2 Opinion evidence

The general rule is that witnesses should only give evidence of facts that they have perceived themselves without speculating, drawing conclusions and inferences or giving their opinion. There is a distinction between the role of a witness in giving evidence of facts and the court in coming to conclusions; therefore, when giving evidence, the witness should not usurp the role of the court or jury. The 'opinion rule' in the English law of evidence excludes the opinion evidence of lay witnesses by reason that the witness may be unreliable or inexperienced in giving evidence and hence there exists a greater risk of such evidence lacking probative force. Further opinions of lay witnesses are simply irrelevant. The court will determine its opinion in relation to the facts that are in issue and counsel and the court will object to questions that seek to elicit witness opinion.

In summary, opinion evidence is excluded. However, there are three exceptions to the rule; opinion evidence may be admissible if it is:

- expert opinion
- opinion evidence of general reputation
- the opinion of an eyewitness.

Let us take a look at each of these in detail.

14.2.1 Expert opinion

There are notably many occasions where the court is required to adjudicate on a case involving complex and technical issues that are beyond its experience or competence. In an ideal world the presiding judge would be an expert in the discipline of which the case is concerned; in reality the majority of the time this is not true. In such cases the court will seek the assistance of experts or expert witnesses who will be better equipped to express their opinion and make conclusions from the facts; for example, on the time relative to the decomposition of a corpse or facial mapping where closed circuit television (CCTV) is in question. The general rule is well established; in *Folkes v Chadd* (1782) 3 Doug KB 157 the court allowed an engineer to give his opinion on the causes of silting in the harbour of the defendant port owner.

Like any exception, before such evidence can be admitted it must satisfy a series of conditions; in relation to expert evidence these are that the

- witness's opinion is beyond ordinary experience and competence
- witness is a qualified 'expert'.

In addition, admission of such evidence is subject to a series of procedural requirements.

Witness expertise

The court will only hear the opinion evidence of a person who is *qualified* to form an opinion on the matter concerned; for example, a Professor on haematology in relation to blood-clotting or a forensic scientist on dismemberment of a body and its decomposition. Although the witness does not need to have a formal qualification because their skill and experience is enough, having such qualifications will undoubtedly demonstrate competence and expertise.

ASE EXAMPLE

R v Silverlock [1894] 2 QB 766

The evidence of a solicitor on handwriting was permitted by the court even though they had only studied and researched handwriting and had no formal qualification in relation to it.

Where the evidence is admitted, then the weight of it will be affected by the actual level of skill, experience and expertise demonstrated by them. Contrast these cases:

CASE EXAMPLE

R v Oakley (1979) 70 Cr App R 7

An officer of the police was permitted to give opinion evidence on road traffic accidents due the extensive amount of experience in the matter concerned.

CASE EXAMPLE

R v Inch (1989) 91 Cr App R 51

A medical orderly was not permitted to give opinion evidence on medical matters due to his inexperience in the matters concerned.

The full text judgment of both these cases is available on Westlaw, LexisNexis and other reputable legal resource databases. What if the witness's evidence requires the use of a new or developing skill, for example a new method of facial mapping, lip reading or voice identification that is still being rigorously contested? Will the court automatically accept the evidence as being expert opinion? No, the court will first adjudicate on whether the discipline qualifies as a recognized expertise and then whether the witness can be considered to be an expert; see *R v Luttrell* [2004] 2 Cr App R 31 and *R v Robb* (1991) 93 Cr App R 161.

Does the party instructing the expert witness own the evidence to be given by them and hence only such party can make use of it? The court in *Harmony Shipping v Saudi Europe Line Ltd* [1979] 1 WLR 1380 held that there can be 'no property' in an expert witness which means the witness, regardless of whoever has instructed or called them, will be an independent witness of the court. Lord Denning:

> J '. . . so far as witnesses of fact are concerned, the law is as plain as can be. There is no property in a witness. The reason is because the Court has a right to every man's evidence. Its primary duty is to ascertain the truth. Neither one side nor the other can debar the Court from ascertaining the truth either by seeing a witness beforehand or by purchasing his evidence or by making communication to him. In no way can one side prohibit the other side from seeing a witness of fact, from

CONTINUED ▶

J getting the facts from him and from calling him to give evidence or from issuing him with a subpoena. That was laid down by the Law Society in their Guide to the Professional Conduct of Solicitors. It was affirmed and approved in 1963 by the then Lord Chief Justice and the Judges . . . that principle is established in the case of a witness of fact: for the plain, simple reason that the primary duty of the Court is to ascertain the truth by the best evidence available. Any witness who has seen the facts or who knows the facts can be compelled to assist the Court and should assist the Court by giving that evidence.

The question in this case is whether or not that principle applies to expert witnesses. They may have been told the substance of a party's case. They may have been given a great deal of confidential information. On it they may have given advice to the party. Does the rule apply to such a case? Many of the communications between the solicitor and the expert witness will be privileged. They are protected by legal professional privilege. They cannot be communicated to the Court except with the consent of the party concerned. That means that a great deal of the communications between the expert witness and the lawyer cannot be given in evidence to the Court. If questions were asked about it, then it would be the duty of the Judge to protect the witness (and he would) by disallowing any questions which infringed the rule about legal professional privilege or the rule protecting information given in confidence – unless, of course, it was one of those rare cases which come before the Courts from time to time where in spite of privilege or confidence the Court does order a witness to give further evidence. Subject to that qualification, it seems to me that an expert witness falls into the same position as a witness of fact. The Court is entitled, in order to ascertain the truth, to have the actual facts which he has observed adduced before it and to have his independent opinion on those facts. It is interesting to see that it was so held in Canada in *McDonald Construction Co Ltd v. Bestway Lath & Plastering Co Ltd* (1972) 27 DLR (3d) 253 . . . it seems to me . . . that the expert witness is in the same position when he is speaking as to the facts he has observed and is giving his own independent opinion on them, no matter by which side he is instructed.'

The effect of this is to render the opinion neutral, ie either party may use it. As the judgment outlines, the exception to this rule, although legal and professional privilege is discussed in Chapter 4, there are a few points to note at this stage. Is privileged information information that does not need to be disclosed? Information is privileged if it involves communications between a lawyer and a client in the normal course of litigation or communications between a lawyer, client and a third party; for our purposes the expert witness, where the dominant purpose in litigation

does not need to be disclosed. This information, subject to certain limitations, may only be disclosed where the client receiving it waives the privilege, ie their right. The position of the law can be summarized as follows:

Expert witness opinion evidence	
Privileged if communication obtained with a dominant purpose of litigation	Not privileged where privilege waived or if communication not obtained with a dominant purpose of litigation
Use: only by party instructing expert	Use: by any party to the proceedings

■ Figure 14.1 Opinion evidence of an expert witness

ASE EXAMPLE

R v R (1994) *The Times* 2nd February

The court held that both the opinion and sample of an expert witness who had carried out testing on the defendant's DNA sample were privileged because they had been created in connection with contemplated legal proceedings where the dominant purpose was litigation.

As the status of the expert witness is one of an independent witness the court can validly reject their evidence; see *R v Lanfear* [1968] 2 QB 77. In *Anderson v R* [1972] AC 100 the court stated that where the expert opinion evidence is clear and not contradicted, then it should not be disregarded.

KEY FACTS

Opinion evidence

The *general rule* known as the *opinion rule* prohibits the admission of opinion evidence as it may be unreliable, it may lack probative force and the opinion of a witness is irrelevant, unless it is:

- the opinion of an expert
- evidence of general reputation
- eyewitness opinion.

CONTINUED ▸

KEY FACTS

Expert opinion

The established principle in *Folkes v Chadd* (1782) 3 Doug KB 157 is to the effect that the opinion of an expert is admissible as evidence if the:

- witness's expert opinion is beyond ordinary experience and competence, for example matters that are complex or technical
- witness is a qualified expert although a professional qualification is not required
- certain procedural conditions are satisfied.

Property in expert witness evidence

In *Harmony Shipping v Saudi Europe Line Ltd* [1979] 1 WLR 1380 the court held that there can be 'no property' in the evidence of an expert witness which means the expert is classified as an independent witness of the court whose evidence can be utilized by another party subject to the law on privilege.

Subject matter of expertise

An expert witness will only be called to give evidence on matters that are beyond *normal* experience or expertise. If the matter falls within the capabilities of the jury, then the expert witness's opinion becomes redundant and therefore will be unnecessary. There are a number of examples that are commonly cited where the opinion evidence of an expert witness has become redundant and unnecessary. They include:

- defences: provocation (*R v Turner* [1975] QB 834)
- personality disorders (*R v Weightman* [1991] Crim LR 204)
- the general truthfulness of witnesses (*R v MacKenney* (1981) 76 Cr App R 271).

CASE EXAMPLE

R v Land [1999] QB 65

L was charged with possession of the indecent photographs of a child (unidentified). The prosecution sought to adduce the opinion of an expert paediatrician in relation to the issue of the child being under 16 and therefore under age. The Court of Appeal held that this was unnecessary as the jury were just as competent as the paediatrician to ascertain the child's age.

In contrast, the courts have decided that expert evidence can be validly adduced where the following defences are raised: insanity (*R v Holmes* [1953] 1 WLR 686), diminished responsibility (*R v Bailey* (1977) 66 Cr App R 31) and automatism (*R v Smith* [1979] 1 WLR 1445). In *R v Lowery* [1974] AC 85 two defendants were charged with a murder; from the evidence it was obvious that it must have been committed by one or both of them. The court allowed the prosecution to adduce the opinion evidence of an expert witness to show which one of the two defendants was more likely to have committed it, as *per* Lord Herschell partly quoting the decision of the Court of Criminal Appeal:

> **J** '. . . "it is, however, established by the highest authorities that in criminal cases the Crown is precluded from leading evidence that does no more than show that the accused has a disposition or propensity or is the sort of person likely to commit the crime charged"; and further, "It is, we think, one thing to say that such evidence is excluded when tendered by the Crown in proof of guilt, but quite another to say that it is excluded when tendered by the accused in disproof of his own guilt. We see no reason of policy or fairness which justifies or requires the exclusion of evidence relevant to prove the innocence of an accused person."
>
> The evidence of Professor Cox, as will have been seen, was not as such evidence in regard to the character of Lowery and King but rather was evidence as to their respective intelligences and personalities . . . Lowery and King were each asserting that the other was the completely dominating person at the time when Rosalyn Nolte was killed: each claimed to have been in fear of the other. In these circumstances it was most relevant for King to be able to show, if he could, that Lowery had a personality marked by aggressiveness whereas he, King, had a personality which suggested that he would be led and dominated by someone who was dominant and aggressive. In support of King's case the evidence of Professor Cox was relevant if it tended to show that the version of the facts put forward by King was more probable than that put forward by Lowery. Not only, however, was the evidence which King called relevant to this case: its admissibility was placed beyond doubt by the whole substance of Lowery's case. Not only did Lowery assert that the killing was done by King and not only did he say that he had been in fear of King but, as previously mentioned, he set himself up as one who had no motive whatsoever in killing the girl and as one who would not have been likely to wreck his good prospects and furthermore as one who would not have been interested in the sort of behaviour manifested by the killer. While ascribing the sole responsibility to King, he was also in effect saying that he himself was not the sort of man to have committed the offence . . . the evidence was relevant to and necessary for his case which involved negativing what Lowery had said and put forward . . . the evidence was admissible.'

It should be noted that this precedes the changes to admission of character evidence rules brought in by the Criminal Justice Act 2003.

More generally, expert witnesses will be called to give evidence on matters that are complex, scientific or technical. In modern criminal justice evidence has become far more sophisticated and as a result evidence of a forensic nature may carry much weight and therefore an expert's opinion would normally be required to meticulously examine exhibits. Other areas where experts are instructed include: detailing professional or trade practice, proving foreign law and examining handwriting. *Lowery* (above) highlights the nature of opinion evidence and its potential use, although it has been distinguished in *R v Rimmer* [1983] Crim LR 250 on the basis of its peculiar or special facts.

The Ultimate issue rule

Let us move on to the subject-matter of the opinion evidence itself. In general terms in criminal cases an expert should only give their opinion in evidence on matters that are not directly in issue; this is known as the ultimate issue rule. *Lowery* (above) provides a good example where the psychiatrist gave evidence on which defendant was more likely to have murdered the victim and not whether or not they actually had committed the crime. The ultimate issue rule seeks to prevent experts from usurping the function of the trier of law and fact, namely the judge and jury, for it is for them to decide on those matters. More recent case law, see *DPP v A & BC Chewing Gum Ltd* [1968] 1 QB 159, shows that judges in criminal cases are not too strict where it comes to policing the rule and will allow an expert to give their opinion in evidence on an ultimate issue so long as the jury do not attribute excessive weight to it. In civil cases the position is slightly more lax where expert witnesses can give evidence on any matter that is relevant; see s 3 of the Civil Evidence Act 1972.

Expert opinion as hearsay evidence

Generally, expert opinion evidence can be presented to a court either orally or in writing in the form of a report. What if the expert worked alongside other scientists in their scientific work and therefore has personal knowledge of some but not all the facts? When assessed on a technical basis, such a report would be classified as an inadmissible hearsay statement of opinion. We will discuss the position in criminal cases in a moment; the position with regard to civil cases is far simpler. Such hearsay statements of opinion are permissible under s 1 of the Civil Evidence Act 1995, which in effect means that the expert making the report does not need to give oral evidence themselves. As *ES v Chesterfield and North Derbyshire NHS Trust* [2004] Lloyds Rep Med 90 (below) shows, the Civil Procedure Rules 1998 (CPR) encourages the use of expert reports where necessary, the result of which is a saving in court resources and time taken to adjudicate. Lord Justice Brook stated that:

 '. . . *judges* have a . . . responsibility under the CPR to . . . restrict expert evidence to that which is reasonably required to resolve the proceedings'.

In criminal cases the agreed use of expert statements of opinion in the form of reports are permissible under s 30 of the Criminal Justice Act 1988; see *Jackson* [1996] 2 Cr App R 420. Once again the evidence is admissible regardless of whether the experts themselves give oral evidence; however, leave of the court to adduce the reports will be required if they do not. Where the court seeks to grant leave it will consider the following:

• the contents of the report

• the reason for the expert not testifying

• any risk of unfairness that may result from the expert not testifying because, in effect, the evidence will be uncorroborated

• all the circumstances of the case.

Where the report is not controversial and is uncontested, then the court is likely to allow it to be adduced; if the opposite is true, then the expert should give evidence along with the admissible report. In criminal cases the issue of admissibility of such evidence was based on the negative views of hearsay held by others; the problems with the admission of expert reports has somewhat been rectified by Part 24 of the Criminal Procedure Rules 2005 (SI 2005/384) and the Criminal Justice Act 2003. First, s 114(1)(b) of the CJA 2003 preserves expert reports as evidence of facts stated therein; second, s 127(3) states that where such evidence is admitted it must be treated as '. . . evidence of what it states' and the court retains the power to make an order against the use of it where the interests of justice so require, thereby safeguarding the rights of the party against whom the evidence is being adduced. In making an order the court will take into account the costs, practicalities and summoning of the expert witness upon whose opinion the report is based so that they may be cross-examined on it. In summary, expert reports, namely hearsay opinion statements, are admissible in both civil and criminal cases with the latter being subject to certain conditions.

KEY FACTS

The ultimate issue rule
The *general rule* in criminal cases is that a common law expert should only give their opinion in evidence on matters that are not directly in issue so that they do not usurp the function of the trier of fact.

CONTINUED ▶

KEY FACTS

Expert opinion as hearsay evidence

Where an expert does not give oral evidence, their opinion, for example, a report, can be technically classed as an inadmissible hearsay statement; however:

- section 1 of the CEA 1995 and the CPRs encourage the use of such statements in civil proceedings
- section 30 of the CJA 1988 made their use permissible subject to the leave of the court, a problem rectified by s 114(1)(b) and s 127(3) of the CJA 2003 and the CrPRs.

The presentation of expert opinion evidence

Most experts will have been experienced in writing reports and giving oral evidence (testifying). Normally the expert will work closely with the instructed advocate so that they can develop and present the report in court in the most effective manner. The advocate will normally question the expert on how they formulated their conclusions as this will most probably be the line of questioning pursued by the opposition when seeking to undermine. Let us look at an example: two facial mapping experts each instructed by opposing parties to assess some low-quality CCTV footage of the part of the face of an individual dressed in a hoodie committing a crime.

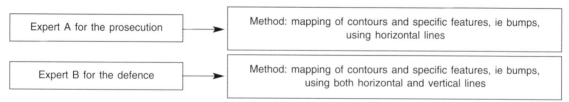

■ Figure 14.2 The presentation of expert opinion evidence in court

The methods of each of the experts were slightly different; expert A had 25 years' experience using a 'traditional' method of facial mapping. In contrast, expert B had only 10 years' experience but used a newer method of facial mapping. The evidence of expert A only indicated that the person in the CCTV footage and the defendant were 'likely' to be the same person. Expert B claimed that the person on the CCTV footage and the defendant were not the same person. The evidence of expert A was contradicted in cross-examination by counsel because he could not give a valid enough reason why he had rejected the use of the 'newer' method. The outcome was that the jury could not decide whom to believe and therefore could not return a verdict; the case had to be retried with a new jury.

In *English Exporters (London) Ltd v Eldonwall Ltd* [1973] Ch 415 the court outlined the extent to which an expert may refer to the hearsay data that they used to formulate their opinion when writing the report. The case at hand concerned the valuation of leases; the court confirmed that although an expert could express their opinion based on matters that may not be within their personal knowledge, they cannot testify as to those facts unless they have actual personal knowledge of them.

ASE EXTRACT

R v Abadom [1983] 1 WLR 126

The defendant was charged with robbery. The evidence of an expert witness showed that the glass that was found on his shoes was very likely the same as that of the window that had been broken during the commission of the offence. The broken glass had the same refractive index which, according to Home Office statistics, was only found in around 4 per cent of all glass samples. The defendant appealed arguing that the statistics were technically hearsay that the expert should not have been allowed to refer to it.

J   The Court of Appeal disagreed, the expert could refer, in the course of his testimony to research of which he had personal knowledge because the details of the research, although not directly evidence themselves, added weight to his evidence.

The current position is neatly outlined by the courts in *H v Schering Chemicals Ltd* [1983] 1 WLR 143 where it was stated that medical or research reports that are technically hearsay statements if used by an expert to formulate their opinion can be referred to when assessing the weight of the experts evidence.

Issues of disclosure

Let us now take a look at how expert reports are disclosed; this diagram summarizes the position:

Proceedings	Reason for disclosure and source for reference
Civil	Part 35 of the Civil Procedure Rules 1998 requires the parties to comply with pre-trial disclosure. In compliance with the overriding objective; to reduce costs, save time and increase efficiency in the way in which the case proceeds, ie clarification of the issues. See: http://www.justice.gov.uk/civil/procrules_fin/menus/rules.htm
Criminal	The Crown Court (Advance Notice of Expert Evidence) Rules 1987 govern disclosure of opinions and any test or observation used to formulate it (3(1)). A failure to follow these rules will result in the evidence being inadmissible unless the court grants leave for it to be adduced. See: http://www.justice.gov.uk/criminal/procrules_fin/rulesmenu.htm

■ Figure 14.3 How expert reports are disclosed

14.3 Non-expert opinion evidence

Let us now focus our discussion on the opinion evidence of non-experts or lay witnesses. In civil cases the position is clarified by the Civil Evidence Act 1972; s 3(2) states that where the testimony of a witness is of their opinion in conveying the perception of facts by them, then that evidence is admissible as evidence of what they perceived. The effect of this is to render admissible the evidence of a witness that expresses a common-sensical observation or opinion of their perception. In criminal cases, although such clarity has not yet been achieved by statute, it is likely that the position is the same.

The next question, logically, concerns the subject-matter upon which a non-expert can give evidence. Commonly cited and accepted facts upon which a non-expert can give evidence of perception include:

- the intoxication of the defendant, ie she was drunk

- identification

- the common value of an item other than a rare antique, ie that an iPod Nano is worth about £100

- speed of travel of a car, ie they were driving very fast

- the physical fitness of a defendant.

Where non-expert evidence is concerned, the issue of such evidence being classified must be kept in mind because the opinion of a non-expert is irrelevant. In civil cases the notice procedure discussed earlier applies.

KEY FACTS

Non-expert opinion evidence
Generally, the opinion of non-expert witnesses is:
- in civil cases admissible under s 3(2) of the CEA 1972 so long as it purveys their perception of facts
- in criminal cases the position is not clear; however, the jurisprudence of the courts suggests that it is essentially the same.

14.4 Opinion evidence of reputation

In civil cases the position generally accepted is that evidence of reputation is admissible, without giving notice, under s 7 of the CEA 1995 to show pedigree, good or bad character, public right.

In addition to this, evidence of opinion is also admissible, as already discussed. In criminal cases evidence of bad character is governed by the Criminal Justice Act 2003; this is discussed in Chapter 11 and there also exists a variety of rules that impact on reputation which are discussed throughout the book.

14.5 Previous judgments – hearsay?

In certain instances a party may wish to rely on a previous judgment because it is factually relevant to their cases. It could be argued, technically, that such evidence is hearsay and therefore the argument against the use of previous judgments centres on the risk of prejudice; for example, there is a risk that court A will be prejudiced after learning of the opinion of court B on a factual issue. Exclusion of such evidence would result in unnecessary and repetitious arguments being pursued, not to mention the inconsistency in judgment; it is therefore tantamount that in some situations evidence of this type be admissible with limitation. The principle of *res judicata* has the effect of debarring the same parties to an action from reopening the same issue in subsequent proceedings. Think about this: A sues his plumber for negligence and loses; he is not happy and decides he would like to sue him again, and again until he wins. This would be an absurd situation. The current position of the law is as follows: an estoppel operates to bar subsequent actions based on the same issue(s).

14.6 Common law rule: *Hollington v Hewthorn* [1943] KB 587

What, then, was the position at common law? On the issue of using previous judgments as evidence in subsequent civil cases, the common law frequently shifted between admission and exclusion. The matter was finally ambiguously settled in *Hollington v Hewthorn* [1943] KB 587 where the court decided that reference to previous judgments should be excluded. In this case the claimant, at that time referred to as the plaintiff, was the victim of alleged negligent driving on the part of the defendant's employee. The Court of Appeal decided that the employee's previous conviction for driving without due care and attention was inadmissible because the opinion of the previous court could not match the opinion of the High Court in a contested personal injury action.

The effect of the decision was to prevent previous judgments being used as evidence in a subsequent case; this was inconvenient and resulted in much inequity. The rule was somewhat reversed by the Civil Evidence Act 1968 (CEA) which provides exceptions to the rule in the form of ss 11–13 which respectively provide for the use of criminal convictions, findings of adultery and paternity and convictions for defamation as evidence in civil cases.

Previous judgments

Generally, the arguments centring around the inadmissibility of previous court judgments focus on the risk of prejudice in the opinion of the current court based on something decided by a previous court, duplicity and inconsistency in judgment:

- in civil cases:
  - The principle of *res judicata* has the effect of *estopping* a party to an action from subsequently reopening the same issue in subsequent proceedings
  - The *common law rule* in *Hollington v Hewthorn* [1943] KB 587 meant that reference to previous civil judgments was excluded; this was partially reversed by ss 11–13 of the CEA 1968 which provide for reference to criminal convictions, findings of adultery and paternity and convictions for defamation
- in criminal cases:
  - The use of previous criminal convictions as evidence is admissible under the CJA 2003 and s 74 of PACE 1984.

14.6.1 Section 11 CEA 1968

The discussion begins with s 11 which provides for the use of previous criminal convictions in civil cases.

Section 11(1) of the CEA 1968 states that:

S '. . . in any civil proceedings the fact that a person has been convicted of an offence by or before any *UK* court or by a court-martial *in the UK* or elsewhere shall be admissible in evidence for the purpose of proving, where *it is* relevant to any issue in those proceedings, that *they* committed that offence, whether *they were* so convicted upon a plea of guilty or otherwise and whether or not *they are* a party to the civil proceedings; but no conviction other than a subsisting one shall be admissible as evidence by virtue of this section.'

Section 11 contains a statutory persuasive presumption which means that the court will *presume* the offence was committed by the defendant unless they can show otherwise; see *Wauchope v Mordecai* [1970] 1 WLR 317. The effect of s 11(1) is to allow the use of a criminal conviction in a *subsequent* civil action; one of the main underlying reasons for this includes the fact that the burden of proof on the prosecution in criminal cases (beyond reasonable doubt) is far higher than that in civil actions (on the balance of probabilities). Therefore, if a particular point has been proven to the judge and jury's satisfaction at the higher standard of proof, it makes sense to

accept it as having satisfied the lower one. Most interestingly, the conviction does not need to be a conviction of a party to the action but it must be relevant to an issue. A question arises; if a criminal conviction is admissible in evidence in subsequent civil actions, is, then, a finding in a civil case admissible as evidence in a criminal case? The provision only deals with convictions and does not state anything in respect of this situation and hence must be read as not having that effect.

The condition for admissibility, apart from relevance, is that the conviction must be one by a UK court or court martial or court martial under the authority of the British Forces. A conviction by a foreign court will not suffice; for example a Spanish conviction for careless driving could not be used as evidence of careless driving in the UK. The use of the conviction does not depend on whether the defendant pleaded guilty or not guilty; however, it must exist without a lodged appeal. If the conviction is being appealed, then the civil action must be adjourned or continued without that evidence.

The conviction will be proof of the fact that the person convicted committed the offence unless they can prove the contrary (s 11(2)); that does not mean a reopening of the case but it may mean that there was an error on the record of the court convicting or the conviction was successfully appealed and quashed. The burden of proving that the conviction does not represent the true facts is on the party asserting that. Discharging this burden is difficult. Remember, the decision is one of 12 jurors who have been satisfied so that they are sure that the defendant committed the offence. In *Stupple v Royal Insurance Co* [1970] 3 All ER 230, Paull J stated:

> J   '. . . for at least the best part of 1,000 years it has been the law of England that it was not for a lawyer or for lawyers in any case of serious crime to pronounce whether an accused person was guilty of the crime and should be punished accordingly. Lawyers can pronounce that a man charged is not guilty if there is not sufficient evidence upon which his fellow citizens can properly find him guilty, or can pronounce that a summing-up by a judge was not a satisfactory summing-up; but once there is proper evidence, and the law and the facts have been satisfactorily explained to the accused's fellow citizens, it is for his fellow citizens, and for no one else, to pronounce whether he is guilty or not.'

In effect the party discharging this burden is arguing that the decision of the jury was wrong or mistaken; therefore, the discharge of this burden must be evidenced by the provision of convincing supporting evidence; see *Taylor v Taylor* [1970] 1 WLR 1148. The Court of Appeal in *Stupple* outlined how difficult this requirement could be, even though it was divided as to whether the conviction gave rise to a presumption or the very fact of the conviction was a factor that would be taken into account when considering whether the standard of the balance of probabilities had been satisfied.

14.6.2 Sections 12–13 CEA 1968: adultery, paternity and defamation

Let us move on to look at some specific instances in which 'findings' in other judgments can be used subsequently. Section 12 of the CEA 1968 provides that where a UK court, in matrimonial or other relevant proceedings, has made a finding of adultery or paternity, then that finding can be taken as evidence of adultery or paternity. It is obvious that adultery or paternity must be relevant to an issue in the subsequent proceedings. The effect of s 12 is to create a statutory presumption, on the person disputing the earlier finding, placing a legal burden of proof on them to prove the alternative.

Section 13 of the same Act provides that in defamation cases, the fact that a person has been convicted by a UK court or court martial of a criminal offence, where it is relevant to the subsequent proceedings, is conclusive evidence that they have committed the offence. This presumption was amended by the Defamation Act 1996, allowing the presumption in relation to the conviction of a non-party, ie a witness, to be rebutted.

14.6.3 Issues in the use of ss 11–13 CEA 1968

The party seeking to rely on s 11 or 12 must plead that they are seeking to rely on the conviction as part of their case in their particulars of claim; this is not necessary in those situations falling within s 13. All three provisions apply to criminal convictions, therefore criminal acquittals, ie where the person is not convicted and the charge is discontinued against them, are not covered because there would be no way of ascertaining what the fact the person was acquitted is attempting to prove and what the probative value of such evidence would be. For example, Hannah cannot plead that James was tried for a criminal offence but acquitted and thereby assert that circumstantially there must be some truth in the allegation because charges were levied although unproven.

14.7 The use of previous criminal convictions in criminal cases

The law on the admissibility of a previous criminal conviction as evidence proving that an offence was committed by the person convicted in criminal cases is contained in the Criminal Justice Act 2003 (CJA) and s 74 of the Police and Criminal Evidence Act 1984 (PACE), the CJA 2003 is discussed in depth in Chapter 11; therefore, our discussion in this chapter will be limited to s 74. Both provisions make previous criminal convictions admissible, within constraints, as evidence proving that the person convicted committed the offence. A major difference between the two provisions is that s 74 distinguishes between the criminal convictions of the accused and those of other persons, ie witnesses.

Section 74(1) PACE 1984 states that

S '. . . In any proceedings the fact that a person other than the accused has been convicted of an offence . . . shall be admissible evidence for the purpose of proving, where it is relevant to any issue in those proceedings, that that person committed that offence, whether or not any other evidence of his having committed that offence is given.'

In addition, s 74(2) PACE 1984 provides that the conviction, unless proven to the contrary, is proof that the person convicted committed the offence. The outcome here is similar to that under s 11 of the CEA 1968; let us take a look at a criminal law example. Donnette and Bindu are respectively charged with handling stolen goods and theft. Bindu is convicted of theft and sentenced to imprisonment. At Donnette's trial for the handling offence the prosecution may wish to adduce as evidence Bindu's conviction for theft; the effect of this is to prove that the goods were stolen.

The life of s 74 has not always been so easy; the provision has encountered other problems. What if the 'guilt' of the other person is not relevant to an element of the offence that the defendant is charged with but implicates them? In this instance the use of the previous conviction is likely to be excluded under s 78 PACE 1984. An interesting point to note concerns the meaning of conviction within the provision; does it mean conviction after a plea of guilty and hence no trial, or does it mean a conviction after a plea of not guilty and therefore after trial? Section 74 refers to a finding of guilt after a plea of not guilty being entered and the trial having taken place. Furthermore, once the person has been convicted, proof of the conviction can be used straightaway; the party seeking to adduce it does not need to wait until the person has been sentenced; see *R v Golder* [1987] QB 920.

CASE EXAMPLE

R v O'Connor (1987) 85 Cr App R 298

A was charged with conspiring with B to defraud C. Even though B had been convicted after having pleaded guilty, hence no trial had taken place, the trial judge allowed for B's conviction to be adduced at A's trial. The Court of Appeal stated that the Judge had erred; he should have excluded the evidence because of the greater likelihood of prejudice to A, ie the jury thinking that if B had admitted it, then A must have done it. The Court declined to comment on the technicalities of s 74.

In contrast to the decision of the Court of Appeal in *O'Connor* a differently constituted Court of Appeal (different judges) in *R v Robertson* [1987] QB 920 decided that s 74 was not so restricted. In *Robertson* the Court of Appeal held that the provision applied so long as the conviction of the other person was relevant to any issue in the subsequent proceedings. However, the judge should be careful when directing and summing up to the jury.

R v Curry [1988] Crim LR 527

A was convicted of allowing his credit card to be fraudulently used. The Court of Appeal held that the use of his conviction in the trial of B would have resulted in unfairness. Although the conviction was technically admissible it was excluded on the ground that ' . . . where the evidence expressly or by . . . inference imported the complicity of the accused it should not be used'.

R v Warner (1993) 96 Cr App R 324

A was accused of supplying drugs (heroin). The police had witnessed a number of people visit the premises and speak to the defendant, after which he would run to his car to collect small packages to give to them. From the visitors at least eight were known drug dealers with previous convictions for such offences. The prosecution sought to admit these previous convictions as part of their case against A under s 74. The defence objected on the basis that the evidence was hearsay; the Court thought otherwise. The evidence was not hearsay because the purpose in tendering it was not to prove what was either said or done or both, nor was it to prove the intention of the visitors. The convictions allowed a circumstantial inference as to the reason for the visits to be drawn by the jury.

R v Warner supports the idea that convictions with a wider relevance can be admitted under s 74. You should refer to the recommended additional reading at the end of this chapter for further information on the topics discussed so far.

14.8 Documentary and real evidence

14.8.1 Documentary evidence

Documents are an important type of evidence because they may be direct evidence, for example in the form of a contractual agreement that evidences the existence of the agreement or admissible hearsay – evidence pointing to the truth of a particular statement under either the CJA 2003 or the Civil Evidence Act 1995. Interestingly, a document is not evidence in its own right when used as an *aide memoire*, ie a memory refreshing document; however, in order for it to be used as evidence the document must be admissible.

The first question is: what is a document? In modern-day colloquial terms, ie everyday language, a document is something that contains and conveys information that can be viewed and understood. This has a wider meaning today because of the advancement in technology, ie e-mails, fax, etc. Section 10(1) of the Civil Evidence Act 1968 states that documents include films, photographs, tape recordings, soundtracks and other methods of recording data, ie dictaphones.

The common law requires the party that seeks to rely on a document to produce the original version of it; a copy was unacceptable. The reason for this was the extent of fraud in hand-copied documents, an issue largely reduced as a result of modern copying methods and newer forms of document, ie DVD. The current position is different; the courts are not as stringent with this requirement. Lord Justice Ackner and Mr Justice Woolf confirmed this in *Kajala v Noble* (1982) 75 Cr App R 149 stating that:

> **J** ' . . . the old rule, that a party must produce the best evidence that the nature of the case will allow, and that any less good evidence is to be excluded, has gone by the board long ago. The only remaining instance of it is that, if an original document is available in one's hands, one must produce it; that one cannot give secondary evidence by producing a copy. Nowadays we do not confine ourselves to the best evidence. We admit all relevant evidence. The goodness or badness of it goes only to weight, and not to admissibility: *Garton v Hunter* [1969] 1 All ER 451, *per* Lord Denning MR at 453e . . . in our judgment, the old rule is limited and confined to written documents in the strict sense of the term, and has no relevance to tapes or films.'

The case of *Augustien v Challis* (1847) 1 Exch 279 is a good example as to how important an original document (primary evidence) could be. In this case the court refused to accept other documents (secondary evidence) as evidence as to the terms of a lease. This rule does not apply where the purpose of the document is to establish that a lease exists and not the terms it contains. It should be noted that other statutes contain rules for the admission of other types of documentary evidence, for example s 71 of the Police and Criminal Evidence Act 1984 allows the contents of a document to be evidenced by an authenticated microfilm copy of the document. The Criminal Justice Act 2003 (CJA) and the Civil Evidence Act 1995 govern the admissibility of documentary hearsay. Let us now take a more in-depth look at the differences between primary and secondary documentary evidence.

A good example of primary documentary evidence is an original document, for example a lease, a contract or a receipt. If, for some reason, only a copy of a document was given to the person, then they must produce all copies, ie when you submit your assessments, the assessment office normally will return to you a carbon copy of the front slip as proof that you have submitted it –

you would need to produce more than that carbon copy for the document to amount to primary evidence. What if the document is one that was purposefully duplicated so that each party signed all copies which were thereafter distributed amongst them, such as a tenancy agreement? Then that agreement is enough. Where the person no longer has the original copy because they have had to submit it somewhere, ie deeds to a bank or contract to a court, then an official copy produced by the body where it is submitted will count as primary evidence. In contrast, secondary evidence can come in a number of forms; it can be oral or written. For the majority of the time, secondary evidence will be inadmissible unless:

- the original has been lost or destroyed
- production of the original is impossible
- the document is a part of a Bankers Book
- someone who is not party to the litigation refuses to produce the original
- a party fails to produce the original after having been given notice to do so.

This diagram summarizes the requirements for admissibility where one of the above reasons applies:

Reason	Admissibility of secondary evidence in lieu
The original has been lost or destroyed	Reasonable effort to locate or trace the original after which secondary evidence can be received by the court.
Production of the original is impossible	If it is impossible or difficult to produce the original then the court may receive secondary evidence.
The document is a part of a Bankers Book, ie accounts	The Bankers Book Evidence Act 1879 allows the use of copies of the book if the book is used in the custody of the bank and is used in the ordinary course of its business. Proof will be required that the copy was inspected alongside the original.
Someone who is not party to the litigation refuses to produce the original	Where someone that is not party to the litigation possesses the document and is entitled to refuse production, then the court may receive secondary evidence unless they can be compelled by the court to produce it.
A party fails to produce the original after having been given notice to do so	Party A can serve party B with a notice requiring them to produce the original document in their possession failing which secondary evidence can be received by the court.

Figure 14.4 Requirements for admissibility

A collateral issue concerns facts that can be presumed from documentary evidence. Documentary evidence will be proof of primary facts so long as it is over 20 years old and is produced by appropriate authority. A good example is the production of paper deeds in unregistered land proving ownership (subject to the rules contained within the Land Registration Acts). Secondary

facts that can be presumed from the production of a document include the date on which it was executed such as the date upon which a contract came into force.

14.8.2 Real evidence

Let us move on now to our final topic for discussion; real evidence. This is evidence that can be tangibly put before the court and which the court can observe and draw inferences from. Examples of real evidence include:

- objects, ie a knife, gun or hacksaw

- physical appearance of persons, for example bruises, responses and behaviour

- physical appearance of animals, such as emaciation

- video recordings including CCTV footage

- photographs or film

- views, where the court may relocate, as in the Soham murders, where the jury visited the site itself.

It is common for the court to come across real evidence whether it is the blood-stained axe with which someone was killed or seeing the post-attacked victim at court. Real evidence must be authentic; if there is any doubt or if it is of low quality, then it will be excluded; see *R v Stevenson* [1971] 1 WLR 1.

KEY FACTS

Documentary evidence

Documents can be direct evidence or hearsay.

- A *document* is something that contains or conveys information which can be viewed and understood, including e-mails, tape or video recording, DVD, Blu-Ray and fax:

- *Generally* the law requires the primary document to be produced, for example the original contract. Secondary evidence, ie a copy of a lease falls into the provisions of the CJA 2003, the CEA 1995 or PACE 1984.

Real evidence

This is evidence that can be tangibly put before the court and which the court can observe and draw inferences from, ie the knife used to dismember a body.

14.9 Summary and examination tip

In this chapter we have discussed two important types of evidence, evidence that can make the difference between proving and disproving a claim or allegation. These topics tend, very rarely, to appear as questions in their own right; therefore, you can rest assured that these topics will usually pervade other questions; hence, it is important to have a practical grasp of the issues we have discussed.

Opinion evidence

Witnesses should only give evidence of facts that they have perceived themselves without speculating, drawing conclusions and inferences or giving their opinion. The English law of evidence excludes the opinion evidence of witnesses because they may be unreliable or inexperienced in giving evidence and hence there exists a greater risk of such evidence lacking probative force. Opinion evidence is excluded unless it is:

- expert opinion
- opinion evidence of general reputation
- the opinion of an eyewitness.

Expert opinion

Expert opinion evidence is used where the court requires assistance on matters beyond its competence or experience, ie complex and technical issues. Expert witnesses are better equipped to express their opinion and make conclusions from the facts, for example on the time relation to the decomposition of a corpse or facial mapping. The court will receive expert evidence where the witness's opinion is beyond ordinary experience and competence and they are a qualified expert.

Witness expertise

The court will only hear the opinion evidence of a person who is *qualified* to form an opinion on the matter concerned, for example a Professor on haematology. The person need not have a formal qualification because their skill and experience is enough, although the level of skill and expertise will affect the weight attributed to the evidence.

Subject-matter

An expert witness will only be called to give evidence on matters that are beyond *normal* experience or expertise.

The Ultimate Issue Rule

The Ultimate Issue Rule states that in a criminal case at common law an expert should only give their opinion in evidence on matters that are not directly in issue, even though in practice they may do so. In civil cases the expert witness can give evidence on any matter that is relevant.

Expert opinion as hearsay evidence

The opinion of an expert can be presented to a court orally or in writing in the form of a report. A report could be classified as a hearsay statement of opinion. In civil cases such hearsay statements of opinion are permissible and in fact encouraged under s 1 of the Civil Evidence Act 1995. In criminal cases the use of expert statements of opinion in the form of a report is permissible under s 30 of the Criminal Justice Act 1988.

Non-expert opinion evidence

In civil cases the Civil Evidence Act 1972, s 3(2) states that where the testimony of a witness is of their opinion conveying the perception of facts by them, then that evidence is admissible as evidence of what they perceived. The effect of this is to render admissible the evidence of a witness that expresses a commonsensical observation or opinion of their perception. In criminal cases such clarity has not yet been achieved; it is likely that the position is the same.

Non-experts can give evidence of their perception, ie the intoxication of the defendant, ie she was drunk.

Opinion evidence of reputation

In civil cases the position generally accepted is that evidence of reputation is admissible, without giving notice, under s 7 of the Civil Evidence Act 1995 to show pedigree, good or bad character, public right. In criminal cases evidence of bad character is governed by the Criminal Justice Act 2003.

Common law rule: *Hollington v Hewthorn* [1943] KB 587

In *Hollington v Hewthorn* [1943] KB 587 the Court of Appeal decided that reference to previous judgments in civil cases should be excluded. The employee's previous conviction for driving without due care and attention was inadmissible because the opinion of the previous court could not match the opinion of the High Court in a contested personal injury action. The effect of the decision was to prevent previous judgments being used as evidence in a subsequent case; this was inconvenient and resulted in much inequity. The rule was partially reversed by the Civil Evidence Act 1968 (CEA) which provides exceptions to the rule in ss 11–13. In summary, s 11 provides for the use of criminal convictions, s 12 for findings of adultery and paternity and s 13 for convictions for defamation.

The use of previous criminal convictions in criminal cases

The law on the admissibility of a previous criminal conviction as evidence proving that an offence was committed by the person convicted in criminal cases is contained in the Criminal Justice Act 2003 (CJA) and s 74 of the Police and Criminal Evidence Act 1984 (PACE). Both provisions make previous criminal convictions admissible, within constraints, as evidence proving that the person convicted committed the offence.

Documentary evidence

Documents are an important type of evidence because they may be direct evidence in the form a contractual agreement that evidences the existence of the agreement and the form it takes, ie the terms and conditions. Documents are things that contain and convey information that can be viewed and understood. There are two forms of documentary evidence, first, primary documentary evidence – this is an original document, for example a lease, a contract or a receipt. In contrast, secondary evidence can come in a number of forms; it can be oral or written. The common law requires the party that seeks to rely on a document to produce the original version of it; a copy is unacceptable. The courts are not as stringent with this requirement.

Real evidence

Real evidence is evidence that can be tangibly put before the court and which the court can observe and draw inferences from such as a knife, gun or hacksaw.

ACTIVITY

Self-test questions

1. What is expert opinion evidence?

2. In civil cases is non-expert opinion evidence admissible?

3. Are the judgments of a previous court admissible as evidence in a subsequent case?

4. How is expert evidence presented in court?

5. Summarize how criminal convictions may be used as evidence in civil cases.

6. Repeat Q5 for criminal cases.

7. How is s 74 PACE 1984 restricted?

8. John and Martha are charged with theft and handling respectively. John is convicted after a guilty plea. Is evidence of his conviction admissible in the subsequent criminal trial of Martha?

9. What is documentary evidence?

10. Define real evidence with examples.

Further reading

Blom-Cooper QC, Sir L., 'Witness Immunity: the Argument Against' (2006) NLJ Vol 156 (7232), 1088–1089.

Chippindall, A. C., 'Expert Evidence and Legal Professional Privilege' (2003) JPI Law, Jan, 61–70.

Gooderham, P., 'Witness Immunity: the Argument in Favour' (2006) NLJ Vol 156 (7232), 1086–1087.

Jackson, J. D., 'The Ultimate Issue Rule – One Rule too Many' [1984] Crim LR 75.

Keane, A., *The Modern Law of Evidence* (5th edn, Oxford University Press, 2008). Chapter 18 has an excellent discussion on both expert and non-expert evidence.

Munday, R., *Evidence* (Oxford University Press, 2007). Chapter 8 of this text has a very good discussion on opinion evidence including an interesting discussion on the use of psychologist and psychiatrist opinion.